The Gift of Music

Crossway books by Jane Stuart Smith and Betty Carlson

Favorite Women Hymn Writers
Favorite Men Hymn Writers
The Gift of Music

The Gift of Music

Great Composers and Their Influence

Jane Stuart Smith
Betty Carlson

CROSSWAY

WHEATON, ILLINOIS

*This book
is dedicated with deep appreciation
to June Samson, who first introduced me to great music.*

The Gift of Music

Third edition copyright © 1995 by Jane Stuart Smith and Betty Carlson

Second edition copyright © 1987 by Jane Stuart Smith and Betty Carlson

Orginal edition copyright © 1978 Good News Publishers

Published by Crossway
        1300 Crescent Street
        Wheaton, Illinois 60187

Scripture verses marked Berkeley are taken from *The Modern Language Bible, the New Berkeley Version in Modern English* © 1945, 1969 by Zondervan Publishing House.

Unless otherwise marked, Scripture is taken from the King James Version.

Cover illustration: "The Month of May" from *Les Très Riches Heures du Duc de Berry* by the Limbourg brothers, A.D. 1416. Used by permission of the Musée Condé à Chantilly, France.

First printing 1995

Printed in the United States of America

Library of Congress Cataloging-in-Publication Data
Smith, Jane Stuart.
   The gift of music : great composers and their influence / Jane Stuart Smith, Betty Carlson. — 3rd ed.
     p. cm.
   Includes bibliographical references and index.
   1. Composers—Biography. 2. Music—Religious aspects.
I. Carlson, Betty. II. Title.
ML390.S642 1995   780'.92'2—dc20   95-32685
ISBN 13: 978-0-89107-869-2
ISBN 10: 0-89107-869-X

Crossway is a publishing ministry of Good News Publishers.

VP		21	20	19	18	17	16	15	14	13
27	26	25	24	23	22	21	20	19	18	17

A man that has a taste
of music, painting, or architecture
is like one that has another sense,
when compared with such as
have no relish of those arts.
—JOSEPH ADDISON

Contents

Foreword

*T*here are things in the Christian world that cause us to be sad. One of these is that for many Christians classical music is a complete vacuum. This robs individual Christians and their children of one of the very rich areas of joy in this life. Incidentally, an ignorance of classical music separates Christians from many people with whom they might wish to speak, and this is a hindrance in communication with them. But the chief sadness of knowing little about classical music consists in the loss the Christian experiences in one of the areas of the affirmation of life.

In this book is a wealth of detail concerning classical music that many Christians will not have thought about at all, and those who do know something of classical music will certainly find added detail to enrich their enjoyment of it. I really do hope that this book stimulates interest in classical music among many Christians. One does not need to be an expert to begin to enjoy such music. I remember what opened the door to classical music for me when I was young—suddenly hearing the *1812 Overture.* Though it would be far from my favorite now, the dynamic force of this music grasped me, and from that time on I went from composer to composer with a growing interest. Music has been a rich source of enjoyment in my own life.

Of course, tastes differ, and many interested in classical music might have chosen different composers to deal with in writing a book and different selections by those composers. As in all discussions in the area of art, there will also be different conclusions. This is inevitable in any area in art and may perhaps be especially true in music. On the other hand, I think everyone will find stimulating insights and fresh ideas.

Betty Carlson came to us while we lived in Champéry, and she became a Christian at Chalet Bijou there. Later she bought Chalet Chesalet in

Huémoz and has been very much a part of the community ever since. She is a worker in L'Abri.

Jane Stuart Smith was singing opera and studying in Milan when she first visited us after L'Abri began in Huémoz. She became a Christian here and was instrumental in opening the first door for us to work among the musicians in Milan. Eventually we held a Bible study class there. Later she became a worker in L'Abri and then, later still, a member of L'Abri, which she still is.

Chalet Chesalet has been a real shelter to many hundreds of people who have stayed at L'Abri through the years. People all over the world now understand something of classical music and have a deep enjoyment of it because of their times at Chalet Chesalet. They have profited from the discussions about music and from listening to the large library of recorded classical music available. Jane Stuart Smith has made a very special contribution to L'Abri, and we look for this book to open the doors to a new affirmation of life in the area of music for many Christians.

—Francis A. Schaeffer

Prelude

TO THE THIRD EDITION

*S*ome years ago I told my friend Jane Stuart Smith that she should write a book about some of the great composers she has given lectures on at L'Abri Fellowship in Switzerland. I have observed how carefully she prepares for each lecture—researching, reading stacks of books, and writing down pages of notes. Then, what I find amazing, she condenses her material so that her lectures rarely last more than one hour.

I kept after her to get going with the book because great music is one of God's gifts to help us through the snarls, noise, and confusion of our world. Over and over I have experienced how cheering it is on a gloomy, trying day to put on Schubert's *Trout* Quintet or Vivaldi's *Four Seasons* or Mozart's *Haydn* Quartets. I began to get a happy feeling thinking about how Jane's book could help open the minds and ears and hearts of many people beyond the circle of those privileged to hear her lectures.

But she did not write the book. She said she would not write it because she could not write a book. Then she informed me I should write it!

As it worked out, we more or less wrote it together with a great deal of help from the Lord, and we have had the joy of receiving favorable comments from readers and even critics. But one criticism we heard repeatedly was, "Why did you leave out Chopin?" "Don't you know that Berlioz is one of France's greatest composers?" "Where are Ravel, Ives, and Rachmaninoff?"

Similar postcards, telephone calls, and letters have kept coming our way. Thus we decided a revised and expanded edition of *The Gift of Music* was the answer. And now we are expanding it again. I will admit this has been a splendid time of learning for me, as several of these composers I knew little about, and I have come to love and appreciate these hard-working, dedicated, gifted musicians and what it has cost them to give us their gifts of music.

Both Jane Stuart Smith and I will be thankful we took the time and effort to write this book if it proves to be an encouragement to you as a listener of good music or as one who wants to be but needs a little help. Also if you are a musician, artist, or writer, there are many vivid and helpful lessons to learn from each one of these amazing composers.

When considering composers who are among the greatest in Western history, the more important question is not "What do we think of Handel (or Mozart or Stravinsky)?" but "What would Handel think of us?" I believe Handel would be surprised that we only listen to some of his music, such as *Messiah* and the *Water Music* Suite, when he wrote so many other magnificent compositions. And in listening to the elegant, carefree sounds of Mozart, it is only fair that we remember he scarcely ever received just payment for his works and was buried at an early age in a pauper's grave. Stravinsky might want us to keep in mind that, yes, his music is at times "lean," but he was trying to strip away the heaviness of sound left over from the nineteenth century.

Most of all, the purpose of this book is to encourage listening to the finest music with understanding and pleasure and to stretch one's imagination. The more people acquaint themselves with what is truly great and beautiful, the more they will dislike and turn away from that which is shallow and ugly. Also we want to show that what each artist believes in his heart and mind affects his creativity and influences those who follow him.

Concerning certain limitations in the following chapters: this is not a history of music, nor is it a book only on Christian composers. Obviously, there is no attempt to discuss all types of music (that would require several volumes). We have chosen to restrict our choice of composers to the area of art music, or classical music, as it is also called. For the sake of brevity some of your favorite composers (and ours) have been omitted. We are aware that one cannot avoid reflecting subjective judgment and personal taste, but we have attempted to present the historical facts accurately and to speak of the weaknesses and foibles of "our" composers with compassion, recognizing that no one is perfect.

Jane Stuart Smith has gathered the material for her lectures over the years from a variety of books and encyclopedias, a file of clippings and notes, and through an active musical life in various countries. I hope the reader has the same excitement in learning that has been my experience while shaping the rather sketchy lecture notes into book form.

In particular we are indebted to Donald Jay Grout for his outstanding book, *A History of Western Music*. Also we give special thanks to Shirley Henn, Mildred Mitchell, and Thelma Diercks for their help in our research in the Hollins College library and to Mary Burnett Hatch for her outstanding help in writing the new chapters for the third edition. We are grateful for the encouragement given by Liggie Smith and our friends in Switzerland who carried on our work while we were away to write the original book, and in particular Rosemary Sperry, who took care of Chalet Chesalet, the chickens, and Owl in our absence.

—Betty Carlson

Psalms in Western Music History

*Sing unto the Lord with the harp; with the harp,
and the voice of a psalm. With trumpets and sound
of cornet make a joyful noise before the Lord,
the King.*

Psalm 98:5-6

*D*o you know that Psalm 98 inspired Isaac Watts to write "Joy to the World"? That Martin Luther's great Reformation hymn "A Mighty Fortress" is a paraphrase of Psalm 46? That the often-sung "Doxology" dates back to Calvin's sixteenth-century Genevan Psalter?

"Psalms are sweet for every age, and they create a bond of unity when the whole people raise their voice in one choir," said Ambrose, bishop of Milan, in the fourth century.

This most wonderful of all hymnbooks has been cherished by God's people in every age. The book of Psalms has been the single most productive source of texts for musical compositions in Western music. Psalm-singing is the earliest recorded musical activity of the church, perhaps in response to the Apostle Paul's admonition to "be filled with the Spirit, speaking to yourselves in psalms and hymns and spiritual songs, singing and making melody in your heart to the Lord" (Eph. 5:18-19). The very backbone of sacred music has been the book of Psalms.

Psalms have been in the center of worship just as we find them in the middle of the Bible. The Psalter is an anthology of poems written by various authors over a period of about one thousand years, but David probably wrote more than half of the 150 psalms.

Psalms were central in Christ's devotion and worship. He often quoted from them and verified that they were referring to Him, as in Luke 24:44: ". . . all things must be fulfilled, which were written in the law of Moses, and in the prophets, and in the psalms, concerning me." Before going to the Garden of Gethsemane and later to His crucifixion, Christ sang psalms with His disciples.

Paul and Silas sang hymns of praise to God in the Philippian jail. Throughout the Middle Ages the walls of European monasteries echoed with the chanting of psalms, and the great reformers planted the Psalter in the heart of their service. Even today psalms are read more widely than any poetry and are used regularly in all Christian churches and Jewish synagogues.

Trust in the living God who hears and answers prayer is the basic theme throughout the book of Psalms. God is a person who acts in nature and history and in the lives of men and women. He is a God of mercy and truth, full of compassion for suffering human beings. Psalms were not written as cold liturgy, but as personal expressions in relation to the sovereign God of the universe who cares for those who trust Him. Human emotions are dealt with in a personal way. John Calvin said that he saw himself in the psalms and applied them to his own situation.

The key word of the book of Psalms is *worship*, and this is heightened by musical settings. Poetry is the form of expression most appropriate to describe feelings, and with music added, the emotional intensity is increased. The word *psalm* comes from the Greek word *psalmoi*, meaning "twangings of harp strings," which reminds us that psalms are to be sung.

The history of music until A.D. 200 is shrouded in darkness because of the problem of notation. We have none of the original music that the psalms were set to, although we know that Hebrew music was mainly vocal with much use of antiphonal singing and some instrumental accompaniment.

Because composers use psalms as texts for musical compositions does not necessarily mean that they believe the content. One must examine a person's life as well as what he professes to believe. Even then there are mysteries that belong only to God. However, we can ask: why have great composers used the book of Psalms as a source of texts more often than any other book? Why are the psalms so important—even to the non-Christian? One obviously knows objectively that they are great literature, but we sense that there is something more. Yes, there is the honesty of the psalms, the melody and beauty, but more important is the truth that the book of Psalms is the inspired Word of the living God.

As we follow the flow of music history, we can start with Ambrose, bishop of Milan (339-397), who emphasized a true biblical Christianity. Ambrose introduced antiphonal psalmody and hymns to the West, and the Ambrosian chant is still sung in Milan today. Augustine (354-430) became a Christian through the powerful preaching of Ambrose. Augustine later said that hymns are praises to God with singing. According to tradition, as Ambrose baptized Augustine, the two improvised the "Te Deum Laudamus" (We Praise Thee, O God) in alternate verses. This may well be true since it was the practice of the early church to create hymns when inspired by strong religious feeling. The "Te Deum" is believed to have been written about that time (late fourth century) and is one of the few prose texts composed then.

Pope Gregory I (reigned 590-604) brought many musical reforms into the church. He was responsible for having all the modes of worship of the Western church arranged into a systematic whole. In his honor this music is called the Gregorian chant. All musical instruments were restricted, and only men were allowed to sing the Gregorian chant in the services. This music, with its impersonal mystical quality, is a powerful expression of Romanesque art. It is startling to realize that three-fourths of the Gregorian chants are made up of either entire psalm texts or selected verses. These chants were the source and inspiration of a large proportion of all sacred Western music up to the sixteenth century. They are one of the great treasures of Western civilization, illustrating again the importance of Psalms in music history. Throughout the Renaissance the psalm settings of Andrea and Giovanni Gabrieli and Sweelinck continued to inspire great music.

Martin Luther (1483-1546) included music as a vital part of worship in the form of congregational chorale singing (with all voices included). This practice helped to sow the seeds of a musical renaissance in the German-speaking lands. The chorale was an effective representation of Scripture. Luther, described as an accomplished amateur, wrote a number of chorales. His best-known, "A Mighty Fortress Is Our God," helped to spread the Reformation through Europe. Luther called the Psalter "a Bible in miniature," and it was his constant companion. It is said that whenever he heard discouraging news he would say to his family or friends, "Come, let us sing the forty-sixth psalm." Luther undoubtedly inspired others to write chorales or to sing them when he said, "He who despises music, as do all the fanatics, does not please me. Music is a gift of God, not a gift of men. . . . After theology I accord to music the highest place and greatest honor."

As John Calvin (1509-1564) prohibited the singing of texts not found in the Bible, the only notable productions of the Calvinist churches were the various translations of the book of Psalms set to music. Elaborate music was prohibited, so the Genevan Psalter is a compilation of simple four-part settings that are excellent for devotional music. In his preface to the Genevan Psalter of 1542 Calvin connects religious music with prayer: "As for public prayers, there are two kinds: the ones with words alone, the others with singing."

The principal French Psalter, published in 1562 with music composed by Louis Bourgeois, includes our often-sung "Doxology." The French Huguenots sang psalms in court and camp. It has been said that the Protestant Reformation exercised a greater influence upon the historical course of religious music specifically and European music generally than any other movement initiated in the Renaissance.

Heinrich Schütz (1585-1672), the greatest German composer of the middle seventeenth century, was one of the most important musical figures of the Baroque period, which culminated in the towering works of Bach and

Handel. Schütz wrote his music in a clear, careful style so that people would get the message of the words. His desire was to proclaim biblical truth. His settings of psalms to music throughout his long, creative life are the heart of his work.

Johann Sebastian Bach (1685-1750) is considered by many Christians and secular critics to be the greatest composer of all time. Bach spent his life in musical service to God. He wrote some of the greatest devotional music the world has ever known. The core of his creative work is a vast treasure of cantatas that make up more than half of his music. These are often based on psalms. Cantata 131, for example, is a setting of the moving penitential Psalm 130.

Unlike many intellectuals of today, who know little or nothing about the Bible, educated persons of the eighteenth century were acquainted with Scripture. George Frideric Handel (1685-1759), "the prince of music," was thoroughly familiar with the Bible, and he delighted in the psalms. He used them in such monumental oratorios as *Messiah* and *Israel in Egypt*. The antiphonal singing we hear in his settings of Psalms 110 and 113 has roots in Jewish worship. His *Chandos* Anthems with psalm texts brought Anglican music of the Baroque period to its culmination.

Franz Joseph Haydn (1732-1809) was a God-fearing man. He wrote his masterpiece *The Creation* in the later years of his life, having been inspired by Handel's *Messiah*. One of the supreme moments in the oratorio is "The Heavens Are Telling," Haydn's setting of verses from Psalm 19. His friend Wolfgang Amadeus Mozart (1756-1791), perhaps the most purely musical composer, did a magnificent arrangement of the shortest of all psalms, the praise-filled Psalm 117.

Ludwig van Beethoven (1770-1827), at one time the rebellious pupil of Haydn, was the great revolutionary composer whose music was the bridge from the Classical period to Romanticism. In his setting of verses from Psalm 19, "The Heavens Are Telling," one can almost see the stars shining.

These composers will be discussed in more detail in subsequent chapters; I am mentioning only a few here to show how in all periods of history the psalms have acted as the "salt of the earth" in music. Countless composers have not been included. To do justice to this theme, one would need to write volumes. What riches have come from the psalms right down into the last half of the twentieth century!

The early Romantic Jewish-Christian composer Felix Mendelssohn (1809-1847) set many psalms to music. One example is "Lift Thine Eyes to the Mountains" from Psalm 121, found in his great oratorio *Elijah*.

The German Classic-Romantic composer Johannes Brahms (1833-1897) said that he could find his Bible in the darkest night because he kept it always with him. The music of Brahms, like that of Schütz and Bach, is inspired by a deep concern with man's mortal lot and his hope of heaven. In his beautiful *German Requiem* there is a setting of Psalm 84. As one hears the different languages of these psalm settings, one is aware of their international influence.

Arthur Honegger (1892-1955), one of "Les Six" (a group of French composers), became famous after his oratorio *King David* was performed in a barnlike theater at Mezières near Lausanne, Switzerland. The text contains many psalms and has as its theme, "Be not afraid; put your trust in God."

A distinguished piece of the twentieth century is Stravinsky's *Symphony of Psalms*. Stravinsky was one of the prime shapers of contemporary music in this century.

After introducing to the twentieth century a composition theory known as the "twelve-tone row" or "serial technique," Arnold Schoenberg (1874-1951) at the end of his life seemed unable to live with it himself. His last completed work was the choral setting of Psalm 130, "Out of the depths have I cried unto Thee, O Lord." He dedicated it to the Israeli nation.

Krzysztof Penderecki (1933-), born in Poland, is one of the outstanding composers of our time. His first published work was *Psalms of David*.

The vast treasure of Christian hymnology has its wellspring in the book of Psalms. The grand note of the great hymns is praise to God through His Word. The father of English hymnody, Isaac Watts, wrote many paraphrases of psalms including "O God, Our Help in Ages Past," a paraphrase of Psalm 90, as well as "Joy to the World," based on Psalm 98. Even today the book of Psalms contributes to our hymns.

Countless others have set psalms to music. Among the best known are Johann Walther, Praetorius, Buxtehude, Vivaldi, Marcello, Schubert, Dvorak, Liszt, Bruckner, Distler, and the Americans William Billings, Charles Ives, Paul Creston, and Bernstein. It is interesting to note that the first book known to have been both written and printed in the English colonies of America was the *Bay Psalm Book*.

It is the prayer of those of us who live and work at L'Abri Fellowship that we turn continually to the Bible for knowledge and wisdom, not only to learn how to live with hope in a fallen world, but to receive inspiration to be more creative. To the Christian musician in particular, I urge you to live in the midst of the psalms, singing them and writing your own music to the glory of God.

Recommended Reading

King James Version of the Bible

Meyer, F. B. *Gems from the Psalms*. Wheaton, Ill.: Good
News Publishers, 1976.

Scroggie, W. Graham. *Psalms*. London: Pickering and
Inglis Ltd., 1965.

Recommended Listening

Gregorian Chant (Solesmes Recordings)
Luther: "A Mighty Fortress Is Our God"
Schütz: "Psalm 121"
Handel: *Chandos* Anthems; *Dixit Dominus*
Bach: Cantata 131
Haydn: "The Heavens Are Telling" (*The Creation*)
Mozart: "Psalm 117" (*Laudate Dominum*)
Beethoven: "The Heavens Are Telling"
Mendelssohn: "Lift Thine Eyes to the Mountains" (*Elijah*)
Brahms: "How Lovely Are Thy Dwellings" (*German Requiem*)
Honegger: "Be Not Afraid" (*King David*)
Stravinsky: *Symphony of Psalms*
Penderecki: *Psalms of David*
Watts (words only): "O God, Our Help in Ages Past"
Ives: *Psalms*

CHAPTER 1

Heinrich Schütz
1585-1672

Thy statutes have been my songs in the house of my pilgrimage.

Psalm 119:54

*I*magine two choirs, six soloists, two violins, and an organ combining to present the account of Paul's conversion. First, from one side of the chancel you hear the deep-toned solo basses asking, "Saul, Saul, why persecutest thou Me?" Soon the tenor, alto, and soprano soloists join in the questioning. The rhythm is accelerated, interrupted by cadences. The choir answers the calls, increasing the volume to a *fortissimo* climax, finally subsiding to an echo effect by the sopranos.

Are you hearing a supernatural invocation?

No. It is one of the impressive works of Heinrich Schütz, whose name is hardly a household word. This German law-student-turned-composer studied music in Italy where the Baroque sound fired his imagination. He returned home to apply Italian methods of word-painting to German texts. He developed the free-style setting of scriptural texts and emerged one of the creative geniuses in musical history.

Too often we don't realize how much someone in the past has influenced what we enjoy today. Schütz's many pupils helped spread his influence—even to Bach who studied under one of them. Had Schoenberg or Cage preceded Bach instead of Schütz, we might not have had Bach—now considered to be among the world's greatest composers and master of the church cantata.

We must be careful not to forget history or the roots of our culture. In cultivating the old, one has a better understanding of the new. Much of what we hear today is dross, but having said that, we cannot dismiss all modern music. We need to be sufficiently informed to understand why it is the way it is. And we must remember that the test of time is often necessary. Great music lives on. Heinrich Schütz is one whose music has survived.

Schütz is considered the greatest German composer of the middle seventeenth century and is one of the most important musical figures of the early Baroque period. He became famous in his lifetime; yet he had a lonely life filled with hardship and affliction, due partly to the upheaval of war. In addition to the musical heritage he gave us, Schütz has something to say to us through the example of his life.

It began in 1585. Schütz was born into the world of Shakespeare and Cervantes, a time of religious strife that climaxed in the Thirty Years' War. Like such outstanding composers as Bach, Haydn, and Schubert, he owed the start of his career to a fine treble voice. He began to study law, but a nobleman who recognized Schütz's abilities and eagerness for knowledge sent him to Venice to study music in 1609.

Venice, "The Queen of the Adriatic," with its lagoons, warm light, and luminous colors, is unique in the world. It was built on 118 miniature islands separated by 160 canals, which are its streets. The islands are connected by 400 bridges. In the time of Schütz, Venice was a spiritual capital of the art and music world. The fascination of light, water, and air is still hypnotic. Quiet, mysterious reflections stir the senses, and gondolas still ply the canals.

When Heinrich Schütz arrived, he was received with great kindness by Giovanni Gabrieli (ca.1555-1612), the most renowned Venetian composer of the time. Schütz, a gentle, humble individual with a desire to learn, was invited to stay in the home of the composer. A rich friendship developed between teacher and pupil, and for four years Schütz was instructed by the great Gabrieli in the "grand Italian style." It became the principal foundation upon which German composers were to build their music.

Gabrieli has been called the "musical Titian" of Venice. His music is brilliant and powerful, and few composers have ever achieved such splendor and grandeur in musical tones. In fact, Gabrieli is considered to have laid the foundation for the modern orchestra. Sometimes he placed as many as four (or more) groups of instruments and choirs, each complete in itself, in the galleries and balconies of St. Mark's Cathedral, resulting in colossal Baroque sound.

This great basilica with its Byzantine domes, its bronze horses, bright gold mosaics, and immense interior bathed in greenish-golden light was the center of Venetian musical culture, whose influence reached throughout Europe. The architectural concept of space-consciousness and echo-effect is a key element in Baroque music, and it was developed at St. Mark's Cathedral. Gabrieli's "Sonata Piano e Forte" is the first score to indicate a change in volume dynamics.

It was traditional that European creative minds sought their final education in Italy. Robert Browning said that Italy was "his university," and it has been and is the university for many artistic people. Some of the students who stop at L'Abri Fellowship in Switzerland are coming from Florence or Venice or are going there. In the same way that the great painter Dürer brought the Renaissance from Venice to northern Europe, so did the music of Schütz show the mellowing influence of Italy.

Schütz studied in Italy for four years, and when Gabrieli died in 1612, Schütz returned to Germany. Gabrieli left his personal signet ring as a lasting token of friendship to his favorite pupil, and Schütz passed on the great teaching he had received from Gabrieli to his many pupils. In a letter included in Moser's biography of Schütz, Schütz stresses the influence of his mentor: "Gabrieli—What a man he was. . . . After I had been but a short time with my teacher, I found out how important and difficult was the study of composition . . . and I realized that I still had a poor foundation in it. From this time on I put away all my previous studies and devoted myself to the study of music alone. Upon the publication of my first humble work, Giovanni Gabrieli urged me with great warmth to continue the study of music."

Schütz's studies with Gabrieli were important to the whole history of German music, as Schütz was a major transmitter of the Venetian style to German composers.

Later Schütz made another trip to Venice to see Monteverdi, the choirmaster of St. Mark's for thirty years and the most universal composer of the early Baroque. Dramatic conflict was the essence of Monteverdi's style. He used dissonance for dramatic expressiveness and believed that rhythm is bound up with emotion. He too had a strong influence on Schütz.

While Schütz was greatly influenced by his studies in Italy, his spiritual roots were in German soil. He was a devout Lutheran composer and is remembered not only for his universal culture and brilliant musical gift, but for his earnest biblical faith. Although he wrote the first German opera, *Dafne*, which is now lost, his enormous output is predominantly religiously inspired.

Schütz's first masterpiece in the "grand Italian manner" was his setting of the *Psalms of David* in 1619. He is often called the father of German music, and it is refreshing and enlightening to observe that he based his music almost exclusively on biblical texts. There is no "magic" in using Scripture, but when the artist believes the words, there is bound to be a wholesome and healthy influence on those who listen to such music. Schütz had as his goal in composition to write the meaning of the words into the hearts of his hearers. "Psalm 121" is an example of a superb union of words and music. It can well be said that Schütz unlocked the music hidden in the psalms. He was the greatest composer of psalm settings in the history of music. A special treasure is the Becker Psalter of 1628 that includes Schütz's plain four-part harmonic settings of psalms. These settings display the earnest simplicity that so enhances religious music.

The Magnificat was a favorite biblical passage of Schütz, and he composed several works to accompany it, including *The German Magnificat*, the last thing he wrote.

He was one of the earliest and among the greatest German composers of oratorio. An oratorio is distinguished from an opera by its sacred subject matter and by the fact that oratorios were seldom, if ever, meant to be staged. The action is suggested or narrated, not presented. Schütz's most famous work of this type is *The Seven Last Words,* a composite of all four Gospels. Schütz used the words of the Bible, and his oratorio presents the essence of Protestant thought. In describing pain he used sharp dissonances. He used rests to focus the listeners' ears on certain passages. And again because he wanted to convey the message, he is more interested in the clarity of the words than in counterpoint. He is a master of declamation. "Is there in the whole literature of music a more dramatic outcry than Schütz's treatment of the words 'My God, My God, why hast Thou forsaken me?'" asks Moser. The quality of this fervent music sums up a quiet, yet deeply felt piety, a personal devotion before the person of Christ. One critic called Heinrich Schütz the most spiritual musician the world has ever known. There is enduring vitality and biblical strength in his compositions.

Like Monteverdi, Haydn, and Verdi, Schütz wrote great music in his old age. He began to lose his hearing and sight, but in spite of these handicaps he created some of his finest music in this period. In 1664 he wrote the *Christmas Oratorio,* a brief biblical history with the high-minded objective to intensify the effect of the Scriptures with music. He achieved his goal. All the words, which fit the music like a glove, are biblical except the beginning and the end. Schütz ends the oratorio this way: "We give thanks to God, our Lord Christ, who by His birth hath enlightened us and by His blood hath redeemed us from the power of the Devil. Let us all, with His angels, give praise to Him with a loud voice, singing, 'Praise be to God in the highest.'"

Schütz wrote the greatest Passions of the seventeenth century. They are like the rest of his music, clean and pure, with a stress on content. These masterly works reveal Schütz as the greatest biblical composer of all time.

The influence of Schütz has been felt even into this century in the fine church music of the German composer Hugo Distler. Every great artist is a product of his times, but because of the profound biblical content in his music, Schütz is for all time.

Schütz was the *Kapellmeister* (master of the chapel) in Dresden from 1617 until the end of his life, except during some especially difficult years of the Thirty Years' War when he was court conductor in Copenhagen.

When Schütz married in 1619, he combined invitations to his wedding with the publication of his *Psalms of David.* The chapter of the Naumburg Cathedral on May 27 has in its minutes: "Heinrich Schütz, Electoral Saxon *Kapellmeister* in Dresden, sends the gentlemen a copy of his published *Psalms of David* and invites them to his wedding on June 1. The gentlemen vote that five Rhenish gold guilden be sent him as an honorarium, which they have taken from the large iron chest."

Schütz, with his gentle heart and spirit, was profoundly affected by the early death of his wife in 1625. He made a decision before the Lord to spend the rest of his life composing church music. He never remarried.

Schütz and the German people were deeply distressed by the long war, and in that tragic time they found strength and comfort in Christian music. After the devastation of the war, Schütz helped with advice, money, and music to restore a number of musical establishments that had deteriorated.

He died in 1672 and was buried in old Fraunkirche beside his wife. In the hall a brass tablet is inscribed, "The Christian Singer of Psalms—A joy for foreigners, for Germans a light."

Schütz is greatly loved, not only because of his music, but for his Christian way of life as well. Despite his many trials he never allowed his faith to waver. His great intelligence, personal integrity, and staunch character earned him universal affection and esteem.

We learn from Schütz that choices are significant. He chose Christianity and dedicated his life to the praise of God, and his music did not suffer from the choice. God enhanced the talents of this gifted musician. Schütz also teaches us to learn from our "university," but to maintain a true biblical base for all learning, to turn to the Scriptures in hardships, and not to give up—even in old age.

Recommended Reading

Moser, Hans. *Heinrich Schütz: His Life and Work.* St. Louis: Concordia Publishing House, 1959.

Recommended Listening

Schütz: *Christmas Oratorio*
Deutsches' Magnificat
Psalms of David
Seven Last Words from the Cross
Giovanni Gabrieli: Music for Organ and Bass
Monteverdi: Vespers

CHAPTER 2

Antonio Vivaldi
ca. 1678-1741

A merry heart doeth good like a medicine.
Proverbs 17:22

*T*he splendor and intensity of the musical life of Venice during the first part of the eighteenth century centered around Antonio Vivaldi. He has been described by his biographer Pincherle as "that whirlwind of music, perpetually pouring forth melodies, rhythms, harmonies, still as alive, for the most part, as on the day of their creation." Yet the music of this original composer, affectionately known as "Il Prete Rosso" because of his red hair and early training for the priesthood, for many years after his death was no longer performed. He must have died poor and unknown, as there is no trace of his grave. His music disappeared into obscurity, lying forgotten in public and private libraries.

As Pincherle says, "Most forgotten composers deserve nothing better than to be forgotten . . . but now and then it happens that an obvious injustice is revealed." A perusal of the latest *Schwann Catalog* proves that the music of Vivaldi deserved to be resurrected. Currently over twelve pages are devoted to Vivaldi recordings, with some concertos performed by ten or twelve different artists. However, even the lively music of Vivaldi probably would have remained lost if Bach had not transcribed some of his works.

Ironically, Bach had suffered a fate similar to Vivaldi's. He too had slipped into oblivion. Then in 1829 the twenty-year-old Mendelssohn introduced Bach's *Passion According to St. Matthew* to the music-lovers of Berlin, and it met with tremendous success. The new admirers of Bach eagerly began to gather his scattered manuscripts. In the course of their research, someone came upon a score dating from 1739 titled "XII concerto [*sic*] di Vivaldi elaborati di J. S. Bach . . . " (Bach is known to have copied at least nine of Vivaldi's concertos.)

The natural question came to mind: who was this Vivaldi whom Bach had honored by transcribing his music? The "detectives" went to work, and finally a few original scores used by Bach were found in old engraved editions in an Amsterdam library. At first these originals were declared to be of slight value, but in the beginning of this century more enlightened scholars recognized Vivaldi as a powerful innovator, an inspired composer in his own right, and the actual creator of the solo concerto prefigured by Corelli and Torelli.

Antonio Vivaldi was born in Venice around 1678, the son of the leading violinist of St. Mark's Chapel. He was educated by his father and Legrenzi, the director of music at St. Mark's and a fine organist and composer. Vivaldi was trained for both music and the priesthood, and he became a priest in 1703. Because of ill health, he was excused from active service the following year, and afterwards he devoted himself wholly to music.

Vivaldi became the head of the Conservatory of the Ospedale della Pietà, which was connected with four institutions organized like convents and paid for by the state. The asylums sometimes held as many as six thousand orphan girls. Those admitted to the Pietà were generally illegitimate. According to Pincherle, before the erection of these charitable institutions, "multitudes [of these children] used to be found which had been thrown into the canals of the city." What was unusual about these semi-convents was that musical training formed an important part of the curriculum. In all music history there seems to be no parallel to the extent and quality of the music that rang through the corridors of the Ospedale della Pietà.

The girls were taught to sing and to play the violin, flute, organ, oboe, cello, bassoon. In short, there was no instrument, however unwieldy, that could frighten them. Music was the heart and soul of their lives. Every Sunday and on all holidays there were musical performances in the chapels by these young ladies, and about forty of the best musicians would take part in each concert. All who wanted could attend the concerts, and they attracted large crowds. The people were allowed to stay as long as they remained in their seats. Applause was not permitted, and so instead there was coughing, loud nose-blowing, and much shuffling and stamping of feet. Many musicians, including Handel, commented on the excellence and liveliness of these performances. It was for these programs that Vivaldi wrote more than four hundred concertos.

Wherever Vivaldi was, there was abundant music-making. Vivaldi was a progressive composer seething with ideas, and the Pietà was a wonderful environment in which to experiment with music. He was a man of contrasts—quick to be irritated, quick to calm down. This characteristic is reflected in his music by dramatic contrasts of dynamics and harmony and varied rhythms, but the haste with which he composed was one of his weaknesses. There is much invention in Vivaldi's music and beautiful melodies, because he was always looking for new sounds. Vivaldi always had instruments and voices at hand to try out fresh ideas.

Venice in the eighteenth century was like a perpetual opera. In the daily life there was scarcely a time or place where the sound of music was not present. One is reminded of the wonderful contemporary paintings by Longhi with costumes and masks, all like a continual festival. The Venetian mania for music nearly consumed them.

The Pietà where Vivaldi served nearly forty years was located on the Riva degli Schiavoni a little before one reaches the Ponte del Sepolcro coming from St. Mark's. A colorful painting by Canaletto (1697-1768), the first great chronicler of Venice, brings to mind what Vivaldi saw as he frequently walked from the Pietà along the Riva degli Schiavoni, past the Bridge of Sighs, turning at the Piazza (the center of Venice), looking at the magnificent Ducal Palace before entering St. Mark's basilica (where he was soloist) to play his violin in the morning service. The Grand Canal with its myriad colors, the gondolas and gondoliers with their songs, and the cheerful activity surely helped to fill Vivaldi's thoughts with bright sounds and melodies.

In spite of his poor health (it is thought that he suffered from asthma), Vivaldi was an incredible worker. His duties at the Pietà included teaching, composing, purchasing instruments, and conducting. Besides all this, he wrote over forty operas, for some of which Canaletto assisted his father in painting theatrical scenes. Also Vivaldi was allowed frequent leaves of absence to travel and conduct concerts elsewhere. Because of his health, he could never travel without a retinue of four or five people, a clue that he knew how to delegate tasks into the hands of others; otherwise it is impossible to understand how he accomplished so much in the sixty-three or sixty-four years he was given in this life. Vivaldi's popularity today illustrates the truth that productivity is an integral part of greatness.

Vivaldi's European reputation was built on a set of twelve concerti grossi. A concerto grosso is a composition involving a few select soloists, usually three, and a full orchestra. A concerto involves one solo instrument and the orchestra. The Baroque idea of the instrumental sound of *solo-tutti* resulted in new sounds and contrasts. Vivaldi was the greatest Italian master of the concerto, and the influence of this original genius on future generations is incalculable. In the works of Vivaldi the concerto was definitely standardized as a cycle of three movements, usually with a slow introduction. Vivaldi was the first to bring the pathos of Venetian operatic arias into the slow movement of his concertos. He was also the first to give the slow movement the same importance as the fast movements. The performer was expected to add his own embellishments.

The two great Italian mediums were the voice and the violin. The violin comes closest to the sound of the singing voice and is capable of many possibilities. Every art depends on its means of expression; so it is no accident that the great Italian school of violin composition flourished at the time when Stradivari had found his own style of violin-making. Antonio Stradivari (ca.1644-1737), born in Cremona, was the greatest of all violin-makers. His violins are beautifully formed and perfect in every detail. This prodigious worker never repeated a design exactly but always made some change, seeking for perfection.

Another person important in relationship to the violin and the concerto grosso is Arcangelo Corelli (1653-1713). Born in Bologna, he spent his creative life in Rome and was one of the greatest of the early violinists. He is considered the founder of the modern method of violin-playing and was also a noted teacher. He wrote no vocal music. His interest was centered in string instruments. Corelli is considered the co-creator of the concerto grosso, and he had a strong influence on Vivaldi, Handel, and Bach. In fact, eighteenth-century music was built on the foundation established by Corelli. His works were the fruit of slow and considered deliberation, and he had a noble concern for measure and balance. One of the great Classicists, he and Vivaldi were incomparable masters of the string orchestra. Corelli lived simply and, like Handel, spent most of his money on paintings. He was calm, reflective, and cultured, contemplating his art with a religious respect. Music, painting, and friendship graced his life.

The Baroque period saw the development of the opera, the oratorio, the cantata, the creation of the solo sonata, the trio sonata, and the chamber duet. It instituted important forms of the concerto grosso and the solo concerto. The three central figures of the concerto are Corelli, Torelli, and Vivaldi. The Baroque composers wrote a great deal of music because the public was ever clamoring for new works; so we can forgive these great composers if some of the vast output sounds stylized. Hardly any other age has been as prolific.

The Four Seasons is perhaps Vivaldi's most popular work. It is one of the masterpieces of descriptive music, and it left its mark on the musical life of Vivaldi's century. His style became the style of the moment. His bird sounds are as vivid as some of the wonderful bird mosaics in St. Mark's Cathedral. The work is often performed today. Vivaldi, a poet full of lyrical power, wrote a sonnet for each of the seasons and the music to go with each season. *The Four Seasons* represents an important Baroque parallel to Haydn's oratorio, *The Seasons*. Later came Beethoven's *Pastoral* Symphony. Vivaldi is one of the towering figures in the transition from late Baroque to the early Classical style. Possibly the greatest paintings of the seasons are *Les Tres Riches Heures* of the Duc de Berry.

Vivaldi, like his contemporaries, composed every work for a definite occasion—not simply "art for art's sake." He composed a great deal of music for plucked instruments, including the lute and guitar. His concertos for mandolin are delightful. We can always admire Vivaldi's seemingly inexhaustible creative power and vitality. His keen, often capricious imagination finds external expression in the variety of instrumental combinations that reflect the Venetian fondness for coloristic effects. One can speak of Vivaldi's music as energetic, nimble, and full of life. Only a small part of his prolific production has been published.

His sacred works were written for the Pietà and hardly ever were performed beyond there. His splendid work the Gloria in D kindles a sense of rapture due to Vivaldi's own spiritual depth. Vivaldi often recited psalms and prayed out loud while walking in the corridors of the Pietà.

While listening to Vivaldi, do not forget that he was rediscovered after Bach's rediscovery. Vivaldi's music would have been lost to us if Bach had not learned by transcribing contemporary composers, especially the Italians. Today our problem is almost the opposite. We have too much available. One has a sense of bewilderment upon entering a music store or bookstore or a library. How does one know what to listen to or what to read? A good plan is to start with the best.

Vivaldi is among the best, but like all human beings, he has his limitations. After one listens to Vivaldi over a period of time, one becomes aware of a sameness in the music. It does not have the depth and spiritual content of Bach; but it has life. It is never old music. When one turns to the radio and suddenly there is Vivaldi, the music brightens the room. When I open the shutters of Chalet Chesalet and see the sun rising above the Swiss Alps, listen to the singing of birds and the ringing of cowbells, I call it a "Vivaldi day."

Recommended Reading

Pincherle, Marc. *Vivaldi: Genius of the Baroque.* New York: W. W. Norton, 1957.

Recommended Listening

Vivaldi: Concerto for Flute, Oboe, and Bassoon
      Concerto in C for Mandolin
      Concerti for Recorder
      Concerto for Two Trumpets
      Concerti for Violin and Orchestra
      The Four Seasons
      Gloria in D
      Pastor Fido, Op. 13
Corelli: Concerto Grosso in G Minor
      Op. 6, No. 8, *Christmas*

CHAPTER 3

Johann Sebastian Bach
1685-1750

*Praise him with the sound of the trumpet: praise
him with the psaltry and harp. Praise him with the
timbrel and dance: praise him with stringed
instruments and organs.*

Psalm 150:3-4

J ohann Sebastian Bach, who may be described as a very determined person, was the outstanding member of the greatest musical family the world has ever known. The Thirty Years' War was remembered by the Bach family because the Bach ancestors left Hungary rather than give up their biblical faith. The earliest musical Bach was a miller. When he went into the mill to grind his corn, regardless of the clatter of the millstones, he would take along his zither and play it, foreshadowing his descendants' love for music.

Bach and Handel were the culminating figures of the Baroque period (1600-1750) in music history. At this time Vivaldi was composing in Italy; Rameau was the court musician of Louis XIV in France; Handel was the central figure in London musical circles; and Bach, known best as an organist in Germany, was creating a world of music. The Baroque period follows the Renaissance and Reformation. The term *Baroque* comes from the Portuguese word *barroco*, meaning a pearl of irregular shape. The word *Baroque* has long been used to denote the period of painting and architecture that includes the names of Rembrandt, Rubens, Velázquez, and Bernini.

It is valuable to examine the interrelationships of the creative activities of artists working in architecture, music, painting, poetry, and sculpture. It helps us to understand and appreciate the other disciplines more deeply. As one takes time to study various artists that make up a period, one sees that the doors of the arts are constantly opening upon each other.

In the city of Eisenach, Germany, Johann Sebastian Bach was born on the first day of spring in 1685. In the same city over 150 years earlier, Martin Luther had translated the Bible into German and also had written some of the hymns that were so influential on the music of Bach. Eisenach is also important to remember as the seat of the minnesingers and the location of the Wartburg Castle, which Wagner would later use for his opera *Tannhauser*. This is the very castle where Luther had translated the New Testament.

It can be said that if there had not been a Luther, there would not have been a Bach. The focus of Bach's spiritual life was in Christianity and in the service of religion through music. It is easy to pass over the previous statement and not realize the truth of the fact that Bach's Christian faith and his music are inseparably united. I have read countless contemporary books and various articles on Bach discussing the mystery of Bach's greatness, and the authors rarely mention his self-acknowledged indebtedness to his Lord and Savior. His belief in the reality of heaven caused his music to be timeless. As one critic said, "Without knowing it, he divided music history into two basic periods: pre-Bach and post-Bach. And in the post-Bach era he is a perpetual presence."

Bach spent his life in the musical service of God without being conscious of the extraordinary greatness of his work. In writing his music to the glory of God and doing his work as a conscientious craftsman who believed in doing a job well, he undoubtedly would have been astonished to learn that over two hundred years after his death his compositions would be more often performed *and* studied and his name more deeply respected by musicians than any other composer's.

After the death of his parents, Bach at the age of ten went to live in Ohrduf with his elder brother who had been a student of Pachelbel. Johann Christoph was a good but stern teacher. He owned one volume of contemporary compositions that the young Bach was not allowed to use; and so over a period of six months, in the still of the night and by moonlight, he copied it all down. When the brother discovered it, he took away the manuscript, but Bach at this early age had begun a lifelong habit of copying and learning from others. Unfortunately, however, this probably contributed to the eye-strain that eventually led to his blindness.

After the death of his brother, Bach was a boy soprano in Lüneberg for several years where he also went to school and came into contact with serious musical culture. There he distinguished himself as a violinist and viola player. When he left Lüneberg, before he was eighteen years old, he was also recognized as a master clavichordist, organist, and a promising composer. He began his professional career playing violin and viola in the court orchestra at Weimar. He was not unhappy there, but the organ was his first love. Bach was next employed in Arnstadt where he wrote almost entirely organ music.

A major influence on Bach that helped to release his creative energies was his two-hundred-mile walk in 1705 to hear the greatest organist of his generation, Dietrich Buxtehude. Buxtehude directed the *Abendmusiken* (evening musical devotions) in the cathedral of Lübeck. Much of Buxtehude's music was composed for these evening devotions, which were held during the Advent season in Lübeck. Bach was almost fired because of his long absence, but his music was never the same afterwards. Buxtehude is in the unique position of being a link between the founder of Protestant Baroque music, Schütz, and its supreme master, Bach. All three of these great composers were Christians and knew and appreciated the Bible and its truthfulness.

Not only did Bach mature earliest in his organ compositions, but he was happiest at this noble instrument and remained absorbed in it throughout his career. During his lifetime he was known as a brilliant organist rather than as a composer, and his advice in organ-building was sought all over Germany. In appraising an organ, Bach always pulled out all the stops first to test the lungs of the instrument. Bach was praised for his performing ability, pedal technique, and art of registration. His habit of astonishing the congregation by trying unusual sounds on the organ stirred criticism, but it aided Bach's independent creative growth.

His next position was as organist in St. Blasius, Mülhausen, in 1707. There he married his cousin, Maria Barbara, who was also a musical Bach, and she bore him two of his famous musical sons, Wilhelm Friedemann and Carl Philipp Emanuel. Within less than a year he was back in Weimar as court organist to Duke Wilhelm Ernst. Here Bach reached his zenith as an organist.

The foundation of Bach's music was the German chorale. In Weimar he wrote some of his chorale preludes, which are organ meditations on hymn tunes. Throughout Bach's life the Lutheran hymnbook was an unfailing stimulation for his genius. These great Reformation chorales were not meant to create a mood but to convey a message. They were a confession of faith in the Scriptures, not simply personal feelings. Bach's first composition was a simple exercise on a hymn tune, and at the end of his life he was still at work on a chorale, "Before Thy Throne I Now Appear."

Bach's ideal was both unity and diversity. His desire was to create unity with diversity in whatever he produced, and he found ways to tie together even the separate parts of a collection, most often by the use of familiar hymn tunes. His organ style was calculated to stimulate devotional feeling, and nowhere more so than in the *Orgelbüchlein*. In this wonderful "Little Book for the Organ," we feel the Dürer-like quality of his music. On the title page Bach wrote, "To the glory of God alone in the highest and to further the learning of everyone."

While in Weimar, Bach became interested in Italian music, especially that of Corelli and Vivaldi. His cousin, Walther, introduced him to the newest Italian music, and he learned musical architecture from the Italians. The Bach style is really a fusion of Italian and German characteristics.

A man of strong opinions, Bach often had squabbles with those for whom he worked. Most often he was right. But the many struggles and hardships he had only drove him closer to his Lord. For example, when he was offered a better position in another city, the prince in Weimar put Bach in prison for a month in order to keep him from leaving. Always an overcomer and an incredibly hard worker, Bach used this time to work on his *Orgelbüchlein*. Temperate, industrious, devout, Bach was a home-lover and family man. He was genuine, hospitable, and jovial. Frugality and discipline ruled in the Bach home, but there was also unity, laughter, loyalty, and love. Bach was a very disciplined person who made the most of all the events— good and bad—in his life.

In 1717 Bach left Weimar and became the court conductor to the Prince of Cöthen. These years are known as the secular period of his life because of the dearth of music in the Calvinist Reformed Church with which he was identified there. Like Rembrandt, Bach suffered under the control of the Calvinists, who believed that artistic music had no place in the church and that it was not right for an artist to depict biblical scenes. But Bach, who never shrank from the "impossible," was not deterred.

Even though we speak of this as his secular period, Bach did not shed his religion when he composed for secular purposes or for instruction. He did not write cheap or trivial works. He believed that the primary reason for music should be for the glory of God and the recreation of the mind. In Cöthen he wrote his central instrumental works, including the *Well-Tempered Clavier* (tempered means tuned). It revolutionized the tuning of instruments and is one of the most amazing works ever written. Along with Bach's other music, it has had an enormous influence on such composers as Mozart, Beethoven, Mendelssohn, Chopin, Schumann, Brahms, and Hindemith. No composer has had an inventive faculty as profound and rich as Bach's. He has been rightly spoken of as "a composer for all seasons."

In 1720 when Bach returned from a musical tour with the prince, he was met at the door of his home with the shocking news that his wife had died and was already buried. His faith sustained him in this black hour. Later he married a soprano, Anna Magdelena, who was a superb helpmate to him, both in caring for the home and their children and also in his work. She helped to copy many of his manuscripts. For her beautiful soprano voice Bach wrote many of his most inspired arias. In all, Bach had twenty children, of whom ten died in childhood. The youngest, Johann Christian, later became the famous "English" Bach composer.

From the music book Bach wrote for his wife, Anna Magdelena, he used a sarabande melody for his *Goldberg Variations*. These were written for a wealthy man who suffered from insomnia. On the nights when he could not sleep, the gentleman would say to Bach's pupil, "Dear Goldberg, play me one of my variations." Everything Bach touched he improved. He did not invent anything new, but it was the way he brought his many musical ideas together that made his music so rich. Many critics consider Bach the greatest of all composers. In him we have a supreme uniting of a person's faith and his talent. Cellist Pablo Casals, who at ninety-three began his day by playing from the *Well-Tempered Clavier* on the piano, once said, "There is always something left to discover in it." Helmut Walcha, the blind German organist, added, "Ultimately Bach opens a vista to the universe. After experiencing him, people feel there is meaning to life after all."

The fusion of national styles in the unique Bach style is one of the most remarkable qualities of his music. This merging of Italian, French, and German styles is most fully exemplified in his six *Brandenburg Concertos*. They continue the coloristic tradition of Venice and of Vivaldi's concertos. The wealth of counterpoint and variety of instrumental color make these concertos unique in this form. Bach loved the recorder and used it in the concertos. He felt that its pure sound carried the soul's devotion to the throne of God. There is always sense of direction in Bach's music. Even when it wanders, there is always a place of return and resolution.

After six years in Cöthen, Bach went to Leipzig in 1723. His crowning years of creativity were spent as cantor at the St. Thomas Church here. It was here that he wrote a vast amount of vocal music, including the heart of his work, the cantatas. Of the nearly three hundred cantatas he composed, only about two hundred survive today. Stravinsky once said that Bach's cantatas should be the heart of every musician's study. The cantatas join the Bible, music, and history into a unified whole—the same thing Rembrandt did in his etchings and paintings, expressing scriptural truth by means of great art.

Bach stressed the words and the message in his cantatas. One could do an entire study listening to passages that illustrate this. This same literalness can be observed in the fifteen woodcuts of the book of Revelation, early masterpieces of the great Dürer. Bach, in a sense, placed himself "in the pulpit" to expound the Gospel, and his cantatas reflect the depth of Christian truth. Bach wrote his music as an act of worship in the true mystical sense, and his faith and music are unified.

Along with the crystalline logic underlying all of Bach's works are the rhythms and controlled but seemingly spontaneous harmonic modulations. One explanation as to why the music of Bach is popular today among young listeners is its living pulse. Pianist Glenn Gould said, "There is a bridge between Bach's ideas of rhythm and those of the mid-twentieth century, and it has been created by popular music and jazz." That may or may not be true, but what eventually captivates the young listeners (according to a *Time* editorial) "is Bach's granite solidity that young people seem to respond to. It is as if he provided a firm ground-base for their improvisatory life-style." We can say as fellow believers with Bach that there is no "as if" about it. The firm base Johann Sebastian Bach has given to the world is Christianity.

Cantata No. 21, *I Was in Much Tribulation*, is in two sections. Part I depicts the sorrow and distress of the sinful soul, and Part II describes the spirit of rejoicing in the salvation brought by Jesus Christ. Bach also includes in this cantata one of his favorite hymns, "If Thou But Suffer God to Guide Thee." The final chorus of this cantata begins with a setting of the words "Worthy Is the Lamb That Was Slain," which is strikingly similar to Handel's setting of the same text in his *Messiah*. Bach longed to know Handel whom he greatly admired, but they never met. Bach traveled in a small radius within Germany, whereas Handel enjoyed international fame.

For years I have been giving Farel House lectures at L'Abri Fellowship. The first one I ever gave was on Bach cantatas. This was before the chapel when we had all meetings in the living room of Chalet les Mélèzes. After our neighbor and dear friend Herr Lengacher built our chapel, one of the first duets a friend and I performed was "Hasten to Jesus" from Cantata 78. As D. F. Tovey says, "Bach's Heaven always rests on a very solid foundation."[1] That foundation is Jesus Christ as truly God and truly man.

The culmination of Bach's work as a church musician were his *St. John Passion* and *St. Matthew Passion*. Often he wrote on manuscripts, "With the help of Jesus," or "To God alone be the glory," acknowledging that his gift of music was from God. The *St. Matthew Passion* is considered one of the richest and noblest sacred works in existence. It is the creation of a mind intimately familiar and profoundly moved by the gospel texts. It is indeed one of civilization's incomparable masterpieces, and yet it was produced in a tense atmosphere of unfriendliness.

One critic said that Bach's move to Leipzig was a "monumental miscalculation." It is true that his salary and social status were lower than before and also true that he entered into fresh difficulties with church officials and choirboys, but in God's overall plan for his life it was not a mistake. It is certain that Bach would not have written as much and as well and pioneered in almost every field of music if in these last years he had been famous and financially free to travel.

Bach in his old age did have one exciting triumph. He was invited to the court at Potsdam to play for King Frederick the Great of Prussia who was a gifted amateur musician. Upon his arrival, the king dismissed everyone else, exclaiming, "Old Bach is here!" It was a memorable evening for the two of them, with the musician delighting the king by improvising a fugue on one of Frederick's themes. Not too long after the court visit, Bach's eyes began to fail. After two operations, which weakened him further, he died at sixty-five, totally blind. While Bach lay upon his bed, shortly before his death, he dictated his last composition—the chorale "Before Thy Throne I Now Appear."

Bach was mourned by many after his death, but only as a brilliant organist and teacher. Exactly one hundred years after the first performance of the *St. Matthew Passion*, Mendelssohn, at the age of twenty, resurrected it. The 1829 performance was received with enthusiasm and awe. Mendelssohn helped to establish Bach's place in the musical world, but in all likelihood no other age than our own has better appreciated the true nature of Bach's wide-ranging giftedness. We have benefited today from the research done by eminent musicologists who have brought the works of Bach into clearer focus, and the advent of records has created a vast new

---

1. D. F. Tovey, *Essays in Musical Analysis* (London: Oxford University Press, 1946), p. 42.

audience for Bach by making available countless Bach albums. According to the *Bach-Werke-Verzeichnis (BWV)*, Bach wrote more than one thousand works, of which nearly three-quarters were intended to be performed at Christian worship services.

Bach's influence in music history has been one of wholesomeness and strength. He is difficult to perform, but he never wrote empty virtuosity. His music has content. Another of his sublime works, the B Minor Mass, with its monumental choruses, was written for the Church universal with a thoroughly Protestant spirit. Bach considered the German mass as arranged by Luther as a memorial and not a sacrifice. The B Minor Mass has only one companion, and that is Handel's *Messiah*. The aim of both creations is the artistic presentation of the essence of Christianity, Handel writing from the historical viewpoint and Bach from the doctrinal.

Bach, a true mystic in the proper biblical sense, lived life to the fullest. Yet he understood that our days upon this earth are numbered. In "Come Sweet Death" he expresses the height and depth of his faith. Biographer Alfred Einstein says, "It can fairly be said that no composer thought more about death or stood in greater awe of it than Bach. Bach welcomed death, although he feared it; and between his fear and his longing stood only an indomitable and rock-like faith." Johann Sebastian Bach was one of the spiritually wisest musicians the world has known.

Martin Luther not only chose to stand for the truth of Scripture, but he surrounded himself with artists, poets, musicians, philosophers, and theologians. As a result the Reformation reached into every realm of culture. Few in our age have even dreamed of, let alone fulfilled, such possibilities— based on a clear understanding of Christianity—the way Bach, Schütz, Handel, Dürer, Rembrandt, and Milton did. As Machen said, "The vast majority of those who reject the gospel do so simply because they know nothing about it. But whence comes this indifference? It is due to the intellectual atmosphere in which men are living. The modern world is dominated by ideas which ignore the gospel. Modern culture is not altogether opposed to the gospel. But it is out of all connection with it. It not only prevents the acceptance of Christianity. It prevents Christianity from getting a hearing."[2]

As it will often be expressed in these pages: "We need to go back in order to go forward." Listen to Bach, appreciate the richness and diversity of his music, but hear his message too.

Recommended Reading

David, Hans T. and Mendel, Arthur, eds. *The Bach Reader: A Life of Bach in Letters and Documents.* New York: W. W. Norton, 1945.

---

2. J. G. Machen, *Christianity and Culture* (Huémoz, Switzerland: L'Abri Fellowship, 1969), p. 8.

Field, Laurence N. *Johann Sebastian Bach*. Minneapolis:
Augsburg Publishing House, 1943.

Geiringer, Karl. *Johann Sebastian Bach: The Culmination of an
Era*. London: Allen and Unwin, 1967.

Newman, Werner. *Bach, A Pictorial Biography*. London:
Thames and Hudson, 1961.

Recommended Listening

Six *Brandenburg Concertos*

Cantatas: No. 4, *Christ Lay in the Bonds of Death*

No. 21, *I Was in Much Tribulation*

No. 80, *A Mighty Fortress Is Our God*

No. 106, *God's Time Is the Best Time*

No. 140, *Wake! Awake!*

No. 211, *Coffee Cantata*

Chorale Preludes: *Orgelbüchlein*

Christmas Oratorio

Goldberg Variations for Harpsichord

Magnificat in D

Mass in B Minor

St. John Passion

St. Matthew Passion

Toccata and Fugue in D Minor

Well-Tempered Clavier

Jesu Meine Freude (Motet)

Four Orchestral Suites

CHAPTER 4

George Frideric Handel
1685-1759

This noble prince of music.

Paul Henry Lang

*I*f an artist could live to read his biography," says biographer Paul Henry Lang, "he would recognize not so much himself, as the mask that covered his face." But I do not believe Handel would mind too much what we say about him as long as we listen to his music. He said little about himself in his lifetime. The central fact of his life was his music. He would be happy to know of the joy and pleasure his music, particularly *Messiah*, gives to so many people, but he would probably be surprised at how few of his works are known today. Handel had an immense genius. The magnitude of his gift from God and the avalanche of great music he wrote is scarcely suspected in this generation except by musical experts.

George Frideric Handel was born in Halle, Germany, within a month of Bach. His father, a barber-surgeon, was a strong individual with an acute business sense and the ambition for his son to be a lawyer. His mother, the daughter of a Lutheran pastor, was a good and pious woman, and Handel had deep respect and affection for her all his life.

Handel's musical gifts must have been noticed early, but his father paid no attention to such "frivolities" as music. When George Frideric was eight or nine, the duke of Weissenfels heard him play the postlude at a church service, and he summoned the boy's father and told him he ought to encourage such talent. As Handel's father was the court surgeon, there was nothing to do but give in, and Handel began studying music instead of law.

His only teacher was Friedrich Wilhelm Zachow, a most learned and imaginative musician and teacher, who instilled in his young pupil a lifelong intellectual curiosity. Zachow gave Handel instruction in organ, harpsichord, violin, and oboe. (Handel learned to love the oboe, and years later in his famous *Fireworks Music* he used twenty-four oboes!) Handel also received from Zachow a solid grounding in harmony, counterpoint, choral writing, and imaginative orchestration. When Handel was eleven, he wrote his first composition, and he played the organ well enough to substitute for his teacher when needed. Handel's appreciation for his instructor knew no end, and after Zachow died in 1712, Handel sent frequent gifts to his widow. Remembering widows and orphans was characteristic of Handel throughout his life. He was a charitable man and very fond of children.

When Handel was seventeen or eighteen, he went to Hamburg. Biographer Newman Flower says that the musician left Halle aimlessly to find fortune. Not so. I agree with Lang who declared that George Frideric Handel never crossed a street aimlessly. As we have seen many talented people come to L'Abri Fellowship over the years for direction in their lives, having crisscrossed Europe and the Middle East after graduating from college, so did Handel go to Hamburg in 1703 to begin his "great search" for ways to work out the ideas flooding his mind. And there in Hamburg he discovered opera with its amalgamation of French, German, and Italian styles. In two years he produced his first opera, *Almira*, and now having something of a reputation, he went to Italy, "the promised land of musicians."

We could write pages about the fertile Italian period, 1706 to 1710, but this at least must be said. While in Rome in 1708, Handel wrote the oratorio *The Resurrection*. It was his first notable religious effort, and he composed it in a month. It was performed under the direction of Corelli. Corelli, who was highly respected in Western Europe, was the great conservative musician of Italy, and he had a profound influence on Handel. Corelli was a meticulous, critical, and gifted musician, and through his diligence he summed up everything that a century of instrumental music had produced. None of it was lost on Handel.

The second opera Handel wrote in Italy, *Agrippina*, was performed in Venice in 1709. It achieved such sensational success that Handel, the Saxon Lutheran, became one of the most noted composers in Italy. The Venetians loved him and spoke of him as *"Il Caro Sassone"* (the dear Saxon). His triumph in Venice brought him world fame, as any successful Venetian production immediately made the rounds of the Italian operatic dependences abroad. During his stay in Venice, Handel and Domenico Scarlatti, one of Italy's most important harpsichord composers, became close friends.

Handel wrote little in Venice, but favors were heaped upon him, and here his fateful meeting with the younger brother of the future King George I of England took place. This younger brother invited Handel to come to Hanover where Handel obtained the post of musical director. But it was only an episode, because almost immediately he was off on a long leave of absence to London where his sparkling opera *Rinaldo* met great success. Back to Hanover he went, and finally in 1712 he moved to England and remained there the rest of his life.

Two factors explain Handel's creativity in England. The country was a beehive of musical activity with Italian opera ruling the day. Within the next thirty-year period Handel wrote about forty operas. He understood the voice wonderfully as a result of his years in Italy. The second reason for his creativity was that the Elector of Hanover became King George I of England in 1714, and the German-born Handel, after the new king forgave him for leaving his post in Hanover, won favor at court. Handel wrote his *Water Music* suite hoping for the king's pardon, and with such glorious music he quickly received it.

Handel's years in Italy were very important to him. He was always interested in melody and beautiful sound (euphony)—the supreme Latin ideal. He retained this all his life. No German surpassed him in writing beautiful melodies. But we must hold in balance the truth that the Baroque was the great period of Protestant music, and of course we know that the Protestant culture was rooted in the Bible.

Both Bach and Handel learned, borrowed, and copied from great men like Corelli and Vivaldi and others, but they were constantly experimenting, inventing, always giving their music their singularly sure touch. As historian Donald Jay Grout explains for the benefit of those who belittle Handel for his eclecticism: "Most of his borrowings were from his own earlier works, but a considerable number were from other composers. . . . If he borrowed, he more often than not repaid with interest, clothing the borrowed material with new beauty and preserving it for generations that otherwise would scarcely have known of its existence."

Handel is really the inventor of the organ concerto with orchestral accompaniment. These original concertos with their warm, expressive melodies are uncomplicated, popular concert music in the best sense of the word. Handel found his way to the hearts of people by the use of simple things. In his oratorios are simple things, as well as sumptuous Venetian double choruses. A secret of great art is to have contrast. The *Messiah* with its majestic choruses and sudden dramatic silences is a good illustration.

Handel's music is as much Italian as it is German. In fact, Handel is the international composer. There is also a sense of French grandeur in his music, and England provided him with the choral tradition. Handel, indeed, may be spoken of as a citizen of the world, whereas Bach remained in Germany all his life. Yet under the hand of God both men were great composers. It should be an encouragement to all of us to be creative with what we have where we are.

Handel was the man of action, the extrovert, the improviser. While still in Italy, he was looking ahead, obtaining most of his best singers for his operas written and performed in England. Bach was also a skillful improviser, but he wished to bring each detail to perfection, whereas Handel desired to have an overall strong effect on his listeners. Handel matured earlier than Bach, and both composers, as we said, appropriated the best from other artists and made the music even better.

Something must be said about Handel the man and why he was an inviting target for critics and for satire. He was a foreigner and an individual no one could help noticing. He had large hands, large feet, a large appetite, and he wore a huge white wig with curls rippling over his shoulders. He spoke English rather loudly in a colorful blending of Italian, German, and French.

He was temperamental, he loved freedom, and he hated restrictions that placed limits on his art. Like Bach, he was often at variance with others. But in his most dramatic fits of agitation there was no real malice, and these scenes frequently were extremely comical. Handel had the gift of command, and even in violent situations (and unless you have been in the theater, you do not know how violent it can be at rehearsals and backstage!) through wisdom and his sense of humor, he had the power to mend fractured relationships.

One evening in an opera performance being played before the Princess of Wales and other noble persons, two prima donnas, in a moment of jealousy, seized one another by the hair. This extra "act" brought forth roars of laughter. Later a farce was written that dramatized this historic "battle of temperament," and the author gave the victory to Handel who walked over to the percussion section of the orchestra and with several blows on the kettledrum brought the struggle to an end.

Between 1718 and 1720, Handel lived on the estate of the Duke of Chandos where he was master of the duke's chapel. Here he composed the *Chandos* Anthems, which are psalm settings. The anthems laid the cornerstone for his future choral compositions. These were the most carefree years of Handel's life. After this interval in the country, he moved back to London, and for the next seventeen years he helped to manage the Royal Academy of Music as well as compose and produce operas.

When Handel first arrived in England, the use of English librettos in the operas had already been abandoned without a murmur; but finally the English people wearied of Italian operas, and Handel gradually began to compose oratorios in English. His first success was *Esther*.

When one speaks about famous people and their successful lives, often the detail of their suffering, anguish, and day-by-day struggles is passed over lightly. It is not fair to do this to anyone and particularly not to Handel. His London years saw ups and downs, unbelievable downs at times. As Romain Rolland has tried to explain it: "He was surrounded by a crowd of bulldogs with terrible fangs, by unmusical men of letters who were likewise able to bite, by jealous colleagues, arrogant virtuosos, cannibalistic theatrical companies, fashionable cliques, feminine plots, and nationalistic leagues. . . . Twice he was bankrupt, and once he was stricken by apoplexy amid the ruins of his company. But he always found his feet again; he never gave in."[3] Handel, the sanest of geniuses, was a hairbreadth from insanity. More than once even his friends thought that he had lost his reason; but no matter how difficult his life was, Handel the musician escaped from his trials into the serenity of his art. In this realm he had supreme self-control.

---

3. Romain Rolland, *Essays on Music,* ed. David Ewen (New York: Dover, 1959), p. 218.

Few suspected his nervous tension and the depth of his emotion in his transports of joy, fury, enthusiasm, or overwhelming sadness. When Handel was writing *Messiah*, which he put down on paper in twenty-four days without once leaving his house, his servant brought him food, which Handel often left untouched. While Handel worked on the "Hallelujah Chorus," his servant found him with tears in his eyes. Handel exclaimed, "I did think I did see all heaven before me and the great God Himself!"

Because Handel lived fully with his heart, his suffering was deep, but out of it came his great music. His power to create a mood with overwhelming poetic depth and suggestiveness is unrivaled. Lesser men who did not understand his genius satirized him as a glutton and a tyrant, but the truth is, his strong personality (with its rougher aspects) was balanced by a sense of humor, generosity, honesty, sincere piety, and superhuman determination.

The music of Handel is lively because he was full of life, and it is intimate yet universal. Always he wrote for his immediate audience, but because there is a timelessness about his music, we are able to appreciate him today.

He drew his music from everywhere. He once told a friend that he got inspiration for some of his airs from the street cries of London. It reminds one of Charles Dickens who received an important part of his education while walking the streets in London. Into the atmosphere of a big, noisy city, Handel brought the beauty of the country. One of his masterpieces, "L'Allegro ed il Penseroso," with words by John Milton, is filled with imaginative musical nature painting. His music is wholesome and communicative. One feels his optimism in his great choruses.

His music is among the most noble ever written, and yet it was misunderstood by church people at first because his biblical oratorios were performed in theaters. The use of a theater for a religious work was revolutionary, and those who opposed Handel went to great extremes to keep his oratorios from being successful. For example, certain self-righteous women gave large teas or sponsored other theatrical performances on the days when Handel's concerts were to take place in order to rob him of his audience, or his enemies hired boys to tear down the advertisements of his concerts.

It is true that Handel hated restrictions and avoided as many official appointments as he could. He took no pains to humor socially minded people, and he had no respect for his unmerciful critics. He was an artist, and he did not alter his God-given ideas to please others. Such a man as George Frideric Handel was not likely to please women, and he troubled his mind very little about them. But he was not unsociable or irresponsible. He simply knew what had to come first. Though he never married, he was not without devoted friends and companionship. Some of his friends were among the noblest intellects of the age.

Two of Handel's greatest oratorios, *Saul* and *Israel in Egypt,* were written in four months, the autumn of 1738, when he was fifty-three. He leased a theater to perform these oratorios during Lent, and as an added attraction he improvised at the organ during the intermission. To appreciate the greatness of Handel and his ability to overcome, keep in mind that one year before he wrote these two works, he had suffered a paralytic stroke and a nervous collapse. And then when you listen to *Israel in Egypt,* also remember that its first performance was an outright failure. It was not performed again for seventeen years; in fact, it never was a success in Handel's lifetime.

Israel in Egypt contains some of his most sublime inspiration. He is at his finest in the choruses. Handel was the master of the basic Baroque principle of contrast, which makes his music so lively and interesting. Much twentieth-century music is extremely dull because of its sameness.

To better appreciate the music of Handel, one must understand that he was an art collector. He owned some paintings by Rembrandt, and he delighted in wandering through art museums. One can see the large man with his enormous hands and feet studying a painting with intensity, undoubtedly talking out loud to himself and with more people looking at him than at the paintings. Because of his interest in art, his music is intensely visual. Handel was like a painter who was at his best in gigantic mural frescoes.

In *Israel in Egypt,* there is a musical description of the plagues sent by God upon the Egyptians. One hears (and practically sees) the hopping of frogs, the arrival of all manner of flies and lice, and the locusts without number that devoured the fruits of the ground. The beginning of the hailstorm is unforgettable, as is the quietness when the chorus sings, "He sent a thick darkness over the land, even darkness which might be felt." It is musical tone painting at its greatest.

Good poetry and particularly the words of Scripture always attracted the composer. He was thoroughly familiar with the Bible, and he probably selected the words for *Israel in Egypt.* They come mainly from Exodus and the historical psalms. In the chorus "But As for His People" Handel gives other Christians the courage to believe in the power of God to do what He says He will do for His people.

Probably the Wesley brothers knew Handel. In the hymnal *Christian Praise,* there is one superb hymn, "Rejoice, the Lord Is King," with words by Charles Wesley and music by George Frideric Handel.

Handel composed the *Messiah* in 1741 at the age of fifty-six. As Newman Flower observes, "Considering the immensity of the work and the short time involved in putting it to paper, it will remain, perhaps forever, the greatest feat in the whole history of musical composition." As we marvel at it, let us not forget to listen to the message. When Handel finished his masterpiece, he put it in a drawer. He did not intend to produce it in London, having been through such turmoils over his other oratorios. But then came an invitation from Dublin, and in the society of cheerful Irishmen, Handel began to recover his good spirits.

The *Messiah* was first performed in Dublin in 1742 and immediately was a huge popular success. When a nobleman complimented Handel on the great entertainment of the *Messiah*, Handel replied, "My Lord, I should be sorry if I only entertained them; I wished to make them better." And better we are because of Handel's *Messiah*, particularly if we too believe the message.

The proceeds went to three charitable undertakings. This was nothing new with Handel. He was always generous. He had his faults, but there was nothing mean or small in him. When he was poor, he was liberal, and when he became rich, he remembered his friends and those in need. He had a particular interest in the Society of Musicians (like Verdi's "Casa Verdi") and the Foundling Hospital. Whenever the *Messiah* was performed afterwards, proceeds were almost entirely reserved for the benefit of charity.

In 1751 when Handel began to write the chorus that ends the second act of *Jephtha*, he noted at the bottom of the page that he was prevented from continuing the work because of "the relaxation of the sight in my left eye." Later when he learned he was really going blind, it was the lowest moment in his life. He had no fear of the coming darkness, but he dreaded the termination of his work. It nearly crushed him, but he struggled through to the end of *Jephtha*.

When he no longer could see to compose, he returned to playing. He practiced the harpsichord for hours each day, and having a dread of idleness, he began to organize performances. Also he still appeared on Sundays as a regular worshiper at St. George's in Hanover Square.

In 1759 when the oratorio season opened in March, Handel announced a series of ten concerts. The almost-blind composer conducted all of them, ending with the *Messiah* on April 6, shortly before Easter. He carried this final performance through to the end seemingly without fatigue, but he knew his time was short. He told some friends that he had one desire left. "I want to die on Good Friday," he said, "in the hope of rejoining the good God, my sweet Lord and Savior, on the day of His resurrection." Shortly before his death a very special person, Selina Hastings, Countess of Huntingdon, visited him at his request. Lady Huntingdon was a true Christian, a remarkable individual, and a generous supporter of Wesley and Whitefield.

When the morning of Good Friday arrived, Handel bade farewell to his friends and then told his servant not to admit anyone else because, as he said, "I have now done with the world." He died that day on April 14, 1759, and was buried in Poets' Corner in Westminster Abbey. Two verses of Scripture come to mind when I think of George Frideric Handel: "A just man falleth seven times, and riseth up again" (Proverbs 24:16), and "When I sit in darkness, the Lord shall be a light unto me" (Micah 7:8).

Handel did not like to traffic in miniatures. Everything was big with him, including his heart. In all his nobility, he could not do things in small, timid ways. His life was rich in melody, and he poured it out generously. Most twentieth-century composers have lost the sense of beauty. One hears few pleasant sounds in music today. That is why many sensitive, artistic people have turned back to listen to Baroque music; it is beautiful, and we need beauty in our lives. Handel has spaciousness in his music, a marvelous sense of timing. His dramatic silences are full of awe. Much modern music batters the listener and adds to the noise and confusion in our already noisy and confusing lives. The music of Handel helps to bring order and joy into living.

In our enthusiasm for *Messiah* we should not neglect some of the other great oratorios. He wrote twenty-six. But let us never cease to marvel at the mighty Handelian hammer strokes on the words, "Wonderful, Counselor, the Mighty God," and the contrast and truth of the words, "He was despised." Also his organ music is marvelous. May this chapter serve as a brief introduction to my favorite composer.

Recommended Reading

Lang, Paul Henry. *George Frideric Handel.* New York: W. W.
    Norton, 1966.
Flower, Newman. *George Frideric Handel: His Personality and
    His Times.* New York: Charles Scribner's Sons, 1948.

Recommended Listening

"L'Allegro ed il Penseroso"
Chandos Anthems
Concerti Grossi (Op. 3 and 6)
Concerto in B Flat for Harp and Orchestra
Concerti for Organ
Dettingen Te Deum
Israel in Egypt
Judas Maccabaeus
Messiah
Royal Fireworks Music
Saul
Solomon
Water Music

CHAPTER 5

Franz Joseph Haydn
1732-1809

God gave me a cheerful heart, so He will surely forgive me if I serve Him cheerfully.

Haydn

*F*ranz Joseph Haydn was one of the sanest, most productive composers in history. His music is played nearly every day over the Swiss FM radio, and I believe there are specific reasons why he still is popular. The music of Haydn has cheer, beauty, logic, order, nobility, freshness of imagination, and humor. These are foreign words to our whole modern culture.

Haydn was in his twenties when Jean-Jacques Rousseau was recklessly urging people to throw over ancient habits, traditions, and laws, demanding absolute freedom for the individual. Rousseau's *Discourse on the Origin of Inequality* excited many intellectuals, students, and artists of the eighteenth century, many of whom enthusiastically accepted its ideas, but not Franz Joseph Haydn. He respected God and the order in His creation. He saw beyond the momentary excitement of violently changing the present political, religious, and educational systems without putting into the void a real base—found only in true Christianity. Those who deny the truth of Scripture never find freedom.

Haydn accepted his life, hard as it was at times, and found it good. He recognized that there are fresh possibilities ahead for those willing to be builders in life rather than destroyers. Haydn wrote some of his richest and happiest music toward the end of his life. He said on one occasion, "God gave me a cheerful heart, so He will surely forgive me if I serve Him cheerfully." When obstacles came into his life, and he found it hard to persevere, he said that often something within him whispered, "There are but few contented and happy individuals here below; everywhere grief and care prevail; perhaps your labor may one day be the source from which the weary and worn, or the person burdened with affairs, may derive a few moments of rest and refreshment." He wrote that in a letter to a group of enthusiastic music-

lovers who had gotten together in the small German town of Bergen to perform his *Creation*. They had written to tell him how delighted and thankful
they were for his music. And some two hundred years later many of us also
are glad Haydn persevered and left to us, as a legacy, his cheerful music. We
delight in the truthfulness of his merry and unequivocal temperament.

Haydn was born in 1732 and raised in a humble but music-loving family in the village of Rohrau in lower Austria. The parents instilled in their
children a love of work, method, and cleanliness, and above all a respect for
religion. As a boy Haydn spent nearly all his time in church and school.

He left home at the age of six for musical training, and when he was
eight years old, he became a choirboy in Vienna. He stayed at the school for
nine years, acquiring enormous practical knowledge of music by constant
performances; but to his disappointment, he received too little instruction in
music theory. Always full of humor and pranks, Haydn could not resist cutting off the pigtail of a fellow singer. He was put out of the choir because of
this incident, but more likely the real reason was that his voice had changed.

For a period of time the seventeen-year-old Haydn made a meager living by giving lessons and playing night serenades in the streets of Vienna.
But he had already set his heart and mind on a life of music regardless of
difficulties. With unusual calmness in an artistic temperament, he persevered
through several years of poverty. Thanks to tremendous persistence Haydn
mastered counterpoint and gradually made himself known to certain influential persons in Vienna. Nicola Porpora, the famous Italian composer and
singing teacher, gave him a few lessons in composition. At one time Haydn
accompanied the pupils of Porpora and lived in the Michaelerhaus in
Vienna. As an opera singer, I studied in this same building some two hundred years later to prepare to sing Brünnhilde in Wagner's *Die Walküre*.

Because Haydn did prevail over his hardships with stubborn tenacity
and resourcefulness, he became one of the most independent spirits in musical history, and one of the most deliberate and disciplined. He always found
composition a labor, and so he set for himself regular hours to compose.
When ideas did not come, he prayed for them. When they came, he worked
with unremitting industry.

His forty-year childless marriage was no joy to either partner. Haydn's
wife did not understand music and showed no interest in her husband's
work. It was reported that she used his manuscripts for pastry linings or hair-
curl paper.

In 1761 Haydn was appointed the musical director in the country
home of Prince Paul Esterhazy, a position that involved a multitude of activities. Haydn carried out these duties extremely well. His service as chief of
personnel revealed tact, good nature, and skill in dealing with people. Living
in the country was no hardship for his contented disposition. He loved hunting, fishing, and other outdoor activities. Here he served nearly thirty years
under ideal circumstances for his development as a composer. There was
always something musical going on at the Esterhazy estate. The Hungarian

prince loved music and was a bountiful patron. As Haydn once explained, "I was cut off from the world; there was no one to confuse or torment me, and I was forced to become original."

We have a somewhat similar environment at L'Abri. It is true that we are here to be a shelter to other people, but it has turned out that living in a small mountain village has been a shelter and a stimulus for some of us interested in the arts. We too have been forced to be creative under the leadership of God.

Besides his many operas, Haydn wrote for all kinds of instruments. Our Christmas record has Haydn's charming flute-clock pieces played on the Flentrop organ. Haydn is often referred to as the father of the symphony and the string quartet as we know them today. The quartet was his natural way of expression—organized simplicity. His quartets are clear, logical, and cheerful compositions.

One writer declared that after listening to Haydn, he always felt impelled to do some good work. This observation could not be made about many twentieth-century composers. They more often irritate the listener, occasionally enrage him. But I find that after the first shock of hearing Berio, Stockhausen, or Boulez, I become quickly bored, and never have I felt like doing a good work after listening to John Cage.

In talking about Haydn, it is impossible to leave out Mozart, who was twenty-four years younger than Haydn. It was he who gave him the nickname "Papa Haydn." They first met in 1781, and a deep friendship followed, with both composers learning from one another. Haydn's best symphonies were written after he met Mozart. Their friendship was one of the rare instances of complete and mutual understanding between two musicians, entirely free from jealousy, each one appreciating the abilities of the other.

About ten years later, when Haydn was invited to go to London, Mozart wrote to him, "Dear Papa, You were never meant for running around the world, and you speak too few languages." Haydn replied, "The language I speak is understood by the whole world." And off to London he went. It did prove to be a fruitful time, and he was right. The language he "spoke" is understood by the whole world. It was a good moment in Haydn's life but also a sad time, as he never saw his younger friend again. Mozart died at the age of thirty-five in 1791.

Haydn's success in England was immediate and emphatic. He left London happy, prosperous, and internationally famous. Indeed, he became the most beloved composer of his time. His truly remarkable fund of musical ideas, his wealth of invention, and the amazing clarity of his works are as fresh today as when he wrote them.

Haydn's twelve London symphonies are his crowning achievement and the works of a consummate master. All that he had learned in forty years of composing went into them, but even so, he remained an entertainer. He was not so concerned with making the world better but happier. His best-known work in this group is the *Surprise* Symphony. The title comes from the andante movement where there is a surprise chord to wake up the audience. Haydn said that it would make all the women scream. Such jokes came naturally to Haydn because of his inherent good nature.

The *Clock* Symphony with its iron logic and coherence is unsurpassed, and the *La Poule* (Chicken) Symphony is charming, amusing music. It received its name from a peculiar cluck in the second theme. The first theme sounds like a rooster chasing a hen, and in the last movement of the fugue, a prize egg is laid. Cheerful and childlike, Haydn wanted to make people smile, to relieve their hardships and troubles.

The Creation is an oratorio that was inspired as a result of Haydn hearing a mighty performance of Handel's *Messiah*. He was stunned and thrilled with the music and the words and awed at the way it was received by the audience with absolute storms of applause. Haydn told his biographer that while composing *The Creation,* "daily I fell on my knees and asked God for strength." The words are taken from John Milton's writings and from the Bible. One of the sublime moments is the climax of the chorus, "And There Was Light," with its unforgettable, overwhelming fortissimo.

Also in his last years Haydn wrote the oratorio *The Seasons.* It is delightful, pleasing music with charming descriptions of nature, expressing man's innocent joy in the simple, natural life. Certainly Bach and Handel had a clearer Christian witness than Haydn, but one senses the Christian base behind his works. When the emperor asked Haydn which oratorio he preferred, Haydn said, *"The Creation.* Because in *The Creation* angels speak, and their talk is of God. In *The Seasons* no one higher than Farmer Simon speaks."

In 1808 Haydn was brought on a stretcher to hear a performance of *The Creation* in Vienna where he spent his last years. At the glorious moment when the chorus sings "And There Was Light," the audience burst into applause. Haydn said with trembling hands uplifted, "Not from me. It all comes from above."

The Austrian national hymn, "Glorious Things of Thee Are Spoken," was composed by Haydn, and the words are by John Newton. The tune is to be found in the second movement of his *Emperor* Quartet. Haydn played it often, and it was the last thing he heard before his death. Again and again in his last days he expressed the hope, "not wholly to die; but to live on in my music." God has surely answered his prayers.

An entertaining as well as instructive game to play is to turn on the FM radio and attempt to identify the piece of classical music being played. So that you will become a skillful listener, here are some suggestions to help you:

1. First try to distinguish the period. (Is it Baroque, Classic, Romantic, Impressionist, Modern?)

2. Next what instruments are used? (Decide whether it is a symphony, a song, opera, piano concerto, quartet, or otherwise.)

3. If still bewildered, try to identify what nationality is being expressed in the music.

4. Is the composition written by a major composer? Remember that the great composers have a style of their own.

a) Try to name the composer, narrowing it down perhaps to Haydn, Mozart, or Beethoven.

b) If there is a soft, singing passage followed by a very loud chord, it is probably Beethoven. (Remember what Renoir said: "He doesn't spare us either the pain in his heart or the pain in his stomach.")

5. After careful listening, attempt to name the specific piece.

Obviously this game may be played in your home or in a classroom by having one person select records and having the listeners guess what is being played.

Recommended Reading

Geiringer, Karl. *Haydn, a Creative Life in Music.* Berkeley: University of California Press, 1968.

Hughes, Rosemary. *Haydn.* New York: Collier Books, 1963.

Recommended Listening

Concerti for Organ
Serenade Quartet, Op. 3, No. 5
Emperor Quartet, Op. 76, No. 3
The Creation
The Seasons
Farewell Symphony, No. 45
Hunt Symphony, No. 73
La Poule Symphony, No. 83
Surprise Symphony, No. 94
Military Symphony, No. 100
Clock Symphony, No. 101
Mass No. 9 in D Minor—*Nelson Mass*

CHAPTER 6

Wolfgang Amadeus Mozart
1756-1791

His music seemed to come out of an ideal realm
undisturbed by the troubles of life.

Donald Jay Grout

Wolfgang Amadeus Mozart, born in Salzburg, was probably the most sheerly musical composer who ever lived. Whenever Goethe spoke of the nature of genius, he would speak about Mozart, who appeared to him as "the human incarnation of a divine force of creation." Mozart had the single-mindedness of genius. He seemed born to create music. Indeed, his gift of writing music was like a cosmic phenomenon. From the age of four until he died at thirty-five, he scarcely had a day's rest. Mozart wrote so much music that one can hardly hope to hear more than half of it in a lifetime of listening.

His thoughts were always occupied with music, and with him the creative process was to a large extent completed before he put pen to paper. All witnesses of Mozart at work agree that he wrote a composition as one writes a letter. He composed whole works in his mind and retained them in his marvelous memory until he could no longer delay writing them out. His mind never really rested from music. As a critic has said, "Music was going on in his head continuously, probably in his sleep."

Mozart and his wife always lacked money, and one of the "better" places they lived while in Vienna had a ceiling with attractive plaster ornamentation of sprites and cherubim. As biographer Alfred Einstein observes, "I am convinced that Mozart never wasted a glance on it." Mozart said himself, "Composing is my one joy and passion." Composition with him was synonymous with life. He could always forget himself in composing. He was no lover of hunting and fishing like his friend Haydn, nor of communing with nature in the woods and fields like Beethoven, Brahms, and Tchaikovsky. His joy was covering paper with music. Mozart never set out to be original. He wrote music to please the public, though often his music is unique.

This supreme figure among the great composers of the world never had good health, and his life was filled with difficulties. Yet we rarely see evidence of these hardships in his music. Mozart's music is not autobiographical like that of Beethoven, for example. If Beethoven quarreled with a friend, you hear angry sounds in his music. Not so Mozart. He escaped into his music when the problems of life were the heaviest. In fact, his life was so full of cares that his music often has a carefree spirit.

Mozart's lively disposition, his love of fun, and the humanizing simplicity that enabled him to carry gracefully his burden of genius came from his mother. His father, Leopold Mozart, was a composer of some ability, assistant director of the archbishop's chapel in Salzburg, and the author of a well-known book on violin-playing. He probably would not be remembered today, other than for his violin treatise and the *Toy* Symphony, if he had not been the father of Wolfgang Amadeus Mozart. But all the biographers agree that Mozart would not have achieved his character and greatness without the influence of his father, who was an excellent teacher.

Mozart's musical education began when he was four years old, along with his older sister Maria Anna, or "Nannerl," as the family called her. Mozart seemed to know music innately. The main thing his father did was to guide and discipline the boy. At age five, Mozart's international career began, and he was on tour over half of the time between the ages of five and fifteen. Most of his life he was very lively and had difficulty keeping still. He was often singing and jumping about and amused at things other people scarcely noticed. His playful humor comes out in a letter he wrote to Nannerl describing a monk he had met in Bologna on one of the Italian tours: "He is regarded as a holy man. For my part I do not believe it, for at breakfast he often takes a cup of chocolate and immediately afterwards a good glass of strong Spanish wine; and I myself have had the honor of lunching with this saint who at table drank a whole decanter and finished up with a full glass of strong wine, two large slices of melon, some peaches, pears, five cups of coffee, a whole plate of cloves, and two full saucers of milk and lemon. He may, of course, be following some sort of diet, but I do not think so, for it would be too much; moreover, he takes several little snacks during the afternoon. . . . " (Einstein, *Mozart*).

Some critics say that Leopold was a calculating opportunist and exploited his children by taking them to the great European cities to play before the crowned heads and the aristocracy, but in these travels Mozart came in touch with every kind of music being written and heard in his day. The young Mozart absorbed with uncanny aptitude all that he heard. His music is a perfect blending of the Italian, German, and French styles. Broadly speaking, taste was the specialty of the Italian art and knowledge of the German. The French contribution was elegance. Mozart, the Austrian, combined the three in his style.

His career as a composer began early. At six he wrote his first minuets. Shortly before his ninth birthday, he composed his first symphony. When he was eleven, he wrote his first oratorio, and one year later he composed his first opera.

Another strong influence in his youth was the youngest son of J. S. Bach, Johann Christian Bach. They met in London in 1764, and it was Bach's son who first introduced him to the spirit of Italian music. Bach worshiped the Italian ideals of beauty and form, and he gave time to the young Mozart, advising him as well as listening to him, much to the boy's great pleasure.

Leopold saw to it that Mozart was steeped in every form of Italian music. The years 1770 to 1773 were largely occupied with traveling in Italy, studying, learning, observing, absorbing, and giving concerts. The importance of Mozart's Italian travels in his teens cannot be overestimated. He spoke fluent Italian, and he was greatly helped by the counterpoint lessons he had with Padre Martini in Bologna. He learned in Italy his unsurpassed ability to characterize life and humanity in music. Of all the major composers Mozart is the least locally rooted. Like Handel, he united the musical treasures of many nations.

The middle years of Mozart were given over to humiliating service for ungrateful patrons who treated the musicians in their court like servants. Often his pride was wounded by arrogant princes and archbishops, and Mozart truly hated them for their greed and failure to recognize his need. He longed for a sufficient income to allow him to be free, but never in his lifetime did he have it.

It is an irony difficult to comprehend: Mozart received little in payment for his colossal outpouring of beautiful music, and when he died, he was buried in a pauper's grave. To have any understanding of Mozart, however, we must accept the fact that he was a child and always remained one. Consequently, not only was he full of contradictions, but he was not at all practical or businesslike or orderly.

Learning about great artists has been a special study of mine over the past thirty years, and I have come to the conclusion that whether listening to Bach, Haydn, or Mozart, or looking at a Rembrandt etching or a Van Gogh or Pissarro painting, great art cannot be paid for. Today we have an opposite condition. Grants are given to those who call themselves composers, and yet their works prove that many of them have less talent than the cuckoo birds I heard this morning in the woods back of our chalet. Today in our museums we look at paintings that are not paintings, and yet the "artists" have received generous payment. It has been rightly said by a Rockford College professor who was speaking broadly about all the arts: "Never, in mankind's history, have stupidity and abomination been more generously rewarded with fame and money than they are in our time." I should like to say it again—rarely can great art be paid for.

From 1774 to 1781, Mozart lived chiefly in Salzburg. But as he traveled and saw other cities, he became more and more impatient with the provincial life of the town and the lack of musical opportunities. Seeking understanding and support for his career, he embarked on another long journey in 1777, this time with his mother, as he seemed incapable of taking care of himself. They finally went to Paris where every attempt at finding a good position or even appreciation ended in failure. When his mother died in Paris the following year, it was a terrible grief and shock to him. It was a long time before he could even write to his father about what had happened. In the letter he said, "I believe that no doctor, no man, no misfortune, no accident can give or take away a man's life, but only God." Finally he recovered his strength and went home.

Mozart may well be called the father of the modern concerto. He was the first to play a piano concerto in public, and his improvisations were much admired. The piano was his favorite instrument, and he used it for some of his most personal expressions. Mozart believed that music should give delight to the one listening. Some critics consider his gentleness as weakness and think that his music is superficial. Pleasure is the most obvious reaction to his music. As has been said, he wrote a vast amount of music, and some of it, though delightful, can sound empty after a while. But there is always *another* Mozart composition one has never heard. A musician never outgrows the music of Mozart. He is the most sensitive of artists, and his taste is wonderful. He enjoyed sitting in a garden with the sound of birds around him while he composed, but more often he had to work without gardens and birds.

Song dominated his whole musical imagination after his travels in Italy, and it is true that Mozart makes the instruments sing. In writing his music he often used various colors of ink. The most difficult passages were in bright blue. The music of Mozart is clear, transparent, beautiful, and extremely difficult to perform.

Most of the works for which Mozart is still famous were composed during his last ten years. This decade was fulfilling to him as an artist, yet it was heavy with disappointments and misery. After enduring more than his share of humiliating treatment, Mozart finally resigned his appointment by the archbishop of Salzburg and moved to other lodgings. The language of the archbishop upon hearing that Mozart had left the court is unprintable. Michael Haydn, the brother of Franz Joseph Haydn, was also in the service of the archbishop and had been commissioned by him to write six duets for violin and viola. Haydn became ill after writing four, and Mozart, who had a high opinion of both brothers, came to the rescue with two duets in his richest style. Michael Haydn submitted them with his own, and the archbishop did not suspect that they were not Haydn's.

Against his father's will, Mozart married Constance Weber in 1782, and thus began the "pawnshop period." She was a poor and unsystematic housekeeper, somewhat flighty, and his character faults and lack of tact did not add to their fortune. From the day of his marriage until his death,

Mozart was always in difficulties for lack of money. Leopold once said about his son, "With him there is either too much or too little, never the golden mean. If he is not actually in want, then he is immediately satisfied and becomes indolent and lazy. If he has to bestir himself, then he realizes his worth and wants to make his fortune at once."

The young couple moved twelve times in the next nine years of their marriage; however, these moves were not as upsetting as one might think. The frequent change of residence in Vienna gave the composer fresh stimulation. Perhaps another reason they were always seeking new lodgings was the fact that Mozart often spent half the night at the pianoforte—his most creative hours. It cannot be said too strongly: Mozart at times had a phenomenal devotion to work, and yet he found time to play billiards, go dancing, and to solve mathematical problems—another of his hobbies.

He also continued to travel. Thus, to a certain extent, one place suited him as well as another as long as he was productive. He once wrote to his wife, "I live quite retired here and don't go out the whole morning but stick in my hole of a room and write." Whatever shortcomings the happy-go-lucky Constance had, Mozart loved her dearly and wrote some of his best music after their marriage.

In the same year that he married Constance, Mozart met Franz Joseph Haydn. It was for each of them a stimulating and rewarding friendship. Instead of the jealousies and insincerities that often arise between talented people, the two musicians genuinely respected one another and learned from each other. The works of Haydn had a strong influence on Mozart's creativity, as Haydn was more adventurous in his composing than Mozart. Both Haydn and Mozart wrote music either on commission or for a particular occasion. Their goal was that their music would be performed, that people would like it, and that they would make money from it. It worked for Haydn because he had the protection of the Esterhazy princes for more than thirty years.

But despite his continuing reputation and the acclaim he received for his operas, Mozart was a free-lance composer and therefore did not benefit from the patronage of a genial archbishop or prince. Since there were no copyright laws to protect his work in the eighteenth century, he lived all his life seeking financial security and never finding it. All that survive Mozart, besides his music and letters, are a few poor portraits, no two of which are alike. Most people fail to understand that creative works take a great deal of time to accomplish, and during those months or years the artist is earning nothing.

Mozart, in gratitude for all he had learned from his older friend Franz Joseph Haydn, dedicated six string quartets to him. As we have said, song dominated Mozart's musical imagination after his visits to Italy, but Haydn revealed to him that instruments have "souls" too. Thus Mozart began to pour out an avalanche of instrumental compositions. The variety and richness of this music is beyond description. According to some critics, Mozart never surpassed the six *Haydn* Quartets in his later works. Haydn, when he first heard the compositions, said to Mozart's father, "Before God and as an honest man, I tell you that your son is the greatest composer known to me either in person or by name. He has taste, and what is more, the most profound knowledge of composition."

Mozart lived in the period known as the Enlightenment. The complex movement began as a revolt of the spirit, a turning against supernatural religion and the church in favor of "natural" religion and practical morality. In the home of Leopold Mozart, religion held a prominent place. He was a devout and unquestioning Catholic. He was sure his son would emulate him, but these presumptions do not always follow. Towards the end of his life Mozart turned from formal religion to Freemasonry.

His last opera, *The Magic Flute*, is a combination of morals and magic, Freemasonry and fairy tale. It is one of the greatest modern German operas and is a testament to the brotherhood of man. Many of the ideas and rituals of Freemasonry go back to the period of cathedral-building (900 to 1600). Today the Masons emphasize the fact that they do not foster any specific economic, political, or religious creeds. They do spend millions of dollars for hospitals and homes for orphans, widows, and the aged, all of which is commendable, of course. But from a biblical point of view, they have turned aside from much of God's truth. Thus it is not clear if Mozart is writing the *Requiem* (his last composition) to the vague "great architect of the universe" (the Mason's terminology for the pantheistic god they affirm) or to the Lord of Lords and King of Kings.

Obviously we can discuss only a small part of Mozart's music in this brief study, but I should like to mention some compositions with which we all should be familiar. The *Prague* Symphony has been considered by various authorities as one of the most beautiful works in the history of music. The people of Prague were his truest and most consistent admirers and patrons. Mozart's Quintet for Clarinet and Strings in A is one of the most perfect works for the clarinet, and the graceful Serenade in G Major (*Eine Kleine Nachtmusik*) is one of his most popular orchestral works.

In 1788, within a period of six weeks, Mozart composed his last three great symphonies—Symphony No. 39 in E Flat, Symphony No. 40 in G Minor, and the most famous, Symphony No. 41 in C Major, more popularly known as the *Jupiter* Symphony.

It is not only the amount of music that Mozart composed in his brief life that staggers the imagination—over six hundred compositions under the Köchel listing—but the variety. His compositions include concertos, quartets, sonatas, divertimentos, serenades, and symphonies. He is regarded as one of the greatest musical dramatists of all times. To do his operas justice would require many lectures. I will mention *The Marriage of Figaro*, as it set the model for all comic opera of the future. He created living characters for the first time in opera. Mozart's favorite form was opera, and he liked comic opera because it expressed his own love of life. It is not astonishing that a mind as well-balanced as Mozart's should show so great a sense of humor. After his father died, and in a time of sorrow and decline, Mozart composed another of his masterpieces, the opera *Don Giovanni.*

Mozart lived in the period known also as the "Age of Elegance." Another name for eighteenth-century music is rococo, from a French word meaning shell. The time is characterized by an abundance of decorative scroll and shell work and by a general tendency towards elegance, hedonism, and frivolity. The emphasis on pleasantness and prettiness is in marked contrast to the impressive grandeur of the true Baroque style. Rococo elements are present in the works of both Haydn and Mozart.

As a musician I have been drawn to the music of Mozart most of my life. At seven I was enthusiastically conducting the G Minor Symphony in front of a Victrola in my home in Virginia. During graduation services at Hollins College I sang Mozart's beautiful "Psalm 117." Later I performed *Idomeneo* and the *Requiem Mass* with the Boston Symphony Orchestra. When auditioning for opera, I chose a Mozart aria; and at the dedication of the Flentrop organ in our L'Abri chapel, I had the joy of singing Mozart's "Alleluia," composed when he was seventeen years old. I continue to sing the "Alleluia" with the L'Abri Ensemble.

Toward the end of Mozart's life, a mysterious visitor approached him and asked the sick and worn-out composer to write a requiem for a certain nobleman and offered a good fee. The visitor was actually the servant of an eccentric nobleman who commissioned works and then had them performed as his own. Mozart accepted the commission, but he never finished it. He died when it was almost completed, believing even as he wrote it that it would be his own requiem. He did his last composing in bed. The opening theme of the "Kyrie" is one used by both Bach and Handel. This is not surprising. Mozart's encounter with the music of J. S. Bach earlier in his life had caused a crisis in his creativity, and the impact of what he had learned from Bach was deep and lasting.

In one of the last letters Mozart wrote to his father he said, "I never lie down at night without reflecting that, young as I am, I may not live to see another day. Yet no one of all my acquaintances could say that in company I am morose or disgruntled. For this blessing I daily thank my Creator."

Mozart died in misery December 5, 1791, and his body was taken to a pauper's tomb. When the hearse approached the cemetery, a thunderstorm broke, and no one followed the coffin to the unmarked grave. Yet the sheer beauty, perfection, and profundity of his music continues to astonish and delight the world through the years. Great music is costly, not to those of us who listen, but to those who make it.

Recommended Reading

Davenport, Marcia. *Mozart.* New York: Charles Scribners and Sons, 1932.

Einstein, Alfred. *Mozart: His Character, His Work*. London: Oxford University Press, 1945.

Recommended Listening

Ave, Verum Corpus
Concerto for Flute and Harp
Concerto for Piano—C Minor
Don Giovanni
Exsultate, Jubilate
The Magic Flute
The Marriage of Figaro
Haydn Quartets
Serenade, *Eine Kleine Nachtmusik*
Quintet in A for Clarinet
Sonata No. 8 for Piano
Symphony No. 35, *Haffner*
Symphony No. 38
Symphony No. 39
Symphony No. 40, G Minor
Symphony No. 41, *Jupiter*

Ludwig van Beethoven
1770-1827

The genius who was before all others a law unto himself.

George R. Marek

*T*he concept that what a man believes affects his work is clearly exemplified in the life and music of that colossal figure in history, Ludwig van Beethoven. His motto was "Freedom above all." He became a legend in his own lifetime, and his figure overshadows the whole of nineteenth-century music. The slogan of Jean-Jacques Rousseau, "Myself alone," became the rallying cry of all the new movements in writing, painting, and music. Neither Goethe nor Beethoven is imaginable without Voltaire, Rousseau, or the early Romantics. Soon Beethoven became the propulsive force and the idol of the Romantics. With "heroic man" at the center of the universe, humanism reached a pinnacle in the age of Beethoven and Goethe.

Beethoven almost worshiped Goethe, Germany's most famous writer. Like the literary genius, Beethoven believed that it is the artist's task to express both the turmoil and the peace within oneself and to search for one's own perfection. Beethoven's music is full of violent contrasts. Renoir, the French painter, observed that Beethoven is "positively indecent the way he tells us about himself; he doesn't spare us either the pain in his heart or the pain in his stomach." The music of Beethoven has a frenzied, "demonic" energy. It is volcanic and exuberant and then suddenly melts into tenderness and sadness, then again bursts into fury. It is a direct outpouring of his personality.

Beethoven was one of the great thinkers in the realm of music. Early he got rid of the frivolous. His intellectual curiosity was enormous, and he continued to learn all his life. If only subconsciously, he merged the two concepts of the Enlightenment and the Romantic movement, the clear resoluteness of the one and the dark introspection of the other. Both are present in his music. This strong individualist, a born antagonist, was set on conquering. Profoundly convinced of the dignity of man, Beethoven believed fanatically in freedom without limits. Romain Rolland has said, "There is something in him of Nietzsche's superman long before Nietzsche."

Ludwig van Beethoven was born in Bonn, Germany, in 1770. He began studying music at the age of four, but under traumatic conditions. His father and a musician friend would return home late at night after visiting the taverns. They would awaken the boy and force him to have a music lesson until the early morning hours. Drinking to excess was an accepted custom in the Beethoven household. His grandmother was also an alcoholic.

The young Beethoven was unmethodical, and even as a child, he was prey to melancholy. But he had tremendous musical ambition and physical strength. While still very young, he was employed as an organist, though he later gained fame as a piano virtuoso. In 1787 in Vienna he met and played for Mozart, who prophesied a bright future for him. Beethoven was called back to Bonn by the disturbing news of his mother's failing health. She died of consumption at the age of forty, not long after he returned home. She was a good, kind person, and Beethoven loved her. His loss brought on the first of those emotional crises that recurred throughout his life. He never abandoned the search for a woman like his mother, and he never found her. There were many women in Beethoven's life, especially among the nobility. As one historian said, "Beethoven was always in love." He considered marriage a few times, but for various reasons he remained a bachelor.

Five long years after his first visit to Vienna, Beethoven set out again for this city—one of the centers of the musical world. By now Mozart was lying in an unmarked pauper's grave. The French Revolution was soon to enter its most terrible stage, the Reign of Terror. Goethe was in Weimar directing the ducal theater, and Haydn was enjoying fame throughout Europe.

Beethoven had some lessons with Haydn in Vienna, and he dug deep into his studies, though in his opinion Haydn was a poor teacher. Undoubtedly Haydn was too busy to concentrate on teaching, but he did something better for the young, unknown musician. He sent several of Beethoven's compositions to the Elector of Cologne and recommended that the young man receive money to continue his career as a composer.

Beethoven learned to compose like his predecessors before he found his own style. Unlike many twentieth-century composers, he never cut himself off from the past. As a boy he had mastered Bach's the *Well-Tempered Clavier*, and he had a lifelong veneration for the music of Handel and Mozart. Once he said, "Handel is the greatest, the most able of all composers. I can still learn from him." And Beethoven was still learning from Handel the year before he died. Always a student, he was of all composers the least inclined to repeat himself. A friend wondered why he did not have Handel's works. Beethoven replied, "How should I, a poor devil, have got them?" It took his friend two years, but he made a secret vow to send Handel's music to Beethoven—everything he could find. In December

1826, a fine edition of Handel in forty volumes arrived. While Beethoven was lying ill the last few months of his life, he would lean the books against the wall, turn pages, and break into exclamations of joy and praise as he studied Handel.

Sir Julius Benedict described his first sight of Beethoven: "He was a short, stout man with a very red face, small piercing eyes, and bushy eyebrows, dressed in a very long overcoat which reached nearly to his ankles." He also had long white hair that touched his broad shoulders.

Beethoven saw himself as a creator "set apart" from ordinary people. Anything or anyone who interfered with his creativity he brushed aside. He could be up in arms at the most trifling fancied slight to himself. He was full of scorn for nearly everyone—the poor, the aristocracy, those who admired him, those who hated him, common people, the weak and feeble. As Marek says, "The mystery of a complex personality can never be wholly unraveled, and surely not that of a man as complex as Beethoven."

In Vienna Beethoven moved in the circle of the nobility, and a long line of influential people helped his career in spite of his arrogant outbursts and blistering rudeness. At the outset of his career, Beethoven was a virtuoso pianist. In the Second Piano Concerto, the earliest orchestral score he saw fit to publish, the last movement has a haunting flavor reminiscent of Mozart and Haydn.

From time to time Beethoven had a few pupils, but he must have been one of the most unsystematic teachers the world has known, being impatient, slovenly, quarrelsome, unbelievably sensitive, and never on time. That marvelous organizer of music was the most disorganized of persons. I mentioned that Mozart and his wife changed their residence twelve times in nine years; Beethoven, in thirty-five years in Vienna, moved at least seventy times. In the many paintings of the great composer, there is often a grand piano. I wonder how many stairs it was carried up and down in these frequent changes of address.

Always an early riser (5 or 6 A.M.), Beethoven liked to work in the morning and had the habit of composing out of doors while taking long walks. He said, "I love a tree more than a man." Beethoven loved the natural world, but as a pantheist who worships nature rather than the Creator. "Beethoven was not the man to bow to anyone—even God!" said David Ewen. Rousseau, whose ideas influenced Beethoven, believed that the creative person should not be at home in society but should seek solitude "to express oneself, one's feelings" and to delve into the unconscious, to uncover the mystery in one's inner self. On one occasion a friend made for Beethoven a copy of one of his scores. The musician signed it, "With God's help." Underneath it Beethoven scrawled, "O man, help yourself."

Beethoven rarely had to write music at anyone's command. He could afford to "think and think" and revise until it suited him, as he had no deadlines to meet. But he wrote his music with great difficulty, and he subjected himself to severe criticism. He began to keep notebooks as a youth, and these are crowded with a welter of musical ideas in all stages of development, comparable to the notebooks of Leonardo da Vinci. Beethoven felt a titanic force of creation within himself. His life was one of incessant creativity.

Beethoven's increasing deafness, which began as early as 1798 when he was only twenty-eight, forced him to abandon his career as a virtuoso and to use his energy for composition. The first symptoms of deafness must have puzzled and frightened him. He tried various doctors and cures and grew increasingly distrustful of everyone. As his biographer Marek relates, Beethoven wrote to a friend, "My poor hearing haunted me everywhere like a ghost; and I avoided . . . all human society." At one period he was tempted to commit suicide. "But only Art held me back," he explained, "for it seemed unthinkable for me to leave the world before I had produced all that I felt called upon to produce." A little later when he began to take courage again, he uttered the famous words, "I will seize Fate by the throat." He flung out the challenge to himself and a parade of Romantic artists after him. "It shall certainly not bend and crush me completely," he said.

In the years roughly between 1802 and 1816, Beethoven had a prodigious outpouring of creativity. His courage was not steadfast. There were black times, but in those fourteen years he composed six symphonies, the *Coriolan* Overture, *Fidelio*, the last two piano concertos, the middle quartets, and piano sonatas through Op. 90, including the *Appassionata*.

In 1816 he was appointed guardian to his nephew Karl. Even though he loved the boy in his commanding, temperamental way, Karl was a source of constant trouble to Beethoven the rest of his life. At one time Karl attempted to kill himself. Finally they quarreled more violently than all the other times, and Beethoven never saw his nephew again.

By 1817 his hearing was completely gone, but probably he could "hear" music by feeling the vibrations. The burden of his deafness helped him to bring to focus what was to become one of the themes of the nineteenth century—the loneliness of man.

When Beethoven conducted the first performance of his Ninth Symphony, he could not hear the applause, and someone had to turn him around so he could see the enthusiasm of the audience. As his creativity increased, he withdrew more and more, even from friends. Although his fame had spread over Europe, Beethoven lived almost as a recluse.

Historically Beethoven's work was built on the achievements of the Classical period, but his figure towers like a colossus astride the eighteenth and nineteenth centuries, forming a bridge to Romanticism. He is the last in the triad of Viennese Classical composers—Haydn, Mozart, and Beethoven. Before Beethoven, musicians had been creators in an ordered universe. Beethoven wrestled with destiny, and his music became a means of expressing his ideas about humanity. Some critics have referred to him as the prophet of self-will, and his weakness was his pride.

It is generally agreed that the music of Beethoven may be divided into three periods: imitation, externalization, and reflection. The first period, imitation, goes to about 1802 and includes the six quartets, Op. 18, the first ten piano sonatas, the first two symphonies, and two piano concertos. The period of externalization runs roughly between 1802 and 1816. As mentioned before, these were years of great creativity. In the final period, reflection, extending from 1817 till his death, Beethoven wrote the *Missa Solemnis in D*, the Ninth Symphony, the last piano sonatas, and the last five quartets.

The piano occupied a central position in Beethoven's art. He wrote thirty-two piano sonatas, which are to piano literature what the plays of Shakespeare are to drama. For Beethoven the piano sonata was the vehicle for his boldest and most inward thoughts.

Concerto No. 5 (*The Emperor*) was written while Napoleon's guns pounded at the gates of Vienna. It was reported that Beethoven took refuge in a cellar with his head thrust into a pillow to help save the remnant of his hearing.

One of the main features of Beethoven's music is the profoundness of emotional content. In the *Appassionata* he came to the full realization that the piano is a percussion instrument. The piece ends in an orgy of musical fist-shaking. Characteristic are the violent contrasts between pianissimo and fortissimo. Until Beethoven's era, most music held a measure of predictability. One of Beethoven's outstanding characteristics is the element of surprise.

Beethoven wrote ten violin sonatas, the most famous being the *Kreutzer* Sonata. Here the violin has percussive declamations. It is even more celebrated because Tolstoy wrote a novel called *The Kreutzer Sonata* about a jealous husband who murders his wife.

His one opera, *Fidelio*, which is among the greatest, gave him more trouble than any of his other works. Beethoven was a superb dramatic musician, but he rarely wrote well for voices. He disregarded the limitations of the human voice and considered it just another instrument. He is frequently unvocal.

It is impossible to discuss Beethoven's symphonies with adequacy in a few words. Each of them possesses a complete and separate individuality, but we will briefly comment on each one.

The First Symphony is the most Classical of the nine.

The Second Symphony was written during the time he began to realize he was becoming deaf. He wrote it in intervals between black depression. It has a simplicity and a sunshine radiance full of energy and fire.

The Third Symphony stands as an immortal expression of heroic greatness. It is a work of nobility and grandeur. Beethoven dedicated it to Napoleon, whom he idealized as a hero leading humanity to a new age of liberty, equality, and fraternity. But when Beethoven heard that Napoleon had crowned himself emperor, he angrily tore up the dedication page and renamed the symphony the *Eroica*.

Musically the age of Napoleon (1769-1821) is the age of Beethoven. The Age of Revolution took place during the great awakening of the human ego in philosophy and in art. The philosophers of the eighteenth-century Enlightenment prepared the way for the political explosion that is called the Age of Revolution. The symbol of the Enlightenment was a question mark, and the star of the Enlightenment was Voltaire, one of the greatest of all French writers, who questioned the reliability of the Bible and placed his confidence in man's reason. Voltaire's enemy was Rousseau, who had little faith in reason. Rousseau believed in action, freedom, and the goodness of humanity, but his own character and life were something else. His mistress had five children, and Rousseau sent them all to orphanages.

The Fourth Symphony is full of energy. In it Beethoven releases tumults of exultant strength.

The Fifth Symphony is a musical depiction of Beethoven's struggle with deafness. Like Goethe, Beethoven believed in a pitiless fate.

The Sixth or *Pastoral* Symphony is the starting point of Romantic music. It is the only symphony to which Beethoven gave a program. Each of the five movements suggests a scene from life in the country. Beethoven told a friend that the quail, cuckoos, nightingales, and yellow hammers around Heiligenstadt, where he spent several summers, had helped him compose the work.

The Seventh Symphony contains one of the most famous of Beethoven's movements, the second, which perhaps has had the most influence on Romantic composers. The whole symphony is controlled by persistent rhythmic ideas. Wagner called it the "apotheosis of the dance."

The Eighth Symphony is urbane and sophisticated.

The Ninth Symphony is a paean to the universal brotherhood of man. In it Beethoven asserts the arrival of joy through suffering. The most striking novelty of the symphony is the use of chorus and solo voices as if the orchestra had developed to such an advanced stage it could go no further and needed the collaboration of the vocal art.

The last five quartets of Beethoven, together with the Great Fugue, are regarded as the summit of his achievement. As Burk says, "The last five quartets can be looked upon as the crown of all that he did, and all that had gone before as a preparation." These occupied him almost exclusively in the last three years of his life. The tortured, unyielding spirit of Beethoven needed isolation to work, and the five quartets express his unutterable loneliness and alienation as he shut himself off from everyone. Music, for Beethoven, became a matter of withdrawal.

Those of us who live in a century following an artist of such extraordinary talent and supreme dedication as Beethoven cannot escape his influence. Grout says, "Beethoven was the most powerful disruptive force in the history of music. His works opened the gateway to a new world." And, may I add, to a disintegrating world. By saying this, we do not mean his music is not beautiful, amazing, noble, and sublime. God is the giver of gifts, but not all gifted persons acknowledge and give thanks to God. Recently I was asked by a student at L'Abri, "What does philosophy have to do with music?" One of the aims of this book is to show how our beliefs and ideas affect what we do in life. The fact that Beethoven held a worldview that excluded spiritual wholeness caused his music to move in a direction of disintegration toward the end of his life.

As a composer his was one endless quest for the ideal form that would completely express the unity he had envisioned from the beginning. But as Francis Schaeffer has explained in his book *How Should We Then Live?* humanism fails to bring unity and does not answer life's crucial questions. The revealed biblical truth of the triune God offers the only worldview that provides a unity between universal absolutes and the particulars of human existence. In Jesus Christ, God offers an individual believer a spiritual wholeness and intellectual satisfaction that give meaning and content to life.

Beethoven's last quartets, consistent with his worldview, turn to the abstract and mystical. "The late Beethoven," according to biographer Alfred Einstein, "has been considered a destroyer of form." The language of the last quartets is austere and the structure unpredictable. Some movements are unusually long, others astonishingly short. The frequent dissonances anticipate twentieth-century music. As the music of Beethoven became more mystical, it moved toward the complete dissolution of traditional forms. Another feature of his late work is the continuity he achieved by intentionally blurring dividing lines. One senses the beginning of the loss of categories.

In these quartets Beethoven used fragmentary thematic materials and vague tonalities. In fact, the formal use of thematic material was abandoned, and instead theme breaks in upon theme. The fragments of melody are varied, transformed, then almost willfully interrupted and recalled. This principle of variation is later picked up and carried much further by Arnold Schoenberg in his perpetual variations, the topic of another chapter.

Beethoven's last quartets have been called the music of the future, and much of what we are listening to today has come as a result of Beethoven's influence.

Beethoven was born a Catholic, but he never attended church. On his deathbed (he died of pneumonia complicated by cirrhosis of the liver and dropsy), he did take the last sacrament, but he viewed all priests with mistrust. Marek describes Beethoven's death: "The day was very cold; snow had fallen. Around five o'clock a sudden thunderstorm obscured the sky. It became very dark. Suddenly, there was a great flash of lightning which illuminated the death chamber, accompanied by violent claps of thunder. At the flash of lightning, Beethoven opened his eyes, raised his tightly clenched right hand, and fell back dead. It was about 5:15 P.M., March 26, 1827." Huge crowds attended his funeral. Franz Schubert was one of the torchbearers.

People all over the world know and appreciate the music of Beethoven. In one sense, his music appeals to us because much of it expresses his struggle and suffering, and we identify with him. Often in his letters Beethoven asked the question, "What is the use of it all?" But when composing, he rarely asked the question until the latter part of his life. In much of his music Beethoven balanced suffering with solace that gave the impression of strength.

By all means, we should listen to the music of Beethoven. It brings together thoughts and emotions that are often more intense than we can produce. But never listen indifferently and without discernment. Enjoy and appreciate what is good, but keep in mind that it is with composers as with all of us: what we believe affects our total life.

Recommended Reading

Burk, John N. *The Life and Work of Beethoven.* New York: Random House (Modern Library), 1943.

Landon, H. C. Robbins, ed. *Beethoven: A Documentary Study.* London: Thames and Hudson, 1974.

Marek, George R. *Beethoven: Biography of a Genius.* New York: Thomas Y. Crowell, 1969.

Recommended Listening

Five Piano Concertos
Concerto in D for Violin
Fidelio
Last five quartets
Piano Sonata No. 8, *Pathetique*
Piano Sonata No. 14, *Moonlight*
Piano Sonata No. 21, *Waldstein*
Piano Sonata No. 23, *Appassionata*
Violin Sonata No. 9, *Kreutzer*
All nine symphonies

CHAPTER 8

Gioacchino Rossini
1792-1868

A time to weep, and a time to laugh . . .
                                        Ecclesiastes 3:4

A student eager to learn more about music asked Rossini, "How do you compose an overture?" He answered, "Not until the evening of the day before opening night!" He had a love of fun and nonsense with a spontaneous wit for expressing this in music and words.

Then he went on to say, "I composed the overture to *La Gazza Ladra* on the day of the premiere, right under the roof of La Scala where I was imprisoned by the manager, watched over by four stage hands who had been ordered to hand over my manuscript, page by page, to the copyist waiting below to transcribe the notes. In case the music sheets stopped going out the window, they were ordered to throw me out instead!

"Another time I composed an overture while fishing with my feet in the water. . . . Sometimes I didn't write an overture at all. I borrowed it from another of my operas."

He said once, "Composing is nothing—the real drudgery is the rehearsals with temperaments flaring." Because of the inadequacies of some of the singers he was forced to sacrifice his own ideas. However, the overtures he wrote to please himself. Today they are his most popular music.

Rossini had an amazing gift for composing in unusual situations—in the middle of a noisy party surrounded by laughing friends or even while carrying on a conversation. Supposedly, when eating in a restaurant, he would use a napkin to note down a sudden musical inspiration. It seemed that a part of his brain was filled with musical notes. He once told a friend, "Give me a laundry list, and I will set it to music."

Gioacchino Rossini was one of Europe's greatest opera composers. A comedian at heart, he was the most famous Italian maestro of his time, as well as perhaps the most humorous and fascinating of all musicians. He was an eccentric original.

Rossini, an only child, was born on February 29 in a leap year, 1792, in Pesaro, Italy. His parents traveled about performing in third-class theaters. His father played the trumpet, and his mother, whom he adored, was a singer—a prima donna buffa. Though he grew up without a stable environment, there was always music in his life.

As a child Rossini was known for his beautiful soprano voice. His singing experience later helped him write well for the voice. Beyond question he was acquainted with the human voice as few other composers have understood it.

When his parents moved to Bologna, Rossini studied at the Bologna Conservatory where he learned to play the harpsichord, horn, and cello, studied singing, and began to compose.

Born only three months after the death of Mozart, Rossini idolized the Austrian composer. Rossini made a very careful study of Mozart's music, as well as Haydn's. From these great composers he particularly learned craftsmanship and the cantabile (singing) style.

Besides his remarkable talent and love of music, his obligation to support himself and his parents helped push him on in his career. Some critics have said he was lazy because he sometimes stayed in bed to compose. He wasn't lazy. He was trying to keep warm and couldn't afford to pay for extra heat. The vast amount of music he composed in his whirlwind career demonstrates that he is a superb example of Italian genius.

One of Rossini's early desires was to write operas. At age eighteen he dashed off in a few days his one-act opera *The Matrimonial Market* (1810) for Venice. It met with tremendous success, and soon he was famous. By the age of nineteen, he was helping to support his parents.

Rossini knew he was born to write "opera buffa" (farce opera), and many of his early operas were comedies. Another comic opera written for Venice was *L'Italiana in Algeri* (1813). A critic wrote that it was "one of the glories of Rossini's youthful years, when melodies bubbled as birds sing, when his slyness and his incomparable wit had all of their joyous recklessness." The overture has survived precisely because it crystalizes these qualities. As a critic wrote, "Music as pure sound, rhythm as pure rhythm, meant everything to him; words very little." Or it could be expressed this way: "His music is never anything but indisputably musical. . . ."

His overtures are little masterpieces from every point of view. You find in them that rhythm and famous crescendo in which he excelled, and it is because of his overtures that Rossini is most widely known. At the age of twenty-one he was already the most successful composer in Italy and world famous. It was melody above all that made Rossini famous.

The Barber of Seville (1816), perhaps the most popular opera buffa in the world, was written by Rossini at the age of twenty-four in about two weeks. He was able to compose so quickly because he often borrowed from other compositions he had written and also, as Verdi suggested, because Rossini undoubtedly already had much of the music in his mind before writing it down. In this regard, he resembled Mozart, or Handel who wrote *Messiah* in three weeks.

During the first performance of *The Barber of Seville* in Rome, it was almost hissed and whistled off the stage. Poor Rossini, his friends thought, and they rushed to his lodgings to console him but found him sleeping peacefully. This opera soon became very popular in Europe and is as fresh today as ever—with its masterly characterizations and exciting ensemble pieces full of sparkling rhythms. "Rossini's youthful spirits positively explode from the music, and the work dashes along." It abounds in music which for sheer gaiety, brio, and irreverence has never been surpassed. Rossini had inexhaustible melodic gifts, a fertile imagination, and an uncanny knowledge of the theater. Above all his music overflows with merriment, wit, and high spirits.

The Barber of Seville, Mozart's *The Marriage of Figaro*, and Verdi's *Falstaff* are among the supreme examples of comic opera with the hint of pathos that underlies all high comedy.

In 1815 Rossini moved to Naples. He was invited by Barbaia, the director of Italy's most important opera theaters. During the next years, Rossini wrote ten operas for the Teatro San Carlo, one of the great opera houses of the world with a fine orchestra and superb singers. Many of the leading roles in this theater were sung by Rossini's future wife, the fiery Spanish soprano, Isabella Colbran. (Rossini wrote ten operas for her.)

In 1959 coauthor Jane Stuart Smith sang Brünnhilde in Wagner's opera *Die Walküre* at the Teatro San Carlo. Also performing with her was Marilyn Horne, who later became one of the outstanding Rossini singers.

For the Teatro San Carlo Rossini wrote three of his finest scores: *Othello*, *Cinderella*, and *La Gazza Ladra*. His best operas are comedies, and *La Gazza Ladra* (The Thieving Magpie) was one of the greatest successes of his career. Part of Rossini's sly wit was directed at himself. It's almost as if his music chuckles. But he turned easily from comedy to tragedy. His first tragic opera was *Othello*, which contains some of his most poignant music. These works profoundly influenced operatic composition and made possible the developments that led to Verdi.

By 1823 Rossini could boast that twenty-three of his operas were being performed in various parts of the world, including Russia and South America. At the time, he was the most talked-of musician in the world. The greatest singers of his time sang Rossini's operas.

After Rossini's marriage to Colbran, he left Naples in order to become an international composer, first going to Vienna. This city was in a "Rossini craze." Even the philosophers, Hegel and Schopenhauer, were infected, and one can detect Rossini's influence in Schubert's earlier symphonies and concert overtures.

While in Vienna, Rossini visited Beethoven in his filthy, cluttered attic room. Holes in the ceiling let in mice and rain. With the indefinable sadness that emanated from his features, Beethoven earnestly urged Rossini to go on writing comic opera "where you are unequaled—more *Barbers!*" Too bad Rossini did not listen.

Rossini next journeyed to London and then to Paris where he was received like a king. After traveling for a while more about Europe (he hated trains and traveling), he settled for a time in Paris in 1824. There he wrote his operas in French, thus founding modern French opera. Rossini wrote more than forty operas between 1810 and 1829.

At the age of thirty-seven, in 1829, he wrote the grand opera, *William Tell* in French, which took six months to complete. (All his other operas had been dashed off quickly.) It is a masterpiece based on a play by Schiller, and it contains some of his most somber passages and storm music, in which he excelled. The opera was in five acts. At the first performance, the restless audience listened with cold respect; the critics raved. In later performances, one by one the acts were cut out until only Act II was given. Once when a director excitedly told Rossini, "We're performing the second act of *William Tell* tonight!" Rossini replied bitterly, "What! The whole act?"

In Paris Rossini's interest gradually shifted from the stage to the bank vault. After completing *William Tell,* his last opera, Rossini decided to leave music before it left him. He was often in poor health. Psychological or not, his illness lasted many years, partly due to having worked under tremendous pressures. He still had thirty-nine years to enjoy the fame and fortune his composing had brought him. Asked one day why he stopped composing, his wry answer was that he preferred eating.

In 1842 Rossini, after a long period of silence, composed his *Stabat Mater,* which contains excellent choral writing and arias in operatic style, very original and with deep feeling.

Before settling permanently in Paris in 1855, Rossini lived in Bologna and then Florence for several years, going through a dark period of neurosis that sometimes bordered on insanity. After his troubled first marriage, his second wife, Olympe Pélissier, and his move to Paris helped him back to health. His older years were his most serene. He never considered it a waste of time to enjoy himself. By now very fat and still amusing, wearing an odd wig tipped to one side, he was still full of *joie de vivre,* laughter, and tears.

He had a villa built outside of Paris in the shape of a grand piano with flower beds in the form of musical instruments. Rossini's Saturday nights became famous. At the piano he was almost as good an actor as a composer. His mimicry of others was hilarious.

Composers like Wagner, Liszt, Verdi, Saint-Saëns, Paganini, and Clara Schumann, to mention a few, flocked to hear the wit of this great genius. Stendahl, his first biographer, said, "If you like Italy and things Italian, nothing is so delightful as Rossini's conversation which is inimitable. His mind is all fire and quicksilver." Rossini claimed, "All kinds of music are valid except the boring kind." He was a charming host and spent much time inventing recipes (*tournedos* Rossini), eating, and helping young composers.

Among those he encouraged and influenced was Bellini, who wrote ten operas in two years, his greatest being *Norma* with its superb aria "Casta Diva." (Coauthor Jane Stuart Smith sang this role in Italy, which is most difficult for the dramatic soprano.) Bellini, in turn, influenced Chopin. Bellini and Chopin are buried near each other in the Paris Pére-Lachaise Cemetery. Also buried here is Maria Callas, a great interpreter of Rossini, Bellini, Donizetti, and Verdi. Their operas are called "singers' operas."

Another "Rossinist" was Donizetti, who wrote over sixty operas, including *The Daughter of the Regiment* and *Don Pasquale*. From Donizetti's *Lucia di Lammermoor* (1835) Liszt made a beautiful piano arrangement of the sextet. Nearly every composer of Rossini's time was indebted to him.

After a famous meeting with Wagner, Rossini was asked what he thought of Wagner's recent opera *Lohengrin*. With his ever-fresh wit he said, "To understand it I would have to listen to it in the theater, and I would never do that!"

One of Rossini's amusing compositions is "Sins of My Old Age." It includes a cat duet for two sopranos that Jane and Frances Kramer often performed in our L'Abri Ensemble tours. The piece always brought forth laughter.

Rossini was the natural enemy of bombast. He was pushed aside for a while by the inflated, short-lived operas of Meyerbeer. Yet only Rossini lives on.

Rossini, as is true with many creative people, wrote too much. But his best works are among *the best*. When he died, he left part of his fortune to his hometown, Pesaro, where many of his operas are still performed. He smiled to the end of his life and is now buried in Florence next to Michelangelo, Machiavelli, and Galileo in the church of Santa Croce.

Rossini, "The Swan of Pesaro," and one of the most original geniuses of the nineteenth century, was a composer of amazing range, force, and versatility. His music is full of sparkle and gusto, which makes us smile along with him. His orchestral writing is a wonder of mobility, sonority, and color—clear and bright like the skies of Italy. But he also wrote wonderfully for the voice. His music is full of laughter. Rossini was the sun of a sunny people.

Recommended Reading

Alverà, Pierluigi. *Portraits of Greatness: Rossini*. New York:
   Treves Publishing Co., 1986.

Kendall, Alan. *Gioacchino Rossini: The Reluctant Hero*.
   London: Victor Gollancz, 1992.

Toye, Francis. *Rossini: The Man and His Music*. New York:
   Dover Publications, 1987.

Recommended Listening

Rossini: *The Barber of Seville*
      Cinderella
      L'Italiana in Algeri
      Il Signor Bruschino
      Overtures: *La Gazza Ladra*
               La Scala di Seta
               Semiramide
               William Tell
Donizetti: *Lucia di Lammermoor*
Bellini: *Norma*

Franz Schubert
1797-1828

*Nor is that musician most praiseworthy who hath
longest played, but he in measured accents who hath
made sweetest melody.*

William Drummond

*T*he early teachers of Schubert watched in silent astonishment at the rapidity with which he absorbed instruction. Holzer (one of his first teachers) said, "The lad has harmony in his little finger." Later at the choir school of the Royal Chapel, Ruziczka—court organist, teacher, and conductor of the orchestra—in an attempt to explain Schubert's swiftness to learn, exclaimed, "He has learned it from God."

The musical education of Schubert actually began at home. Schubert's father was an amateur cellist, and he was the boy's first music teacher. Between the merciless grind of teaching school and the implacable routine of raising and burying children (of fourteen, nine died in infancy), the parish schoolmaster encouraged and cultivated music in his home. Schubert's father taught him to play the violin, and his older brother Ignaz gave him his first piano lessons. They soon recognized their inadequacy as teachers, and at the age of seven Schubert was apprenticed to the choirmaster of the parish church, Michael Holzer.

During his holidays from the choir school, Schubert formed a family string quartet to try out his music. Another brother, Ferdinand, who remained close to Schubert all his life, once said that the family rehearsals were frequently interrupted by the young composer correcting the faults of the father with a gentle, "Sir, there must be a mistake somewhere."

Early in life Schubert learned to live with hardships. At the Imperial and Royal Seminary the music room was left unheated even in the winter. But in spite of that, there was plenty of music. The school orchestra performed an entire symphony every evening and finished off with the "noisiest possible overture." In warm weather the school windows were left open, and people crowded around to listen to the free concerts until the police complained that the gatherings obstructed traffic, and they finally dispersed the crowd.

At one concert Joseph von Spaun, a student of law and nine years older than Schubert, turned around to see who behind him was playing the violin so well. He discovered a very small boy wearing spectacles. Later in one of the practice rooms Schubert played a Mozart sonata for him. Urged on by Spaun, the shy and blushing Schubert then played a minuet of his own composition. Schubert told his new friend that he "sometimes put his thoughts into notes," but very secretly so his father would not think he was neglecting his studies. Schubert began composing when only thirteen years old, and he wrote his first song the next year. He began his first symphony in 1813.

In his choir school days, Schubert impressed everyone with his musical gifts, but they were also aware of his moral qualities. Because of his reliability, the boy was privileged to leave the school and to have special lessons with Salieri, who had been a friend of Haydn and was one of Beethoven's teachers. As historian Donald Jay Grout summarizes it: "Schubert's training in music theory was not systematic, but his environment, both at home and in school, was saturated with music-making."

The cheerful amateur activities at the choir school and the pleasure he received singing in the church choir, sometimes as the soloist, were the positive side of his schooling; but the negative aspect sounds familiar to those studying the lives of famous composers. Poverty, particularly in early life, seems to be the conventional requirement for the development of a composer, coupled with the person's unending determination to overcome impossible circumstances. Most of his life Schubert was so poor he could not afford to buy paper on which to write his music, and he rarely had his own piano.

Schubert seldom had enough to eat at the choir school. In a letter to his brother Ferdinand, the youthful Schubert wrote:

> *You will know from your own experience that there are times when one could certainly do with a roll and a few apples, particularly when one has to wait eight and a half hours between a moderate-sized midday meal and a wretched sort of supper. . . . How would it be, then, if you were to let me have a few kreuzer each month? You wouldn't notice them, and they would make me happy and contented in my cell. . . . I rely on the words of the Apostle Matthew, especially where he says: Let him who hath two coats, give one to the poor.*
>
> > Your affectionate, poor,
> > hopeful, and once again poor brother,
> > Franz[4]

Even though one might question the accuracy of the biblical quotation, the letters of Schubert are as delightful to read as his music is to listen to. In fact, they are a counterpart of his music. The style is simple, melodic, and diatonic. Schubert, whether in words or music, expresses in the most direct way the fundamentals of things without self-consciousness or the

---

4. O. E. Deutsch, ed., *Franz Schubert's Letters* (New York: Vienna House, 1974), p. 23.

desire to produce a large dramatic effect. Schubert in another letter to Ferdinand, this time concerning his music, said, "What I feel in my heart I give to the world." Schubert's letters, especially in the earlier period, show the contrast of joy and sadness so characteristic in his music.

Franz Peter Schubert was born in 1797 in Vienna. He was the youngest in the family. His father was a God-fearing, strict, but kindly and honorable schoolmaster. Schubert's mother, like Haydn's, was a professional cook. Also like Haydn and several other composers, Schubert was selected to be a Vienna choirboy because of his beautiful soprano voice. Even though his heart was elsewhere, he was educated to be a schoolteacher. His father did not consider composing music a profession, but there was no way to stop the melodies from filling Franz's mind. His art was his life, and his life was his art.

He taught for three miserable years. Then in 1816 his friend Schober, a restless poet, offered him a place to live and opened the door to the freedom so necessary for his creativity. However, even the frustration of teaching school had not stopped his composing, but it had been a physical and emotional strain for him. Schubert was only five feet, one and a half inches tall. He had a warm, gentle, friendly, profoundly simple personality, but he was extremely modest. With his head spinning with music, he could not help being an indifferent teacher.

Shortly before he was freed from teaching, he was in his room reading Goethe's poem, "The Erlking." His friend Spaun passed by to see the young composer and found him in a state of high excitement. Even as Schubert was reading, he could hear the music in his head and was reciting the poem and hurling notes on a piece of music paper at the same time. Within less than an hour his composition was finished. Some critics consider "The Erlking" the greatest of all *lieder*. The accompaniment of "The Erlking" is very effective. Schubert brings the piano into equality with the voice. It is the closest music has ever come to a complete union with poetry. Schubert was to the song what Beethoven was to the symphony, Wagner to the musical drama, and Chopin to the piano.

Of the eight great composers of the eighteenth and nineteenth centuries whose names are closely associated with Vienna—Gluck, Haydn, Mozart, Beethoven, Schubert, Bruckner, Brahms, and Mahler—only Franz Schubert was actually born there. Schubert rarely left Vienna except for a few excursions with friends and two summers spent in Hungary as a music teacher to the two daughters of Count Johann Esterhazy. At first he was in high spirits in Hungary, but soon he missed the stimulation of his artistic friends. He wrote in a letter to one of them, "Not a soul here has any feeling for true art . . . so I am alone with my beloved [muse], and have to hide her in my room, in my piano, and in my heart. . . . It is fairly quiet, except for forty geese which sometimes set up such a cackling that one cannot hear oneself speak" (Flower, *Schubert*). Even though the Esterhazy interludes were not really to his liking, nothing was wasted as far as his music was concerned. Schubert was much influenced by Hungarian and Gypsy music.

It is impossible to discuss the life and music of Schubert separately because they are one. If he was not composing, he was thinking, talking, playing, or listening to music. He was overjoyed when beautiful music was performed. His friends, and he had many who later went on to make names for themselves in the different arts and professions, spoke of his natural simplicity, his frank, open, sunny disposition and generous nature. Flower says that according to one friend, "His was a magnificent soul. I never saw him jealous or grudging of others; the childlikeness of his mind and the lack of guile are beyond expression."

Schubert never married, and for him friendship was the joy of his life. After giving up teaching, he was penniless, but his friends came to his aid. Schober provided lodging, someone else found him appliances, they took their meals together, and the person who had any money paid the bill. Schubert was the leader of the party, and he was known by several affectionate nicknames. Among his friends, besides Spaun and Schober, were the poets Grillparzer and Mayerhofer, the singer Vogl, painters Schwind and Kupelweiser, Dietrich the sculptor, and Franz Lachner, afterwards the court *Kapellmeister* to the king of Bavaria. These friends not only bought paper on which he could write his music, but they organized periodical meetings that they called "Schubertiaden." Other friends and influential people were invited to these musical evenings to hear Schubert's compositions. His songs were usually sung by Vogl with Schubert at the piano. Vogl, a well-known Viennese singer who especially appreciated the Bible, showed unusual kindness to the sensitive Schubert. Schwind's drawing of a Schubertian evening is well-known. These meetings were not only social occasions. Besides playing the music of Schubert's inexhaustible pen, those present read poems and discussed drawings and sketches.

If Schubert had not had his friends, it is possible we would not have his music. They were the ones who listened to it, enjoyed it, and encouraged him to go write more. After his brief teaching career, he spent the rest of his short life doing more or less what he wanted. But he was never lazy nor dissipated. He had a weakness for wine, but his indulgences were brief, and he always came back to his work. Often at night he would meet some of his friends in a favorite restaurant for music, talk, food, and drink, but nearly always Schubert would leave before the others. He composed both carefully and ceaselessly. When someone asked, "How do you compose?" he answered, "When I have finished one piece, I begin another." Daily Schubert studied and composed six or seven hours, a methodical habit he learned from his father.

Apart from his friends and the small circles in which he moved, Schubert never was a success in his lifetime. But posterity has caused his music to become a lasting international treasure. He is the classical example of a composer, artist, or writer so devoted to his art that he never manages to live well or come to terms with publishers and the world. His pitifully brief life illustrates the tragedy of genius overwhelmed by the necessities and annoyances of daily living. But Schubert, with the exception of his years in the choir school, rarely went hungry. He could always sell a song for the price of a meal, and often he did.

Schubert is known as the musicians' musician. Liszt called him "the most poetic musician who ever lived." As Ernest Newman says, "The simplicities of a Schubert or a Mozart may go deeper than the sophistications of many a more intellectual composer."

The contemporaries of Schubert had no idea of his significance. The music critics today speak of Franz Schubert as the greatest writer of songs and one of the supreme creators of melody. It is an overwhelming statement when we consider the multitude of songs that have been composed in the past and are being written today. Like many gifted persons, he wrote too many songs, but his best are the best. In his short life of thirty-one years he wrote an enormous amount of music besides his songs. Schubert followed unreservedly a single impulse—to create.

Schubert can be compared to the great English Romantic poet John Keats, who died at twenty-six. Those who composed in the Romantic period had a strong literary orientation, and the characteristic Romantic form was the *lied* (or song) with its dependence on poetry.

As Schubert wrote more than six hundred *lieder*, only a few numbers can be mentioned. The "Ave Maria" with words by Sir Walter Scott is a good example of a song dependent on poetry. Its simple greatness and magical effect of harmonic shifts is typical of Schubert. "An die Musik" with words by his friend Schober is another exquisite song. One phrase, "To music which leads to a better world," could be regarded as the motto for all of Schubert's music. Also to be cited among the great poetic songs are "Gretchen at the Spinning Wheel," with words by Goethe, and "Hark, Hark, the Lark" and "Who Is Sylvia?" both with words by Shakespeare.

Some critics speak of Schubert as a dreamer who lived a disorganized and easygoing life. It is not true. Even while walking about seemingly doing nothing, he was searching for inspiration. At times Schubert suffered terrible headaches and periods of depression, and the walks undoubtedly helped to relieve him.

The story of how Schubert composed "Hark, Hark the Lark" probably was repeated more than once in his life. According to the well-known story, Schubert was walking past an outdoor cafe when he saw some friends at one of the tables. He joined them and picked up from the table a volume of Shakespeare that one of the friends had been reading out loud. Glancing idly through the pages as the others talked, his eye caught the lines "Hark, Hark the Lark." Immediately his face was aglow. "Such a lovely melody has come into my head," he said. "If only I had some paper!" One friend quickly drew lines across the back of a menu, and Schubert scribbled down the notes as fast as he could. Later he took home his song and the Shakespeare book, and that same evening composed "Who Is Sylvia?" Thus two beautiful songs were born.

The works of Schubert also include overtures, dances, chamber music, operas, sonatas, and symphonies. One of the most delightful compositions Schubert wrote was the Quintet in A, or *The Trout*. It gets its name from the third movement, which is based on a Schubert song. A wealthy cellist who held musical evenings in Vogl's home asked Schubert to contribute a new work, and so he wrote the Quintet. As Schubert often wrote specifically for the musicians at hand, the Quintet has a very exciting part for a double bass. The piece is full of musical charm and the magical Schubertian modulations. Schubert almost always wrote at headlong speed, and much of his work is fresh, vivid, spontaneous, bearing the mark of improvisation.

By the age of twenty-one Schubert had already written six symphonies. The two-movement Symphony No. 8 in B Minor, more often known as the *Unfinished* Symphony, can be called the first truly Romantic symphony. Schubert's inspiration had its roots in Beethoven. He complained to a friend one day, "Who can do anything after Beethoven?" Having said that, he still had the courage to write his symphony. It really is not unfinished, as in it Schubert said everything he had to say on the theme of melancholy. It was first performed thirty-five years after his death, and today the *Unfinished* Symphony ranks with the finest of Beethoven. Schubert's experience should encourage each of us to make our own statement. It might be better than we think.

Schubert worshiped Beethoven from afar, and even though they often ate in the same restaurant, the modest Schubert never approached his hero. When Beethoven was on his deathbed, Schubert was one of the few people he asked to see in his last days, for shortly before his fatal illness Beethoven had seen about sixty of Schubert's songs. He said several times, "Truly this Schubert has the divine fire."

In 1828 Schubert wrote his Ninth Symphony in C Major. It is the last mighty Classical symphony. Though the music of Schubert is Romantic in its lyrical quality and harmonic color, he always maintained a certain Classical serenity and poise. The symphony was refused performance at first because it was considered "too long and too difficult." The work might have been lost forever except that years later Robert Schumann visited Schubert's grave and saw Ferdinand Schubert at his home, where Schumann discovered the Ninth Symphony among "a fabulous pile" of manuscripts.

Schubert's music always sounds good. The beauty of sound was essential to him. He learned to write for orchestras by playing in an orchestra. He had the power of making instruments sing. His ideal composer was Mozart, and during the last months of his life he was studying Handel. One time after hearing some music by Mozart, Schubert wrote in a letter, "Happy moments relieve the sadness of life. Up in heaven these radiant moments will turn into joy perpetual."[5]

During his latter years, Schubert took a renewed interest in church music, which had always stirred him deeply. Franz Schubert was a man who

---

5. O. E. Deutsch, ed., *Franz Schubert's Letters* (New York: Vienna House, 1974), p. 32.

accepted religious principles and strict dogma. In spite of the struggles of his life, his faith remained unshaken, and it adorned some of his richest compositions.

At the end of his life, Schubert wrote the song cycle *Die Winterreise*, which includes some of the best songs ever written; yet Schubert was forced to sell them for almost nothing because of his grievous financial state. He said that these songs affected him more deeply than any of his others. Here he expressed the extremes of pathos. Schubert did have times when he was obsessed by the seeming failure of his life. But even in the tragic music of the final years, there is no bitterness, only a darkening of the wistfulness that makes much of his music so poignant. Schubert died at thirty-one of typhoid fever, and his request to be buried next to Beethoven was fulfilled.

From Bauernfeld's *Diary* (one of Schubert's many friends):

20 Nov. 1828

Yesterday afternoon Schubert died. On Monday I still spoke with him. On Tuesday he was delirious, on Wednesday dead. To the last he talked to me of our opera. It all seems like a dream to me. The most honest soul and the most faithful friend! I wish I lay there in his place. For he leaves the world with fame!

Recommended Reading

Deutsch, Otto Erich. *The Schubert Reader. A Life of Franz Schubert in Letters and Documents.* New York: W. W. Norton, 1947.

Flower, Newman. *Franz Schubert: The Man and His Circle.* New York: Tudor Publishing Co., 1935.

Hutchings, Arthur. *Schubert.* London: J. M. Dent, 1967.

Recommended Listening

"Impromptus"
Quartet in D minor, *Death and the Maiden*
Quintet in A, *The Trout*
Rosamunde, Incidental Music
Any of his songs
Die Schöne Müllerin
Die Winterreise
Symphony No. 8, *Unfinished*
Symphony No. 9, *The Great*
Wanderer Fantasie for Piano

The Strauss Family
Nineteenth Century

*The waltz has brought happiness and enjoyment to
the world.*

Egon Gartenberg

*I*n all ages people have danced for joy or sorrow, for artistic expression, for ceremonial purposes, even in preparation for war, and certainly for health reasons. The love of dancing is passed down from generation to generation, and dancing, along with music, is one of the earliest of the arts.

In Scripture we read about David dancing in worship before the Lord. Ecclesiastes 3:4 tells us there is a time to dance. Of course, there is evil dancing as in the sexual orgy before the golden calf, related in Exodus 32:19. As a result Moses threw down the tablets of the Ten Commandments and broke them.

In chapter 6 of the gospel of Mark, Salome dances before King Herod, resulting in the beheading of John the Baptist. On the other hand the dance is encouraged in Psalm 30:11: "Thou hast turned for me my mourning into dancing."

Verse 3 of Psalm 149 says, "Let them praise his name in the dance: let them sing praises unto him with the timbrel and harp." In Psalm 150:4 we hear, "Praise him with the timbrel and dance; praise him with stringed instruments and organs." We all love Christmas carols. *Carole* (in French) means a dancing choir, and carols were originally dancing songs.

We find a great deal of dance music throughout music history, as many Classical composers loved the dance. The Bach and Handel suites are collections of dances. Mozart, who loved to dance himself, wrote a large amount of dance music, such as minuets. Also Beethoven, Schubert, and Haydn wrote dance music.

Then there is a wealth of ballet music written by Tchaikovsky, Prokofiev, Stravinsky, Ravel, etc., and in the twentieth century jazz, swing, rock and roll, and so on. One can think of many other dances, such as folk dances (which we enjoy doing at Swiss L'Abri now and then). And dancing may have purposes other than sheer enjoyment. Coauthor Jane Stuart Smith had the privilege of studying modern dance for over two years with Martha Graham in New York to help her have a graceful appearance on the opera stage.

One of the most popular of all dance steps is the waltz. It became the craze in Europe in the nineteenth century, centered in Vienna. The waltz is a strong affirmation of life, light-hearted, frolicking with happiness, popular, and in a sense enjoyed by most everyone with its strong downbeat followed by two chords. *Walzen* means "to turn," and its probable ancestor is the *ländler,* a slow alpine dance in three-quarter time.

When the waltz is mentioned, one immediately thinks of the inimitable Strauss family. The "waltz kings," Johann Strauss, Sr., and Johann Strauss, Jr., ruled the social life of Vienna in the 1800s as the Habsburg royal family under Franz Josef ruled the empire. This family represented the true soul of the city during its golden age.

The Strausses must be included among Vienna's important musicians. Because the ruling families and aristocracy of this city loved the arts, and especially music, Vienna produced the most magnificent waves of musical genius anywhere over a span of three centuries. The first wave: Gluck, Haydn, Mozart, Beethoven, Schubert, and the elder Strauss. The second wave: Brahms, Bruckner, Goldmark, Wolf, Mahler, Richard Strauss, and the younger Johann Strauss. And finally the third wave: the twentieth-century geniuses—Schoenberg, Berg, and Webern.

Johann Strauss, Sr., (1804-1849) of humble origin, studied violin as a child. In 1826 he joined with Joseph Lanner, who invented the classic Viennese waltz, and they began to formalize this waltz into what we know today. Eventually the two conductors separated, and each formed his own highly trained orchestra, which played in large, elegant ballrooms such as the "Sperl" and in dance gardens.

Strauss, Sr., lived for his orchestra and to make money. Lavish with the funds to care for his orchestra, he showed little love for his family. He was restless, irascible, demanding, and tyrannical. Even so his sons idolized him and learned a great deal from him. For Strauss, Sr., created a cheerful music that has become one of Vienna's gifts to the world. Hans Christian Anderson said of him, "The melodies were streaming out of him." Strauss, Sr., traveled far and wide with his orchestra (which, by the way, he always conducted using his violin bow as baton). His "Radetzky March" is his greatest success, bringing him immortality. It is the unofficial Austrian national anthem.

He did not want any of his children to become professional musicians, though he made a lucrative business of the waltz by giving the people what they wanted. But secretly encouraged by their mother Anna, Johann's three sons—Johann, Jr., Josef, and Eduard—studied music and eventually contributed even more to the waltz than he did.

After Johann, Sr., abandoned his family for another woman, young Johann, Jr., (1825-1899) became the new "waltz king." He was even greater than his father. Young Johann was already writing music in three-quarter time at the age of six. The composer Richard Strauss (no relation) called him "this God-gifted dispenser of joy." Brahms insisted, "This is a master." Wagner called Strauss, Jr., "The most musical head that I have ever come across."

Strauss, Jr., was inspired by beautiful Vienna. (His music *is synonymous* with Vienna.) At his debut concert when only nineteen with a small orchestra at the Dommayer Casino, Strauss, Jr., included six of his own compositions. Some can be called symphonic waltzes for dancing, such as his greatest, "The Blue Danube Waltz." After Johann, Jr.'s debut, Johann, Sr., refused to speak to him for two years.

Strauss, Jr., himself, was unable to dance, probably because he was too busy conducting and composing. Some evenings he had six orchestras playing throughout Vienna, and he would make appearances at all the concerts in this elegant, aristocratic city—with Eduard and Josef assisting.

Following his historical, highly successful debut, he gradually made the waltz an art form in the highest sense. His waltzes, full of grace and lightness and melodic charm, are authentic contributions to the great musical repertory, just as much as Beethoven's *Fifth Symphony*. Beethoven, near the end of his life, complained that the Viennese were waltz-mad. Perhaps he had a point. Many of the enthusiasts danced through the night until early morning. The large, elegant dance halls of Vienna (some could accommodate at least five hundred people) overflowed. At a memorable Strauss concert at the Imperial Spanish Riding School, one thousand people sang, and five thousand listened.

Like his father, Johann, Jr., was a compulsive worker and paid for his relentless exertions with repeated breakdowns in health, often having to cancel engagements and take cures at spas. He also suffered from restlessness. He wrote music mainly at night and often under stress. Some of his compositions were written at the last moment before the performance.

For twelve consecutive summers, he went on tours throughout Europe, especially in Russia where his performances were called "Russian Summers." Even the czars attended the waltz evenings.

He also had triumphant tours in France and in England where he played for Queen Victoria's coronation. Though he had a fear of traveling and of death, he even went to the United States to perform at a Boston Jubilee for an audience of one hundred thousand. That mammoth concert was a nightmare for him.

"The Emperor Waltz" was written to honor the emperor of Austria, Franz Josef, who reigned for nearly sixty-eight years. It is not the usual cheerful waltz; it is better described as full of bitter-sweet melancholy.

In ill health and urged by his first wife, Jetti, to concentrate on composing, he gradually handed over the responsibility of the family orchestra to his brother Josef. His brother reluctantly took over the conducting, but he handled it with outstanding success. He too wrote beautiful waltzes and was called "the Schubert of the waltz." He suffered from depression, especially after his mother's death, and died young of a brain tumor.

After Josef's untimely death, Eduard directed the family orchestra. He lacked the creative ability of his brothers. Though handsome and a fine conductor, he secretly envied Johann, Jr., all his life.

In Johann, Jr.'s two operetta masterpieces, *Die Fledermaus* (The Bat—greatest of all Viennese operettas) and *The Gypsy Baron*, he took the step that led from the ballroom to the theater—from the waltz to the Viennese operetta. These operettas are widely performed worldwide today. His contemporaries said that he brought the spirit of the café into the opera house, happiness and enjoyment to the world through his music. In this respect he resembled another Viennese musician, Franz Schubert, the greatest of all songwriters, who also wrote piano waltzes and *ländlers*.

The melodies of Strauss, Jr., sparkle like champagne with rhythmic ingenuity, expressing the *joie de vivre* of nineteenth-century imperial Vienna. His art remained fresh and young. His genius went far beyond the realm of light dance music, inspiring many great composers who wrote waltzes.

Strauss, Jr.'s friend Brahms wrote superb waltzes for piano and singers. Chopin's fourteen waltzes are aristocratic through and through—and no longer Viennese but idealized—and not for dancing. Remember that the waltz was the *first* dance in which partners embraced each other. Early on it met with violent opposition, especially in Victorian England. Some considered it the work of the devil. Tchaikovsky's waltzes in his great ballets, *Nutcracker, Sleeping Beauty,* and *Swan Lake,* are universal favorites. *Eugene Onegin* reminds us of Tolstoy's novel *Anna Karenina* where there is a brilliant waltz scene. The great French composer, Berlioz, has a remarkable waltz in his *Symphonie Fantastique.*

There are wonderful waltzes in *Der Rosenkavalier* by Richard Strauss. Then we should also remember *The Invitation to the Dance* by Weber and "The Skaters Waltz" and *Valse Triste* by Sibelius. Swiss folk music is full of waltzes.

Debussy wrote waltzes, and Ravel in his superb *La Valse* was inspired by Strauss, Jr., but here the waltz is the symbol of a dying world. Stravinsky has a waltz in his ballet *Petrouchka,* and there are wonderful waltzes in the *Entertainer Ballet* with music by Scott Joplin. Poulenc, Satie, and Prokofiev all wrote waltzes. So the waltz lives on through great composers. But its real beginning was with the Strauss family.

When the great "waltz king," Johann Strauss, Jr., died in 1899, he had composed nearly five hundred works—waltzes, polkas, quadrilles, marches, galops, operettas, and on and on. He is as assured of immortality in the world of music as Beethoven or Brahms. It has been said of Strauss, "He only speaks German but smiles in all languages." His music has received universal praise. Every New Year's day a marvelous waltz concert is televised from Vienna for the whole world to see and hear.

When life gets hard, the day is gloomy, and nothing seems to cheer you, put on a waltz. Your spirit will be uplifted, and soon everything will look brighter.

Recommended Reading

Gartenberg, Egon. *Johann Strauss: The End of an Era.* University Park and London: Pennsylvania State University Press, 1974.

Kemp, Peter. *The Strauss Family: Portrait of a Musical Dynasty.* Tunbridge Wells, England: Baton Press, 1985.

Recommended Listening

Strauss, Sr.: "Radetzky March"
Strauss, Jr.: *Die Fledermaus*
   The Gypsy Baron
   "Artist's Life"
   "The Blue Danube"
   "Emperor Waltz"
   "Roses from the South"
   "Tales of the Vienna Woods"
   "Tristch–Tratsch Polka"
   "Voices of Spring"
   "Wine, Women, and Song"
Josef Strauss: "Pizzicato Polka"
   "Music of the Spheres"

Hector Berlioz
1803-1869

Whoever wants to know about the nineteenth century must know about Berlioz.

W. H. Auden

*B*erlioz never learned to play the piano well, but eventually it turned to his good. "When I consider the appalling number of miserable platitudes to which the piano has given birth," he said, "I feel grateful to the happy chance that forced me to compose freely and in silence, and this has delivered me from the tyranny of the fingers, so dangerous to thought. . . . "

Over a period of time Berlioz learned to play several instruments and eventually became one of the greatest orchestral innovators in history because he did not limit himself. If he could not play the piano as a virtuoso, he decided to acquaint himself with one hundred instruments—the symphony orchestra. From the beginning of his career Berlioz's conception of a large and sometimes noisy orchestra startled Europe.

A story illustrates his sensitivity to tonal combinations. The dramatist Legouvé was present at an opera performance one evening when there was a commotion in the gallery. A student sitting near him rose to his feet, bent toward the orchestra, and shouted in a thundering voice, "You don't want two flutes there, you brutes! You want two piccolos! Two piccolos, *do you hear?*" Having said it, he sat down, scowling with indignation, indifferent to all around him.

In the tumult that followed the wild outburst, Legouvé turned around to look at the one who had caused it. There he saw young Berlioz trembling with passion, his hands clenched tightly, his eyes flashing, and a head of hair—"such a head of hair! It looked like an enormous umbrella."

Hector Berlioz became France's greatest symphonic composer and was one of the leaders of the Romantic movement. He was also a brilliant critic with an imagination that ran as much along literary as musical lines. Two of his favorite authors were Shakespeare and Goethe. Writing for him was a torture. He said that he could spend eight consecutive hours on his music, but he had to fight with himself to begin a piece of prose. Even though putting down thoughts was mental agony, he kept at it. "The fear of being dull or monotonous," he once said, "makes me try to vary a little the turn of my poor sentences." Because of his diligence, Berlioz added something not only to musical history but also to world literature.

It is not only in his music criticism that one sees his technical expertise and lively writing style, but also in his autobiography. With the idea of leaving posterity his own account of himself, he began his *Memoirs* (1846) in a period of profound discouragement. There are sad moments, highly dramatic episodes, and extremely funny details filled with a bubbling sense of humor.

Turner, one of Berlioz's biographers, considers his autobiography the most extraordinary and gifted literary work ever written by a musician. Berlioz paid to have twelve hundred copies printed, not to be sold until after his death. He also wrote a book on orchestration in 1844, which was the first textbook of any importance on this subject. It has had immense influence on composers since that time.

Besides his other achievements, Berlioz was a masterful conductor and the father of modern orchestration. As early as 1825 he conducted an orchestra of 150, but his dream orchestra numbered 467 instruments with a chorus of 360 voices, besides 30 harps, 30 pianos, 12 cymbals, 16 French horns, and a dramatic variety of percussion—Romanticism at its height. Mahler later realized this dream in his *Symphony of a Thousand*.

In music, as well as art and literature, the Romantic period spans the nineteenth century. Historian Donald Jay Grout said, "Romanticism cherishes freedom, movement, passion, and endless pursuit of the unattainable. Just because its goal can never be attained, Romantic art is haunted by a spirit of longing, of yearning after an impossible fulfillment."

In France the Romantics were led by Delacroix in painting, Victor Hugo in literature, and Berlioz in music. These three artists were mutual friends in their revolution against the eighteenth century's insistence on restraint, logic, and tradition. Reason was no longer key to their thinking, but emotion became their touchstone. From the beginning the Romantic movement had a revolutionary tinge, with an emphasis on the virtue of originality in art.

The restless Romantic impatience with limits leads to a breaking down of distinctions and categories. This is evident when one compares the symphonies of Berlioz, especially his *Symphonie Fantastique,* with the clear, orderly, formal symphonies of Mozart and Haydn. In his intensity and excessiveness, Berlioz was an eminently Romantic personality. One sees it in his life, his appearance, and his works. There was nothing usual about Berlioz, and there has never been anyone quite like him. He was extreme in everything. His humor reflects this enjoyment of excess.

In one of his essays he tells of a competition at the conservatory. There were thirty pianists assembled to play the competition piece, Mendelssohn's G Minor Concerto. After the thirty performances, he noted that a piano began playing the concerto by itself. "Nobody can stop it," wrote Berlioz. "They send for the manufacturer, and he rushes over. The piano has gone berserk and will not listen to orders. The manufacturer sprinkles the piano with holy water. That does not help. They remove the keyboard, which continues to play, throw it in the courtyard, and chop it up with an axe. Now each piece of the keyboard dances around. Finally they throw it into a fire. There was no other way to loosen its grip."

Hector Berlioz was born near Grenoble in the south of France in 1803. His father, a distinguished and intellectual doctor who had a great influence on Berlioz's education, sent his son at an early age to Paris to study medicine. At Hector's first grisly dissection, which he describes hilariously in his autobiography, he jumped out of the window in horror. Though he later went back to the hospital, it was not long before his medical studies took second place to music. He spent far more time at the opera and the conservatory than at the medical school.

After attending an opera by Gluck, for whose music he had a great passion, he wrote, "I vowed as I left the opera that I would be a musician come what might, despite Father, Mother, uncles, aunts, grandparents, and friends."

Christoph Willibald Gluck (1714-1787) had revolutionized the whole art form of opera by using music in its proper function of serving the poetry to help express the plot. Gluck's masterpiece *Orfeo ed Euridice*, in its Classical simplicity, had a profound influence on Berlioz, and especially on Berlioz's magnificent opera *Les Troyens*, one of his last major works.

Finally Berlioz was able to communicate to his father that music was his life, and he entered the Paris Conservatory, but without support from his mother who was very legalistic and vehemently opposed his musical career. She was convinced that all musicians and artists were doomed to perdition.

Years of struggle and poverty followed, and Berlioz had to fight every step of the way. His ambition, vanity, and belief in his own powers had no limit. He felt to the bottom of his heart that music was one of the necessities of existence, not a decoration nor an artificial pleasure. He lived music with all his mind, soul, and body. There is a mixture of flaw and genius in almost all of the works of Berlioz, but as Schonberg remarked, "There is not one piece of his that lacks its incandescent moments."

Obviously Berlioz was a difficult student, contrary and rebellious toward old-fashioned teachers, especially toward Cherubini; but at the same time he was diligent, with tireless energy, and he received an exceptionally long and severe academic training.

The starting point for nineteenth-century program music was Beethoven's *Pastoral* Symphony. Berlioz believed that the root of his art lay in Beethoven's symphonies. "I have taken up music where Beethoven left off," he said. It is no accident that the *Symphonie Fantastique* was conceived the day after Berlioz first heard the *Pastoral* Symphony.

Berlioz wrote the *Symphonie Fantastique* at the age of twenty-five, and it is one of the most original and astonishing works in the history of music. In the strictest sense, it is a masterpiece. There are five movements with a recurring motif called by Berlioz *"l'idée fixe,"* symbolizing the woman he loved. The rhythms are alive with tremendous verve and vitality, and his music is always expressive with its originality of orchestration. He was concerned for the most minute details. His concepts of color and sonority have influenced many composers to reassess the capabilities of the symphony orchestra.

After his fifth attempt Berlioz won the much-coveted Prix de Rome in 1830 and was expected to remain in Rome three years. Berlioz went prepared to dislike Italy, and he did. He called it "a garden peopled by monkeys." However, he loved the countryside and was later inspired to write his second symphony, *Harold in Italy,* suggested by his reading of Lord Byron's *Childe Harold.* The viola solo impersonates Harold himself.

Within eighteen months the homesick Berlioz was back in Paris and soon after took a job as a music critic to support himself. He hated the writing, but he became one of the outstanding music critics of all time. He eked out a poor living for himself and his family for the next thirty years. One of the ironies of his life was the contrast between the demand for his writing and the lack of appreciation for his music, especially in his own country.

While still working on the *Symphonie Fantastique,* Berlioz fell violently in love with the Irish actress Harriet Smithson. Without her even knowing what was going on, he wept to his friends, he raved, he disappeared into the fields outside Paris, and one time Liszt, Mendelssohn, and Chopin went after him, convinced he was going to destroy himself.

Finally, in 1832 he married Harriet after six years of siege. She did not turn out to be what he had hoped for, and his love soon faded. She grew jealous after their son, Louis, was born and made home life unbearable. As James Baldwin said, "Everybody wants an artist on the wall or on the shelf, but nobody wants him in the house." However, his wife, before she became impossible to live with, was the inspiration for the loveliest of all his works, *Romeo and Juliet,* a dramatic symphony with chorus. This composition was made possible because of a large gift of money from Paganini.

Berlioz had a lifelong enthusiasm for Shakespeare, which influenced several of his works such as *Overture to King Lear* and the opera *Beatrix and Benedict.* Like Wagner, Berlioz wrote all the librettos for his operas. Berlioz's purpose as a composer was to develop dramatic music on Shakespearean lines; and like Shakespeare, Berlioz's favorite theater was that of the imagination.

At intervals between quarreling with his wife, Berlioz plunged into European music life and immediately became the leader of the avant-garde. Berlioz was an inconsistent man. Though he screamed against tradition, there is a Classical aspect in his music that became more pronounced as he grew older. His Classic opera *Les Troyens*, inspired by his lifelong love of Virgil, displays the passion of youth tempered by restraint, clarity, and proportion. As Schonberg said, "Berlioz was French, with all the logic and mental organization that implies."

Hector Berlioz was in constant trouble throughout his life; indeed his career was essentially tragic. He was troubled not only that the French people were puzzled by his music, but there was trouble at home, trouble with his colleagues, trouble with mounting debts and failing health; yet discouragement could not stem the flow of major compositions.

Harriet died in 1854, and after several months he married his mistress, Marie Recio, a singer. Berlioz turned more and more to conducting, not because he liked it, but because nobody seemed able or eager to conduct his music. He did so himself in order for it to be heard. He traveled widely as a conductor.

As Berlioz grew older, he became more and more discontented, yet he kept firmly focused on his music. He was possessed and exhausted by his musical emotions, yet was fiercely devoted to his art. He polished his scores time after time in later years, as was his general practice.

One of the first compositions of Berlioz for which he wrote the entire text was *L'Enfance du Christ*. The words are of a high literary quality. It is one of the purest and loveliest works of its kind, and it was recognized as a masterpiece at its first performance.

The "Shepherd's Chorus" is exquisite. Though there is no evidence that Berlioz believed in Christ, those of us who do can listen to this beautiful music knowing that all gifts do come from God. Romain Rolland, in speaking about Berlioz, said, "He believed in nothing—neither God nor immortality." Nevertheless, Berlioz did write a number of religious works. His complete lack of spiritual understanding made him the antithesis of a church composer, and much of his religious music seems more suited to celebrate a pagan rite.

It is impossible to associate his gigantic, grandiose *Requiem* with prayer for departed souls. His spine-chilling "Tuba Mirum" is a vision of the trumpet call that will reverberate through the tombs of the dead summoning them before the final judgment seat of God. His orchestration called for sixteen kettledrums.

There is no doubt of the grandeur and originality of Berlioz's music or its frequent theatrical effect. Sometimes there are bizarre passages, but there are numerous moments of breathtaking beauty. No work of literature inflamed the Romantic imagination as strongly as Goethe's *Faust*. One of Berlioz's finest compositions is his large choral work *The Damnation of Faust*, with its broad conception of the conflict between good and evil, the deification of nature, and invocation of the supernatural.

In the last years of his life, beset by ill health, he was a lonely, tortured man, longing for death, yet haunted by the fear of death. He grew more melancholy and shut up within himself with no comfort of belief in the true

God to sustain him. This tempestuous personality, irritable and excessive in everything, became a martyr to his music, although he believed intensely in the freedom of art.

Loneliness and a sense of separation is a key aspect in Romanticism. Part of Berlioz's misery came from his longing for the impossible and his rejection of the Lord who had given him his extraordinary gifts. St. Augustine's thought, "We shall never find peace until we find it in God," tragically sums up Berlioz's final days.

The death of his beloved son Louis at Havana in 1867 was a crippling blow and a direct cause of his own final decline. He died two years later in despair. Only in the second half of the twentieth century, after years of neglect and misunderstanding, has there been a growing revival of interest in Berlioz's achievements.

Recommended Reading

Berlioz, Hector. *Memoirs of Hector Berlioz*. New York: Tudor Publishing Co., 1932.
Barzun, Jacques. *Berlioz and His Century*. Chicago: University of Chicago Press, 1982.

Recommended Listening

Carnaval Roman
La Damnation de Faust
L'Enfance du Christ
Harold in Italy
"Nuits d'été"
Requiem
Romeo and Juliet
Symphonie Fantastique
Les Troyens

CHAPTER 12

Felix Mendelssohn
1809-1847

*It is a relief to find one musician who was really
happy for the greater part of his life, even though
that life was a short one.*

Siegmund Spaeth

*A*t the age of seventeen Mendelssohn composed the enchanting overture to Shakespeare's *A Midsummer Night's Dream*. He never surpassed this music, and it set the standard for all subsequent concert overtures of the Romantic period. It was first performed in 1826 in the family garden house with a private orchestra under Mendelssohn's direction. Its sparkling melodies and brilliant orchestration established the young Mendelssohn as one of the leading composers of his day. Seventeen years later he added about a dozen pieces making this a programmatic orchestral suite.

He made his first public appearance as a pianist when nine years old, and he began to write music when he was ten. His first teacher was his mother, a woman of exceptional culture and refinement. In Berlin, where the family moved in 1812, Mendelssohn studied with Carl Zelter and other excellent teachers who introduced the boy to the finest music. Zelter, for all his gruffness and severity, regarded his young pupil with great pride and affection. In fact, Zelter was so impressed with his eleven-year-old pupil, he took him to Weimar to visit Goethe. The famous poet-philosopher accepted the precocious boy on terms of equality, and the young Mendelssohn and the seventy-two-year-old writer became close friends.

The prospect of their son visiting Goethe threw the Mendelssohn family into great excitement. Felix's sister Fanny wrote to him: "When you are with Goethe, I advise you to open your eyes and ears wide, and after you come home, if you can't repeat every word that fell from his mouth, I will have nothing more to do with you."

It is certain that young Felix did repeat every word that fell from Goethe's mouth. Mendelssohn had a phenomenal memory. In 1829 his overture to *A Midsummer Night's Dream* was performed in England. The score was carelessly left in a hackney coach and disappeared. (It turned up *one hundred years* later at the Royal Academy.) Mendelssohn seemed not at all disturbed by the loss of his music. Immediately he sat down and rewrote the whole overture from memory, and every note agreed with the orchestra parts.

It was through Zelter that Mendelssohn learned to appreciate Bach. When Mendelssohn was only twelve, he had studied Bach's *St. Matthew Passion* in manuscript form in the Royal Library, and he became so excited about this discovery that his mother had a copy made for him as a birthday present. Eight years later in 1829 Mendelssohn performed Bach's *St. Matthew Passion* in Berlin, and it is considered one of the great events in the history of music.

The *St. Matthew Passion* was given the second time on Bach's birthday, March 21, and it again met with great success. Mendelssohn said to a friend in the theater who had helped him to persuade Zelter to perform the passion, "To think that it should be an actor and a Jew that had given back to the people the greatest Christian work."

Mendelssohn, in contrast to the modern school which underrates the music of the past, insisted that one should learn from such masters as Bach and Handel without being merely imitative. Perhaps more than any other conductor, Mendelssohn contributed to shaping public taste for good music. He had excellent musical taste himself and demanded excellence in performance. Besides renewing interest in Bach and Handel, Mendelssohn also deserves credit for increasing the performances of works by Mozart and Beethoven.

Felix Mendelssohn was born in Hamburg, Germany, in 1809. The son of wealthy, cultured Jewish parents who had become Lutherans, Mendelssohn was baptized in the Lutheran church. Both Felix and his sister Fanny were taught music by their capable mother. In the Mendelssohn family the tradition of hard work was strongly established, and self-indulgence played no part in Mendelssohn's life. All through his life he felt an almost religious devotion to his family in general and to his father particularly as head of the family.

The grandfather, Moses Mendelssohn, was a well-known philosopher. It is a great tribute to this man's personality that in the face of much racial prejudice at the time of Frederick the Great, Moses was so widely loved and respected. Felix Mendelssohn's father said of himself after his son became a well-known composer, pianist, and conductor, "Formerly I was known as the son of my father, and now the father of my son!" Even though Abraham Mendelssohn was less distinguished than his father and his son, he was a remarkable character too and a man full of deep family affection.

Of all the composers we have considered, Felix Mendelssohn seems to have been the most versatile. He could paint and draw excellently. He also was a bit of a literary artist as judged by his letters and occasional poems. He was an all-around athlete, and musically he had many talents. He composed and conducted, played the piano and organ amazingly well, and was more than an adequate performer on the violin and viola.

Clara Schumann, the famous German pianist, once said, "My recollections of Mendelssohn's playing are among the most delightful things in my artistic life. . . . He could carry one with him in the most incredible manner, and his playing was always stamped with beauty and nobility." Being able to do so many things and to do them well placed a burden on Mendelssohn. He tended to do too many things, and this plus his natural restless temperament and the emotional tensions that are a part of creativity sometimes resulted in a rather ineffectual fussiness in some of his music.

If there is one thing great musicians have in common, it is their irritability. Being "sensitive" does not alone prove that an individual is a great artist, but as Alfred Einstein explains in his book *Greatness in Music*, "The irritability of the great is caused by the task to which they are committed and the urge to accomplish that task to the utmost degree."

In 1829 Mendelssohn made the first of ten trips to England. He achieved almost immediate fame as a composer, conductor, and soloist. Even today Mendelssohn's works are admired and performed more in England than in any other country. His conservatism, melodiousness, high spirits, and unfailing good manners appealed to the British and still do.

He introduced Beethoven's Concerto in E Flat to English audiences, and on another visit the Concerto in G. Mendelssohn was one of the first artists to play a concerto by heart in public. He was a modest man in spite of his giftedness and high standing in society. At a concert the score for one of his trios was mislaid. Mendelssohn put another volume upside down on the music stand and had a friend turn the pages in order that he might not seem to be playing by heart when his colleagues had to have notes.

Fingal's Cave or the *Hebrides* Overture was composed when Mendelssohn was twenty-one, and it is one of his finest works. He wrote it after a visit to the Hebrides. He loved to travel, and often things he saw and experienced during his journeys inspired him. He said once, "To me the finest thing in nature is the sea."

His wonderful conducting of the festival at Dusseldorf in 1832 led to his appointment as general music director to the town. Here he began his first oratorio, *St. Paul*. Then he received an invitation to take the permanent direction of the Gewandhaus concerts at Leipzig. This was the highest musical position in Germany, and finally in 1835 Mendelssohn went to Leipzig where he was received with acclamation. Shortly after his arrival there, he had a welcome visit from Chopin, and about the same time he met Robert Schumann and Schumann's future wife, Clara.

In 1837 Mendelssohn married Cecile Jeanrenaud, a minister's daughter from Frankfurt. They had five children. His wife was reserved in contrast to Mendelssohn's warm, outgoing personality, but she had great charm, serenity, and good sense. She was an oil painter and the best of wives for Mendelssohn. They were a devoted couple.

In 1841 the king of Prussia called Mendelssohn to Berlin and gave him the title of *Kapellmeister*. It was an honor, and the composer, not wanting to seem ungrateful, could not bring himself to turn it down; but the appointment soon became a vexation and a strain. His early death was definitely related to overwork.

The high point of Mendelssohn's visit to England in 1842 was his invitation to perform for Queen Victoria at the palace. While waiting for her to appear, Mendelssohn and Prince Albert were having an animated conversation, hauling out all manner of volumes of music. Suddenly the young queen arrived, and seeing books and portfolios scattered about the room, she immediately began to tidy up the royal chamber. After Mendelssohn played for the queen, Prince Albert urged her to sing. It took a while to find the music, and Queen Victoria performed to Mendelssohn's accompaniment. She sang in a small but well-trained voice, making a few mistakes and admitting that her nervousness made her short of breath. The visit gave great pleasure to all three. In a letter to his family Mendelssohn described Queen Victoria as "pretty, shyly friendly and polite, and speaks German very well. Her singing is quite delightful."

Mendelssohn in 1843 founded the great conservatory in Leipzig, and two years later he introduced Jenny Lind to the Gewandhaus concerts. He wrote the soprano solo "Hear Ye Israel" for the famous Swedish singer, whom Mendelssohn admired greatly. At the height of her career Jenny Lind left the opera stage to devote her life to oratorio singing. As biographer Philip Radcliffe relates the incident, a friend asked her, "How was it that you ever came to abandon the stage at the very height of your success?" She replied, "When every day it made me think less of the Bible, what else could I do?"

The outstanding instrument of the Romantic era was the piano, just as the organ was for the Baroque and the tape recorder (electronic music) is for the twentieth century. Mendelssohn's *Songs Without Words*, a series of small, intimate piano pieces, contributed enormously to his popularity. His elegant and sensitive style is essentially Classical. His well-known symphonies, the *Scottish* and the *Italian*, show the high quality of Mendelssohn's orchestration and mastery of form. In the *Reformation* Symphony, written for the tercentenary of the Augsburg Protestant Confession, Mendelssohn used Luther's "A Mighty Fortress Is Our God" during the last movement. Of his two hundred musical compositions, one of the favorites today is his Concerto for Violin in E Minor. It is considered one of the finest of all violin concertos.

Mendelssohn was the greatest nineteenth-century composer of oratorios, and like Bach and Handel, he knew the Bible well. He said often, "The Bible is always the best of all." His oratorio *St. Paul* is based on a pure and simple scriptural text. His use of the chorale suggests the influence of Bach.

Mendelssohn always loved England and made many successful trips there. His oratorio *Elijah* (the greatest oratorio since Handel's *Messiah*) was composed for the English public. He was an excellent writer for the chorus.

Like Handel, Mendelssohn could write moving and effective choral music—for instance, the "Baal" choruses or the lovely "He Watching over Israel." "If with All Your Heart You Truly Seek Him," "Lift Thine Eyes," and "He That Shall Endure to the End" are Mendelssohn at his best. The oratorio *Elijah* is a work of the greatest stylistic purity and the highest nobility. It dramatically demonstrates the composer's Christian faith.

Elijah was a great success in England. It was first given in 1846 as a morning performance at the Birmingham festival. The moment the beloved Mendelssohn took his place as conductor, the sun broke forth. The audience spontaneously burst into applause at the dramatic effect, and they continued to applaud throughout the performance; even so, the meticulous Mendelssohn made many revisions before publication. He remained a highly fastidious composer to the end and one of the most intelligent and scholarly composers of the century. Within less than two years after the Birmingham triumph, Mendelssohn was dead at the age of thirty-eight. He had been devoted to his gifted sister Fanny, also a composer, and the abrupt news of her death hastened his own death only six months later. He fell into a state of unconsciousness and never fully recovered.

The music of Felix Mendelssohn breathes goodness and happiness. His name Felix means "the happy one." He was a gifted person, and he used his gifts to the glory of God. All Europe sorrowed over the loss of this amazing man and musician. It was almost like an international calamity, because Mendelssohn with his personal charm and shining Christian purity had left his mark. Some of Mendelssohn's music has faded, and some lacks depth, but the best is on a high level and fills us with admiration. "He That Shall Endure to the End" is not only an inspiration to listen to, but it is great music.

Recommended Reading

Radcliffe, Philip. *Mendelssohn*. London: J. M. Dent, 1957.

Recommended Listening

Concerto in E Minor for Violin
Elijah
A Midsummer Night's Dream
A Midsummer Night's Dream, Incidental Music
Octet in E Flat for Strings
Hebrides Overture
Rondo Brillante for Piano and Orchestra, Op. 29
Songs Without Words
Symphony No. 3, *Scottish*
Symphony No. 4, *Italian*
Symphony No. 5, *Reformation*
Variations Serieuses
Sonatas for Organ

CHAPTER 13

Frédéric Chopin
1810-1849

*It is when working within limits that mastery
reveals itself.*

Goethe

*T*here was always music in the Chopin home, and Frédéric's parents were distressed when they saw their infant son burst into tears at the sound of singing or the playing of the piano and other instruments. They thought he hated music; but one day when he reached up to the piano and with his small fingers picked out several tunes, they understood with laughter and tears that their child had been crying for joy. No wonder Frédéric Chopin grew up to be "the poet of the piano." In a remarkably single-minded way almost everything he wrote was directly for the piano or involved with the piano. He created his own unique world of color in sound.

Chopin spent about half his brief life in Poland and the other half in Paris. Like many bright young people, he craved adventure. Thus he went to Vienna, Berlin, Munich, and a few other places, but Paris was his goal, and he arrived there in 1831. While in Berlin he saw Mendelssohn but was too timid to introduce himself. On one of his travels before Paris he heard Handel's "Ode for St. Cecilia's Day." He wrote home, "It most nearly approaches my ideal of sublime music."

Chopin was born near Warsaw. His father, who was French, came to Poland to work, but after the failure of the company he was associated with, he became a tutor and eventually started a successful tutoring academy of his own. Many of his pupils were of the nobility, and Frédéric early in life liked to mingle with those in the highest society. His mother was the lady-in-waiting for a countess, and she herself was of noble birth.

The atmosphere in the Chopin home was loving, refined, and artistic. There were four children, and they were all musical. As the only boy, Frédéric's choice of a career was never in doubt. At six he was already a good pianist, hailed by many as another Mozart. At age eight he saw his first composition in print. It was a polonaise. This is a national dance of Poland, originally performed by the nobility.

Chopin's first teacher, a well-trained musician, introduced his young prodigy to Bach and also allowed him to improvise freely on the piano. In later years Chopin would warm up for a concert on passages from the *Well-Tempered Clavier* by Bach. He knew them all by heart.

With his next teacher, Joseph Elsner, Chopin studied composition. This was a crucial moment in his musical education. It was perfectly normal for a well-rounded musician like Elsner to urge his pupils to compose sonatas, symphonies, operas, and other forms of music to broaden their understanding of the possibilities for a composer. But Elsner had excellent judgment. He never forced Chopin's style and did everything he could to let the unique giftedness of Chopin develop naturally.

Often we are asked at L'Abri Fellowship, "What does it mean to be creative? How would you define a creative artist?" Chopin is an outstanding example. He concentrated intensely upon his own particular and limited point of view. He decided early in life to write exclusively for the instrument he loved. Music did not pour out of him. He had to work hard and with great anguish at times to accomplish his goals. He preferred short forms of music, and like a jeweler working on rare gems, Chopin would polish his relatively small output of compositions until they were as nearly perfect as he could make them.

Another author expressed it this way: "He cultivated his own garden." Anyone who has done preparation for planting understands the hard work of cultivating flowers and vegetables.

When Chopin left Poland and his beloved family as a young man of twenty, it never entered his mind that he would not return. As biographer Huneker said, "Chopin, his heart full of sorrow, left home, parents, friends . . . and went forth into the world with the keyboard and a brain full of beautiful music as his only weapon." His steadfast love for his family was one of his finest characteristics.

The Poles consider Chopin the most towering cultural figure their country has produced. He is the musical soul of Poland. One of the greatest dramatic outbursts in piano literature is the *Revolutionary Etude* (Op. 10, No. 12). He composed it with deep emotion when he heard that Warsaw had fallen to the Russians.

When Chopin arrived in Paris in the autumn of 1831, it was a time of temporary stabilization in France, and the national revival and prosperity manifested itself in a flowering of the arts. Chopin already enjoyed limited success, but as a composer he knew his "mere piano pieces" would not be highly favored in the Parisian musical life. Thus before he left Warsaw, he had finished many compositions, including the Piano Concertos in F Minor and E Minor as well as mazurkas and most of his etudes.

He had little money but soon made friends among the nobility, and word spread that Chopin was willing to give piano lessons. Almost immediately he had more students than some of the best professors in Paris. His pupils—Princess This, Countess That, Duke Somebody, and the like—never handed Chopin money for the lessons. Instead, they unobtrusively placed twenty or thirty francs on the mantelpiece while Chopin looked out the window or filed his fingernails. He was too proud to reveal the fact that he really needed the money.

The teaching side of Chopin's career is reflected in his magnificent etudes, including what some consider his greatest melody, Etude Op. 10, No. 3, and the pieces composed for his pupils to play. They include the preludes, nocturnes, waltzes, impromptus, mazurkas, and the earlier polonaises. Many of these compositions were dedicated to his pupils.

Fairly soon Chopin was earning enough money to keep his own carriage, live very comfortably, and dress like a count himself. So he was soon known and liked in the higher circles, although he made few close friends. Schumann helped to spread his fame, but even apart from Schumann, Chopin was being recognized as a genius. Liszt, Berlioz, Hiller, Bellini, and Meyerbeer became admiring friends also.

Wherever Chopin went, he was treated as someone special, like a prince, and this noble quality carried over into his music. His compositions are never commonplace or ordinary. Chopin was not a follower. He was a leader.

Although he is known as a great pianist (his improvisations evoking much astonishment), frail health limited his sonority, and early in his career he learned he should not play in large halls. There is no other example in the history of piano-playing of such a legendary reputation. It is built on barely thirty public performances, all that Chopin gave during his whole career. In one of his last concerts, his sound was almost a whisper and the applause nearly as delicate as his playing.

The works of Chopin demand of the pianist not only technique and a flawless touch but an imaginative use of the pedals and a discreet application of "tempo rubato." Chopin described this as a slight pushing or holding back within the phrase of the right hand while the left-hand accompaniment continues in strict time.

It was at private musical parties in the magnificent homes of his many noble friends that Chopin became known and beloved as a pianist as well as a composer. Those must have been exciting evenings. One can picture Chopin and Liszt playing four-hand music with much improvisation and possibly Mendelssohn or Berlioz turning the pages.

It must be said of Chopin that he had a tenacious hold on life in spite of his poor health. His cheerful optimism helped him. In the midst of frustration he could smile and even joke about whatever was irritating him. But one hears the sad aspect of his life in some of his Romantic and melancholy music.

Chopin enjoyed the company of women, and they appreciated him, but because of his physical frailty and his extreme reserve he never married.

Before he came to Paris, he had anticipated marrying a countess he had known from childhood, but her father objected. He did not want a musician son-in-law.

Chopin had several lesser affairs, and his yearning for affection particularly appears in the nocturnes. When he finally accepted the fact that his romance with the countess was terminated, his health suffered, and he became very depressed; but before leaving Poland, he composed a waltz for her, Op. 69, No. 1.

Two friends urged him to come with them to England. They assured him the change would cure him as well as lift his melancholy spirits. It did the opposite. The combination of the English weather and his already lowered vitality damaged his weak lungs. He returned to Paris suffering both in mind and body, and he might have surrendered to complete despair if the writer George Sand, one of the most remarkable women of the nineteenth century, had not entered his life. They had met through Liszt in the winter of 1836, and almost immediately after his return from England, they were seen everywhere together.

She was older than Chopin, and about the time of their meeting she was at the height of her fame as a novelist and feminist. To the casual spectator, it would seem that she, the masterful woman, was in charge of the musician; but it really was not so. Chopin had lived most of his life with delicate health and had learned the art of getting his own way. Because of his extreme weakness at times, he was forced to rely on others for help, but in his art he showed an astonishing degree of self-confidence and independence.

Chopin craved perfection, and this desire came to dominate his whole life. In his unusual relationship with George Sand, he undoubtedly received an emotional stability he needed, and he was allowed time and quiet to compose. In these next nine years Chopin entered upon one of the most productive periods in his life. In his passionate ballades, imaginative scherzos, impromptus, and such inspired works as the Fantaisie in F Minor, Barcarolle, and Berceuse one finds the perfection he strove for.

Early in November 1838 the two of them, along with Sand's children and a maid, went to the Isle of Majorca seeking sunshine and warmth. Instead it was wet, cold, and miserable, particularly because they lived in an abandoned Carthusian monastery. One hundred some years later we visited the monastery on a beautiful, sunny day. Even then it was chilly and bleak inside. The damp cell and poor food almost finished Chopin, and eventually the weary travelers stopped at Marseilles until he was well enough to go to Nohant where George Sand had a summer home.

In spite of the difficulties at Majorca, Chopin returned to France having written two polonaises, the C Sharp Minor Scherzo, the Prelude in A Major, No. 7 (one of his most poignant compositions), and twenty-four preludes (Op. 28). He had taken his copies of Bach's preludes with him and modestly said that his twenty-four preludes were "mere scribblings" when placed side by side with Bach's forty-eight. Chopin wrote his music with heart-rending effort, shutting himself in his room (or in the monastery cell) sometimes for days, doing and redoing a passage.

In 1847 his friendship with George Sand ended abruptly. In a quarrel between George and her daughter Solange, he took Solange's side, and finally George Sand had had enough. The separation meant little to her, as she was extremely occupied with her writing and various liberal causes, but for Chopin it was literally a death blow and marked the end of his creativity. His health deteriorated rapidly, and he never wrote any more music.

At the urging of a Scottish friend, Jane Stirling, one of his wealthy pupils, he went to England and Scotland where he was immediately taken up by fashionable society. He was in the terminal stage of tuberculosis and so depleted that after playing in a salon, he had to be carried to his bedroom and undressed by his valet.

He returned to Paris where the revolution was still raging. He had little money left, but fortunately the Stirlings gave him a generous gift to sustain him in his last days. His sister Louise came from Poland to nurse him. He lingered with much suffering until the early morning of October 17, 1849. The Polish soil that had been given to Chopin when he left Warsaw in 1830 was buried with him. His grave at Pére-Lachaise Cemetery is between Cherubini and Bellini.

There is no doubt that Chopin gained from George Sand's affection and care a sense of security and peace of mind that hastened the final maturing of his genius. The new epoch in his life began with the B Flat Minor Sonata, the G Major Nocturne, Op. 37, No. 2, and the F Sharp Impromptu, all composed during his first stay at Nohant. From then until 1846 his summers were spent at Nohant where he not only composed but enjoyed the visits of the great singer Pauline Viardot and painter Delacroix, whose dramatic painting of Chopin now hangs in the Louvre.

All his life Chopin loved singing, and in particular he had the greatest affection for the Italian opera composer Bellini. The music of Frédéric Chopin requires exquisite phrasing and a singing tone. Because of his unique style, one can readily recognize the music of Chopin, who has rightly been called "the poet of the piano."

Recommended Reading

Huneker, James. *Chopin: the Man and His Music.* New York: Dover Publications, 1966.

Recommended Listening

Ballades
Barcarolle
Concertos for Piano
Etudes, Op. 10 and 25

Mazurkas
Nocturnes
Polonaises
Preludes, Op. 28
Scherzos
Sonatas 2 and 3 for Piano
Waltzes
Fantaisie in F Minor

CHAPTER 14

Robert Schumann
1810-1856

*In no other composer is there such an attempted
fusion of sound with literary idea.*

Schonberg

Clara Schumann
1819-1896

*She became the most celebrated woman pianist of
her time, and she furthered her husband's career by
giving the first performances of his works.*

World Book

*T*he marriage of Clara and Robert Schumann in 1840 was a story of love from beginning to end, but woven into that story were much trouble, anguish, and drama before, in between, and until Robert's early death in a mental institution. Clara's father, Friedrich Wieck, a gifted piano teacher, was vehemently opposed to the marriage. His daughter was already a brilliant pianist at nine, and everything in Wieck exploded at the thought of Clara being out of his control and married to the unsettled poet-musician Robert Schumann. Wieck did everything in his bitterness to separate the two. Blinded by his intense jealousy, he made extravagant charges against Schumann, accusing him of laziness, irresponsibility, and drunkenness. Finally Robert and Clara went to court, and the judge repeatedly had Wieck take back his untrue statements.

Robert and Clara did win their case, but it seemed like forever before they could marry; and even though at times he was disconsolate and restless, finally Robert Schumann escaped into the world of creativity. He wrote to Clara, "I have noticed that my imagination is never so lively as when it is anxiously extended towards you."

In this lonely, nerve-wracking period Schumann revealed that he had within him that musical gift from which masterpieces emerge. He had lived in his inner prison dominated by the conflicts and contradictions of his life, and when he began to compose, he uttered his immortal cry, "I would like to sing like the nightingale, and die of it." Music absorbed him completely.

In 1838 the composer's maturity and supreme mastery was revealed in every bar of *Kinderscenen* (Op. 15). Here are remembrances of childhood by an adult, and the artistry of Schumann makes us forget the hours of work that went into perfecting the tiniest detail.

Schumann was the tone-poet of eternal youth. Even though he had his terrible bouts with depression, his music has a fresh vitality and sparkle. Delacroix believed that the great artists are "those who have kept, until the age when the intelligence has developed its full power, a part of that impetuosity of impression . . . which is the hallmark of youth."

Robert always liked children and was himself a delightfully radiant and enthusiastic young boy. His curiosity and imagination were always on the alert. He enjoyed sharing his ideas with everyone. At the age of twelve he formed a small orchestra, composed music for Psalm 150, and studied Mozart, Haydn, and Weber.

After his father took him to hear Moscheles, one of the great pianists of the period, Robert insisted that his father buy him a piano. He enjoyed playing it, but still literature attracted him the most in his youth, particularly the writings of Jean Paul Richter who inspired Schumann· to write his early piano music, *Papillons*. No one in these early days of Schumann marked him as a genius, but when he began to write his music, he struck off entirely on his own.

After his father died in 1826, his mother, who could see no future for her son in music or literature, sent Robert off to Leipzig to study law, a profitable career, not music—"the breadless art"—as she called it. Nevertheless, Schumann spent most of his time at concerts or practicing the piano or reading to his friends from Shakespeare, Richter, Goethe, or Byron.

It was in Leipzig that he began studying the piano with Wieck. During this period he ruined one of his fingers trying to find a shortcut to finger independence. Several biographers speak of his accident as providential because it turned him in the direction of composition.

At the time that Robert was escaping into the world of creating music, Clara, as a concert pianist, was showing her capability and brilliance. While Robert was in Vienna, she went to Paris alone. Her father should have gone with her to help her deal with the hazards of traveling in the middle of winter and the difficulties of organizing a tour, but at the age of nineteen Clara did everything herself. She chose the dates for her concerts, booked the hall, arranged to have programs printed, looked after the sale of tickets, and then finally played splendidly at each concert. She wrote to Robert, "I see that even without my father I can still exist in this world."

There is no doubt that Clara Schumann was a great pianist. Goethe heard her play when she was twelve or thirteen. He did not have a good ear for music (according to her father), but Clara's playing won him. She was invited to repeat the visit. This time, with his own hands, the aged poet graciously brought a cushion to raise the small figure to the keyboard. After the performance, Goethe exclaimed, "Why, the girl has more power than six boys put together!"

Robert went into another silent period when the wedding was further postponed, but after some happy moments with Clara, he began to compose again. While she was on her next tour, he wrote, "Ah, Clara, what divine happiness there is in writing for the voice! I have been deprived of it too long."

Here began an uninterrupted flow of composition. In what is known as Schumann's song year, he wrote more than 130 songs of exquisite beauty. In the song form he found the union of poetry and music, his two major interests in the world of art.

About five months before they were married, Robert went to Berlin to hear his friend Mendelssohn sing his first song, accompanied at the piano by Clara. Shortly after this joyful reunion, Robert Schumann composed the *Liederkreis* (Op. 39) with words by Eichendorff, the *Dichterliebe* (Op. 48) with text by Heine, and *Frauenliebe und Leben* (Op. 42) with words by Chamisso.

The song cycle *Dichterliebe* (Poets' Love) is one of the most perfect fusions of music with poetry. The songs are of unsurpassed sensitivity and beauty. They express the full, restless tide of Romanticism. "No one alive is as gifted as you," Clara exclaimed. "My growing love and admiration for you can hardly keep pace with each other."

Finally in 1840 Clara and Robert were married in a small village church at Schönfeld near Leipzig. It was a true love match as well as the union of two remarkable artists.

Robert, a very high-strung person, often pushed himself way beyond his physical and mental limits. Still, he wrote a great deal of music in his forty-six years. Clara urged him to try a symphony. Within three months his fresh, youthful *Spring* Symphony was played in Leipzig with Mendelssohn conducting. Eventually Schumann wrote four symphonies, and although some critics claim it would have been better for him to compose as he saw fit, it is interesting that all four of the Schumann symphonies are in the repertoire today.

No doubt, Robert Schumann was a great melodist, and his gift was essentially lyric. He was a miniaturist known for his short piano pieces and songs. That wonderful domestic instrument, the piano, was always closest to the heart of Schumann, and in his piano music he shares his most intimate feelings. More than to the intelligence, it is to the heart that the highly original Schumann revealed himself.

In 1841 Schumann wrote a piece of music, and after a series of rejections, he began to revise the composition and made it so much better that five years later Clara played the premiere of the A Minor Piano Concerto at the Gewandhaus. Soon it was on its way to being one of the best-loved pieces in the entire concerto repertory. We have mentioned some of the high moments in his career, but actually Schumann did not enjoy much success in his lifetime, especially as a conductor and teacher. Even his friends did not really understand or appreciate his music.

The nineteenth century was in the main a secular and materialistic age. Musical Romanticism flourished especially in Germany with Robert Schumann, the central figure who brought this movement to its zenith. In his *Fantasy Pieces* we hear some of the greatest piano music of all time. The first piece is "Des Abends," which expressed the quietness of night. One of the symbols of the Romantic movement is the night with its tranquillity and mystery and ghostly images.

Schumann is the voice of romance, and once heard he is never to be forgotten. His passion for Romanticism did cause a gradual withdrawal from truth and reality. Romanticism leads inevitably to irrationality, because much of it is infused with a kind of idealistic longing that in a vague pantheistic sense might be called religious. One author said concerning Schumann, "He was religious, but had no religion."

The soaring, ardent, impulsive character of Schumann expresses the depths and tensions of the Romantic spirit. In his music, moods and keys change suddenly and often. A divided soul, moving in a world of extreme emotions, he constantly swayed between elation and despair with intermittent mental breakdowns and deep melancholy. In some of his music we can hear the early stages of fragmented music. In *Warum* (Why), Schumann tried to solve the riddle of life by music, but he failed. In the dark universe of Romanticism the eternal "why" remained unanswered.

As early as 1827, when Robert was still a teenager, he came under the influence of Franz Schubert. When he heard of Schubert's death at thirty-one, he wept bitterly. Schumann took everything personally and profoundly, and it was as if he had lost a close friend.

From the beginning Robert pursued an independent musical course. He made detailed studies of Schubert and Beethoven, but the composer he examined the most was Bach. He particularly immersed himself in the *Well-Tempered Clavier*. Once he had discovered the music of Bach, he let Bach be his master for the rest of his life. This could be one reason why the music of Schumann is truly beloved: his Romanticism was enlightened by Bach's Christianity.

Schumann once called Bach "that genius who purifies and gives strength . . . and whose music seems written for eternity." Perhaps because of the influence of Johann Sebastian Bach on his life, Schumann believed that, as he expressed it, "To spend one's strength on religious music remains perhaps the highest aim of the artist." Schumann wrote little religious music, although later in his life he was instrumental in the publishing of Bach's complete works.

In 1833 Schumann started reviewing concerts and new music. One of his early reviews was of Chopin. Schumann was the first to recognize the greatness of Chopin and wrote in the magazine, "Hats off, gentlemen—a genius!"

In writing about other composers, a more generous critic never lived. Maybe he was not as witty as Berlioz, but Schumann was always lending a helping hand to young talent. In his busy life he even found time to help Clara compose a number of piano pieces and songs.

His one strong dislike was Wagner, partly because he had not heard any of the music of Wagner's maturity and also because of a vast difference in temperament. Wagner knew how to promote himself, and even if he was disliked in many places, his music was performed and discussed. The gentle Schumann, one of the most lovable men in the history of music, did not stand up for himself. But as a critic, he was willing to fight for others and to call attention to the fact that people of his day seemed content with "titillating potpourris" in the salons of Europe. Schumann thoroughly disliked sham and pretentiousness. Only a few years had passed since the public had appreciated Beethoven, Schubert, and Weber, and so the aim of his writing was to bring again "the poetry of art to honor among men."

Schumann was the editor of the *New Magazine for Music*. In his articles he gave pen names to a society he called "Davidsbund" in order to discuss music from different points of view. For himself he had two names— Florestan expressed the exuberant side of his nature, and Eusebius was the more quiet, reflective side. Then he also had Chiara, who was Clara, and Master Raro, who expressed himself as if he were Friedrich Wieck.

Even with his mental and nervous handicap, which worsened in the last fifteen years of his life, he persevered in an amazing way, although his compositions lack youthful inspiration as he was involved in a constant struggle with poor health.

On a trip to Vienna for the magazine he made a wonderful discovery. In the possession of Schubert's brother was the great C Major Symphony that Franz Schubert had written at the end of his brief but overflowing life. It had never been performed.

One of the last triumphs in Schumann's life was his recognition of the great future ahead for Brahms, who was only twenty years old at the time.

In 1854 Schumann began to suffer from an acute and painful attack of an ear malady that had troubled him before. He heard a continual ringing in his head. Then when he could not sleep at night, he thought he heard choirs of angels and cries of demons. On February 27 he threw himself into the Rhine River, but some boatmen nearby saved him. He was taken to a mental institution near Bonn. There he lived for over two years, a mere shadow of his former self.

It was an extremely troubled time for Clara, but she did not give way to despair. The Schumanns had eight children, of whom five had lived, and so Clara, to help pay the mounting bills, began giving concerts again. Brahms was a faithful friend during these hard years. Brahms had a deep attachment to Clara, though he was much younger. People have speculated about why they did not marry after Robert died, but Clara was single-minded now, and Brahms also needed freedom for his creativity. His motto was "Free but glad." As the greatest woman pianist of her century, Clara dedicated herself to performing the music of Robert Schumann until he was known and accepted all over Europe and England.

Toward the end of Robert's life, he became very agitated when Clara or Brahms visited him, because he could not communicate with them. But one of the last times Clara saw Robert, with great effort because his body was so weak, he put his arm about his beloved wife. In her diary Clara wrote, "I will never forget it. That embrace I would not trade for all treasures."

Clara Schumann continued to give concerts for forty years after Robert died, helping to make him one of the unforgettable composers in music history.

Recommended Reading

Schauffler, Robert Haven. *Florestan: The Life and Work of Robert Schumann.* New York: Henry Holt and Co., 1945.
Reich, Nancy B. *Clara Schumann: The Artist and the Woman.* London: Victor Gollancz Ltd., 1985.

Recommended Listening

Robert Schumann: *Carnaval*
Concerto in A for Piano
Dichterliebe
Fantasiestüke
Frauenliebe und Leben
Kinderscenen
Papillons
Quintet in E Flat
Symphony No. 1, *Spring*
Symphony No. 3, *Rhenish*
Clara Schumann: Trio in G

Franz Liszt
1811-1886

It is not genius he lacks, but the capacity to sit still.
Princess Carolyne Wittgenstein

*F*ranz Liszt was born in the year of Halley's comet, and his life itself was like a brilliant phenomenon. His dates span much of the nineteenth century, and he was one of the most colorful figures in the history of music and a legend of the Romantic period.

He is difficult to describe, as he was a *very* complex individual. In a worldly sense he seemingly had everything: magnetism, extraordinary energy and strength, good looks, and the ability to get from people what he wanted, plus great musical talent. Yet at heart he was a restless, unhappy man.

Liszt was generous and kind but could quickly become arrogant and capricious. He was also excessive and extreme in everything he did. He never married, but he was always in love with some lady and obviously enjoyed being surrounded with beautiful, rich, and noble women. His "Liebestraum" (Dream of Love) is one of the most popular piano pieces of all time.

Franz Liszt was probably the greatest master of the keyboard the world has ever known, not only because of his prodigious feats, but also because of the incredible technical demands his piano music makes on the performer. At the height of his fame as a pianist (at the age of thirty-seven), he gave up playing concerts in order to compose and help other musicians. One could say that he was an important, rather than a great, composer, and with his "ceaseless industry" he wrote an enormous amount of music. Obviously, with such a torrent of notes, it is not all of the highest quality.

Liszt was one of the noblest, most unselfish, exciting figures in the musical world, and his generosity to other artists is almost unbelievable in as gifted an individual as he was. It is far more common for a person of his abilities to exalt himself. He loved the world and worldly pleasure, but within

Liszt there was also a spiritual hunger that certainly could explain his thoughtfulness to others. Certainly Franz Liszt was a mass of contradictions. His "seething Romanticism" kept him restless and on the move all his seventy-five years, and though he eventually received four of the seven degrees of priesthood, he continued to be torn between a longing for spiritual security and a love of worldly sensations. One can only hope he found peace with God before he had to meet the Maker and Giver of all gifts.

In a letter to his mother in 1862, Liszt wrote, "You know, dearest mother, how in many of the years of my youth nothing seemed so rich in blessedness as the goodness and compassion of God. Despite all the errors of my life, nothing and nobody have been able to shake my faith in eternal salvation."

Franz Liszt was born in the small town of Raiding in Hungary where his father, Adam Liszt, a musical enthusiast, was steward of the Esterhazy properties. His father remembered Haydn and also had been acquainted with Hummel and Cherubini.

Liszt, like many of our other composers, was a child prodigy. At seven he was already playing the piano very well, at eight composing, at nine making concert appearances, and at ten studying in Vienna with Czerny and Salieri. He was introduced to Schubert and Beethoven. Beethoven was so thrilled when he heard the young Liszt perform that he kissed him on the head.

Following the Vienna period, the family moved to Paris. Soon afterwards Liszt was the darling of the French salons. Then in 1827 his father died suddenly with these words on his lips: "I dread women on your account; they will trouble and dominate your life." The warning proved prophetic.

His first notorious love affair with a married woman, Countess d'Agoult, occurred when he was twenty-two. She deserted her husband, and they eloped to Geneva, Switzerland, in 1835. After three children, they parted in bitterness. One of their illegitimate daughters, Cosima, eventually married a pupil of Liszt, Hans von Bülow. And following her father's pattern, after a time she ran off with Wagner. During these happy, turbulent years Liszt wrote *Années de Pèlerinage*, the first version of the Paganini Studies, and the twelve Grandes Etudes. Artistically the countess had a good influence on Liszt, turning him to the sort of thing he could successfully accomplish.

A few years before his liaison with Countess d'Agoult, he met three incredible personalities—Paganini, Chopin, and Berlioz. Liszt's whole approach to music was transformed after he heard Paganini, the greatest violinist of all time. For about two years, Liszt practically lived the life of an ascetic in order to practice with an intensity and diligence that few have exercised before or after. He emerged from his hard labor and became known almost immediately as the Paganini of the keyboard. Some of his finest music are his Paganini Studies, dedicated to Clara Schumann.

Chopin opened up new sources of poetry to Liszt, and his piano style was based on that of Chopin. In a letter Chopin wrote, "Liszt is playing my etudes and transporting me out of my respectable thoughts. I should like to steal from him the way to play my own etudes."

The third powerful influence on Liszt was Berlioz, particularly his *Symphonie Fantastique*, for which Liszt made a piano transcription. Later when Liszt wrote his symphony *Faust*, he dedicated it to Berlioz. It is considered a masterpiece.

When Liszt was at the height of his power as a pianist (1840-1848), he stunned his audiences with the brilliance and dynamics of his playing. Women would swoon at his concerts. Others fought for his belongings—a handkerchief, a flower, or a snuffbox. Within these seven or eight years his playing took him to Berlin, Copenhagen, Constantinople, Leipzig, Lisbon, London, Madrid, Moscow, St. Petersburg, and Warsaw, as well as to scores of smaller towns. Liszt really invented the solo piano recital.

When he gave a concert, he would be dressed in some startling outfit. As he played, he constantly tossed back his long hair, with his lips quivering and his nostrils palpitating. He held his audience with his great playing, but the theatrics of it all also made people adore him.

Novelist George Eliot described her reaction to Liszt: "Then came the thing I longed for—his playing. I sat near him so I could see both his hands and face. For the first time in my life I beheld real inspiration—for the first time I heard the true tones of the piano. . . ."

In 1847 Liszt made his last grand tour, and in Kiev he met the fabulously wealthy, cigar-smoking Princess Carolyne Wittgenstein, whose brother was the czar of Russia. She joined Liszt in Weimar, scandalizing everyone. From 1848 to 1861, Liszt was court music director at Weimar.

The princess persuaded him to give up his career as a traveling virtuoso, which was ruining his health, and to concentrate on composition. During the next twelve years he wrote or revised most of the major works for which he is known. It was a remarkable period of productivity. After 1847 Liszt made no money by playing, teaching, or conducting.

Liszt and the Princess Wittgenstein lived at the Villa Altenburg. In this period he wrote and published the Sonata in B Minor (one of the masterpieces of nineteenth-century piano literature), the Hungarian Rhapsodies, Paganini Etudes, and the Transcendental Etudes. Also in these years he wrote twelve symphonic poems (including the well-known *Les Preludes*), the *Faust* and *Dante* Symphonies, and a host of minor works.

As the court music director at Weimar, he zealously encouraged the Romantic movement by conducting many new compositions, including Wagner's *Tannhauser* and *Lohengrin*. Wagner and Liszt were friends, and eventually Wagner became his son-in-law. Wagner said to Liszt, "Ours is the music of the future."

Liszt really only liked the music of his time. He had hardly any interest in old music, with the exception of Bach, and by producing the modern works of composers like Wagner, Berlioz, and Schumann, Liszt made Weimar the musical capital of Europe.

At a time when there were no radios, television, or recordings, Liszt's remarkable and extremely difficult piano transcriptions of operas and songs not only did a great service to the original composers, but also helped to spread interest in important music. A fine example is his *Grand Fantasy* on Bellini's *Norma*, an opera that influenced Chopin, Wagner, and Liszt profoundly.

One cannot comprehend how Liszt had time for pupils, but it was an ongoing part of his life to teach and encourage younger musicians. Many of his students went on to have very successful careers. The names of his pupils would fill many pages, including such excellent musicians as Albéniz, Bizet, Saint-Saëns, Smetana, etc. Others who had their music published because of Liszt's influence were César Franck, Borodin, Dvorak, Vincent d'Indy, Grieg, and MacDowell. The world is richer because of these composers, and we are indebted to Franz Liszt. One of the most difficult tasks for a new artist is to get into print. Liszt never charged money for his lessons and help.

As we said earlier in this chapter, there was a part of Liszt that was drawn to religion. In 1841 he had become a Freemason, encouraged in this direction by Princess Wittgenstein, a mystical-religious person. They wanted to marry, but the church interfered, and soon afterward they went their separate ways.

By 1865 Liszt had received four of the seven degrees of priesthood. He was not allowed to become a priest because of his reckless past, but after he began to wear his religious frock, everyone knew him as "the Abbé." During this time he composed a setting of Psalm 13, two immense oratorios (*The Legend of St. Elizabeth* and *Christus*), and two piano pieces ("The St. Francis Legends").

Being an abbé did not change his way of life much. In fact one historian described Liszt as "Mephistopheles disguised as an abbé." He was first given an apartment in the Vatican opposite the Loggie of Raphael. Later, through a friend of his who was a cardinal, Liszt spent at least part of each year at the Villa d'Este at Tivoli and the remaining months in Budapest and Weimar.

The Villa d'Este has one of the three or four most beautiful gardens in the world. As Sitwell says in his excellent biography of Liszt, "The giant cypresses in the garden and the voices of all the waters could not be improved upon for poetry and music. It was amid this enchantment that he grew into old age, and it is certain that he worked more at Villa d'Este than anywhere else in those years." Such fine piano pieces as "Cyprés de la Villa d'Este" and "Les Jeux d'Eaux à la Villa d'Este" were inspired there. It was in his piano music that Liszt was at his greatest. His two piano concertos are unsurpassed in their grandeur and authentic virtuosity.

Liszt's love of traveling continued to the end of his life. He could not remain still for long, and on one of his visits to Hungary he stayed in the home of a rich baron with two other guests, von Bülow, the conductor, and an extraordinary and talented violinist, Reményi.

It was shouted through the streets that Liszt was in town; soon a crowd of seven or eight thousand people gathered at the square outside the baron's home. Liszt went to the open windows and, rather than making a speech, had the piano moved over so the people could see and hear him. First he played a rhapsody with Reményi and then the "Rákóczy March" for four hands with von Bülow. It created a sensation.

Around this time, a correspondent wrote and asked Liszt if he had given up his music since becoming an abbé. "It is true," he answered, "that I have joined the ecclesiastical profession, but not a bit through disgust of the world, and less still through lassitude for my art."

When Franz Liszt was seventy-five years old, he made his last concert tour, playing in Paris and then in London for Queen Victoria. He returned to Bayreuth to attend a Wagner festival. There he contracted pneumonia and died in 1886. His last word was "Tristan."

Today Franz Liszt is regarded as one of the great innovators of the nineteenth century. His music has ingenuity and brings to life a specific period in musical history in which the virtuoso was the monarch and virtuosity an end in itself. As Schonberg said, "It is music intended to amaze."

Recommended Reading

Sitwell, Sacheverell. *Liszt.* New York: Dover Publications, 1967.

Recommended Listening

Années de Pèlerinage
Piano Concertos E Flat and A
Faust Symphony
Hungarian Rhapsodies
Mephisto Waltz
Opera Transcriptions
Les Preludes
Sonata in B for Piano
Sonetti del Petrarca
Transcendental Etudes
Un Sospiro

Richard Wagner
1813-1883

*He rejected history and chose mythology, creating a
world of his own.*

Paul Henry Lang

Richard Wagner was familiar with the theater from childhood. His step-
father, Ludwig Geyer, probably of Jewish blood, whom historians as well as
Wagner regarded as his real father, was a gifted actor, singer, and artist. As
early as ten, Wagner was studying Greek tragedy (so he said). When he
learned English, he promptly fell in love with Shakespeare. One of Wagner's
first literary ventures was *Leubald and Adelaide,* a bloody tragedy vaguely reminiscent of *Hamlet.* The young Wagner had so many characters die in the first
act he had to bring them back as ghosts to complete the drama.

His musical interests had a slow awakening. His talent for music as a
youth was so unpromising that his piano teacher said, "Nothing will ever
come of him." But in 1827 his lifelong passion for Beethoven's music was
aroused when he attended the Gewandhaus concerts in Leipzig. He was particularly stirred by hearing Beethoven's Ninth Symphony. Later Wagner said
that his operas were a continuation of Beethoven's Ninth Symphony.

He studied music secretly, learning counterpoint from Beethoven,
orchestration from Mozart, and harmony by instinct. Wagner was regarded
as an "intelligent but lazy" pupil. At eighteen he entered Leipzig University
and studied briefly with Weinlig, a successor of Bach at the St. Thomas
Church. But he continued to be an erratic and careless student and interrupted his studies with frequent drinking bouts, gambling, and affairs with
women. The theater was his world, and loose living was part of it.

He was offered a post as musical director at Magdeburg, and there he
fell in love with the actress Minna Planer. Although she was uncultured, she
was experienced in the life of the theater. They finally married after two
years of living together, but their marriage was a torture for both of them.

Wagner's years of bohemianism had encouraged a pattern of irresponsibility, extravagance, and dishonesty that was to become a way of life for him.

Six months after their marriage, Minna left him; but she rejoined him in Riga when Wagner was appointed the music director of the theater in 1837. Wagner wrote most of *Rienzi* there. But after two years with debts piled high, the Wagners fled Russia by way of the Norwegian fiords and across the channel to England. The composer, inspired by the storms they encountered while aboard ship, conceived the idea for his next opera, *The Flying Dutchman*, which is outstanding for its musical description of a storm-tossed sea and the theme of salvation through the love of a woman.

The next three years, spent in Paris, were a time of poverty and misery, but he wrote *The Flying Dutchman* during this period. No obstacle could hinder his creativity. The word *impossible* was unknown to Wagner. He arrived in Paris full of hope, but nothing worked out for him. He quickly ran out of money, and he and Minna lived in quarters far worse than anything they had experienced in their fifth-rate theatrical world in Germany. "The almost incredible bitterness of the Paris years left an indelible mark," writes Abraham, "as large as it was ugly, on Wagner's soul."[6]

After experiencing such poverty in Paris, Wagner seemed determined to never know want again. His love of luxury and his living above his means on other people's money kept him constantly in debt, but it was no great burden to him. He simply borrowed more money from friends, relatives, and strangers he had charmed, without a thought of paying them back. Wagner believed the world owed him a living—and a good one at that.

In 1843 after *Rienzi* and *The Flying Dutchman* were performed successfully, Wagner was offered the coveted position of conductor of the Royal Theater in Dresden. There he remained six years. With his restless nature he was never content, but he did write *Tannhauser* (1845) and *Lohengrin* (1848), two masterly treatments of the Romantic view of medieval life. These operas clearly dealt with the subject of the conflict between the two worlds, the world of the flesh and that of the spirit. Besides composing the music, Wagner wrote all the words for his operas. *Lohengrin* was the last important German Romantic opera, and we see changes prophetic of the music dramas of Wagner's next period. *Lohengrin* was first performed in Weimar under the direction of Franz Liszt in 1850. Liszt championed Wagner's music and later became his father-in-law.

Richard Wagner was the key figure of Romanticism, in which we have the abandonment of categories. He searched for the unattainable Romantic ideal, the universal, all-embracing art work. A born reformer, an insatiable idealist, and a monumental egoist, he set out to create a world of his own; but his egomania was supported by genius. Romanticism by nature must be fragmentary with its longing for the infinite, which cannot be attained. Wagner was one of the first philosophical composers placing mythology in

---

6. Gerald Abraham, *A Hundred Years of Music* (New York: Longwood, 1938).

the central position of his Romantic thought. Like Nietzsche, Wagner felt that mankind was in need of a new mythology. He felt that history was insufficient for the purpose of art. Even in his youth Wagner had the dramatist's instinct to seek escape from this world by contriving another, and we shall see later that in *The Ring* he created his own mythological world.

In 1849 revolution was brewing in Germany, and Wagner participated in an unsuccessful revolution. A warrant was issued for his arrest, and he fled to Switzerland and was in exile there for the next ten years.

During his first years in Switzerland, Wagner wrote no music. Always an omnivorous reader, he began to examine his own thinking on subjects ranging from anti-Semitism to vegetarianism. He put his conclusions in writing. These *Swiss Essays* reveal how unbalanced, yet brilliant, egocentric, and calloused Wagner really was. In his essay "Jewishness in Music" Wagner advocated the complete elimination of the Jews from German society and culture, though later Jewish musicians were some of his finest interpreters. As Sigmund Spaeth once commented, "It is easy to like the music of Richard Wagner; it is almost impossible to like him as a man." Finally Wagner came back to his music, and in 1853 he began the libretto for his monumental creation, *The Ring of the Nibelungen.*

In 1857, still unable to go back to Germany, Wagner and his wife Minna were invited to live in a cottage near Zurich on the estate of Otto Wesendonck, a wealthy industrialist. Wagner, who not only in his music but in his life was "looking for salvation in the ideal woman," thought he had found her in the person of the beautiful wife of his benefactor. Matilde Wesendonck returned the love of the composer, who seemed to have had a hypnotic fascination for practically all women and even a number of men. This ugly little man with his protruding forehead and prominent nose and mouth must have caused a stir every time he came into a room. Having been in the theater all his life, he demanded the center of attention, and in spite of his immoral character, he had remarkable personal magnetism. His own life would make a fascinating opera story.

In this latest "love" interval Matilde Wesendonck wrote five poems that Wagner set to music. Some of this music was later included in *Tristan,* which Wagner was then working on. He wrote the libretto in four weeks, an astonishing feat. The affair was eventually discovered by Wagner's enraged wife, who intercepted a love letter. Wagner was forced to flee to Venice where he wrote the yearning second act of *Tristan,* inspired by his violent desire for Matilde. In this opera the passion of love becomes almost a delirium with its ever-intensifying chromaticisms, its unbroken deluge of emotion. Completed in 1859, *Tristan* is a unique conception for the stage. It deals with the emotional lives of the characters rather than the external events or actions. There is not one happy note in it. Schnorr, the first to sing the role of Tristan, died after four performances at the age of twenty-nine.

There is tragic gloom in the music, and yet as historian Donald Jay Grout says, "*Tristan* is in many respects the quintessence of Wagner's mature style. Few works in the history of music have exerted so potent an influence on succeeding generations of composers." And yet when *Tristan* was first performed, all that many critics could see and hear were two large persons screaming at each other!

According to Thomas Mann, a great event in Wagner's life was his becoming acquainted with the philosophy of Schopenhauer, particularly his masterpiece *The World as Will and Idea*. It was the uniting of two brilliant but neurotic minds. Schopenhauer was a cynical, solitary man influenced by Eastern religions, but basically his philosophy is atheistic. For him, blind will is the ultimate reality. Schopenhauer sought relief from suffering through the contemplation of works of art, especially music. He preached the worship of heroes. He saw the ultimate good in beauty and ultimate joy in creating or cherishing the beautiful.

Wagner's discovery of Schopenhauer confirmed his own instinctive pessimism. His preoccupation with *The World as Will and Idea* and his yearning for Matilde Wesendonck brought forth *Tristan*. The second act of the opera is filled with Schopenhauer's pessimistic philosophy of hopeless love longing for night, death, and oblivion. The music critic Lang says, "The music of Romanticism reached its peak and its ruin in Wagner." Richard Wagner was one of the most influential personalities of the nineteenth century, and what came out of his mind has altered the course of history. He wrote for the illness of the nineteenth century and furnished a magic potion—his seductiveness.

One of many talented artists influenced by Wagner was the French poet Baudelaire. The poet had two gods—Poe and Wagner. Baudelaire spoke of Wagner's music and its "opium influence" on him. He tried to imitate Wagner by living a life free from restraints and by longing for the unattainable. Baudelaire, his mind destroyed by drugs and alcohol, died at the age of forty-six paralyzed from a venereal disease; he wrote from his deathbed, ". . . feeling the wind of the wings of madness."

In 1860 Wagner went to Paris where the productions of *Tannhauser* were fiascoes owing to riots by members of an influential group, the Jockey Club, angered because the opera lacked the traditional second-act ballet. Wagner then spent three years based in Vienna but traveling widely as a conductor. Again he was forced to flee the city to avoid imprisonment for debts. Trying to explain his conduct, his irresponsible way of living, Wagner said, "Mine is a highly susceptible, intense, voracious sensuality, which must somehow or another be indulged if my mind is to accomplish the agonizing labor of calling a nonexistent world into being."

At the most desperate moment in his life, Wagner was summoned to meet the nineteen-year-old King Ludwig II, who had just come to the throne of Bavaria. The date was May 3, 1864. Ludwig, a very unstable man himself, had already come under the "opium" spell of Wagner's music. The young king promised Wagner financial independence and fulfillment of every artistic wish. If Ludwig had not entered the scene at this time, the later works of Wagner probably would not have been written. The musician moved to Munich and enjoyed a short period of triumph where many of his operas were performed.

But Wagner's insistence on luxurious surroundings, rooms filled with priceless rugs, paintings, velvet and satin hangings, and his profligate life had a negative influence on King Ludwig politically and incensed the Bavarian people. Wagner was forced to leave, but his music continued to be the obsession of Ludwig's life. Later the king helped build the Wagnerian Theater in Bayreuth before he lost his mind, was deposed, and committed suicide by drowning at the age of forty-one. The extraordinary castles that Ludwig designed, such as Neuschwanstein with its Wagnerian rooms, are worth visiting.

In his fifty-third year Wagner returned to Switzerland, and with money from King Ludwig he secured a home at Triebschen on Lake Lucerne. Wagner had already had a child by Cosima von Bülow, the wife of the first great Wagnerian conductor. She and the child came with him to Triebschen. The disillusioned von Bülow said, "If it had been anyone but Wagner, I would have shot him." Cosima, the illegitimate daughter of Liszt, became Wagner's mistress, and they had three children. Finally they were married in 1870 after von Bülow granted a divorce. (Minna had died of a heart attack in 1866.)

Wagner believed that a woman fulfills her highest function in sacrificing herself for a man, and Cosima did this in a complete sense. She was the ideal, self-effacing, and worshipful wife essential to Wagner's creativity. In the beautiful home at Triebschen, Wagner spent some of his happiest and most creative years, if a person like Wagner could ever be said to be happy. Here he completed the opera *Die Meistersinger* and started his two-volume autobiography, which wallows in self-deception and presents a twisted view of the facts.

One of many distinguished visitors at Lake Lucerne was the philosopher Nietzsche. As a boy of fourteen, he fell in love with the music of Wagner. Nietzsche is known as the apostle of the "superman" and the prophet of doom. He predicted the end of the common man. A follower of Darwin, Nietzsche created a god in his own image. Along with Schopenhauer, he believed that human behavior is irrational. Man's only hope lay in a "superman"—that is, the developing of an aristocratic, ruthless, superior human race that could dominate the world. In Wagner's music dramas Nietzsche saw a revivifying of the pagan power that he thought would triumph over the disintegrating weakness of the "meek" Christian tradition.

After Wagner wrote *Parsifal*, Nietzsche attacked his former friend in a paper entitled "The Case of Wagner," accusing the composer of making music ill. Nietzsche misinterpreted *Parsifal*. He thought it had Christian overtones, but quite the contrary. Wagner was not bowing down to Christ. Some parts of the work are considered among the finest music composed on a religious theme, especially the "Prelude" and the "Good Friday Spell." But even though the plot involves the sword with which Christ was struck during the crucifixion and the chalice used at the Last Supper, this work is in no way a Christian opera. It is typically Romantic music infused with idealistic longings that might be called "religious" in a vague pantheistic sense. The American Wagner critic Robert W. Gutman points out that Wagner clearly detested Christianity, which he saw as "Judaic error perpetuated."

Finally we have arrived at Wagner's immense work, *The Ring of the Nibelungen*—the most monumental musical achievement to weather the test of time. It took Wagner twenty-six years to complete. The libretto, which includes *Das Rheingold, Die Walküre, Siegfried,* and *Die Götterdämmerung,* was conceived backwards. The basic theme of the cycle concerns the desire for world power and gold, and it ends in destruction.

The musical fabric of *The Ring* is constructed of leading motifs, a type of musical label, with the ascending themes referring to life and the descending themes to death. These are woven into Wagner's technical method of continuous music and filled with psychological meaning. The stupendous climax of *The Ring* is Brünnhilde's immolation scene.

Wagner's desire was to merge the different arts—poetry, dance, music, and painting—into one super experience. He sought to express a world philosophy in music drama—the "universal artwork" capable of freeing modern man. He believed that human redemption was achieved by love, but because of his humanistic base, the story pessimistically ends with everyone being destroyed. Wagner's concept of man finding redemption through a woman leads to death. In contrast, God's love for the world through Christ and whosoever believes in Him leads to life everlasting.

The will to power that the philosopher Nietzsche preached inspired Hitler's Holocaust in World War II. It should not surprise us that Hitler's favorite composer was Wagner. He refused to listen to anything except military bands and Wagner's Nordic music dramas. I read recently that Hitler hailed Wagner as his only predecessor.

Wagner's thirteen operas generally have superb beginnings and endings with much too much in between. There are long stretches of boredom, loudness, and bigness. His music dramas are static, heavy, and at times tedious, but they have a sweep, grandeur, and spaciousness uniquely their own. Undoubtedly Wagner has written some of the most exalted music ever composed. It enchants and overpowers the senses. The orchestra is of central importance. He enlarged its resources enormously and created a vast new musical language. Suffering and sorrow constitute the basic tone of the music dramas. There is little humor in Wagner's life or music with the exception of *Die Meistersinger*.

Richard Wagner, the man of iron determination, controversy, and raw energy became more inconsiderate (if that is possible), self-obsessed, and melancholy as he grew older. By this time he was living at Wahnfried in Bayreuth with frequent trips to Italy to find relief for his skin disease, erysipelas. Finally he was able to construct his "temple," a new kind of theater with lowered orchestra pit, at Bayreuth, which opened in 1876 with a complete performance of *The Ring*. Wagner died of a heart attack in 1883 in Venice at the Vendramin Palace, and he was buried at Wahnfried. His was an obsession to an artistic ideal that overrode all other obligations, but his music lives on in the great theaters of the world. Crowds flock to Bayreuth every summer to hear his colossal music dramas.

In Louis Untermeyer's excellent book *Makers of the Modern World*, the first four men he writes about are Darwin, Kierkegaard, Wagner, and Karl Marx. Untermeyer opens his essay on Wagner with these words: "A self-pampered voluptuary who preached the gospel of self-denial and renunciation, an unscrupulous opportunist who, deceiving his wife, assured her that 'your suffering will be rewarded by my fame,' an importunate cadger who was also an accomplished cad, Richard Wagner not only changed the whole course of modern music but built a monumental edifice which has withstood the controversial assaults of battering animosity, critical scorn, and wildly changing taste."[7] When you listen to the music of Wagner, be aware of his "opium" influence.

Recommended Reading

Newman, Ernest. *Wagner as Man and Artist*. New York: Garden City Publishing Co., 1941.
Osborne, Charles. *Wagner and His World*. London: Thames and Hudson, 1977.

Recommended Listening

Götterdämmerung (from *The Ring*)
  "Funeral Music"
  "Rhine Journey"
  "Immolation Scene"
Lohengrin—Preludes
Die Meistersinger—Preludes
Parsifal—"Good Friday Spell"
"Siegfried Idyll"
Tannhauser—Overture
Tristan and Isolde—Prelude and Liebestod
Die Walküre (from *The Ring*)
  "Magic Fire Music"
  "Ride of the Valkyries"
Wesendonck Songs
Wagner Arias

---

7. Louis Untermeyer, *Makers of the Modern World* (New York: Simon and Schuster, 1966), p. 12.

CHAPTER 17

Giuseppe Verdi
1813-1901

*The man that hath no music in himself, nor is
moved with concord of sweet sound, is fit for treason,
stratagems, and spoils.*

Shakespeare

A few months after Giuseppe Verdi was born in Italy, Russian and Austrian soldiers swept down from the north killing as many people as they could seize. To protect herself and her child, Luisa Verdi found refuge in the village church in a narrow staircase to the belfry and thereby saved herself and the future composer. It is said that Verdi's operas are performed more often today than those of any other composer.

Verdi was born in 1813 in Le Roncole, a tiny village in the province of Parma, at that time occupied by the French. His father kept a small inn that was also a sort of village store. They were poor people, peasants actually, but to be a peasant in Italy is not demeaning. A national characteristic of these humble people is the humane spirit found among them. Italians are kind-hearted, hospitable folk who laugh and cry easily. They have a strong feeling of solidarity, which makes poverty bearable. They are quick to help each other.

The parents of Verdi were not musical, but when their son showed an interest in learning, the father bought an old spinet, and the boy pounded on it with great delight. Verdi received the rudiments of his musical education from the village organist in the same church where his mother had saved his life. The organist was impressed with the boy's exceptional gifts, and when the organist died suddenly, Verdi at the age of twelve was able to succeed him.

As a boy, Verdi used to visit the neighboring town of Busseto where his father bought supplies from Antonio Barezzi, a well-to-do shopkeeper. Barezzi liked the boy and took him into his shop. As Barezzi was also a lover of music, through him Verdi was put in touch with other musicians who were able to teach him what they knew. In a few years Verdi became the assistant conductor in Busseto and was a person of some importance in town. As early as sixteen Verdi was writing songs, piano pieces, church music, and particularly marches, which were played by the Busseto Municipal Band to great applause.

When Verdi was eighteen, he tried to get the position as organist in a larger town nearby, but he failed. However, by this time the general feeling in Busseto was that young Verdi was very talented musically and should go to Milan and study at the conservatory. He was granted some money from a music fund in Busseto, and his friend and future father-in-law, Barezzi, added a contribution of his own.

In 1831 Verdi arrived in Milan, excited about being able to study at the music conservatory. However, he was refused admission on the grounds that he lacked sufficient musical knowledge and that he was too old. Verdi was bitterly disappointed, but he was a tough-minded young man who did not easily accept defeat. Soon he became the private pupil of the composer Vincenzo Lavigna, who gave him a solid grounding in the music of Palestrina and Marcello and taught him harmony and counterpoint and everything he knew about opera. Best of all, they became friends.

After three years of study in Milan, Verdi returned to Busseto. In 1835 he married Margherita Barezzi. They had known and cared for each other since Verdi had worked for her father. At this time Verdi was composing an opera, and he hoped to have it produced in Parma. But it was rejected; so in 1839 Verdi, his wife, and their two small children moved to Milan.

Again he met with disappointment. His opera was accepted, but soon after rehearsals began, the tenor fell ill, and the production had to be postponed. This discouraged Verdi so much he decided to return to Busseto, but his wife and Merelli, the new impresario at La Scala, persuaded him to remain in Milan and to try again. It was not that Verdi lacked confidence, but he had a wife and two children to care for. He had a strong sense of right and wrong and did not want to be obligated to others to support him. Finally, in November of 1839 Verdi's *Oberto* was produced. As Verdi himself said about the opera, "It was not very great, but good enough."

It led to a commission. He was asked to write a comic opera, *King for a Day*. Just as he began to write it, Verdi fell ill with angina, and his wife cared for him through difficult and anxious weeks. They were poor, and it was a burden to Verdi that he could not pay the rent on time, not being well enough to do anything about it. Margherita pawned her last trinkets and paid the rent. In time, Verdi was able to work again. But soon complete disaster struck the loving family. Between 1838 and 1840 Verdi's two children and wife died. These sudden tragedies were so shocking to him that years later when he was telling a friend about it, Verdi thought his wife and children had all died within three months rather than two years. Ever afterwards he was inclined to melancholy.

In this black time in his life, the composer was reduced to the point of despair. He sent back to Busseto the furniture and few effects his wife had carefully and lovingly collected for their little home in Milan, and he moved into a dismal furnished room on the Piazzeta San Romano. He had one friend who occasionally visited him, and Verdi would mumble something about taking students, but he never did. Most of the time he was alone, eating alone at a dreary *trattoria* on the piazza or having a "sea biscuit" dipped in water in his room. To add to the grimness of these months, he had to finish the comic opera.

King for a Day was produced in 1840, and it was a complete fiasco. People booed and hissed, which is a frightful but all too common experience in an Italian opera house. It left Verdi stunned and resentful, having recently endured such deep personal tragedy. He said years later that if the audience had only endured the opera in silence, he could have borne that. This experience affected his outlook on life and art during the rest of his career, and his immediate reaction was never to compose again.

In his biography of Verdi, Toye recounts this crucial incident. He relates that finally Merelli at La Scala knew something had to be done, and he sent for Verdi. As Verdi said years later, "He treated me like a capricious child! . . . He refused to believe I could turn my back on music because of a single failure." But Verdi, still in mourning for his wife and children, was adamant. He would not compose, as he found no consolation in it.

Time dragged on. "One evening in the winter as I was leaving the Galleria," Verdi said, "I ran into Merelli who was on his way to the theater. It was snowing with large flakes. Taking me by the arm, he asked me to accompany him to his office at La Scala. We chatted as we went, and he told me of his troubles with a new opera he had to produce."

Merelli went into great detail about the opera, and when Verdi was about to leave, Merelli put the troublesome, thick manuscript into Verdi's hands. When he got to his room, Verdi threw the manuscript on the table, and the libretto fell open to these words, *"Va, Pensiero, Sull'ali Dorate"* ("Go, Thought, on Golden Wings"). As Verdi said, "I glanced through the verses following and was deeply moved, particularly because they almost paraphrased the Bible which I have always loved to read." Verdi read the libretto three times, and *Nabucco* kept running through his head all night.

However, Verdi, still determined never to compose again, returned the manuscript to Merelli. But Merelli, even more determined, stuffed the libretto back into Verdi's overcoat pocket shouting, "Put it to music; put it to music!" He shoved the composer out of the office and locked the door. Again Verdi went home with *Nabucco* in his pocket. He later explained how he composed the music: "Today a verse, tomorrow another, one time a note, another a phrase . . . little by little the opera was done."

In three months, Verdi had completed *Nabucco*, the opera destined to be the foundation of his fame and fortune. The story is about Nebuchadnezzar, but for purpose of song the name is changed to Nabucco. It was the best of Verdi's early operas, and with excellent singers it was a great success.

To understand why Verdi became famous so quickly, one must understand the political climate in Italy at this time. The Italians were weary of being under the heel of Austria, and the wonderful chorus, "Go, Thought, on Golden Wings," which concerns the longing of Jewish exiles for home and freedom, perfectly expressed the Italians' longing for their independence. *Nabucco* premiered March 9, 1842. From then on, Verdi, himself a fiery patriot, became a national hero, idolized as no composer had ever been. He became a symbol of Italy's struggle for independence. With strictly enforced censorship the Italian people had no way to express their great desire to be free. "*Viva* Verdi" became a popular war cry throughout Italy, for the Italians associated the letters in Verdi's last name with the slogan, "Vittorio Emmanuele Re d'Italia" (Victor Emmanuel King of Italy). In 1861 the people's dream of a free nation came true when Victor Emmanuel was crowned king of Italy.

One of the outstanding singers in the *Nabucco* opera was Giuseppina Strepponi who, after a scandal-ridden interlude, became Verdi's devoted second wife. She brought love, stability, and a reason to go on back into the life of Verdi. Also what helped to draw out the alternately shy, fierce, and stubborn composer were the salons held in the home of the Contessa Maffei. She was an intelligent woman with gentle manners, and she saw the worth of the young composer who had experienced such sorrow. She became a good and kind friend. It speaks well of Verdi's self-education that he could hold his own among the intellectuals who attended the salons. But by nature Verdi was taciturn, and he became a favorite, as good listeners are always popular among those who love to talk! These evenings stimulated, taught, and disciplined Verdi.

The operas of Verdi's early period are clearly influenced by Rossini, Bellini, and Donizetti, but they also reveal his own extraordinary lyrical and dramatic gifts, which so ably generate theatrical excitement. There were several productive years after *Nabucco*. In 1847 Verdi took a definite step forward and chose a theme from Shakespeare. The result was the opera *Macbeth*. Verdi had felt a lifelong attraction to Shakespeare, but he had to wait forty years before he found the right librettist.

By 1853 Verdi had composed his three most popular and widely performed operas—*Rigoletto, Il Trovatore*, and *La Traviata*. These were epoch-making works. When *La Traviata* was first performed in Venice, it was a complete failure. It was not the fault of the opera but of poor casting. The soprano, who is the main character, was *very* stout, and the audience broke out into roars of laughter in the tragic scene when the doctor announces that she is in the last stages of consumption and has only a few hours to live.

Verdi, in his composing, never broke with the past or experimented radically with new ideas. He said at one time, "Let us return to the old; it will be an advance." This became a famous maxim. He also said that he was not a learned composer, only a very experienced one.

Verdi was a sound businessman, honest, true to his word, and thoroughly competent to deal with impresarios, publishers, prima donnas, and tenors. As soon as he was financially able, he bought a farm near Busseto. This was no whim of the composer. He said of himself after he became famous, "I am and always will be a Le Roncole peasant."

All his life Verdi loved the land in that corner of Parma where he was born. He is the only eminent composer in history who was also a successful farmer. Around his own country home, Sant' Agata, Verdi developed a model farm that employed two hundred farmers and their families. When times were hard, instead of lowering salaries, he raised their wages. Verdi, like Handel, did not forget those who helped him when he was poor. He provided well for his relatives and frequently sent gifts to those who had a need.

Because of his love for the country and seclusion, Verdi retained his simplicity. He loved Sant' Agata best of all with its superb horses and dogs, but because it was cold and damp in the winter, Verdi rented an apartment in Genoa for his wife's sake. However, they never could stay very long at either place, as there were always rehearsals and performances in Milan, Rome, Venice, Paris, and other European cities.

Nearly every year Verdi brought out another opera, and one year even three. They were not all successful, but the faults nearly always stemmed from poor librettos. Verdi said, "In the theater the public will stand for anything but boredom." Therefore, even though some of the librettos are inferior and downright foolish, Verdi's operas continue to live because they do have drama, no matter how primitive, and most of all because they do have great music. In all Verdi wrote twenty-six operas.

A few of the better-known operas from the period between 1857-1871 were: *Simon Boccanegra*, first produced in Venice; *The Masked Ball*, Rome; *The Force of Destiny*, St. Petersburg; *Don Carlos*, Paris; and *Aïda*, composed for Cairo to celebrate the opening of the Suez Canal. As Aïda is dying, she sings, *"O terra addio, addio valle di pianti"* (literally, life is a vale of tears). The summing up of all Verdi was reaching for in his middle period is found in *Aïda*, called by some critics the perfect grand opera.

For a long time Verdi was falsely considered a musical adversary of Richard Wagner. (Both were born in 1813, and both composers died in Italy.) Today one sees that Verdi is a totally different spirit with totally different aims, yet no less belonging to the "small company of great masters." Verdi admired Wagner's music, but because of his innate musicianship and Latin grace, he was intellectually and musically Wagner's antithesis. The orchestra of Verdi is always in the background, and there is the irresistible triumph of melody and voice. Because of his temperament and teaching, Verdi despised excessive length.

There are scenes in all of Verdi's operas that may be counted among the most extraordinary and moving ever written. He was an explosive composer from the beginning to the end. What is decisive is Verdi's grandeur as an artist, his sincerity, and his integrity as a man. Verdi was always a conscientious craftsman. He felt that simplicity spells strength, and one hears it in his impassioned melodies. In his works Verdi shows that he is a totally committed artist. As Lang says, "Verdi's music is eternally human, bold, dramatic, full-bodied, and Italian in every atom." It will be seen that Verdi produced more slowly as the years went by, not because he lacked inspiration, but the works required a longer time for gestation. There was no longer the "guitar" accompaniment in the orchestra but richer, broader, more ambitious instrumentation.

In 1874 Verdi produced the *Requiem Mass* to honor Italy's greatest prose writer, Alessandro Manzoni. The writer's *I Promessi Sposi* (The Betrothed) was the most famous Italian novel of the nineteenth century. As Verdi said, "It is a truthful book, as true as truth itself." Verdi admired Manzoni from boyhood, and even after he became a famous composer, he always felt that Manzoni was above him. The *Requiem* is a colossal work, deeply moving, vividly dramatic, and glorious in sound. It is unlike any other requiem and has been criticized by some for its theatricality. Verdi conducted it for the first time in Venice, and it was an immediate and permanent success. To understand in depth the conversation of many Italians, it is helpful to read *The Betrothed* and listen to Verdi's operas, as Italians are forever spicing their talk with quotes from Manzoni or snatches of song from *La Traviata* or *Falstaff*.

In the 1870s Verdi seemed to have reached the summit of his career. Apart from supervising productions in Italy, he spent more and more time at Sant' Agata, which he managed himself down to the smallest detail. For a few years he even sat in the Parliament as a member from Busseto. In his country home he had a library of several thousand volumes, most of which he had evidently read. He loved to read in the evenings. By his bedside were the complete works of Shakespeare, Dante, Byron, and Schiller. Also within reaching distance were his King James Bible, Milton's *Paradise Lost*, all kinds of dictionaries and histories, and the complete string quartets of Haydn, Mozart, and Beethoven.

In 1887, after a silence of sixteen years, news spread around Milan that Verdi was writing another opera, this one set to a play by Shakespeare. Meeting the poet Arrigo Boito had fired the imagination of the seventy-four-year-old composer. Today Boito ranks among the best librettists in the entire history of opera. He submitted the best libretto Verdi ever had for *Otello*, and in this work Verdi brought together everything he had learned in a lifetime. *Otello* is the greatest tragic opera to come out of Italy. In it Verdi proclaims the glory of the human voice. He was convinced that the voice has an inexhaustible capacity for expression.

But *Otello* was not Verdi's last triumph. Six years later he wrote another masterpiece, this time a comic opera, again using words from one of Shakespeare's plays. Verdi was close to eighty and as excited about doing *Falstaff* as anything he had written in his life. As Lang shows, it did not come from the top of his head. "What shall I say?" asked Verdi in trying to explain it to a friend. "For forty years I have wanted to write a comic opera, and fifty years I have known *The Merry Wives of Windsor,* but the usual 'buts' stood in the way. At last Boito has settled all the 'buts' and has given me a libretto like no other."

As biographer Ernest Newman says, "It was a piece of singular good fortune both for Verdi and for the world that at the height of the musician's imaginative and technical powers he should meet with a poet who could place Shakespeare at his service in a form thoroughly practical for the operatic stage." The first performance of *Falstaff* drew celebrities from all over the world, and from the beginning it has been recognized as one of the three or four masterpieces in comic opera.

Strepponi, Verdi's wife, lived to see the triumph of *Otello* and *Falstaff,* and then she died in 1897. He missed her deeply, but he did not suffer from loneliness. The years had taught Verdi to cherish solitude, and he believed passionately in privacy for himself and others. He spent his last years at Sant' Agata, Genoa, and Milan continuing the routine of his life. In Genoa everyone knew the great Verdi, but the people also understood and respected his desire for privacy. When he would enter his usual café, everyone in the room would rise in his honor, bow, and then leave him alone.

In spite of his fame and fortune, there remained in Verdi something of the durability and resilience of the peasant in his outlook upon life to the end. His last compositions were settings of sacred texts called *Quattro Pezzi Sacri* (Four Sacred Pieces). Verdi died of a stroke in Milan in 1901. He left the royalties from his works to the Casa Verdi, a home for aged musicians in Milan. It is called "The House of Rest," and it still continues today. He and his beloved wife are buried there. Verdi's was a long and glorious career. He lived a rich and honest life, filled with a deeply felt humanity. Above all, he loved the human voice and farming.

Recommended Reading

Hussey, Dyneley. *Verdi.* London: J. M. Dent, 1948.
Toye, Francis. *Giuseppe Verdi: His Life and Works.* New York: Alfred A. Knopf, 1931.

Recommended Listening

Aïda (Nile Scene)
Un Ballo in Maschera (*"Eri Tu"*)
Don Carlos (*"O Don Fatale"*)
Falstaff ("All the World's a Jest")
La Ford del Destino (*"Pace, Pace, Mio Dio"*)
Macbeth (Sleepwalking Scene)
Nabucco (*"Va, Pensiero, Sull'ali Dorate"*)
Otello (Act I—Love Duet)
Requiem Mass
Rigoletto (Quartet, *Caro Nome*)

Simon Boccanegra ("Il Lacarato Spirito")
La Traviata ("Ah! Fors e Lui")
Il Trovatore ("Miserere")

Anton Bruckner
1824-1896

His whole being shows a personality quietly in contact with God.

Erwin Doernberg

I read someplace that the aim of Bruckner's music was to make the supernatural real. Having just bought his *Te Deum*, I put on the record and picked up the needlepoint pillow I was working on. I stitched away for a while and then quietly put down my work. Something about the music called for full concentration.

As the orchestra approached the last movement, I recognized the theme from the Seventh Symphony that ushered in the greatest climax imaginable. Bruckner interwove contrapuntally the words *"Non confundar in aeternum"* (Let me not be confounded forever) with *"In te, Domine, speravi"* (In Thee, O Lord, have I trusted), and the *Te Deum* thundered to a victorious C-major conclusion. It made me think of something I had heard years ago: "Once you love Bruckner, you love him forever." After one hearing of the *Te Deum*, I knew I had to learn more about this great composer.

Most people's judgment of others depends on immediate impressions. Anton Bruckner, because of his small-town background, his quaint way of dressing (he always wore rather short trousers), his frequent speaking in the upper Austrian dialect, his passion for learning, and his way of eating made him an ideal subject for the faultfinders; but there is a logical explanation for each of his eccentricities, which I'll discuss later.

Like most important composers, Bruckner began to write music in his early childhood. But he differed from the others in that he did not compose a great work until he was forty-one, and he was not widely known until he was over sixty.

He was born in Austria at Ansfelden in 1824. There were eleven children in the family, and Anton was the oldest. His father and grandfather taught school, and his mother was a singer. By the age of four Bruckner showed a precocious interest in music, which his parents encouraged.

The church at Ansfelden had a small orchestra, and on special occasions some trumpeters and a timpanist were invited to play. Anton was thrilled with the sound of the trumpets. Very likely it was right in his hometown church that the foundation was laid for the rich brass climaxes Bruckner put in almost all of his later works, a foundation strengthened by hearing Wagner's music.

In 1835 Anton was sent to the home of his godfather for further musical education. He remained for almost two years studying particularly the art of playing the organ from a figured bass. In Horsching, Anton was privileged to hear Haydn's *Creation* and *The Seasons* as well as Mozart's masses. In this period he made his first attempts at organ improvisations, for which he became famous years later.

These two happy years were followed by deep sorrow. His father died, and his mother did not want her oldest son to stop studying music out of obligation to help support the family. She arranged for him to be a choirboy at the nearby monastery school, St. Florian. With two other boys he lived in the home of the headmaster. Here his musical education intensified, and he also studied reading, writing, and arithmetic.

By 1840 Bruckner had decided to be a teacher so he could help to care for his mother financially. He went to Linz, and by the end of the year he had his certificate as an assistant teacher for elementary schools. He received his first appointment in the small village of Windhaag. But before starting to work, he spent a few weeks in St. Florian, which eventually became his spiritual home for the rest of his life. He also visited his mother, which must have been an occasion of pride and joy for her that her son was to be a teacher, like his father.

His year-and-a-half stay at Windhaag was far from ideal. His superior treated him like a servant. He had many duties in the school and church as well as outdoor work, including the spreading of manure. He took his meals with the servant girl. Fortunately he had the use of an organ and used his few free moments studying Bach's *Art of the Fugue*. He also did some composing and played his violin at dances to earn money.

His next position was in Kronstorf, a smaller town than Windhaag, but he was much happier. Part of his joy came from studying with the choirmaster Zenetti in nearby Enns. Zenetti based his teaching mainly on Bach's chorales and the *Well-Tempered Clavier.*

Through the daughter of a French general in the town of Steyr, he was introduced to the music of Schubert. Also he was allowed to improvise on the organ in the beautiful Gothic church in Steyr. Baroque and Gothic, Bach and Schubert—these are the roots of Bruckner's music, to which the great Italian masters of polyphony were to be added. But Bruckner had twenty years ahead of him before he began to write his great symphonies.

In 1845 a vacancy occurred at St. Florian, and he returned to be the first official assistant teacher in the parish school. He remained in St. Florian ten years. Bruckner was intensely industrious and, like a true artist, worked and studied throughout his life. In 1848 he became the organist at St. Florian. A successful performance of his Mass in B gave him the courage to leave teaching and dedicate himself to composition and performance, despite uncertainty over lack of finances (a pattern throughout his life).

When the organist of the Linz cathedral died, applicants for the position were invited to play before a commission on November 13, 1855. Bruckner did not apply and had no intention of doing so, but he went to Linz to hear the candidates play. They both failed. A committee member noticed Bruckner and asked him if he would like to play. In his typical uncertain way he was not sure he wanted to try out, but the committee persuaded him to come forward. He played brilliantly. After a series of other tests and much indecision on Bruckner's part, he became the cathedral organist in Linz at thirty-two.

Over a period of five years he studied with the well-known Simon Sechter, a master in theory. Sechter said that he had never had a student as conscientious as Bruckner. Schubert had planned to study with Sechter also but had died suddenly at the age of thirty-one before he could carry out his intention.

After Sechter, Bruckner began studying with Otto Kitzler, who was nine years his junior. Kitzler was a practical musician with a modern outlook. Under his influence, Bruckner began to turn his attention to symphonic forms. It was Kitzler who introduced Bruckner to the music of Wagner.

During these years critics began making poor jokes about "the cathedral organist who never left off studying." Bruckner was admonished to dress more carefully, speak more clearly, and not eat such large meals. He was a bachelor, an eccentric in the best sense of the word. He had no interest in spending the little money he had on clothes when he knew his mother had needs. All his life he was generous with the little he had. He studied because he truly loved learning and knew it was essential to learn all through one's life. He ate large meals because often he was occupied during the day, and he would wait until late in the evening to have his one meal.

Someone said, "We are not in the world to see through each other, but to see each other through." Happily, Bruckner had good friends, and his best friend was the Lord. Biographer H. F. Redlich said, "Bruckner is perhaps the only great composer of his century whose entire musical output is determined by his religious faith."

In 1863 Bruckner heard the complete performance of Wagner's *Tannhauser*. It was a great turning point in his life and opened the door to his power of creativity, which had been mounting up inside him. One of the first things he wrote after being inspired by the grandeur in Wagner's music was the Mass in D Minor, a work of masterly power and individuality with no more than a passing trace of Wagnerian influence. Bruckner, though he was a great admirer and later a friend of Wagner, did not imitate him. He took only that which suited his own spirit. Actually Bruckner was more Schubertian than Wagnerian. And so at forty-one Bruckner wrote his first symphony, and in the space of twenty years his greatest works were written.

In 1868 Bruckner moved to Vienna, but typically he went through all manner of doubts and feelings of insecurity about making a change. Yet his friends stood by him. Also because of friends, he was accepted at the Vienna Conservatory as a teacher. There he spent the last twenty-eight years of his life teaching, composing, and playing the organ.

He was asked in 1868 to come to Nancy and play on a newly constructed organ, and the following year he was requested to come to Paris and try out their new organ. Both performances were great. His audience in Paris at the Notre Dame Cathedral included César Franck, Saint-Saëns, Auber, and Gounod. His concerts consisted largely of his own magnificent improvisations.

Two years later he was invited to play the organ in London. He wrote excitedly to a friend about the posters he saw all over the city advertising the recitals: "Everywhere my name appears in letters bigger than myself!" Bruckner, even in old age, always remained youthful at heart. He wrote very little organ music. When asked why, his answer was, "How can I write down music when I am playing it?"

Bruckner, as a teacher, was strict and severe in all matters of musical craftsmanship, be it composition, organ-playing, or theory. He wanted his students to know the rules. "Here in school everything must go according to the rules, and you are not allowed to write one single forbidden note." Then speaking in his dialect and with dry humor, he would add, "But if you bring me something which is so strictly in accordance with the rules once you have finished your schooling, I'll throw you out!" One of his pupils was the eminent songwriter Hugo Wolf, and Gustav Mahler was one of Bruckner's followers.

His students loved him. Though he was a disciplinarian, he was never dry or boring. He was always inventing amusing stories to make the subject under discussion vivid, and he also used many illustrations from everyday life to help the young musicians better understand the intricacies of the musical craft.

After a hard day of working, Bruckner enjoyed going to an inn with some of his students and friends. Conversation centered chiefly around music, and there was a great deal of laughing and joking, but Bruckner would never tolerate anything of an obscene nature. On these occasions he also enjoyed dancing, which helped him relax and relieve some of the tension from his long hours of work and the pressure of the unfair criticism that was always upon him.

While still working on his Second Symphony in 1872, he directed the first performance of his Mass in F Minor in Vienna. It proved to be an enormous success. His friend Herbeck said, "Bruckner, I only know two masses:

this one and Beethoven's *Missa Solemnis!*" There is a glowing sense of devotion in the F Minor Mass, no doubt because of the depth and purity of
Bruckner's love and respect for God.

However, Bruckner was foremost a composer of symphonies. He
spoke of his compositions as his children, and he took as much time wash-
ing and scrubbing and dressing them as any good parent does. Some of the
critics enjoyed saying that Bruckner did not compose nine symphonies but
one symphony nine times. This is foolish talk. Bruckner's symphonies are all
different, and yet, as with every true artist, they have a likeness of style. He
did not repeat himself, because his vision deepened from work to work. In
his music Bruckner never made the slightest concession to the taste of his
time, nor did he ever leave off studying. If one listens carefully, there is a vast
amount of learning in his symphonies.

Bruckner's Third Symphony is dedicated to Wagner. Because of his
friendship with Wagner, he became known as a Wagnerian symphonist, a
totally wrong conclusion. The main influence Wagner had on Bruckner was
challenging him with what could be done with a large orchestra, brass instruments, and particularly tubas.

It was the critic Eduard Hanslick who equated Bruckner with Wagner
in the silly, though tragic, Brahms-Wagner war. Most of Bruckner's creative
life was lived under the hatred and virulence of Hanslick, who tore
Bruckner's works to pieces and because of the composer's extreme sensitivity made him miserable for years. Bruckner once said about his critics, "They
want me to write in another way. How would the Father in heaven judge me
if I followed others and not Him?" The great artist Dürer had the same
understanding. He accepted the truth that one day he too would have to
answer before the throne of God for every work of art he made. It is an
admonition for all artistic people to take seriously.

When Bruckner conducted his Third Symphony, it was a fiasco and
did him great harm. His friends and pupils, dismayed by the failure, urged
him to revise the work. They meant well, but the humble Bruckner became
a victim of self-doubt, and revising his scores became a mania of his.

His Fourth Symphony, known as the *Romantic*, has become one of
Bruckner's most popular works and is widely performed. Like Beethoven,
Bruckner loved the countryside. In the third movement we hear the music
of huntsmen's horns with the poetry and sound of the forest all around.

When he was sixty, Bruckner's Seventh Symphony brought him the
greatest success of his lifetime, along with the *Te Deum*. The trumpet theme
in the scherzo was suggested to Bruckner by the crowing of a rooster. The
much-neglected and misunderstood Bruckner began to win international
acclaim after the brilliant performance of this symphony, conducted by
Arthur Nikisch. Two other great Bruckner conductors were Hermann Levi
and Hans Richter.

The heart of Bruckner's music is in the slow adagio movements. The
adagio in the Seventh Symphony was written as a lament after Wagner's

death. "The character of this music is like the light, lofty interior of some great cathedral," commented Simpson. "The architectural lines of Bruckner's orchestration are as finely colored as the very best stained glass."

Bruckner's health began to deteriorate in 1885. He suffered from a weakness of the heart, a form of dropsy, that made it difficult for him to walk because of swollen legs and feet and hampered his organ-playing. Nevertheless it is interesting to note that in 1886 Bruckner played the organ at the funeral service of Franz Liszt in Bayreuth at the request of Cosima Wagner.

Bruckner's Ninth Symphony, this angelic music, is the last thing he wrote. He called it his farewell to life and was still working on it the day he died in 1896.

Like all of us, Bruckner had his foibles. They are not hard to explain, however. The short trousers, for example, made his organ-playing easier. Then all his life he longed to marry. Nothing wrong with that, but even as an older man, Bruckner was always drawn to young ladies, very young ladies, though nothing was ever concluded. One thing is certain—any relationship with the opposite sex outside of marriage was out of the question for him, and what saved him from despair in his loneliness was his deep piety. As Edmund White said, "In an age of growing religious doubt, Bruckner remained almost childlike in the unquestioning certainty of his faith." Bruckner was so well read in the Scriptures that he was a match for any theologian. Whenever he made those marvelous improvisations on the organ, before he wrote his music or taught, he always spent time in prayer.

The last cruel blow in Bruckner's career was the rejection of his colossal Eighth Symphony by his conductor friend Levi in 1887. Levi, who had so successfully conducted the Seventh Symphony and the *Te Deum* and made Bruckner's name known far beyond Austria, was simply unable to grasp the magnitude of the Eighth Symphony. This, along with Bruckner's poor health, caused the composer to put aside the Ninth Symphony, which he had just begun. It took him three years to get back to it, and even though he did not finish it in his lifetime, the symphony is left incomplete only in a superficial sense.

Bruckner's *Te Deum* is dedicated to his dear Lord, and in his music he makes the supernatural real. On my first hearing of Bruckner's *Te Deum*, that was exactly how I responded—this is heavenly music.

We can learn much from Bruckner today. His firm, unsentimental Christianity would not allow separate departments for his faith and his creativity. One becomes aware that Bruckner's compositions are somehow different from those of Beethoven, Wagner, Mahler, and Schoenberg, and it is the spiritual dimension heard in his music. Anton Bruckner took literally the words of the psalmist: "Praise Him with the sound of the trumpet. . . . Let everything that has breath praise the Lord."

Recommended Reading

Doernberg, Erwin. *The Life and Symphonies of Anton Bruckner.* New York: Dover Publications, 1960.

Schonzeler, Hans-Hubert. *Bruckner.* London: Marion Boyars, 1978.

Recommended Listening

Mass No. 3 in F Minor
Psalm 150
Symphony No. 4, *Romantic*
Symphony No. 7
Symphony No. 8
Symphony No. 9
Te Deum

CHAPTER 19

Johannes Brahms
1833-1897

*For all flesh is as grass, and all the glory of man as
the flower of grass. The grass withereth, and the
flower thereof falleth away: But the word of the Lord
endureth for ever.*

1 Peter 1:24-25

*A*t the age of thirteen Johannes Brahms helped support his family by
playing the piano in the lowest sorts of sailors' dance halls, taverns, and
restaurants in Hamburg. But since he detested wasting time, often he
propped a book on the music rack in front of him. It did not take long for
this unhealthy and questionable atmosphere to undermine his delicate con-
stitution, and finally his father rescued him by securing for him a teaching
position in a pleasant country village away from the narrow, dirty streets and
the dilapidated, overcrowded, age-blackened houses and taverns of the poor
neighborhood in Hamburg where Brahms grew up. The change of air and
environment helped him greatly, and years later he looked back on those
cheerful months in Winsen as among the happiest in his childhood. They
helped to establish the rugged health he enjoyed most of his life.

Johannes Brahms was born in Hamburg in 1833. His father played the
double bass in the civic orchestra, and he was the first to teach young Brahms
the basic elements of music. But Brahms revealed such talent he had to be
passed on to another teacher. He had two teachers as a boy. Friedrich Cossel
and Eduard Marxen both recognized Brahms as remarkably gifted. They
taught him well and without pay. Brahms made his debut as a pianist at ten.

The mother of Johannes was seventeen years older than her husband.
Though she was not well educated, she was a woman of great sensitivity and
spiritual resources. Brahms was devoted to her. In spite of their poor circumstances, his parents did their best to create a secure home and to foster
the natural talents of their children.

Even though he had many struggles in his early years, Brahms developed into an outstanding pianist. Nevertheless, he considered playing the

piano an avocation since he was determined to devote himself mainly to composition as soon as he could afford it.

In 1853 Brahms accepted an engagement as accompanist to the Hungarian violinist Reményi for a concert tour. In Göttingen the piano on which Brahms was to play the *Kreutzer* Sonata by Beethoven was a half-tone below the right pitch. Brahms transposed the piece from A to B flat and played the part by memory, doing it so skillfully that the great violinist Joseph Joachim, who was in the audience, was astonished and wanted to meet Brahms. Joachim immediately liked the shy and unpretentious twenty-year-old Brahms, and a lifelong friendship began.

Joachim, happy to recommend such a talent, gave Brahms introductions to some of the leading musicians of the day, including Robert and Clara Schumann. After Brahms played some of his compositions for them, Robert Schumann wrote an enthusiastic report about Brahms in the *New Magazine for Music*. He proclaimed Brahms to be the great composer of the future, "called forth to give the ideal expression of the time."

Schumann was also the first to recognize the genius of Chopin. Frédéric Chopin (1810-1849), born in Poland, was one of the most original, creative geniuses in musical history. He composed relatively little but was born into a world suited to his prodigious talents. The Romantic period was the time of the gigantic piano virtuosos. Like a jeweler polishing rare gems, Chopin worked on his pieces until they were as perfect as he could make them. His etudes are landmarks in the history of piano music and are among his greatest works. Chopin made the piano sing. He was a great melodist, and he created a new realm of piano sound. There is no greater specialist than Chopin. One can nearly always recognize a Chopin composition. There is scarcely one in his repertoire that we could dispense with.

Because Robert Schumann was highly respected in the musical world, his endorsement of Brahms and Brahms's unusual individuality caused his name to become known, and the publication of Brahms's works was eagerly awaited. This is one of the rare instances in the history of music of an established composer recognizing the genius of a newcomer. Schumann was twenty-three years older than Brahms. From the first, Schumann tried to interest Brahms in composing a symphony. "The beginning is the main thing," he said. "If only one makes a beginning, then the end comes of itself." Brahms owed much of his early style in writing music to Schumann.

One cannot speak about Robert Schumann without mentioning his wife, Clara. She was the most celebrated woman pianist of her time. She was trained by her father, married Robert in 1840, and continued to tour after her marriage, furthering her husband's career by giving the first performance of many of his works.

Robert Schumann, because of several personal tragedies in his life, showed signs of depression and even mental illness as early as 1843. He kept hearing the note A sounding in his ears. He recovered somewhat and had several busy years writing music, traveling, and directing; but in 1854 he had a renewal of the symptoms that threatened him before. Besides hearing the ringing A, he now imagined he heard voices too. He threw himself in the Rhine, but he was rescued and spent his last years in a private asylum where he died in 1856.

When Brahms heard of the tragic circumstances, he moved to Düsseldorf to help Clara and her children, and he was a strength to them during this time. He stayed for several years, living on piano lessons, composing incessantly but publishing little. A lifelong friendship developed between Clara Schumann and Brahms. After leaving Dusseldorf, Brahms continued to submit his compositions to her before publishing them.

Undoubtedly Johannes Brahms was very much in love with Clara Schumann. She was one of the most fascinating women of the nineteenth century, but they never married. She was fourteen years older than Brahms, for one thing, and they both needed their freedom—she to give concerts to support her family, and he to compose. After 1856 Clara Schumann frequently played in England and became noted as an interpreter of Brahms's music.

Between the years 1853 and 1857, Brahms taught, toured as a pianist, and composed. From 1857 to 1860 he was a teacher and conductor at the small German court of Lippe-Detmold. Twice the position of conductor of the Philharmonic Orchestra in Hamburg became vacant, but Brahms was not appointed, and so he resolved to forget his hometown. In 1863 he went to Vienna.

Some years later he finally settled in the enchanting city of Vienna where he was stimulated by an artistic and congenial atmosphere. Vienna, called the "Queen of the Danube," is a world center for literature, music, and learning. The inner city's most renowned street is the Ringstrasse with its parks and lilac trees, its opera house, Imperial Palace, and the famous St. Stephen's Cathedral nearby. The Viennese people are known for their liveliness, charm, wit, and ability to enjoy life. Music is a necessity to them.

As soon as Brahms was financially able, he devoted more and more time to composing. His publisher and friend Simrock helped him achieve independence. He did not need a large income for himself, as he felt more comfortable when leading a simple life. But Brahms did derive pleasure in helping others, notably Anton Dvorak, and he was especially generous to his family. Brahms, who enjoyed a wide range of great literature, delighted in giving books to friends and relatives. There were also several struggling young musicians who secretly received financial gifts from Brahms, as did Clara Schumann and her children. He delighted in doing good secretly.

Johannes Brahms was a gruff, humorous, sometimes lonely individual touched with melancholy. His outlook on life, as of so many Romantics, was mingled with pessimism. He was a modest man, sane, and with a lovable personality. His stubby, plump appearance was often somewhat untidy, and he had long hair and an untrimmed beard and mustache. His rough humor was bearish, and he had a temper if interrupted in his work. Privacy for

Brahms was a ruling passion. He loved independence, solitude, and freedom. He set great store by undisturbed solitude, and his friends knew he was not to be bothered when he was working.

Basically he was kindhearted and had a sense of politeness which knew no class distinctions. There was no haughtiness in Brahms. As an example, while staying in an Italian inn on one of his working holidays, he would go about in stockinged feet in the evenings rather than keep a poor servant waiting to polish his boots. He was profoundly thoughtful.

As he grew older and more independent, he established the pattern of spending the winters in Vienna in his simple three-room apartment. Always an early riser and a man of rigid self-discipline, Brahms would prepare his morning coffee and get to work. What brightened his days were the twice-daily trips to the Red Hedgehog Inn where he ate his meals in the congenial company of musical and artistic friends.

To Brahms, travel and the enjoyment of nature were necessities of life. In the springtime he loved to travel in Italy and to bathe in its beauty. He enjoyed a good table too. Brahms received lasting inspiration from Italian art. One hears the Italian influence in the balanced serenity of his Piano Concerto No. 2. Brahms's summers were nearly always spent in the country. Like Beethoven, he was an outdoor person who received much inspiration on long walks. He loved Italy and Switzerland.

Traveling was no burden for Brahms, as it is for some people. His method of packing for a journey was to pile all his clothes upon a table, then tilt it so that everything tumbled helter-skelter into the open trunk! Brahms never liked to write letters when on a trip; so he used postcards for a large part of his correspondence. Once he wrote a card containing two brief lines saying that there was a sixteen-page letter to follow. Naturally it never was written. Brahms had the heart of a child, and he especially loved children and pets. He enjoyed playing with toy soldiers, which gave him musical ideas. One of Brahms's favorite books, even as an adult, was *Robinson Crusoe*.

The famous "war" between Brahms the Classicist and three other composers—Wagner, Bruckner, and Wolf—was stirred up mainly by the critics, in particular Eduard Hanslick. When Brahms sent flowers to the funeral of Wagner in Venice, Wagner's wife, Cosima, sent them back.

Brahms began as a true Romantic composer, but in his mature works he succeeded in fusing opposing trends and wrote expressive yet concise music structurally rooted in the past. In a period that emphasized revolution in art, he held to the great musical traditions. His music shows the Classical influence of Bach, Handel, Haydn, and Beethoven, but his compositions are not mere imitations. He used the old forms so skillfully that they are filled with an entirely new spirit.

He never worried unduly about originality, believing that workmanship was fully as important as invention. Brahms said, "It is not hard to compose . . . but it is hard to let the superfluous notes fall under the table." He was highly critical of his own work and destroyed many superfluous notes, thus producing a consistent high quality in his compositions.

Brahms, a true Classicist among the Romantics, never composed an opera, although he considered it at various times. Rather, he chose to develop the forms of Beethoven's period. He was interested in Hungarian music and used many folk song tunes in his compositions. In 1869 his Hungarian Dances met with phenomenal success, and they were played all over the world.

Brahms was one of the great songwriters of the nineteenth century, and the song occupies a central position in his art. Schubert was his model for songwriting. Brahms also composed many notable pieces for piano solos. His piano waltzes are delicious little masterpieces. Brahms was a great admirer of the Viennese waltzes of Johann Strauss.

In 1873 Brahms wrote the masterly *Variations on a Theme by Haydn*. This was followed by his four magnificent symphonies, called the *Indian Summer of the Symphony*. They sometimes suffer from sluggish orchestration and a feeling of heaviness. Brahms also was the giant among composers of chamber music in the Romantic period. His Piano Quintet in F Minor and the profound Clarinet Quintet are among his contributions to good listening. Brahms showed notable rhythmic originality, often using conflicting rhythms. He was a true musical scholar, and he always continued his reading in literature and history.

Clara Schumann wrote to a friend telling about a symphony he was hoping to write: "Brahms is in good spirits, delighted with his summer holiday, and has a new Symphony in D Major ready in his head; the first movement he has put on paper." Brahms must have absorbed much sunshine and fresh air, as the mood of the second movement is bright and cheerful.

Brahms completed the soul-stirring *German Requiem* in 1868—he had been working on it since 1857. He directed the first performance on Good Friday. It met with success, and Brahms moved into the front rank of German composers. News of his mother's death reached him in Vienna on February 1, 1865. A friend found him at his piano weeping while playing Bach's *Goldberg Variations*. The incident recalls Beethoven's and Tchaikovsky's use of the "music cure" in times of special need.

Brahms's *Requiem* is a fundamentally Protestant one. Not only does it depart from the Latin and the well-known movements of the Catholic requiem mass, but its spirit is totally different. The heart of the Catholic requiem mass is the "Dies Irae" (Day of Wrath) or the last judgment that threatens the departed with purgatory or the pains of hell. The *Requiem* by Brahms professes faith in the resurrection and reunion with God through the atoning death of Jesus Christ. The choice of words for the *Requiem* reveals an understanding of the vanity and emptiness of life when lived apart from knowing the consolation of Christian truth. The *Requiem* was partly motivated by the death of his mother and of Schumann, especially the fifth movement. Brahms's music, like that of Schütz, Handel, and Bach, is inspired by a deep concern with man's mortal life and his hope of heaven.

It was at school that the Bible first came into his hands, and as he matured his knowledge of the Scriptures increased. He was a great admirer of Luther's translation of the Bible. Brahms said once, "In my study I can lay my hand on my Bible even in the dark."

The final illness of Clara Schumann resulted in Brahms's "Four Serious Songs." They were the supreme achievement of his last years. A few months after Clara's death, Brahms died of cancer. His death was hastened by his catching a chill at Clara Schumann's funeral. The Scripture text of the last movement of the German *Requiem* was read at Brahms's funeral: "Blessed are the dead which die in the Lord from henceforth: Yea, saith the Spirit, that they may rest from their labors; and their works do follow them" (Revelation 14:13).

Speaking of two influences that decidedly shaped Brahms's music, biographer Walter Niemann says, "The fact that Brahms began his creative activity with the German folk song and closed with the Bible reveals better than anything else the true religious creed of this great man of the people."

Brahms's last works were the eleven chorale preludes for organ. The last of these is entitled, "O World, I Must Depart from Thee." Brahms was buried in Vienna near the graves of Beethoven, Schubert, and Mozart. He was one of the few major composers whose greatness was recognized in his lifetime.

Recommended Reading

Geiringer, Karl. *Brahms: His Life and Work*. New York: Oxford University Press, 1947.
Niemann, Walter. *Brahms*. New York: Alfred A. Knopf, 1941.

Recommended Listening

Academic Festival Overture
Alto Rhapsody
Concerto No. 2, B Flat for Piano
Concerto in D for Violin
"Four Serious Songs"
German Requiem
Piano Music, Op. 116, 117, 118, 119
Quintet in F Minor for Piano and Strings
Songs—"*Wiegenlied, Von Ewige Liebe*," etc.
Four Symphonies
Variations and Fugue on a Theme by Handel
Variations on a Theme by Haydn
Waltzes, Op. 39

CHAPTER 20

Camille Saint-Saëns
1835-1921

*As an eclectic, Saint-Saëns nourished himself in
Bach and Handel as well as others and turned all
into French elegance.*

Arthur Hervey

O ne of France's leading composers, Saint-Saëns's musical career lasted almost seventy years. He had a powerful influence in the period extending from 1870 to the end of the nineteenth century, which resulted in a genuine renaissance of French music.

An awesome child prodigy, Saint-Saëns began his career early in life. By the age of three, already able to read and write, he had composed his first piece of music and at ten made his debut as a pianist. By then he was able to play Beethoven's thirty-two piano sonatas from memory. He had total recall. If he read a book or heard a piece of music, it was in his memory forever. His was a fabulous musical mind; he had almost too many abilities without one being supreme.

Saint-Saëns was born in Paris in 1835. His father died a few months after his birth, so he was brought up by his mother and a great-aunt. Both of them taught him much about the wonder of music, as they themselves were avid musicians. As a child, he loved to listen to sounds—the creaking of a door, the striking of clocks, the boiling of a kettle. He found music everywhere.

After his studies at the Paris Conservatory, Saint-Saëns became one of the important pianists and organists of his day. He was also a fine conductor and a brilliant score reader. At first sight he played the full, complex orchestral score of a Wagner opera—a feat that even astounded Wagner.

Saint-Saëns was a composer who wrote in all forms, an outstanding musicologist and a lively critic with a biting sense of humor. He also wrote poetry and had an interest in astronomy and archeology.

A small, dandified, peppery man, dangerous to cross in spite of his foppish looks, he strangely resembled a parrot. He had a sharply curved profile, a beaklike nose, and lively, restless, piercing eyes. Small of stature, he strutted like a bird and talked rapidly with a curious affected lisp.

Saint-Saëns said, "I live in music like a fish in water." He composed as easily "as an apple tree produces apples." Playing the piano was very much the same, and so it is no wonder that he was the first one to perform all five of his piano concertos. His music has a certain coldness, and it is more brilliant than emotionally moving.

The logic of his music, its neatness, finish, and clear outlines make him what we call today a true professional. He was the most perfect of technicians, but many critics say his music is all technique and no ideas—empty form, elegant but superficial. The Piano Concerto No. 5 is one of the best of his later works. The French tradition is essentially Classical—order and restraint are fundamental. Saint-Saëns, with high craftsmanship, managed Classical forms easily.

He, like other prominent composers, including Albéniz, Bizet, and Smetana, studied with Franz Liszt in Weimar and was greatly influenced by him. Liszt never missed a chance to give possible genius a hearing. It is remarkable that Liszt never charged for his lessons. Through the influence of Liszt, Saint-Saëns's grand opera *Samson and Delilah* was first performed in Weimar. Saint-Saëns wrote many operas, but only *Samson and Delilah* is still performed today. One of its great arias is "My Heart at Thy Sweet Voice."

Saint-Saëns had an enduring friendship with Liszt. Probably Liszt was the greatest pianist who ever lived, and he described Saint-Saëns as the finest organist in the world, a master of improvisation.

Inspired by the symphonic poems of Liszt, Saint-Saëns was the first Frenchman to write in this genre. His most famous symphonic poem is the brilliantly orchestrated *Danse Macabre* (a death dance). The scene is a fantastic graveyard. The clock strikes midnight. Death appears and plays a strangely tuned violin. Skeletons rise from graves and dance a ghostly waltz. The clattering of bones is suggested by the xylophone and the *Dies Irae* (Day of Judgment) sounds. A cock crows; all disappear, and deadly stillness reigns in the graveyard.

In 1878 Saint-Saëns lost both of his sons. The older, at two and a half, fell out of a window and died. The other son died soon after. Saint-Saëns blamed his wife for their deaths, and three years later he left her. They never met again. An aggressive, irritable character by 1890, his sarcastic tongue made him many enemies. He was a bitter, ill-tempered, restless person with a great love for traveling. Yet he always worked feverishly.

Perhaps he realized he had not lived up to his glorious potential, as he is not one of the great masters. With a bitter sense of the futility of life, he wrote a study of pessimism that advocated atheism. He maintained that art and science would take the place of religion. "As science advances, God recedes. Life has no purpose. Nature is without aim; she is an endless circle and leads us nowhere. . . . People have always been disappointed in their search for final causes. It may be that there are no such things."

Existentialism in France had a spokesman in Saint-Saëns long before Jean-Paul Sartre. Perhaps Saint-Saëns's only passion in life was a love of liberty. He was a remarkable thinker with an insatiable thirst for knowledge. As a church organist at the Madeleine, he must have missed the church's true message. That church's message may have, unfortunately, been false, turning him away from Christianity. How easy it is to miss the truth of Christianity.

One of his most delightful compositions is *The Carnival of Animals* for orchestra and two pianos. He did not allow this work to be published in his lifetime. Now it is one of his most popular works, a zoological fantasy with lions, hens and cocks, an elephant, a cuckoo, the famous swan melody, and so forth. Satirical, it is one of the best of all musical jokes, superbly orchestrated. It is full of the kind of humor that became a part of the French tradition.

Saint-Saëns left hardly any branch of music untried, including teaching. He was an inspiring teacher. His most prominent pupil was Gabriel Fauré, who represented the French love of logic and tradition. Saint-Saëns had a close relationship with Fauré and his family and was most helpful in Fauré's career. Hearing "Sanctus" from Fauré's *Requiem* is like sitting in the calm of a vast cathedral seeing the sun sparkling through the stained-glass windows.

Saint-Saëns was often hostile to others, especially women composers such as the brilliant Nadia Boulanger (1887-1979). Nadia was not only a composer, but she was one of the most influential composition teachers of the twentieth century. Saint-Saëns considered a woman composer a freak of nature—like a dog walking on its hind legs. He had a somewhat arrogant musical mind. However, he did help found the Société Nationale de Musique in 1871 to encourage new French music. Among the composers helped were César Franck, Gabriel Fauré, Vincent d'Indy, and Claude Debussy.

A contemporary of Saint-Saëns was the Franco-Belgian César Franck (1822-1890), an ardent church musician and, unlike Saint-Saëns, an evangelical Christian, humble and modest. Franck was an inspiring teacher. Among his outstanding students were the composers d'Indy, Duparc, and Chausson. Coauthor Jane Stuart Smith often sang Duparc's great song "Chanson Triste."

Franck's still widely performed Symphony in D Minor (dedicated to Duparc) expresses Franck's profoundly mystical attitude toward God and is like a religious meditation in music. Yet it reveals Franck's strong and ardent personality. The instrumentation has an organlike texture, showing his love for the organ. The strong chromatic harmony was influenced by Wagner, which Saint-Saëns was able to avoid. Saint-Saëns did not like Franck, as Saint-Saëns had become an arch conservative and considered Franck his rival.

Another contemporary of Saint-Saëns was Charles Gounod (1818-

1893), best known for his ever-popular opera *Faust*. Among his religious compositions is "The Song of Ruth," which Jane has sung in many, many weddings, including all four children and a granddaughter of Francis and Edith Schaeffer.

Saint-Saëns was on good terms with his friend Bizet (1838-1875), whose opera *Carmen* was produced a bit earlier than *Samson and Delilah*. *Carmen* was at first a failure but now is considered one of the greatest of all operas. Bizet wanted passion and life above all in his music, while Saint-Saëns sought purity of style and perfection of form.

Claude Debussy (1862-1918) was another contemporary of Saint-Saëns. Briefly an organ student of César Franck, Debussy is one of the great originals in music history and one of the greatest French composers. He has had a vast influence on twentieth-century music. Debussy deliberately broke the rules that Saint-Saëns never had the courage to break (he was too much of a traditionalist). Debussy's tone poem *La Mer* is a wonderfully Impressionistic description of the sea. Typical when one has very strong opinions, Saint-Saëns hated Debussy's music.

Another contemporary of Saint-Saëns was Charles Widor (1844-1937), an outstanding organist. He is best known for Symphony No. 5 for Organ. The "Toccata" is exciting, particularly when played by contemporary organist Diane Bish.

One of Saint-Saëns's instrumental masterpieces is the C Minor Symphony with organ, which was dedicated to the memory of his friend Liszt. Saint-Saëns said of this symphony: "With it I have given all I could give." Saint-Saëns, a French Romantic, was "a Parisian of the finest culture, the finest taste" (Einstein) with an extraordinary mind. This French genius combined German technical thoroughness with the French qualities of clarity and order, wit and tunefulness. As Romain Rolland said, "He brings into the midst of our present restlessness something of the sweetness and clarity of past periods, something that seems like fragments of a vanished world."

Saint-Saëns was a progressive force in his day. Today generally there is a rather low estimation of his work. But it is amazing how much of his music is still performed. Perhaps Saint-Saëns is a better composer than many think. His music is rooted in the Classical tradition, and perhaps a new assessment is due. He was a master craftsman "and wrote in many forms but . . . " failed to create his own unique style.

Recommended Reading

Hervey, Arthur. *Saint-Saëns*. London: John Lane Bodley Head Ltd., 1921.

Vallas, Leon. *César Franck*. London: George G. Harap & Co. Ltd., 1951.

Recommended Listening

Duparc: Songs
Saint-Saëns: *Carnival of the Animals*
Concerto No. 5 for Piano and Orchestra
Danse Macabre
Fantaisie in A for Violin and Harp
Samson and Delilah
Symphony No. 3 for Solo Organ and
Orchestra
Franck: Sonata in A for Violin and Piano
Symphony in D Minor
Widor: "Toccata"

Peter Ilich Tchaikovsky
1840-1893

*Truly there would be reasons to go mad were it not
for music.*

Tchaikovsky

*T*chaikovsky, though not a concert pianist, wrote one of the most brilliant of concertos, the Piano Concerto in B Flat. He dedicated it to his friend Nicholas Rubinstein, who told him it was impossible to play. Tchaikovsky was not convinced. He changed the dedication and gave the concerto to the German pianist and conductor Hans von Bülow, who, not daring to present it in Europe, played it successfully for the first time in Boston. With Tchaikovsky's mastery of orchestral effect, rhythmic vitality, flair for the dramatic, and largeness of gesture, the Piano Concerto in B Flat is rightly a very popular work and is played often. It is a pageant of wonderful melodies—Tchaikovsky's first masterpiece.

Peter Ilich Tchaikovsky was born on May 7, 1840, in Votkinsk, Russia, but where he came from, musically speaking, is a mystery. He picked up a smattering of musical knowledge as a boy along with his brothers and sisters, but he was never suspected of possessing any special musical talent. There had been no traces in his family. He studied to be a lawyer and later worked as a clerk in the Ministry of Justice, but finally his creative talent was clearly revealed. Hearing the music of Mozart's *Don Giovanni* helped him make the decision to devote his life to music.

At the age of twenty-three he entered the newly founded Conservatory of St. Petersburg, which was begun by Anton Rubinstein. Tchaikovsky was the first Russian to receive systematic training in music fundamentals. Working intensely hard, he completed the course in three years. He was then recommended by Rubinstein for a teaching position at the Conservatory of Moscow in 1866, and about that time he began to compose seriously. He remained there for twelve years as a professor of harmony, and he was highly regarded as a teacher. Despite the long hours and hard work, he continued to compose.

Tchaikovsky's melancholy and introspective temperament was clearly reflected in his music. He loved his mother with all the ardor of an acutely sensitive boy, and when she died of cholera when he was fourteen, his emotions were deeply affected. To alleviate the distress caused both by her sudden death and by his easygoing father's seeming indifference to it, Tchaikovsky composed a short waltz. Escaping into music when overwhelmed became a pattern in his life. He wrote some of his most lighthearted ballets in times of mental anguish.

Tchaikovsky's life was founded on raw nerves and abnormal sexual instincts. He was tormented over his homosexuality. He also suffered from epilepsy, migraine headaches, insomnia, and attacks of depression. His life contained all the elements of tragedy, and yet he continued to produce music with unchecked ardor, and he lived a life of ever-increasing artistic achievement. In their biography *Beloved Friend*, Bowen and Meck include this excerpt from one of Tchaikovsky's letters: "I have some very low moments, but an insatiable thirst for work consoles me. . . . If one lacks the right mood, one must force oneself to work, otherwise nothing will be accomplished." Another time he wrote, "Without work, life has no meaning for me." He was a very humble man who rarely believed in the excellence of his work.

While still teaching at the Conservatory of Moscow, Tchaikovsky at the age of twenty-nine composed his fantasy *Romeo and Juliet*. It is one of his finest works and marks the beginning of his career. Considering how late Tchaikovsky came to the serious study of music, the quickness of his technical development is amazing. He greatly admired Shakespeare and Dickens, especially *Pickwick Papers*. Tchaikovsky found great pleasure in literature and the theater. The form of *Romeo and Juliet* is similar to Mendelssohn's overture, *A Midsummer Night's Dream*. *Romeo and Juliet* was received coldly at first, but now the work is an international favorite. In it we hear some of his great melodies, particularly the lovers' theme, his ripe harmonies, and vigorous rhythms.

For his mature, masterly piece, *Francesca Da Rimini*, Tchaikovsky chose a subject from Dante's *Divine Comedy*. The story is of the love of Francesca and Paolo whom Dante places in the Inferno where they are seen as two lost souls wandering disconsolately. The tale is expressed musically by Tchaikovsky with deep sensitivity and compassion.

Hoping for stability in his life, at the age of thirty-seven Tchaikovsky married Antonina, one of the students at the Moscow conservatory. She had cunningly pursued him, and the marriage was a disaster. She was an unsavory person and ended her days in a mental institution. Close to a nervous breakdown, Tchaikovsky attempted suicide. At this moment of desperate need, Madame Nadejda von Meck, a wealthy widow with eleven children, who had already heard some of Tchaikovsky's music and was deeply moved by its beauty and sensitivity, commissioned him to write other works.

In 1877 this support took the more substantial shape of an annual allowance to free him so he could compose. The immediate result of her patronage was Tchaikovsky's Fourth Symphony. Madame von Meck was passionately musical in the Russian manner where one loses oneself completely in sound. (For a while she had Claude Debussy in her palatial home to instruct her children in music.)

Thus began an extraordinary correspondence between the two that lasted thirteen years and has served as the principal source for biographies of Tchaikovsky. *Beloved Friend*, an excellent book about Tchaikovsky, includes these interesting letters. The nineteenth century was a great time of letter-writing. Tchaikovsky was a compulsive correspondent. He also kept a diary, some of which he destroyed. Madame von Meck and Tchaikovsky mutually agreed never to meet; yet the love between them was profound. He respected her for understanding his need for privacy and solitude. Through their correspondence and the gifts of money, she gave him the encouragement and confidence he desperately needed. It is one of the most celebrated friendships in history, but it ended tragically.

Throughout his life Tchaikovsky was obsessed with the idea that he was fighting a battle against fate. In his Fourth Symphony, dedicated to Madame von Meck and one of his finest works, we encounter the fatalism that reflects the pessimism of both of them. Russia is a land of sorrow and tragedy, which is reflected in its literature and music. Tchaikovsky, like many Russians, habitually drank too much as a temporary escape from an oppressive world, but he was certainly not an alcoholic. He was a sensitive, high-strung individual, easily depressed about his life and work.

Tchaikovsky laid great weight on the Russian element in his music. Stravinsky said, "Tchaikovsky is the most Russian of us all." Michael Glinka, who wrote operas in the early 1800s, is considered the father of serious Russian music. After Glinka's death, his sister lived for fifty years spreading propaganda for his music. Her home became a salon for "The Five"—Balakirev, Cui, Rimsky-Korsakov, Borodin, and Mussorgsky, who were contemporary with Tchaikovsky. They were all amateurs except their leader, Balakirev. Balakirev urged Tchaikovsky to write *Romeo and Juliet* but later accused him of being too much an admirer of Western culture.

Like Dvorak and several other composers, Tchaikovsky had a great love of nature and his native soil. In 1885 he bought his own house in the vicinity of Moscow after many years of roaming. Here he lived until the year before his death when he moved to the nearby town of Klin. The Moscow house is known today as the Tchaikovsky House Museum. Ever a generous man, when he heard there was no school for children in the village, he promptly gave money to establish one. Tchaikovsky was deeply patriotic, although he was ashamed of the contrasts of life in Russia and of the injustices of which the czarist government was guilty.

Once Madame von Meck freed him from teaching, he formed the habits of work that remained with him for the rest of his life. Even when traveling he tried, not always successfully, to follow the same routine. From eight to nine in the morning he would drink tea and read his Bible. Then he would work. Later in the afternoon, he would walk. Having read someplace that in order to keep healthy a person should walk for two hours a day, this he did with scrupulousness. It was on the walks, many times, that the work of composition was initiated, ideas tried and jotted down in little notebooks. He felt strongly that an artist must not give in to that powerful human trait of laziness. Like most artists, Tchaikovsky craved solitude so that his ideas would not be stolen from him in breezy, indifferent conversation.

Tchaikovsky dedicated the *Serenade for Strings* to Madame von Meck. In the first movement he attempted to adopt the style of Mozart, his favorite composer. The second movement exemplifies his marvelous gift for melody. As one critic said, "There is always a waltz in his music." The second movement is actually a *valse triste* and brings to mind the nineteenth-century salon with its superficial gaiety tinged with melancholy.

Like many artists and musicians, Tchaikovsky loved Venice and Florence. He also spent time in Switzerland in the village of Clarens near Montreux. As one walks along the lake stopping now and then to look at the mountains and flowers and to feed the swans, it is easy to picture Tchaikovsky having done the same. He was always composing, even when traveling about to conduct his music. When Carnegie Hall was built, Tchaikovsky was invited to conduct in New York City and was a resounding success. His great personal charm and handsome appearance won him friends in many countries. Saint-Saëns said, "He was the gentlest and kindest of men."

The music of Tchaikovsky is a mixture of folk melody, cosmopolitan Italian opera, French ballet, and German symphony, but still very Russian. His immense popularity is due to tunefulness and beautiful melodies that sweep over one like a wave, and also his brilliant orchestration. He was one of the finest orchestrators of all time, and Tchaikovsky is at his best in the ballets. Even his symphonies have ballet-like touches. Lack of form, so apparent in his early symphonies, was his worst musical defect. Tchaikovsky was the first Russian composer to gain international fame.

The home of his sister Alexandra and her husband and children provided a place of stability and comfort for Tchaikovsky. He had a genuine affection for children. His first ballet, *Swan Lake*, was originally planned as entertainment for his nieces and nephews. Yet always underneath, this gentle man was lonely and frustrated. He said, "Regretting the past and hoping for the future without ever being satisfied with the present—this is how my life is spent."

His three ballets have become classics. In *Swan Lake* (1875-1876) Tchaikovsky strove for a simple fairy-tale style combined with theatrical brilliance to meet the needs of the classical Russian ballet. His superb orchestral technique and delicacy of touch make it a masterpiece.

In 1888 and 1889 he wrote *Sleeping Beauty*. The waltz in it, which is rightly famous, has a melodious, lyrical style. Some of the most delightful music he ever wrote is in *Sleeping Beauty*. Tchaikovsky was passionately fond of the waltz all his life. It was his way to escape from the troubling reality of life into the lovely but artificial world of ballet and music.

Three years after *Sleeping Beauty*, Tchaikovsky wrote *The Nutcracker Suite*. It is a Christmas Eve ballet about a little girl who dreams that the nutcracker she received as a present has turned into a handsome prince. In the "Dance of the Flowers" we find the modern orchestra in full color and Tchaikovsky at his best.

One can see clearly how he found consolation from his personal sorrows through writing charming, cheerful music, because shortly before he wrote *The Nutcracker Suite*, Madame von Meck, in a cruel and unexpected manner, broke off their friendship. Her favorite son became desperately ill, and she imagined that she had neglected him by showing so much attention to Tchaikovsky. Another biographer explained that she discontinued the allowance imagining herself to be financially ruined, which apparently was pure delusion. By then Tchaikovsky no longer really needed the money, but he was deeply wounded by the way she terminated their friendship. Within a few months he became an old man. He never got over the shock, and on his deathbed three years later he called over and over for Madame von Meck. She died soon after he did.

Madame von Meck was a strong atheist, an intense and dominating woman. She was proud of her independence of God and society and often chided Tchaikovsky for longing to feel Christian truths more strongly and to have a more secure faith. In their biography of Tchaikovsky, Bowen and Meck include this revealing excerpt from one letter Tchaikovsky wrote to Madame von Meck: "On one side my mind refuses to be convinced by dogma . . . on the other hand, my education, and the ingrained habits of childhood, combined with the story of Christ and His teaching, all persuade me, in spite of myself, to turn to Him with prayers when I am sad, with gratitude when I am happy."

Tchaikovsky wrote eight operas, but only *Eugene Onegin* and *The Queen of Spades* are now regularly performed. *Eugene Onegin,* with its famous letter scene in Act I, was only a token success at its Moscow premiere, but enjoyed great popularity in St. Petersburg because of the czar's admiration. The Violin Concerto is one of the most popular as well as one of the best. Of his songs, "None but the Lonely Heart" is best known. Of prime importance are Tchaikovsky's last three symphonies. They are rich in content, tension, and melody. His love of percussion instruments is noteworthy.

Concerning the Sixth Symphony, Tchaikovsky said, "I have put my whole soul into this work." He wrote it after the shattering break with Madame von Meck. Again Tchaikovsky, taking refuge from the sorrows of life, wrote his finest music. With his Sixth Symphony the nineteenth century is completed—from the optimism and triumphant finale of Beethoven's symphonies to the twilight anguish of Tchaikovsky's last musical statement. Tchaikovsky's brother Modeste gave it the name *Pathetique*.

After completing his last symphony, he went to St. Petersburg to conduct it, but the public did not appreciate it. This great symphony had a cold and indifferent reception, but the verdict was speedily reversed—too late for Tchaikovsky who, like his mother earlier, died of cholera. He was fifty-three. The Sixth Symphony is one of the most popular of the nineteenth century, with its sweeping climaxes and tragic beauty. The music of Tchaikovsky with all its strength and beauty nevertheless expressed the pessimism that attended the final phase of the Romantic movement.

Recommended Reading

Bowen, Catherine Drinker, and von Meck, Barbara. *Beloved Friend: The Story of Tchaikovsky and Nadejda von Meck*. New York: Dover Publications, 1946.
Warrack, John. *Tchaikovsky*. London: Haish Hamilton, 1973.

Recommended Listening

Capriccio Italien
Concerto B Flat Minor—Piano and Orchestra
Concerto D Major—Violin and Orchestra
Eugene Onegin—Selections
Francesca Da Rimini
Marche Slave
Nutcracker Suite
1812 Overture
Romeo and Juliet
Serenade in C for Strings
Sleeping Beauty Ballet
Swan Lake Ballet
Symphony No. 4
Symphony No. 5
Symphony No. 6, *Pathetique*

Anton Dvorak
1841-1904

His music expresses joy in life, love of man and
nature, faith in God, and devotion to his country.
Alec Robertson

It was cold and damp when we flew into Prague some years ago. Czechoslovakia, surrounded by Russia, Poland, Germany, Austria, and Hungary, was at the time also surrounded by Russian soldiers. The weather seemed to reflect the downcast spirit of the Czechs as they watched their beautiful city slowly crumbling into ruin. As we walked in the Old Town Square and circled the John Huss statue and watched the figures turn on the old clock, it appeared upon first glance that they were about to restore some of the ancient buildings. But on closer examination, "restoration" was actually outright neglect or total abandonment. It was one way the people fought against the Russian occupation, by deliberately being poor workmen. One Czech explained, "Our national disaster is occupation. Perhaps, therefore, our greatest quality is patience."

Another characteristic of the Czechs is their love of music and dancing. "We have none of Dostoyevsky in us," this man explained. "It is better to laugh than weep." This has been true of the Czechs down through history. No matter what nation dominated them, the saving factor for the future of Czech music and dance was that the country people remained obstinately Czech, and they kept in their hands a torch by which Smetana and, after him, Dvorak lighted fires that the whole world could see. Today in the Czech Republic Dvorak enjoys great popularity as his music represents the people's true spirit.

Burney, writing in 1772, spoke of the Czechs as the most musical people in all Europe. He noticed on one of his tours that in the villages boys and girls are taught music in the schools. He saw them playing the violin, oboe, and bassoon, and little children industriously practicing on four clavichords owned by the schoolmaster.

In such a village Anton Dvorak was born on September 8, 1841. His father was the local butcher and innkeeper of Nelahozeves in Bohemia, a small village that lies on the banks of the River Moldau about forty-five miles north of Prague. At the door of his father's inn young Anton first appeared as a musician, taking his place among the fiddlers who were there to play for the spontaneous dancing in the streets during a national festival.

Anton Dvorak was the eldest son, and though they were a poor family struggling for the bare means of existence, he grew up healthy and high-spirited. At an early age he showed his love for music. The village teacher taught him to sing and play the violin and organ. Dvorak truly thirsted for musical knowledge. When he was twelve, his father sent him to nearby Zlonic where he went to school. There he made friends with the organist and chief musician in town, who instructed the boy in theory, organ, and pianoforte. His teacher admitted that Dvorak was "extraordinarily full of promise," but in spite of it, Dvorak's father ordered him to come home and learn to be a butcher.

Dvorak tried to obey his father, but it was a depressing, terrible time in his life. Finally the sixteen-year-old Anton was allowed to go to Prague and attend the Organ School. He lodged for a while with a cousin who was married to a tailor. Dvorak was not happy there. It is possible that his relatives looked down on him. The boy was a peasant, not very sociable, a quiet person, and his only interest in life was music, to which he was completely dedicated. His early years were beset with difficulties. He had to support himself by playing the violin and viola in cafes and theaters and playing the organ in church.

For a while he lived with another relative, but there was no piano. A friend by the name of Anger who played with him in the theater orchestra invited Dvorak to share his room. Anger said that he had an old spinet that Dvorak could use for composing. The instrument was in the bedroom where, besides the congenial Anger, there lived also a medical student interested in opera, two other students, and a tourist guide. Needless to say, the arrangement did not last long.

Anton Dvorak, always silent and reserved, once grimly declared that in his early days in Prague he always had enough paper to make a fire. What he meant was that he used his early compositions to begin the fire in his stove. In the twelve years after he left the Organ School, and until his emergence before the public as a composer in 1871, Dvorak spent hours each day studying other composers, particularly Beethoven, and then writing much music, which he soon destroyed. "If I ought, I can" might well have been the motto of Dvorak, and he had a firm, inner conviction that he would eventually succeed as a composer. Dvorak was a hard worker and determined to overcome.

Biographer Alec Robertson says that between 1863 and 1869 his burnings were on so large a scale that he must rarely have been cold. But he continued to compose, steadily cherishing an obstinate faith in himself. All through his life he refused to send to the printer music that did not satisfy his own critical standard.

In 1873 Dvorak married Anna, a good contralto singer, and she became a practical, energetic wife. Though they were poor, his home now formed a center in which he could create new works in peace. His was an unusually happy family life. The noises in the home did not worry him at all. His favorite spot for work was the kitchen, where at a small table he sketched out his symphonies and other compositions amid the usual clutter of pots and pans. Steeped in domestic happiness, Dvorak penetrated deeper and deeper to the roots of his own individuality. Finally freeing himself from copying other composers, he now discovered that in his own soul there was music from his rural Czech background.

The artistic life of the Czech nation was given a great boost in 1860 when Italy's victories over Austria brought about a larger degree of political freedom in Czechoslovakia. Smetana, who is called the "father of Czech music" (1824-1884), returned from exile in Sweden and helped to found the Society of Arts. He also became the conductor of the Czech National Theater Orchestra in which Dvorak played the viola. Smetana intended to provide the theater with a repertory of native works. Casting about for ideas about what to write, he decided that the best platform for propagating the national idea in music was the opera, as it appeals to both the eye and ear.

So Smetana wrote his jolly, spirited *The Bartered Bride,* and it eventually brought him worldwide fame; but more immediately, the Prague citizens, "to whom music was as catching as measles," took to their hearts the popular airs by one of their own countrymen. Also notable is Smetana's symphonic poem series *My Fatherland.*

The Bartered Bride is a flawless work of comic art, and of course Dvorak was present in the orchestra pit at all rehearsals and performances; he too caught the "disease" of opera. Anger said that in this period Dvorak frequently and gladly accompanied him to hear Wagner's operas, and finally in 1874 Dvorak produced his own opera. But it was not a success. Nothing daunted, the overcomer Dvorak rewrote the opera in three months. His perseverance was rewarded, and soon his operas began to bring him national acclaim. By 1876 Dvorak was able to give up his various ways of earning a living and devoted himself entirely to composition.

One of the first compositions Dvorak wrote that brought him into notice as a composer of merit was a patriotic cantata. His rise to prominence dates from this successful performance. Around the same time the already-famous Brahms came upon certain duets of Dvorak and, particularly appreciating the freshness and naturalness of his music with the Bohemian flavor, recommended Dvorak for an annual pension. Brahms became a good friend of Dvorak and, remembering himself how appreciative he was of Robert Schumann's help before he had published any music, Brahms introduced Dvorak to his publisher, Simrock. Simrock liked the music and printed the charming *Moravian Duets* in 1876.

Following on this success came a commission in 1877 for a series of Slavonic Dances. When published, this cycle of sparkling, lively pieces swept Europe and established Dvorak's world fame. They also stirred interest in Czechoslovakian music. Commenting on Brahms in a letter, Dvorak said, "What a warm heart and great spirit there is in that man."

A performance of the Slavonic Dances in London in 1879 made Dvorak known to British music-lovers, and he went many times to England to conduct his music. Especially well received was his *Stabat Mater*, written in memory of the death of his oldest daughter. It is the noblest manifestation of Dvorak's religious inspiration.

Dvorak continued to write chamber music, symphonies, operas, and songs. His most famous in the last group is "Songs My Mother Taught Me." It is a near-perfect little work of art ending with a phrase of unforgettable beauty. The operas, though popular at the time, have failed to enjoy lasting success, although *Rusalka* is the best loved of his stage works. In 1883 Dvorak wrote the brilliant Hussites Overture, a powerfully built work based on the chorale "St. Wenceslaus" and the Hussite hymn "All Ye Who Are Warriors of God."

It should be remembered that the national hero of Czechoslovakia is John Huss (ca. 1369-1415). He was a priest and professor of philosophy at the University of Prague, a man of high moral character and life. Huss was an outstanding preacher and very popular with the people because he spoke out clearly and fearlessly against ecclesiastical greed and corruption. Huss was "a reformer before the Reformation," strongly influenced by John Wycliffe. He insisted that the Holy Scriptures are the only rule in matters of life and religion. Following his excommunication, the whole nation rallied around him, but the enemy was stronger. After being deceived and cruelly tortured, John Huss was burned at the stake in 1415. As he was dying, he sang, "Jesus Christ, the Son of the living God, have mercy on me." Under King Wenceslaus, the Czech Reformation began in 1424. This resulted in the Hussite Wars in which the blind general John Zizka led the Czechs against the Catholics and Germans and conquered Prague.

In 1890 Dvorak enjoyed a personal triumph in Moscow where two concerts were arranged for him by another composer friend, Tchaikovsky. Then in 1892 Dvorak accepted the post of director of the newly established National Conservatory of Music in New York. It was started by Jeannette M. Thurber, an enthusiastic music-lover and wife of a wealthy grocery magnate. It was not easy for Dvorak to leave his beloved Bohemia and go to New York City, but accompanied by his wife and two of their numerous children, he accepted the position.

Now a famous man, Dvorak was still basically a conservative, quiet son of the soil, not very sociable and rather suspicious, preferring to keep within a narrow circle. He turned down the social invitations showered on him because he had work to do, and he needed to go to bed early in order to do it. He proved to be a fine teacher but an indifferent administrator. One of his delights in New York was to go to the railway stations and watch the trains thunder by or to Central Park and listen to the birds, which reminded him of home.

It has been said that the harvest of Dvorak's American visit is not rich numerically, but it may be compared to a full harvest of the purest and heaviest wheat without chaff. Dvorak's talent for composition was of the highest order, and in his Symphony No. 9 in E Minor, *From the New World*, he seemed to please everyone. There are few notable works of permanent value that have been immediately accepted and appreciated by the public at large, but the *New World* Symphony is one that has.

Most of the orchestration for the symphony was done in Spillville, Iowa, where the composer went in the summertime. Dvorak suffered badly from homesickness in New York, but in Spillville he found his own people. It was a colony of Bohemians from Czechoslovakia. There he could speak his native tongue, go to church, sing some of the sweet, sad songs from his homeland, play at the many festivals, and eat and drink among his people. Also in Spillville, he had his whole family together, the other four children having been sent for.

The *New World* Symphony is in the spirit of folk music, and the majority of the melodies are unmistakably Czech. Sweetness of sound is a chief characteristic of Dvorak's music. The largo of the second movement has a hauntingly beautiful melody played by the English horn. There is a sense of longing about it, and a spiritual has been adapted from it, "Going Home." One loves the melodic invention of Dvorak, his transparency and heartwarming simplicity. His is happy music with a touch of sadness. The black singer Henry Burleigh studied with Dvorak at the conservatory and introduced Dvorak to the beautiful songs of his race.

For a while there was a controversy whether Dvorak had used authentic American themes in his symphony. As Robertson shows, he settled it in a letter he wrote to the Berlin conductor Nedbal: "Please omit the nonsense about my having made use of 'Indian' and 'American' themes—that is a lie. I merely tried to write in the spirit of these national melodies."

Also in America, Dvorak wrote his masterly Cello Concerto, the American String Quartet, Humoresque, and *Ten Biblical Songs*. The latter are a fervent and intimate expression of Dvorak's deep piety. Today they are played often in the Czech Republic, and it means something much deeper to the Christian people living there who have only recently gained the freedom to worship the living God.

After three years Dvorak returned to Prague. He was very homesick for his beautiful little country. Success never spoiled him. He remained what he had always been—a simple, rather obstinate God-fearing man, almost always silent and reserved, neither asking for advice nor receiving it. After the stunning success of the *New World* Symphony in New York, Boston, and Vienna, Dvorak commented simply, "May God be thanked."

Happiness for him lay in his family circle, and for the most part in pleasures that money cannot buy. He spoke of his genius as "the gift of God" or "God's voice" speaking to him. After finishing a great work, he was always afraid lest that voice might not be heard again and his creative faculty withdrawn. With Handel and Haydn, Dvorak's music was among the healthiest of all composers.

Dvorak caught a chill standing at the railway station in Prague on his regular visit to see the locomotives, and he died suddenly at the dinner table shortly afterwards on May 1, 1904. His music is the most inventive and spontaneously musical of all national composers. It is joyous and untouched by tedium and continues to bring comfort, not only to the people of his beloved land, but to all nations. Anton Dvorak is one of the most human and lovable of the great composers.

Recommended Reading

Robertson, Alec. *Dvorak*. New York: Collier Books, 1962.

Recommended Listening

Dvorak: *Ten Biblical Songs*
   Carnival Overture
   Concerto in B Minor for Cello
   Quartet in F, *American*
   Slavonic Dances
   Stabat Mater
   Symphony No. 7 in D Minor
   Symphony No. 8 in G
   Symphony No. 9 in E Minor, *New World* Symphony
   Trio in E Minor, "Dumky"
Smetana: *The Bartered Bride*–Overture
   "The Moldau" (from *My Fatherland*)

CHAPTER 23

Gabriel Fauré
1845-1924

Fauré's refined, highly civilized music embodies the
aristocratic qualities of the French tradition.
Donald Jay Grout

G abriel Fauré was born in Paniers, France, in 1845. He was the youngest of six children, and because of financial problems in the family, he was put out "to nurse" in a neighboring village for four years. Then he was allowed to return to the family circle, as his father had received a promotion.

It is obvious that Gabriel was not brought up in an atmosphere of intimate tenderness. He had four brothers and one sister, and one of the brothers was a practical joker. Once he threw a plateful of spinach in Gabriel's face to awaken him from his meditations. This early background helps to explain Fauré's reticence, thoughtfulness, and reserve.

Fortunately, when Gabriel was eight years old, a blind woman heard him playing the harmonium in the village church. She urged his parents to allow him to study music, and within a year he was in Paris where he began his musical training and general education at the École Niedermeyer.

A native of Switzerland, Louis Niedermeyer was an outstanding educator in music history. His goal was to train organists and choirmasters, hoping to improve church music. The students' "daily bread" were the masterpieces of J. S. Bach. Niedermeyer became a person of distinction in Parisian musical life.

Here in this excellent school Fauré learned to play the piano and organ, had courses in harmony and counterpoint, especially Bach, and was given a thorough grounding in Gregorian chant. This became important in the writing of his music, as Fauré often used the modal sound.

As in most boardinghouse schools, conditions were not ideal. It is reported that there were at least a dozen pupils placed in the same room, each playing a different piece on a different instrument; however, it turned to good for Gabriel Fauré, as it intensified his capacity for concentration.

Probably when the other students ran out to play after the long hours of studying and practicing, Fauré was absorbed in thinking about writing music and actually doing it.

When Niedermeyer died in 1861, Camille Saint-Saëns joined the staff at the Niedermeyer school. He was only ten years older than Fauré but was already launched on a brilliant career as a concert pianist and composer. As a musician, he not only could instantly sight-read anything, but he was a musicologist long before the term came into use. He introduced Fauré to the whole range of music, and later in life Fauré said that he owed everything to his professor Saint-Saëns.

It was the beginning of a wonderful and lasting friendship. Saint-Saëns did for Fauré something that nearly every artistic person wishes would happen to him or her. First, he recognized Fauré's abilities and encouraged him to get the best training possible in the areas where he appeared to be the most gifted, as an organist and composer. Next, when Fauré was ready, Saint-Saëns found jobs for him as a church organist and put him in contact with publishers for his music.

Fauré studied at the Niedermeyer school for eleven years, graduating with first prizes in piano, organ, harmony, and composition. At the age of eighteen, he published his first piano work. When he was twenty, he had already written his first twenty songs.

In 1877 his engagement to Marianne Viardot, who was from a distinguished musical family, was broken off. He was very much in love with her. During a three-week period Fauré had written Marianne thirty-five letters, and almost immediately after that summer, she said she could not marry him.

Six years later, Fauré married Marie Fremiet, the daughter of the sculptor, Emmanuel Fremiet. She proved to be a good and faithful wife, content to be a homemaker. They had two sons.

For thirty years Fauré held various posts as an organist. In 1896 when he was fifty-one, he became the organist at the Madeleine Cathedral as well as a professor of composition at the Paris Conservatory. He was an excellent teacher. His influence on his pupil Ravel and on the outstanding teacher Nadia Boulanger, who went on to teach many other composers, is one of the important factors in the history of twentieth-century music. It was an influence that brought greatly needed order.

The biographer Suckling divides the works of Fauré into three periods—apprenticeship, maturity, and further exploration. One critic observed that in chamber music Fauré found himself with completeness at an earlier date than in any other branch of his art. His Violin Sonata in A and the Quartet in G Minor are outstanding.

Fauré rarely wrote his music in the spirit of Rimsky-Korsakov and many other artistic people who simply write regularly to keep in training. Fauré did not hesitate "to lie fallow" when he had nothing important to say. Throughout his life Fauré only had time to compose during the summer holidays, and generally he went to Switzerland where he found the quiet atmosphere he needed.

He had superb technique in writing, and yet his music, because of its transparency, seems simple. This is not because it is shallow, but because it is free of impurities. Along with Debussy he helped to free French music from German influences. As an example, Fauré did not waste time over "introductions" of the Lisztian kind. He once said, "The essence of musical art consists, to my mind, in raising us as far as possible above things as they are."

The music of Fauré has elegance and reserve. It flows easily and has a Hellenistic beauty so well suited to his opera *Penelope*. Someone spoke of his piano music as pieces of "winged fantasy." Yet his piano pieces, such as his wonderful Nocturne No. 6, are not easy to play. Even though he was influenced by Chopin in writing preludes, impromptus, barcarolles, and waltzes, he does not have flashy virtuosity. One writer described it as "the highly sensitive but never exhibitionist art of Fauré."

In 1877 Saint-Saëns took Fauré to Weimar where Saint-Saëns's opera *Samson and Delilah* was given its first performance, with Liszt conducting. In the course of the visit Saint-Saëns introduced Liszt to Fauré. Then two years later Fauré visited Germany again to hear Wagner's *Ring*. When he saw Liszt, Fauré showed the great master of the piano his *Ballade* (Op. 19).

After trying a page or two, Liszt returned the music to Fauré with the comment, "It was too difficult." Obviously if Liszt could not play it, no one could; but the critics believe it was more a question of taste rather than a technical problem. There was never a more un-German composer than Fauré.

Gabriel Fauré ranks with the greatest of all song composers. He preferred working in small forms. In his music Fauré not only interpreted and complemented the poems he selected, but as Chantavoine explained, "In some cases, he has actually revealed them, by opening up for them that region of our minds which the choicest words in poetic speech have otherwise failed to penetrate."

Fauré, in one sense, can be compared to Schumann of the Romantic period in Germany, being both musician and poet. He belongs not only to the history of French music, but to that of French poetry and artistic sensibility. Fauré wrote nearly a hundred songs.

His characteristics are most fully revealed in such songs as "Nell," "*En Sourdine*," "*Automne*," "*Après un Rêve*," "*Clair de Lune*," "*Les Berceaux*," and the masterly song cycle "*L'Horizon Chimérique*." When coauthor Jane Smith was a student at Hollins College, her friends called her Nell, as she often sang this touching song.

Fauré is often spoken of as the "French Schubert." In many of his songs his emotion does not overflow, but in exquisite restraint he writes music that is extremely moving. His songs have great elegance and reserve, yet they communicate in a profound way.

As a composer Fauré was constantly developing, but he never relinquished beauty, logic, moderation, and tradition. This musician's musician held fast to the poetry of pure musical form in an age when these ideals were considered old-fashioned. In contrast to Schoenberg, whose music has no rest, Fauré was able to combine chromaticism and repose.

Concerning how he composed, he would laugh when students asked where he got his inspiration. "For example," one of his young admirers inquired, "where did you receive the inspiration for your sixth nocturne?" Fauré replied gravely, "In the Simplon tunnel." As the Count de Caylus said, "Natural gifts consist simply of greater aptitude in one person than in another to receive impressions and allow them to germinate."

In 1886 Fauré composed his beautiful *Requiem*. It had its first performance at the Madeleine two years later. No more tender or consoling funeral mass than this one has ever been written. The "Sanctus" is particularly moving. It has healed many a painful wound and quieted many a desperate heart.

Nadia Boulanger wrote, "The *Requiem* is not only one of the greatest works of Gabriel Fauré, but also one of those which do most honor to music and thought. Nothing purer, clearer in definition, has been written. . . ." (Her biography is well worth reading.)

His father had died in 1885, and because Fauré's wife was not well at the time, he was not able to be present for his father's last hours. Part of his problem was also financial. Even though some of his compositions had already brought him fame, there was little money. This was one of the most burdened times in his life.

Fauré's worries and troubles continued into 1890, and there was scarcely a day without a neuralgic headache and dizziness. Then an American woman made it possible for Fauré and some of his friends to take a holiday in Venice. This brief but precious vacation restored his health. Also in this fascinating, picturesque city he wrote five superb songs with words by Paul Verlaine.

After considerable difficulty, Fauré became director of the conservatory in 1905 and remained its head until 1920. Though he was a small, mild, seemingly reticent person, Fauré proved to be an excellent administrator and had the courage to introduce needed reforms. The conservative professors were replaced by musicians like Debussy and d'Indy who shared Fauré's ideas.

At this period in his life when he was being appreciated more and more, tragedy came in the form of deafness, reminding us of Beethoven's similar problem. As early as 1903 Fauré observed the first signs of it, complicated by distortion of pitch, and by 1910 it had become an agony. Partly from his unwillingness to advertise his sorrows and also because he did not wish to lose his professional work, he said little about his perplexing situation. Finally, in 1920 he was asked to retire from the conservatory directorship. The same year he was promoted to the highest class in the Legion of Honor.

In spite of his deafness, his last twenty years were the period when he composed some of his best music. Almost to the day of his death he continued to write music, finishing his String Quartet in 1924.

At the age of seventy-six, Fauré played at a concert in Tours, but he was unable to hear the music. The following year there was a benefit concert of his works at the Sorbonne. Charles Panzéra and his wife, Madeleine Baillot, contributed to the program, as well as other outstanding performers. (Years later at Juilliard, Jane Smith had the joy of studying with these two superb musicians.) As Suckling said, "The concert lasted until one o'clock in the morning and left no doubt of the honor in which Gabriel Fauré was held by musicians and other friends young and old," including "Les Six."

The life of Gabriel Fauré extended over the periods of early Romanticism, Wagner, the post-Romanticism of Brahms and Mahler, the Neoclassicism of Stravinsky, and Schoenberg's atonalism; and in spite of all these very different influences, he went his own way. Fauré, always an impeccable workman, was one of the most elegant and refined of all composers and one of the most influential musicians of his time.

Recommended Reading

Suckling, Norman. *Fauré*. London: J. M. Dent, 1946.
Rosenstiel, Leonie. *Nadia Boulanger*. New York: W. W. Norton, 1982.

Recommended Listening

Ballade for Piano and Orchestra
"La Bonne Chanson"
"Dolly"
Masques et Bergamasques
Nocturne No. 6
Pavane
Pelléas et Mélisande
Quartet No. 2 in G Minor
Requiem
Sonata in A for Violin and Piano
Songs: *"En Sourdine," "Nell," "Les Berceaux," "Clair de Lune," "Après un Rêve," "L'Horizon Chimérique"*

CHAPTER 24

Giacomo Puccini
1858-1924

These are the laws of the theater: to interest, to
surprise, to move. And musical drama must be
'seen' in its music as well as heard.

Giacomo Puccini

*A*s anyone who has been in the opera world knows, the drama among composers, conductors, and singers is often as colorful as any opera. Puccini and the conductor Toscanini would get along well for a while, and then abruptly there would be a fiery encounter. One Christmas Puccini sent Toscanini a "panettone" (a tasty Italian cake), and suddenly he recalled they were not on speaking terms at the moment. He sent a telegram: "Panettone sent by mistake. Puccini." The following day he received an answer: "Panettone eaten by mistake. Toscanini."

It is this mixture of intense emotion, humor, and high spirits that causes many of us to love Italians. Puccini had these qualities, but his spirits dropped often. As he said himself, "I have always carried with me a great sack of melancholy."

Giacomo Puccini was born in Lucca, Italy, in 1858. He was one of eight children, and at the time of the father's early death, his mother was only thirty-three. As Puccini came from a line of musicians extending over an uninterrupted period of 150 years, his mother, Albina, was determined Giacomo would not have to accept a menial job. He was first to study the "classics" and then music. With little income, the family would survive on spaghetti.

At first it appeared that Giacomo would not arrive at anything. He was a sullen and unambitious child. His chief interest was trapping birds. An uncle taught him to sing and to play the organ, but the uncle reported to Puccini's mother that the boy had no talent for music. Albina refused to believe it and soon found another teacher, Angeloni. The teacher had been a pupil of her husband, and she begged him to do something for her son.

Angeloni was not only a good music teacher, but he had a passionate interest in hunting. The first day the two met, they did not mention music, but they spoke of owls and finches and the best way to catch them. Soon Puccini would do anything for his new teacher, and the same stubborn force he had applied to indolence he now poured into music.

At fourteen Puccini was already playing the organ in several of the churches in Lucca and earning a little money. He improvised snatches from Verdi's operas *Rigoletto, Il Trovatore,* and *La Traviata* in his organ pieces, which quite surprised the congregation.

As he could also play the piano now, he was useful at weddings and dances. The nuns connected with one of the churches liked him, and often he played for them. As a reward he would always receive a cup of hot chocolate. Puccini was very Italian. He adored sweets.

When he was still a teenager, one memorable day in 1876, he and two friends walked the nineteen miles to Pisa to hear Verdi's opera *Aïda*. While the boys walked home in the dark, arriving in Lucca as the sun began to rise, deep thoughts were going through Puccini's mind. From that time on he knew what he wanted to do with his life—he too would write operas. He also realized he needed more musical training.

In order to give some proof of his ability so he could gain support to attend the Milan Conservatory, he entered a composition contest. He did very poorly, but it did not deter him. He quickly wrote something better.

This composition, a motet, which is quite theatrical, won favor with the people of Lucca. He even got a good review from a doctor who was a relative of the family. The doctor agreed to advance Puccini a small amount of money to help get him started in Milan, and his mother wrote a convincing letter to Queen Margherita in Rome, who was known to award scholarships to talented students.

Without the support of his mother, the doctor, and the queen, Puccini probably would have spent his life in Lucca being an organist. Not that being an organist is unimportant, but the musical world would not have had *Manon Lescaut, La Bohème, Tosca, Madame Butterfly,* and *Turandot,* some of Puccini's most popular operas. Had Puccini known what hard work was ahead for him, he might have stayed in Lucca. But the creative force was already driving him on.

And so at the age of twenty-two, Giacomo Puccini arrived in the teeming city of Milan. The year was 1880. At the conservatory the shy but determined student was assigned to Ponchielli, who loved to teach and took the liveliest interest in those pupils who had talent and were willing to learn. Puccini became one of his favorites. The very month Puccini entered the conservatory, Ponchielli was finishing an opera, *The Prodigal Son,* which was produced that same year at La Scala. Ponchielli is mainly remembered for his grandiose opera *La Gioconda* with its setting in Venice, so full of Italian drama and melody. One often hears the colorful ballet from this opera, "The Dance of the Hours."

Puccini worked very hard in Milan, went hungry, and lived in very crowded, dumpy quarters with two other students. Their antics make one think of the artistic young men we meet later in *La Bohème*.

He received a good review of his composition *Capriccio*, which he wrote during his last year at the conservatory. He read and reread with satisfaction the favorable review of it and bought many copies of the newspaper to send home to his mother.

At the end of his days at the conservatory, he went through a period of wondering what was next. He knew he wanted to write operas, but where was he to find money for a libretto? He still had many lean years ahead, but with the help of his wonderful professor, Ponchielli, he made some good and necessary connections.

While he was still in his bohemian phase (for a time one of his roommates was Mascagni, who later composed *Cavalleria Rusticana*), he and a friend found a restaurant called Aïda where they were able to eat on credit.

About this time, Puccini entered his new opera *Le Villi* in an important competition. It did not even receive a mention in the contest, partly due to its illegibility (Puccini never improved his notoriously bad musical notation). In particularly flagrant cases he would write *"scusi!"* (please forgive) in the margin of his opera scores. However, thanks to the help of the librettist Fontana, the publisher Giulio Ricordi, and the composer Boito, the opera was performed and proved to be a success that same year, 1884. Puccini had to take eighteen curtain calls. Even though it was not really great music, he showed that he was able to create the theatrical mood. The melody and his dramatic instinct communicated to the audience.

The day after his success, Puccini walked into the Aïda Restaurant, drew from his pocket an Italian bill equivalent to $100, and placed it nonchalantly on the counter. Then in a voice that all could hear, he said, *"Il conto, per favore!"* (The bill, please!).

But as often happens in life, joy abruptly changed to sadness. Puccini received word that his faithful, beloved mother was dying. How he wished she could have attended the concert and heard the applause and seen her son take eighteen curtain calls. He rushed home to be with her, and she died a few weeks later. His grief was shattering. He knew how much he owed to her. He went into a period of profound depression, but he was encouraged to go on with the help of his friend Giulio Ricordi, who saw him through those hard years.

Ricordi was the head of a famous Milan publishing firm founded in 1808 and had worked closely with Verdi. Ricordi truly believed in Puccini's abilities and stayed with him even though for several years it appeared as though he had made a poor investment. We will not go into the complicated story about the opera *Edgar*, which Puccini himself called a blunder and eventually disowned.

Then in 1893 *Manon Lescaut* was premiered—a brilliant triumph. It laid the foundation for Puccini's international fame. George Bernard Shaw wrote, "Puccini looks to me like the heir of Verdi."

Ricordi was finally rewarded for his patience and faith in Puccini. *La Bohème* was not a success at first, but each time it was performed, the enthusiasm grew because of Puccini's extraordinary sense of the theater and his thrilling melodies. When the season was over, twenty-four sold-out performances had been given with the young Arturo Toscanini conducting. That year, 1896, Puccini not only became famous but wealthy, and Ricordi even more so. The publisher deserved it. There never would have been a Puccini opera without the wise, gentle, and patient Ricordi.

It was another four years before Puccini's verismo opera *Tosca* appeared. It became popular almost immediately. Puccini united grand opera with verismo. This term literally means truth (or true truth), and sometimes it is translated as realism or life-as-it-really-is. Verismo reached its peak in the operas of Puccini. His librettos present everyday people in familiar situations acting violently under the impulse of heightened emotion. The veristic opera is the grandfather of such television programs as "Days of Our Lives" and "As the World Turns."

Shortly after his mother died in 1884, Puccini ran off with a married woman, Elvira Gemignani, who was difficult, possessive, and narrow-minded. They lived in Chiasso, Switzerland, for a while, then moved back to Milan, but they were put out of their lodgings for playing the piano at night. Puccini was tired of Milan by this time and was happy to leave. Finally he found the place he was looking for, a home on a lake in an obscure village near Pisa, called Torre del Lago. There he could fish, hunt, and work on his operas.

In 1904 Puccini married Elvira after her husband died, though their life together was filled with interminable quarrels. Their passion for each other had cooled by this time, and she grew increasingly jealous of her handsome, popular husband—and with good reason. Puccini described himself as "a mighty hunter of wild fowl, opera librettos, and attractive women." One of his friends described him as "permanently adolescent."

In private he was lovable, gentle, and unassuming with a sense of humor; yet his whole life was tinged with melancholy. He was a slow worker, plagued by self-doubt and sadness. His music is not ennobling like Verdi's, but it is endearing.

Whenever he needed inspiration, he would find another woman. One time he had an automobile accident, and the maid at Torre del Lago took care of him—such good care that it brought out all the jealousy and rage in the heart of his wife. The maid was innocent, but Elvira stirred up the whole village, and the young girl committed suicide. From this time on Puccini was a miserable, sad man. He was famous and wealthy, but he nevertheless wallowed in self-pity, finding life an intolerable burden and at the same time tormented by the thought of old age and death. Having no faith in the God of all comfort, he suffered spiritual loneliness and isolation.

The first performance of *Madame Butterfly* in 1904 was a fiasco, but after Puccini struggled a long time rewriting it, *Butterfly* along with *Tosca* and *La*

Bohème became the three most successful operas of the early twentieth century.

His other works are *The Girl of the Golden West* (1910), a story of life among the gold miners of California, and *Il Trittico*, which includes the comic opera *Gianni Schicchi*, taken from Dante's *Inferno*. It is a masterpiece of brilliance and wit. *Il Tabarro* is outstanding for its somber atmosphere and dramatic concentration, and *Suor Angelica* is the moving story of a nun who has had an illegitimate child.

Melody in a sense came naturally to Puccini. He said once, "Without melody, fresh and poignant, there can be no music." His melodies are beautifully written for the voice. "Somewhere, somehow, he evolved a personal, inimitable style," said Schonberg, "that stands out among the Italian operas of his time like the song of a nightingale in a flock of starlings."

Whenever Puccini composed an opera, he researched and spent time on its geographical and historical background. Many of his singers admired his exactitude, and he was patient with those he worked with, but firm. He knew more about the voice than many voice teachers and had an uncanny flair for the theatrical.

Puccini was influenced by Wagner, Verdi, and Debussy. His admiration for Wagner continued to the end of his life. He said, "The genius of Wagner is beyond all description." It should be remembered that the list of operas performed today consists basically of the works of five composers—Mozart, Verdi, Wagner, Strauss, and Puccini.

Puccini's last and unfinished opera, *Turandot*, is considered by Newman his greatest score. It has its defects, but it is a uniquely beautiful work. Jane Stuart Smith, my coauthor, made her European operatic debut as Turandot in Venice and sang it throughout her career as an opera singer in many different theaters. It is a very demanding role, yet rewarding because of the gorgeous music and costumes.

Turandot is an exotic Chinese tale in which Puccini introduced Chinese melodies and for the opera invented a new style—dissonant, complex in orchestration, and full of choral writing. Puccini was a master in handling big choral scenes. Unfortunately he did not live to finish this beautiful opera, which was completed by Franco Alfano. Puccini died in Brussels of a heart attack in 1924 after undergoing an operation on his throat for cancer.

"Just think of it!" Puccini told some friends. "If I hadn't hit on music, I should never have been able to do anything in this world." He died rich, leaving nothing to charities, the people of Torre del Lago, or struggling young composers. He had been stingy all his life, probably due to his early financial struggles and lack of Christian understanding. He is buried at Villa Torre del Lago with his wife and son. Mass is said there every month. Yet in spite of his splintered, neurotic personality, Giacomo Puccini has left to the world beautiful and unforgettable music.

Recommended Reading

Marek, George R. *Puccini*. New York: Simon and
  Schuster, 1951.

Recommended Listening

Arias and operas: *La Bohème*
  The Girl of the Golden West
  Gianni Schicchi
  Madame Butterfly
  Manon Lescaut
  Il Tabarro
  Tosca
  Turandot

CHAPTER 25

Gustav Mahler
1860-1911

Where do I go? I go wandering in the mountains,
seeking rest for my lonely heart!
"The Song of the Earth"

*B*runo Walter in speaking about Gustav Mahler said that his spirit never knew escape from the torturing question, "For what?" Few people worked harder or accomplished more than Mahler, but he was rarely content. All his life was a conflict between belief and unbelief, and he was obsessed with themes of death and the life beyond. Mahler was Jewish, and like many Austrian-Jewish intellectuals, he became a convert to Roman Catholicism. But he remained a perpetual doubter all his life, yearning for the ecstasy of faith and the "wholeness of soul" that comes from certainty.

Gustav Mahler was born in Kaliste, Bohemia, in 1860. Around the age of four, fascinated by the band music he heard in the street near his father's inn (which was also the family home) and the folk music sung by the Czech people, he began writing his own pieces and trying them on the accordion. Later he found an old piano in the attic, and gradually he learned to play it. His vocation was never doubted. By fifteen he was so proficient musically that he was accepted as a student at the Vienna Conservatory and was thankful to leave the village of Iglau where he grew up. At the conservatory he was a friend of Hugo Wolf, who later became one of the great songwriters.

Mahler's father was an Austrian-Jewish tavern keeper, a cruel man of "fierce vitality." He was self-educated and resented his wife's social superiority. He mistreated her, and young Mahler's childhood was complicated by the quarrels between his parents and the illnesses and deaths among his eleven brothers and sisters. This may help to explain Mahler's obsession with death and his unceasing quest to discover some meaning in life. Mahler had such empathy with his fragile mother that he copied unconsciously her slight limp. As one friend commented, "He walked with a lopsided gait." He also inherited his mother's weak heart. His father's brutality haunted the sensitive musician throughout his life. Add to that the racial tensions he had to endure, both in Bohemia and Vienna, and one sees he had a difficult beginning.

After getting his diploma from the conservatory in Vienna, Mahler, a prodigious worker, supported himself by occasional teaching while trying to gain recognition as a composer. His poverty during these years was chronic. Reluctantly he decided for a career as an operatic conductor, since at that age he probably was unaware of his rare, almost uncanny talents in that direction. Finally, at the age of twenty he turned to conducting as a livelihood and set aside time in the summers for composing.

When his parents died in 1889, Mahler took on the responsibility of caring for his remaining brothers and sisters. In one of his illnesses Mahler went to Italy, and his sister Justine went along to care for him. Later she became his faithful housekeeper. The radiance of the Italian springtime helped to restore his health.

After seventeen years of conducting in various European opera houses, Mahler rose to the top of his profession and was asked to be the musical director of the Imperial Opera House in Vienna in 1897. Though he became one of the greatest conductors of modern times, he was frustrated. He wanted most of all to be a composer.

The years Mahler spent in Vienna were brilliant because he was an eminent interpreter, especially of Wagner and Mozart. But the time was also discordant and strife-ridden. Mahler was a relentless conductor. His striving for perfection gained him the enmity of the performers but the adulation of the audience. As one critic said, "Mahler, whose neuroses made Tchaikovsky's neuroses look healthy," was a tempestuous, restless, irritable, impatient personality who inevitably provoked storms wherever he went. His motives were never really mean but stemmed more from confusion, as his life was a tug-of-war. He longed for freedom to compose, but had to continue conducting in order to live. Invariably he carried a parcel of books and music under his arm. He was always intent on learning. Of Mahler's dedication to music there was no doubt.

Mahler easily made enemies with his intensity, arrogance, and insecurity dating back to his childhood. All his life he suffered from fearful headaches (which would explain some of his irritability), but he almost never canceled a rehearsal or performance. Mahler had fanatical energy, ruthless zeal, and musical genius. Even though his health was poor, he was determined to overcome. He was a tireless swimmer and an indefatigable hiker. His appearance was that of a slim yet well-muscled sportsman.

Mahler married Alma Schindler in 1902 after having had a long series of unhappy affairs. Much could be said about Alma. Books have been written about her, and she has written one herself. Although Mahler's love for Alma was genuine, it was a frustrating marriage for both of them. Mahler was forty-one and Alma twenty-three, and the conductor-composer (who lived for his music) could not devote himself exclusively to his beautiful, young wife. He said once, "I cannot do anything but work."

She was a brilliant pianist and gifted composer herself, and soon she became an accurate copyist of his scores and an understanding and sympathetic critic of his music. Alma introduced him to many artistic people with whom she was acquainted. With her originality of mind and strong ambition, she was worthy to become the wife and companion of Mahler. Alma could be extravagantly generous and inordinately mean. As one person said, "If Mahler was selfish, Alma was more selfish still."

Gustav Mahler did most of his composing with frenzied speed in the summer between hectic seasons of conducting, and he would orchestrate his works during the winter in the morning before rehearsals. He was happiest when he was in his studio far away in the woods at Maiernigg, wearing his oldest clothes, walking and composing. The balcony of his studio-bedroom had a magnificent view over the lake. His music is filled with sounds of nature he must have heard there and in other places where he worked during the summer.

Mahler spoke of himself as "the summer composer," and the great dream of his life was to earn enough money so he could retire when he was fifty and devote his entire time to composing. It was one of the reasons he drove himself relentlessly. It is surprising when one first considers that Mahler turned to symphonies and songs for his creative expression because his life as a conductor centered in the opera house, but his autobiographical music was more effectively expressed in programmatic symphonies and songs.

The first years of Gustav and Alma's marriage were brightened by the birth of their two children and Mahler's increasing productivity as a composer. In 1904 he read some poems by the German poet Friedrich Rückert lamenting the death of his children. The tragedy so affected Rückert that he poured out his sorrow in countless poems. When Mahler began to write the beautiful and heartrending music known today as the *Kindertotenlieder* (Songs on the Death of Children), Alma declared that she found his choice of such a sad text "incomprehensible." "For heaven's sake," she said, "don't tempt Providence."

When three years later their beloved Maria died of diphtheria and scarlet fever at the age of five, Mahler was inconsolable. Even though he had many character faults and was egotistical, he possessed a childlike simplicity and idealism that made his suffering unbearable. The *Kindertotenlieder* is one of Mahler's most intimate and profoundly moving compositions.

Mahler's Sixth Symphony reveals a superstitious element in his personality. In the finale are three climactic hammer blows that represent the three blows of fate that fall on the hero. In 1907 Mahler identified the three blows of fate with his own life: (1) His resignation from the Vienna Opera House. (After Mahler came under a venomous attack in the press in 1907, he asked for his discharge.) (2) The death of his daughter Maria. (3) The diagnosis of his fatal heart disease by a doctor.

Mahler was told that his whole way of life would have to change and that his favorite long walks would have to be given up. It was a time of dejection, but Mahler was not yet through. Music was his only way of life, and so he went on a concert tour to St. Petersburg and Helsinki. Then he accepted an invitation to conduct Mozart and Wagner at the Metropolitan Opera House in New York, and he and Alma crossed the Atlantic for the first time in December 1907. Upon arriving in New York, Alma said, "We were so excited that we forgot our cares."

Mahler's last three years were spent in New York City where he was invited to conduct both the Metropolitan Opera and the New York Philharmonic Orchestra. Summers were devoted to composing and conducting in Europe. From the proceeds of his American engagements he started to build a home in Austria where he could retire and compose in peace, but this dream was never realized. Toward the end of his life a crisis in his marriage, in addition to the perpetual inner doubts, persuaded Mahler to consult Sigmund Freud. But he found no spiritual help, and the meaning of life for him remained as obscure as ever.

In 1911, now a very sick man, Mahler returned to Europe, and after a brief time in Paris he was brought back to Vienna. He died there at the age of fifty. His last words were, "Mozart . . . Mozart." Gustav Mahler was buried next to his daughter Maria in Grinzing near Vienna.

The music of Mahler was not always well received. After the premiere of the Third Symphony in Germany in 1902, a reviewer concluded that "the composer should be shot." When Mahler first performed the Fourth Symphony in Vienna, it drove the audience to such fury that fist fights broke out all over the concert hall. When he met with such incomprehension and lack of appreciation, he said obstinately, "My time will come!" And Mahler's time has come. As one of our recent conductors has said, "Mahler was a high-strung genius who speaks today to a high-strung generation."

Mahler is an important forerunner of twentieth-century techniques of composition. Such widely differing composers as Schoenberg, Berio, Shostakovich, and Britten have acknowledged his influence. He was a profound admirer of Wagner, in whose music we find the culmination of the Romantic agony. Mahler was the last in a great line of Viennese symphonists that included Haydn, Mozart, Beethoven, Schubert, Brahms, and Bruckner. One could say that Wagner was the door, and Mahler, the last of the diatonic composers, opened it to Schoenberg and twentieth-century music.

Mahler spoke of himself "as a pupil of Bruckner." Although he probably never actually studied with him, Mahler was the devoted disciple of Anton Bruckner, yet without his religious beliefs.

Bruckner was a solitary, simple, and devout soul. His religion was the foundation of everything he did. He even introduced masses into his symphonies. Bruckner was born of a poor family in upper Austria. He was a fine organist and at first expressed himself in church music. He was a humble man, never at home among the intellectuals in Vienna. He dedicated his Ninth Symphony "to the good Lord." His was a medieval soul living in the nineteenth century struggling with the problems of how to find an artistic relationship to God. When Mahler used a chorale tune in his Fifth Symphony, his wife said, "Bruckner, yes, but not you."

The compositions of Mahler consist of nine symphonies (a tenth unfinished), some songs, and four song cycles somewhat in the manner of Schubert and Schumann. He wrote nothing for the stage in spite of his vast experience conducting operas. His symphonies are long and programmatic (like Richard Strauss's) and demand enormous performing resources. "To write a symphony," Mahler said, "is, for me, to construct a world." He conducted one thousand performers in the premiere of his Eighth Symphony. Today it is referred to as the *Symphony of a Thousand.*

Lyricism is the essential ingredient of Mahler's music. The melody is long of line with intermittent extravagant leaps that help to heighten the power to communicate intense emotion. (Schoenberg also used this technique.) One finds in the music of Mahler great beauty and power along with banality and even vulgarity. Mahler was a pioneer of brilliant orchestration with a unique sense of color.

The main themes of Mahler are typically Romantic: the beauty of nature (he said once, "My music is, throughout and always, but a sound of nature"), love and faith, destiny and death. His music is full of unrest and nostalgia. He usually ended a symphony in a different key than he began with, and he has the Schubertian wavering between major and minor. Even in his music Mahler was never satisfied, constantly making revisions. He was one of the most adventurous and fastidious of composers in his treatment of instrumental combinations. In spite of massive orchestras, he maintained clarity of line and lightness of texture. Mahler's style is based on orchestral counterpoint. He was a master of technique.

Mahler required many unusual instruments—harness bells, mandolin, guitar, glockenspiel, and harmonium—and employed a variety of original percussion instruments, including a hammer. Mahler was fascinated with band music, and his symphonies resound with the sound of drums and horns. His use of foreign elements in his symphonies has been ascribed to lack of originality, but more correctly it is a specifically modern approach. Stockhausen has said that what Mahler did was to integrate all the elements, from the most banal and commonplace, into a whole that transcends them. Mahler used instruments in their extreme range and had some instruments offstage to achieve a sense of distance. His music has flashes of haunting beauty that speak to questing, doubting souls.

Let us now turn briefly to several of his symphonies. The introduction to the First Symphony represents the awakening of nature at early dawn to spring without end. One of the important motifs is the cuckoo call.

The second movement is a scherzo-waltz *ländler* so typical of Viennese music. Mahler had absorbed much of Austrian popular song and dance.

The third movement is an ironic funeral march with the simple French children's song, "Frère Jacques." A funeral march was one of Mahler's favorite symbols, and it expressed his obsession with death. Most all of his symphonies have marches. He also used chorales to create the atmosphere of religious faith.

In Mahler's first four symphonies he gave out detailed programs. Words were important in his creative process. Later he suppressed these when the critics accused him of not being able to write absolute music. In the First, Second, Third, and Fourth Symphonies Mahler used music from his *Wunderhorn* cycle (Youth's Magic Horn). These symphonies, like Beethoven's Ninth, employ the human voice.

The Second Symphony is his famous *Resurrection*. In Mahler's own program notes are the following observations: "I have called the first movement 'funeral rites.' . . . it is the hero from my Symphony No. 1 whom I am laying in his grave. And the question asked of him is, 'To what purpose have you lived? What next? What is life and what is death? Is it all a hollow dream?'"

Second movement—"Remembering the past . . . a ray of sunshine, pure and unspoiled, from the hero's life."

Third movement—"When you awaken from the wistful dream of the second movement . . . life appears senseless . . . and like a dreadful nightmare."

Fourth movement—"The stirring voice of simple faith reaches our ear; I am of God and will go back to God."

Fifth movement—"The voice in the desert sounds: the end of all life has come. . . . The earth trembles, the graves are opening, the dead rise and march past in endless procession. The great and the small of this earth— kings and beggars . . . the trumpets call—in the midst of a horrible silence we seem to hear a distant nightingale . . . a choir of saints sing, 'Resurrection'—And the glory of God appears . . . and lo and behold! There is no judgment. . . . An overwhelming Love shines. We know and are."

While Mahler was a great composer and conductor and his music beautiful, it is nevertheless foolish to get one's doctrine from someone who never found peace in his life. What Mahler is expressing in the Second Symphony is humanism and high Romanticism, certainly not the truth expressed in the Scriptures. There will indeed be a final judgment, and Christ Himself will be the judge. There will be condemnation for those who have rejected the Savior and forgiveness for all who have believed in Him during this life.

In the Eighth Symphony Mahler reverts to the programmatic and philosophically motivated symphonies of his early period. Mahler had the idea of an infinite, cosmic music. But unable to understand the infinite, personal God as revealed to us in Christ Jesus, he leaped into a mystical, irrational, and humanistic religion that ends in emptiness and despair. Mahler strove for the monumental, but he floundered in this gigantic work.

One is aware that Mahler tried to do too much. His excesses can be heard in the exhaustive tension in some of his music and in the repetitions. His symphonies are long, and they lack unity. They all begin to sound alike, and many times the composer finds it difficult to bring the music to a close. But having said that, there are many passages of overwhelming beauty.

Mahler the symphonist cannot be separated from Mahler the song composer. He was at his best when writing for the voice. For Mahler, music was a vision, intoxication, and fulfillment—"a mysterious language from beyond." His best-known work and masterpiece, which he never heard performed, is *Das Lied von der Erde* (The Song of the Earth). It is a song cycle for solo voices and orchestra. Mahler seeks to describe a problem fundamental to all human beings—the reality of loneliness and death. In the music one hears the dualism of joy and despair, and one feels the fierce clinging to the beauty of earthly things, but mingled with resignation. It is a work that is solitary and unique, an expression of an artist upon whom darkness has fallen.

The haunting motif of the first movement is "Dark is life, dark is death." The last movement may be regarded as Mahler's farewell to life. He wrote *The Song of the Earth* soon after his physician had told him he had a fatal heart ailment. It contains some of the saddest music ever written. The bitter poignancy of the contralto's last word, *"ewig"* (everlasting), is unforgettable. Bruno Walter says that most people of his time were able to make some kind of peace between themselves and the universe. Mahler never could, just as fewer and fewer people can today. Mahler questioned the whole basis of his existence, never really finding an answer to the tormenting question, "For what?" But God has given us sufficient evidence in the Bible and in the person of the Lord Jesus Christ and through the glory and wonder of His creation that our lives do have significance now and forever. No one has to go through life yearning for faith. Each person who places his or her hope in Christ can echo the truthful words of Paul: "For I know whom I have believed, and am persuaded that he is able to keep that which I have committed unto him against that day" (2 Tim. 1:12).

Recommended Reading

Mahler, Alma. *Gustav Mahler: Memories and Letters.* New York: The Viking Press, 1946.

Redlich, H. F. *Bruckner and Mahler.* London: J. M. Dent, 1955.

Recommended Listening

Mahler: *Kindertotenlieder* (Songs on the Death of Children)
  Des Knaben Wunderhorn (Youth's Magic Horn)
  Das Lied von der Erde (The Song of the Earth)
  Lieder eines Fahrenden Gesellen (Songs of a Wayfarer)
  Nine symphonies
Bruckner: Symphony No. 9
  Te Deum

CHAPTER 26

Claude Achille Debussy
1862-1918

A lost soul under a sky full of stars.
                                        Oscar Thompson

*E*verything he does is wrong," said one of his teachers, "but he is wrong in a talented way." Claude Debussy went to the Paris Conservatory and studied there for eleven contention-filled years, questioning and breaking away from all the rules of the past. "Why must dissonant chords always be resolved?" Debussy asked, and when he was not given a satisfactory answer, he began to experiment with chromaticism, modal technique, the whole tone and pentatonic scales, the avoiding of a definite key, and using chords that tended to produce vagueness of tonality. With his fastidious ear he had a natural affinity for the exotic and old as well as the most avant-garde. He acquired a reputation as an iconoclast, violating all rules, and it is not surprising that some years later the twentieth-century revolution in music began in France with Claude Debussy.

One of his professors at the conservatory inquired, "What rules do you observe?"

Debussy answered, "None—only my own pleasure!"

"That's all very well," came the reply, "provided you're a genius." They soon began to suspect that he was.

One critic said of Debussy, "It is the beginning of the twentieth-century breakup of music." In fact, everything in Western music has been called into question since 1910, and the two contemporary composers involved were Debussy and Schoenberg, both rejecting what they considered "the straitjacket" of tonality. Oscar Thompson says that Debussy's music was the determining factor in the music of at least the first third of the twentieth century. Other critics say that Debussy led straight to Webern.

Claude Debussy was born near Paris of a middle-class family. His father ran a not-very-successful china shop. It makes one think of the painter Renoir, who worked in a china factory and was enchanted with color. A born rebel, Debussy attended no formal school. But because he played the piano well, he came to the attention of a wealthy woman who had been a pupil of Chopin. She taught him for three years without pay, so carefully that Debussy entered the Paris Conservatory in 1873 when he was eleven years old.

The years at the conservatory were stormy because of his marked originality, and his youth was spent in unusual circumstances, even for a talented musician. Unexpectedly, at eighteen, while still living with his parents in a poor suburb of Paris and attending the conservatory in the daytime, he came under the patronage of Madame Nadejda von Meck of Russia, the beloved friend of Tchaikovsky.

Madame von Meck, an extremely wealthy widow, engaged Debussy to play duets with her and her children. In the long summer vacations he traveled with the family to their palatial residences in Europe to teach the children music. Through Madame von Meck, Debussy's musical horizons suddenly widened. While they were in Venice, he met Wagner and immediately fell under the spell of *Tristan and Isolde.*

Debussy was with the von Mecks for several summers. In Russia he was influenced by the music of Mussorgsky and Borodin. A remarkable sight-reader, Debussy was especially entreated to play Tchaikovsky's music. Becoming accustomed to luxurious living as a youth had an unhealthy influence on Debussy. Later he delighted in confessing his fondness for every kind of indulgence. He had aristocratic tastes and especially liked caviar.

In Paris around this time (he was nineteen), Debussy fell in love with a singer, Blanche Vasnier, the young wife of a well-known Parisian architect. She inspired many of his early compositions. When he was twenty-two, Debussy won the Grand Prix de Rome, the highest award a French composer can achieve. He received the prize because of his composition, a cantata, *The Prodigal Child.* He went to Rome intending to stay three years in the Villa Medici to pursue his creative work, but he hated being there. His only memorable experience in Rome was hearing Liszt play for the last time in his life at the Villa Medici. Before returning to France, he made a long pilgrimage to Sant' Agata and chatted with Verdi as the beloved Italian composer planted vegetables with the assistance of a small boy. It was in Rome that he composed the orchestral piece *Printemps* (Springtime), inspired by Botticelli's *Primavera.*

After two years Debussy returned to Paris—to Blanche and several other women. So that I will not have to repeat a number of unpleasant stories, it is enough to say that Debussy lived a life of extreme intemperance. One of his mistresses, "Gaby of the green eyes" (his favorite color), threatened suicide; his first wife, Lily, a dressmaker, shot herself, though not fatally, and Debussy thought of killing himself too. Instead, he divorced Lily and married Emma Bardac, the mother of his illegitimate daughter. This last marriage seemed to succeed, although Debussy was never out of financial trouble because of his gourmet tastes. For his daughter Chouchou he later wrote the piano suite *The Children's Corner* and the ballet for children *The Toy Box*.

Debussy has been described by numerous epithets—unsociable, amorous, catlike, sensual, hedonistic, voluptuous, rebellious. He was supremely indifferent to the opinions of others. Unattractive physically, he had a large forehead that gave him an unbalanced appearance. He cared little for people, preferring cats to human beings. He had a sullen "I-don't-care" attitude toward life. Debussy thought only of himself and was incapable of making any sacrifice. A convinced atheist, he once said, "I have made a religion out of mysterious nature." He was lazy about everything but his music.

On his return to Paris, he began to frequent salons where the avant-garde gathered. At Stephane Mallarmé's home he met some of the leading Impressionist and Symbolist painters. Debussy was a product of the movement called Symbolism, and he much preferred this term to Impressionism. A key to the Symbolists were the writings of Edgar Allan Poe. Baudelaire had translated and introduced Poe and his strange, horror-filled, hallucinated world to the French. The refined poetry of Verlaine, Baudelaire, and Mallarmé suggested to Debussy a new type of music—a music that seems to hint rather than to state, music that is vague, with tonal colors taking the place of logical development. Debussy thought of music as an expressive or suggestive medium. Romain Rolland called him "this great painter of dreams."

In the Exposition of 1889 Debussy heard some musicians from the Far East perform, and he was fascinated by their intricate percussive rhythms and bewitching instrumental colors. They seemed to open a new world of sonority for him. Debussy felt closer to poets and painters than to other musicians. He especially liked Whistler. There was scarcely any Western music that he liked. He showed very little sympathy for or interest in what other musicians were creating.

In 1894, when he was thirty-two, he completed his first major orchestral work, *Prelude to the Afternoon of a Faun,* and here his style was fully formed. In this tone poem inspired by Mallarmé, a sensuous, enchanted world seems to rise before us, but far off and misty. It evokes the warmth of a summer day. With its color, mood, and harmonic opulence, it is a late offshoot of Romanticism, actually a bridge between Classical and twentieth-century concepts of tonality. In this beautiful composition we are listening to one of the great inventors in the history of music. Though not loud music, in a sense it broke sound barriers because it was unlike any music of the past. It is fragmented, with shimmering vibrations, and the emphasis is on individual voices rather than the massive effects of Wagner. There are no superfluous notes in the scores of Debussy.

He had his years of being under the spell of Wagner. A fellow composer, Erik Satie, urged Debussy to return to simplicity and clarity, expressing the French spirit in concise, luminous pieces, not to imitate the overblown Wagnerian forms. Satie was an early Dadaist, and his music is anti-Romantic. After Debussy freed himself from the Wagnerian influence, he fought Wagner the rest of his life. As Thompson shows, Debussy once said, "Wagner has led music astray into sterile and pernicious paths. Already for Beethoven the art of development consists in repetition, in the incessant restatement of identical themes; and Wagner has exaggerated this procedure to the point of caricature."

In 1900 the *Three Nocturnes*—*Nuages* (Clouds), *Fêtes* (Festivals) and *Sirènes* (Sirens)—were performed with great success. The most obvious thing about these nocturnes is their relationship to Impressionist painting. It is as if the "sick room" of Romanticism had opened into a garden filled with flowers. Debussy may have borrowed the names from Whistler. Specifically, *Nuages* has been likened to Monet, *Fetes* to Renoir, and *Sirènes* to Turner. As contrasting moods and evocations of light effects, these nocturnes are unique in music.

The turning point in Debussy's career came in 1902 with the premiere of his opera *Pelléas and Mélisande*, with words by Maeterlinck. It is the most important opera that Impressionism produced and is absolutely original, unlike any other opera. There is a flow of inner life in *Pelléas and Mélisande*, and Debussy forces us to listen less with our minds and more with our nerves. Debussy called it the "old and sad tale of the woods." The opera stirred up controversy because of its unconventional style and mysterious atmosphere. Debussy and the librettist declared that they were haunted in the work by the terrifying nightmare tale of Edgar Allen Poe's "The Fall of the House of Usher." For years Debussy worked on two operas, *The Devil in the Belfry* and *The Fall of the House of Usher* (both stories by Poe), but for various reasons neither was completed. In *The Devil in the Belfry* Debussy was going to have the Devil whistle rather than sing.

With his second wife, Emma Bardac, who had divorced her banker husband, Debussy fled to Eastbourne, England, in 1905 to seek refuge from the gossip and scandal they had stirred up in Paris. These troubles did not interfere with Debussy's creativity. The fifteen years following *Pelléas and Mélisande* were productive ones for the composer.

La Mer (The Sea), written in 1905, is a masterpiece. This symphonic work presents three aspects of the sea—"The Sea from Dawn Until Noon," "Sport of the Waves," and "Dialogue of the Wind and the Sea." It is a world of sheer fantasy—the very essence of the sea, yet vague and mysterious. The sound is transparent and airy. The orchestration is full of surprises and shattering climaxes, and Debussy exhibits rare strength and energy. *La Mer* reminds one of what Mallarmé said: "I think there should be nothing but illusion." Debussy never tells a story; he gives an impression. He had a passion for the sea. His father had wanted him to be a sailor, but Debussy wanted to be a painter. In *La Mer* we hear a "musical painting." Some composers are imitative followers of others and lack a unique, distinctive style, but not Debussy. He is one of the most original of all composers. One quickly learns to recognize the works of this most intimate, personal musician.

Debussy wrote some exquisite songs, including "La Chevelure" (Tresses) in the set *Chansons de Bilitis* with words by his friend Pierre Louÿs. Among the chamber works, Debussy's Quartet in G Minor is one of the greatest quartets written by a Frenchman.

In 1912 Debussy wrote *Images* for orchestra, which includes "Iberia," one of the most famous interpretations of Spain. Debussy is concerned with sights, sounds, and a feeling for the Spanish dance. Here the objective universe has disintegrated into a world of dream and illusion, of mist and shadows. In the second movement, a tender night song called "Perfumes of the Night," we have veiled, languid sounds. This slow movement is one of Debussy's finest.

In his solo flute piece "Syrinx" (Panpipes), also written in 1912, many features of Debussy's style occur in a short piece. Here there is sound for sound's sake rather than stress on content. It is full of wavering uncertainty, and intricate rhythms tend to free the music from the bar line. There is a sense of hesitation and vagueness. Debussy opened up new regions of sound and functionless harmony. He tends to write in patterns rather than with a sense of direction. There is fragmentation and a feeling of disintegration; yet the music is still beautiful.

The piano was Debussy's favorite instrument, and here he achieved his most sensitive speech. Three composers have been essential to piano music—Beethoven, Chopin, and Debussy. The aim of Debussy was to liberate the piano from its percussive sound. He said, "Beethoven definitely wrote badly for the piano." Debussy wanted the piano to sound like an instrument without hammers. Even though there is a nebulous quality in his piano pieces, Debussy had a superb command of compositional technique. He detested variations and obvious devices of formal development. He once said, "I think it is altogether disastrous to repeat oneself."

One of his best-known pieces is "Claire de Lune" from the *Suite Bergamasque*. His glittering preludes for piano are pieces with a perfect sense of proportion for small things. "Reflections in the Water" (from *Images*) is a lovely piece written in excellent taste that reminds one of Monet, who lived in a houseboat so he could paint the water and light at different hours of the day. Someone has remarked that in Debussy's music there is always the sound and movement of water.

One learns to love the cool pastel colors of Debussy. But there is a sadness because one hears in the compositions of Debussy and sees in Monet's paintings the adoring pantheist loving creation rather than the Creator.

Another famous water piece is Maurice Ravel's *Jeux d'eau* (Fountains) with its use of the pentatonic scale. It was written before any of Debussy's important piano compositions and proves that Ravel was far less indebted to Debussy than some would claim.

Debussy acted as a music critic for several periodicals to help out financially at times. Often he wrote under the pseudonym M. Croche, and he was considered one of the wittiest critics of the century. His last years were less productive because of cancer, yet he always got back to music. It was there that he really lived his life. "I have no hobbies," he explained. "They never taught me anything but music." I am certain his professors at the conservatory were impressed to hear that the unteachable Debussy learned something from them.

In his last works he turned to the heritage of the French Enlightenment composers Rameau and Couperin, and his style became more austere. His sonatas for cello and piano and for violin and piano are almost Neoclassical. He became more depressed as his illness weakened him. In one of Debussy's last letters he wrote, "I am a poor traveler waiting for a train that will never come anymore." During the bombardment of Paris in March 1918 Debussy died. The funeral procession passed through deserted streets while his beloved city was being bombarded by enemy shells. His daughter Chouchou, whom he loved dearly, died one year later at the age of fourteen.

Debussy adhered to no religion, although he was very superstitious. Lockspeiser says, "His atheism was sensual and instinctive. Quite simply he experienced no desire for a religion." He wrote no sacred music. Debussy once said, "We have not the simple faith of other days."

I personally appreciate the music of Debussy—as does anyone who loves what is beautiful. But it makes me sad when I think of his life and the influence he has had on the musicians who have followed him. We must not forget the message of Debussy's music: humanism disintegrating into fragments and despair.

Recommended Reading

Lockspeiser, Edward. *Debussy*. New York: McGraw Hill, 1972.

Thompson, Oscar. *Debussy: Man and Artist*. New York: Tudor Publishing Co., 1940.

Recommended Listening

Chansons de Bilitis
Children's Corner Suite
Danses Sacrée et Profane
Ibéria
Images pour Piano (Books 1 and 2)
La Mer
Nocturnes
Pelléas et Mélisande
The Afternoon of a Faun
Preludes for Piano (Books 1 and 2)
Quartet in G Minor

CHAPTER 27

Frederick Delius
1862-1934

No matter what the motive, withdrawal from the world, if even for a brief period, has usually been the first step that a man has taken on the road to high endeavor.

Eric Fenby

A blind cellist once said, "Only the music of Delius can convey to me some idea what it must be like to see a glowing sunset." As one of Delius's friends said, "Delius was on the whole a watercolorist of music, not a filler of canvasses with oil."

Frederick Delius, who was to become one of the most poetic and artistic of composers, had an adventurous, often dissipated, troubled life. He was a sickly child, but he grew into a vigorous, lively, and handsome young man. He was one of twelve children.

Delius's father, a proud, unbending individual, was a successful German manufacturer who made a fortune in the wool business. He became a British subject in 1860 and settled in Bradford, England, where Delius was born. Even though his father appreciated music and invited musicians to perform in their home, he was indignant to think that his son wanted to devote his life to what he regarded "a pleasant pastime" with little possibility of earning money. Sir Thomas Beecham, in an attempt to defend Delius's father and the hard stand he took against his son becoming a musician, says, "Neither he nor anyone else in his circle had the slightest idea that Frederick had in him a spark of original talent as a composer."

Delius's mother, also proud and unbending, gave him no encouragement either. Even after their son had become a famous composer, his parents never forgave him for choosing to be a musician, and they refused ever to hear one note of his music.

Delius had no choice but to attend the International College to learn how to work in an office, and when he was nineteen, he entered the family business. He was not exactly an asset in the office and soon was transferred to Germany. There he spent the greater part of his time taking violin lessons, practicing, and going to concerts. In 1882 he was moved up to Sweden. At first he seemed to be doing well, and orders came in to the Bradford office from the north. But then Delius discovered the beautiful Swedish countryside and the Norwegian mountains and fjords . . . and so it went.

In 1884 after a violent family scene, Frederick, at the age of twenty-one, sailed for Florida where he was supposed to superintend an orange grove. Delius was fascinated by the music he heard while sitting on the porch of his cottage on warm summer nights near the bank of the St. Johns River. Anything natural and unspoiled appealed to him, and he was amazed at the exotic beauty around him. Years later he said, "Hearing the Negroes singing in such Romantic surroundings; it was then and there that I first felt the urge to express myself in music."

One day when he was in Jacksonville, he went into a music store, and finding a piano in a back room, he sat down and began to improvise. Another visitor in the store was struck by the uncommon sounds coming from the back of the shop and introduced himself. Delius was delighted to meet another musician. His new friend was Thomas F. Ward, an organist and gifted teacher who had come south for his health. Years later Delius declared that the only teaching of any real value he ever received was from Ward. The organist must have enjoyed teaching him the next six months, as Delius was enthusiastic and hungry for musical knowledge. Among many things, Ward taught Delius counterpoint, fugue, and good work habits. The one thing that saddened the teacher was his pupil's strong rejection of Christianity.

Within a year Delius had had enough of managing the orange grove—by now in a ruinous state—and when a brother came to see him, he was glad to turn over the responsibility to him. After a short stay in Danville, Virginia, as a music teacher at the Roanoke Female College where he made his only appearance as a soloist in Mendelssohn's Violin Concerto, his father finally agreed to finance his musical study in Leipzig. His parents were amazed to learn that Frederick had been heralded as a celebrity in Danville and had also earned money teaching music. They thought that if he had a European diploma, he could return to America and "do even better."

Delius felt that he learned little in Leipzig, but there he met Edvard Grieg, who was a tremendous help and encouragement to him in his musical understanding. Grieg, who became Delius's friend and believed he had talent, met the elder Delius on a trip to England. Even though the wool merchant was not convinced his son would amount to anything, Grieg interceded for the composer, and the father refrained from cutting off his allowance. Delius was not a good student, but finally he received his diploma because of the compositions he wrote.

After graduation he moved to Paris and lived there for over eight years with frequent long visits to Norway that inspired some of his most beautiful music. He had a generous uncle in Paris who also helped him financially. During one of his stays in Norway, he was aimlessly looking over the books in the library of a friend when he came across a copy of Nietzsche's *Thus Spake Zarathustra*. Even as a boy, Delius was at heart a pagan, and finding this book was one of the most important events in his life. As Eric Fenby says, "Nor did he rest content until he had read every work of Nietzsche that he could lay his hands on, and the poison entered into his soul."

In his Parisian period Delius associated mainly with writers and painters. Two of his close friends were Strindberg the playwright and Edvard Munch the painter—as one critic commented, "two super-egoists like himself." Another friend was Alfred Sisley, the Impressionist painter. Both Delius and Sisley were of English origin and the sons of prosperous industrialists. Delius in a real sense may be thought of as the Sisley of music. They were both "painters" of water and light, and both men disliked excess in their artistic expression. Gauguin was also a friend of Delius. After Delius's uncle died and left him a legacy, he bought Gauguin's now-famous painting *Nevermore* (he was later forced to sell it).

It was in Paris that Delius met his future wife, Jelka Rosen. Jelka was a gifted young painter with a Danish-Jewish background. She also loved music, poetry, and the philosophy of Nietzsche. He found her a stimulating companion, but that was all at the time.

The years Delius spent in Paris were strange. He had a period when he showed a decided preference for the "low life." Dressed in shabby clothes, he frequented all sorts of dubious quarters, the morgue included. He did work at his music on and off, hardly ever writing in the daytime, but he destroyed a considerable amount of it. Then for a while he moved into the aristocratic "high life." Speedily he became a success, particularly among the women because he was handsome and cosmopolitan. One of his talents that won him friends was making horoscopes.

It is not surprising that he tired of this life and one day abruptly returned to Florida—ostensibly "to attend to his orange grove," but mainly to try and find a young black woman to whom he had become attached many years before. His search proved futile. He returned to France, and shortly after turning up unannounced on Jelka's doorstep, they were married.

In the meantime Jelka and another artist, Ida Gerhardi, with the help of Jelka's mother, had purchased a charming old house in the village of Grez-sur-Loing on the southern border of the Fontainbleau Forest. Close to the garden, which is bordered by huge trees and slopes leading gently down to the river, stands an old bridge that has been the subject for many well-known paintings by such artists as Corot, Sisley, Edvard Munch, and Carl Larsson. Larsson was fascinated with Grez. The studies he made there were the first to bring him fame and now are in the National Museum at Stockholm.

Grez-sur-Loing, which is about forty miles from Paris, is still a charming old village with narrow streets and houses all wearing the color of antiquity. Not too long ago we had the privilege of visiting Delius's two-storied home. The present owner, Madame D'Aubigné, was very gracious. She showed us Delius's music room and even took time to walk with us in the garden down to the Loing River where Delius derived much inspiration for his music. The composition *In a Summer Garden* captures the beauty and tranquillity of this sun-drenched, riverside garden. It is one of Delius's small masterpieces.

Delius lived over thirty-five years in Grez, from 1897 until his death in 1934. After he settled in Grez, he seldom heard or thought about any music but his own. Delius, the poet always, was able to recollect emotion in tranquillity. Here he lived a very sheltered existence that revolved wholly around his work. Jelka was the ideal wife for him. As Fenby observed, "Her name deserves a very prominent place on the scroll of those who have given themselves unstintingly for others." Had Delius not married Jelka, we might never have heard of him, because he was not a man who knew how to organize his life. Jelka did it for him because she believed in his genius, and she loved him.

It was never easy to be in the company of Delius, even in the early years at Grez, because of his aloofness, his indifference to whether he hurt the feelings of people or not, his colossal egotism, his contempt for "ordinary" village people, his unbearable selfishness, and his inability to be interested in anything other than his music. He did enjoy a good table, and there was always a well-stocked wine cellar in the Delius home.

It took many years, but finally Delius's works aroused interest in Germany and later in England. Sir Thomas Beecham, who was responsible for introducing the music of Delius to the English people and who was a great interpreter of his works, was amazed when he first met Delius because he looked so unlike an artist. "He must be a cardinal," thought Beecham upon the first meeting. Delius did have an air of sober elegance, shrewdness, and fastidiousness one associates with high-ranking ecclesiastics.

His life became more difficult and his appearance even more austere as he approached the age of sixty. He fell victim to blindness and creeping paralysis because of syphilis, which he had contracted as a young man. The last twelve years of his life were spent as an invalid. After he lost the use of his hands, he resumed composing when an unusual young man came to be his amanuensis. Eric Fenby has written a very readable book about his experiences in Grez entitled *Delius As I Knew Him*.

Delius the man (like Wagner) is difficult to like, but not his music. Those who respond to the magic of his sound find it some of the most beautiful ever written. He was a composer of instinct rather than intellect. His was a "still, small voice," but an absolutely unique one. The music of Delius is suffused with rapture. It is fluid, like light and water. He was a sensitive nature poet, and his music has the emotional quality we associate with British poetry. Delius was a watercolorist using notes instead of paint. Because he was an ardent lover of that which is beautiful in nature, we not only hear his music, but it is as if we are seeing Impressionistic paintings of hills, trees, birds, sunrises, and sunsets.

Many critics think the compositions of Delius are suggestive of England, but Eric Fenby felt that the mellow French countryside near Grez-sur-Loing and Delius's own garden, as well as what he had heard and seen in Florida and Norway in his earlier years, were the true source of his inspiration. In speaking about composition, Delius said, "You can't teach a young musician to compose anymore than you can teach a delicate plant how to grow, but you can guide him a little by putting a stick in there. . . . How can music ever be a mere intellectual speculation or a series of curious combinations of sound that can be classified like the articles in a grocer's shop? Music is an outburst of the soul."

The development of Delius as a composer was unusually slow. By the age of forty-one he had written five operas, six large works for orchestra, several suites, a number of short pieces, and about fifty songs, and of this output only a few of the songs had been published.

One of his earliest compositions was *Over the Hills and Far Away*. Delius, having rejected the God of history, found his inspiration in nature. His early works display a certain vigor and freshness, but as he grew older, his attempts at gaiety have an air of sadness. His later efforts possess an increasing atmosphere of despair and melancholy, which have a deep effect on the sensitive listener.

He dedicated his orchestral suite *Florida* to the people of Florida. He first arranged to have it performed when he was a student in Leipzig and paid the members of the orchestra by treating them to a barrel of beer.

Delius's Piano Concerto shows the influence of Grieg. Delius tended to begin his works softly, but not in this composition. The one-movement concerto has a forte opening. It is strong, rhapsodic music. There are moments in the music of Delius that are meandering and dull, and one is often aware of his lack of formal training. The best of music is more than "an outburst of the soul."

In 1902 he wrote *Appalachia*. It refers to North America and especially the Mississippi River. The Civil War had ended only nineteen years before Delius went to Florida, and he saw some of the tragedy of the Reconstruction Era. In *Appalachia* Delius uses variations on an old slave song, "No Trouble in That Land Where I'm Bound." The second tune he uses is "Oh, Honey, I'm Goin' Down the River in the Morning." It is a song of separation and heartbreak. "Goin' down the river" meant to be sold and separated from one's family.

In *Sea Drift* (1904) Delius uses a text from Walt Whitman's *Leaves of Grass*. It is a setting of the middle section of the poem, "Out of the Cradle Endlessly Rocking." The music evokes the surge of the sea, which symbolizes the intensity of love and longing—the composer's real theme. The story is of two birds and their nest of eggs hidden in a briar close to the seashore.

The she-bird disappears. The he-bird, watching the nest, continues looking out at the sea, waiting in vain for her return.

His most outstanding opera is *A Village Romeo and Juliet*. The orchestral interlude "A Walk to the Paradise Garden" is exquisite. One notices the Wagnerian influence of the *Tristan and Isolde* chord at the end.

One of Delius's compositions, *A Song Before Sunrise*, captures in a sweeping cadence the exhilaration and freshness of an early morning in the Swiss Alps.

Brigg Fair (1907) is one of Delius's most widely performed works. It is an English rhapsody in the form of variations on a popular tune. It was first performed in Basel, Switzerland. Some critics say that after *Brigg Fair* Delius only repeated himself. It may be true, but he bears repetition.

One of the most exquisite pieces ever written about the springtime is his composition *On Hearing the First Cuckoo in Spring*. It is for a small orchestra and probably was inspired by the beautiful countryside of Norway, which Delius loved. As Sir Thomas Beecham says, "There is a world of sorrow in one little song."

Before mentioning the composition *A Mass of Life*, with words from Nietzsche's *Thus Spake Zarathustra*, it would be helpful to give some background information about the German philosopher Friedrich Nietzsche. His father was a Lutheran minister, and behind each of his parents was a line of clergymen. Nietzsche's father died when he was five, and the delicate, brilliant child was raised in a household of adoring women who did not equip the boy for the shocks of the real world outside. At the university he quickly succumbed to the philosophy of Schopenhauer, and within a few years Nietzsche had developed the doctrine of the "superman." But because he, like Schopenhauer, worked out his philosophy without a true base and reference point, after some years he learned that his new values did not satisfy him. He became more and more cynical. He thought of himself as a nihilist, but he found out that it is nearly impossible to live wholly negatively. He suffered dreadfully in his life. He had syphilis, became a drug addict, and at the age of forty-five lost his reason. The tragedy is that already he had put into print the ideas he no longer believed in.

Delius wholeheartedly adopted Nietzsche's philosophy as his gospel, and *A Mass of Life* not only gives insight into Nietzsche's thinking but also Delius's. It is loud, unattractive music. Delius often does not write well for the voice. But as in much of his work, there are the moments of beauty. Some consider it the climax of his achievement, although it is less often performed than his smaller orchestral pieces.

A Mass of Life is an attack upon Christian doctrine and the Christian way of life as Nietzsche and Delius saw it. They both wanted to correct what they called the "slave morality" of Christianity. Their great emphasis was upon will, not bowing to anyone, and living and dying fearlessly though death be total extinction.

Death, when it came to Delius, was terrible, and within a few months his steadfast wife was dead too.

In speaking about Delius, Eric Fenby observes, "Given those great natural musical gifts and that nature of his, so full of feeling, and which at its finest inclined to that exalted end of man which is contemplation, there is no knowing to what sublime heights he would have risen had he chosen to look upwards to God instead of downwards to man!"

When we drive over the St. Bernard pass to Italy, often we listen to the music of Delius, which heightens the beauty of the world we see around us. But then we are glad to turn to Bach and Handel who fill our hearts with wonder, not only at all the marvel and mystery of our world, but at the God of all creation. When one believes the Scriptures, there is a true reason for hope and rejoicing. Christians are not victims of a "slave morality." They bow down willingly before the everlasting God, "who at sundry times and in diverse manners spoke in time past unto the fathers by the prophets, [and] hath in these last days spoken unto us by his Son, whom he hath appointed heir of all things, by whom also he made the worlds" (Heb. 1:1-2).

Recommended Reading

Beecham, Sir Thomas. *Frederick Delius*. London: Hutchinson, 1960.

Fenby, Eric. *Delius As I Knew Him*. London: Icon Books, 1966.

Jefferson, Alan. *Delius*. London: J. M. Dent, 1972.

Recommended Listening

Appalachia
Brigg Fair
Concerto in C Minor for Piano
In a Summer Garden
On Hearing the First Cuckoo in Spring
Over the Hills and Far Away
Sea Drift
Song Before Sunrise
Summer Evening
"Walk to the Paradise Garden"
Florida Suite

CHAPTER 28

Richard Strauss
1864-1949

Thirty years ago I was regarded as a rebel. I have lived long enough to find myself a classic.

Richard Strauss

Richard Strauss was the most famous of the post-Romantic German composers and one of the great figures of his time. He bears no relationship to the Johann Strauss family of Vienna. He was born in Munich. His mother was the daughter of the city's wealthiest beer-maker. His father, Franz, was an outstanding horn-player and had performed in the world premieres of Wagner's *Tristan and Isolde* and *Die Meistersinger.*

Franz Strauss was always getting into fights with Wagner and von Bülow because he hated the horn parts of Wagner's operas, but Wagner put up with him because he played so beautifully. Richard Strauss inherited his father's musical instinct. Richard was "an alarming child prodigy from the age of five" and was composing by the age of six. Being strongly anti-Wagner, his father taught Strauss in a strictly Classical tradition.

Von Bülow, an outstanding conductor whose wife, Cosima, left him and married Wagner, was a great help in Strauss's youth, taking him as his assistant conductor at age twenty-one and urging him to conduct and compose. In 1888 at the age of twenty-four, Strauss composed one of his most successful orchestral works, *Don Juan,* heroic music and superbly orchestrated.

This philosophical symphonic tone poem is about a superman broken by his own excesses in search of the ideal woman. He rejects order and tries to destroy it, but he is destroyed by it. He loves women, so he must possess them or degrade them. The music of *Don Juan* is a logical successor of Wagner and Liszt. In the Romantic generation both *Don Juan* and *Faust* had great appeal. Liszt, who wrote the *Faust* Symphony, originated the tone poem.

Don Juan was first performed in 1889, and Strauss became famous overnight. The premiere took place in the remarkable German city Weimar, called the "Ilm Athens" because it was located on the Ilm River. Strauss was a conductor here for almost five years, and during this time he married the singer Pauline de Ahne. She was the daughter of a general and gradually came to act like one herself.

Weimar was a city of the highest culture. Bach had been an organist there where his three famous composer sons were born. It was also the home of Goethe, Schiller, and Liszt. Liszt conducted the successful world premiere of *Lohengrin,* which was the turning point of Wagner's career. The granddaughter of Catherine the Great, Maria Pavlovna, lived in Weimar and was a generous patron of the arts.

The influence of Alexander Ritter on Richard Strauss was revolutionary. "Your future lies in the symphonic poem," Ritter said to Strauss, "in the poetic and expressive in music as exemplified in the works of Berlioz, Liszt, and Wagner. That is the music of the future, and that is the line I urge you to follow."

Strauss was also strongly influenced by Berlioz, the greatest orchestral innovator in musical history. Berlioz's *Symphonie Fantastique* is a candid exposition of his emotional life. Berlioz was a man of fantastic imagination and passion, and in times of deep disappointment, he found release in expressing emotion in music—the writing of his own programmatic music.

Sometimes Richard Strauss was called Richard III by von Bülow because, in his opinion, after Richard Wagner there could be no Richard II. Strauss had tremendous reverence for Wagner. Usually, Strauss conducted sitting down; but he stood when conducting a work by Wagner. Throughout Strauss's life Wagner's *Tristan and Isolde* and Mozart's *Cosi fan tutte* remained his favorite operas. Wagner had an enormous influence on musicians after him, including Mahler and Schoenberg, but not Strauss whose influence was minimal on twentieth-century music.

Leaving Weimar, Strauss, at the age of thirty, returned to Munich as co-conductor of the Munich Symphony. A great conductor and composer, he began directing orchestras in many important cities, often accompanied by his wife, who succeeded in alienating many of Strauss's acquaintances. He was forever ready to champion the unfamiliar and the new.

As a wedding tribute to his wife, Pauline, he gave her a very special gift—two of his greatest songs, "Cäcilie" and "Morgen." In "Morgen" one can "see" as well as feel the love of two people walking hand in hand along the seashore.

Probably Strauss's most important tone poem is *The Merry Pranks of Till Eulenspiegel* (Till Owl Glass), a mirthful musical tale in rondo form with its sparkling wit revealing Strauss's sense of humor. Writing at the top of his voice (he loved the hubbub of the orchestra), he produced a complicated score, brilliantly orchestrated, that describes the struggle of the eternal rebel against bourgeois respectability and against his loneliness as an outsider. Till is a practical joker making fun of pompous people, but he is hanged because they make the laws. *Till Eulenspiegel* is a heartwarming and happy masterpiece.

Other tone poems by Strauss are *Death and Transfiguration, Don Quixote, A Hero's Life,* and his *Alpine Symphony,* all with beautiful moments and grandiose orchestral effects. *Also Sprach Zarathustra* (1896) is Strauss's tribute to Nietzsche (1844-1900), of whom he was a passionate admirer. Strauss was a free-thinker, more at home in the atmosphere of wit or depravity and evil.

Nietzsche's theme is the evolution of humanity and the theory of superman. For him God is dead. And he completely rejected Christianity, believing that it teaches man how to die but not how to live. Nietzsche went insane in 1889. Among the many influenced by him were Wagner, Hitler, Delius, and many others. Nietzsche was a brilliant philosopher but very destructive, with imagination, not truth, the stronger. May we not take advice from those who could destroy us.

Richard Strauss was a good, solid German happily married with no scandal in his private life. He was henpecked by his wife, Pauline, who was a singer, strong and grasping, but he was truly devoted to her and put up with her tantrums. She would often scream, "Richard, go compose!" She sang his songs accompanied by him and did much to popularize them. Strauss was one of the outstanding *lied* composers, along with Schubert, Schumann, Brahms, and Wolf. Some of his early songs were genuine masterpieces.

Completely professional, he found work to be his greatest pleasure. He was totally obsessed by his art, claiming to think in terms of music at all times. With a passion for making music and money, he drove a hard bargain and liked the sound of crisp bills. Once when returning from conducting, his young son met him at the station and said, "Papa, how much did you get for the rehearsal?" Strauss, weeping tears of joy, enfolded the boy in his arms. "Now I know you are true son of mine."

His symphonic poems lead into his operas, three of which are masterpieces. As Marek said, "It is a characteristic of Strauss's operas that the female characters spring to life, the men being comparatively pallid." Perhaps the most often performed operas today are those of Mozart, Verdi, Wagner, Puccini, and Strauss.

In 1905 he composed his first operatic masterpiece, *Salome* (in a Wagnerian style). A setting of Oscar Wilde's one-act play, it was a shocker—full of lust and hate expressed in the text and action, not through the music. It contains Salome's "Dance of the Seven Veils," possibly the most famous dance in history.

The secret of Strauss's art is its furious rhythm. With unheard of speed, he is a master of timing, of shock, and surprise. His next opera, *Elektra* is possibly the finest tragic opera since Wagner. Strauss has amazing skill in musical characterization. Shattering the profound in terror, *Elektra* has been called "an opera of horror."

Both *Salome* and *Elektra* depict half-insane women contriving to commit murder and gloating over their victims. A great contralto, Schumann-Heink, who sang at the premiere of *Elektra* said, "We were a set of mad women—truly we were." Strauss was a composer with cultural interests of great breadth. His literary and philosophical interests had a Renaissance intensity.

In *Elektra* for the first time Strauss used a libretto by Hugo von Hofmannsthal from Sophocles' great play. In all, they produced together six operas. Their last collaboration was *Arabella*, as Hofmannsthal died of a stroke in 1929.

Always between Strauss and Hofmannsthal (a well-known Jewish man of letters) there was a tug of war. Strauss seemed to have a constant need to dazzle and overwhelm. From the "Expressionism" of *Elektra* (reminding us of German Expressionism exemplified in the work of the painter Oskar Kokoschka) with its huge orchestra, maddening music, and moments of deliberate ugliness, Strauss, influenced by Hofmannsthal, suddenly turned to Neoclassicism. He wrote his third operatic masterpiece, which is his greatest opera. Under the influence of Mozart and Johann Strauss (the Waltz King), Richard Strauss wrote his comic opera *Der Rosenkavalier* (The Rose Bearer, 1911), an opera of waltzes that abounds in beauty and strokes of genius. In view of its slightly melancholy atmosphere of old Vienna, Strauss said, "How could I have composed this without thinking of the laughing Waltz King Johann Strauss, Jr., of Vienna?"

He admired Johann's natural talent and spontaneity. The champagne atmosphere of *Der Rosenkavalier* was the creative high point of Richard Strauss's career. With the clarity of Mozart he lightened his music and reduced the mammoth orchestra. The opera contains magical orchestral colors and a lively sense of comedy. One of the most beautiful parts is the final trio of soaring sopranos, which reveals what a master of melody Strauss was.

Richard Strauss was a hard-headed, practical businessman with an ambition to become a millionaire—which he achieved when he was fifty. This gave him the freedom to devote himself to his art. He lived to see his early works become classics, but his later compositions deteriorated, partly because he had become very conservative and somewhat repetitious. Critics disagree on this, however. The great musicologist Grout considered Strauss's last opera, *Capriccio*, one of his best.

Undoubtedly, Strauss was a man of genius who probably outlived his inspiration and creative power. Critics feel there was no inner growth because he put effect above substance, and he was thought of as "a musical genius with a small soul." His later operas have pages of great beauty, but they become more eclectic and uneven in inspiration.

When the Nazis came to power in Germany, Strauss was appointed head of the Third Reich music. As an opportunist, amoral and apolitical, he never put up a fight against the horrors of the Nazi regime. He stayed comfortably in his luxurious villa in Garmisch. He knew very well what was going on. All he wanted was to write music, make money, and do what was best for himself. However, he was concerned for the safety of his daughter-in-law who was Jewish. He said, "It is absolutely clear to me that the Germans will only find new strength through the liberation from Christianity." Many, like Thomas Mann, Hindemith, etc., left Germany in protest.

Richard Strauss was the end of a tradition rather than the beginning of a new one. He had little effect on twentieth-century music, in contrast to Debussy and Schoenberg. Some composers, like Schubert, lived too short a life to enjoy success. Strauss outlived his greatest work. Some critics say that his "Four Last Songs" was the death of Romanticism. He composed this beautiful work in Switzerland, partly on Lake Geneva at Montreux. Late in his life he spent three and a half years in Switzerland. He lost much of his money because of the war. He did return to Germany and died in Garmisch, having composed a great deal of beautiful music.

Recommended Reading

Abell, Arthur M. *Talks with Great Composers*. Garmisch, Germany: G. E. Schroeder Publisher, 1964.

Marek, George R. *Richard Strauss: The Life of a Non-hero*. New York: Simon and Schuster, 1967.

Wilhelm, Kurt. *Richard Strauss: An Intimate Portrait*. New York: Rizzoli, 1989.

Recommended Listening

Also Sprach Zarathustra
Ariadne auf Naxos
Don Juan
Don Quixote
Elektra
"Four Last Songs"
Ein Heldenleben
Der Rosenkavalier
Salome
The Merry Pranks of Till Eulenspiegel
Death and Transfiguration

CHAPTER 29

Jean Sibelius
1865-1957

*This is the music of a great man who, refusing to be
distracted by fads and fancies, worked unflaggingly
to develop the gifts he possessed.*

Anonymous

*B*oth parents of Jean Sibelius were musical, and even as a baby, Jean
would creep under the piano and listen when anyone played. But when he
grew older, he complained, "The piano does not sing," and he shifted his
affection to the violin.

Sibelius's father was a doctor. In the summer of 1868 he caught
typhus while treating epidemic victims and died suddenly. The family was
left without resources; so they moved in with his mother's mother, also a
widow. His Swedish grandmother Borg looked severe, but she had a delightful sense of humor and would crumple into laughter at the children's frol-
ics. Jean, his sister, and brother all adored her.

In the summers Jean visited his grandmother Sibelius, who lived on the
Gulf of Finland. Here he became acquainted with an uncle who had a passion for astronomy and music. It was through Uncle Pehr that he became
devoted to the violin.

His childhood was happy, not only because of the love of his mother
and grandmothers, but also because they lived close to the beautiful Finnish
countryside, which he adored all his life. From boyhood his closest companion was nature. He once said, "It is true I am a dreamer and a poet of
nature. I love the mysterious sounds of the fields and forest waters and
mountains. Nature has truly been the book of books for me."

Even though he was born in Finland and lived in the lively, little town
of Tavastehus, Sibelius grew up speaking Swedish, the language of Finland's
educated people during the long Swedish occupation of Finland. When he
was eight, he began to learn his difficult native tongue. He quickly became
fluent in Finnish, but to the end of his life he never overcame certain gram-
matical errors.

He was a shy, dreamy student, though well-instructed in the classics. He admired Homer and Horace for their depth of thought and simplicity of expression. He excelled in mathematics and was intrigued by astronomy, but soon music became his passion, and he was given to scribbling musical notes in the margins of his books.

At the age of ten he composed a piece for violin. For years he longed to be a violin virtuoso, but he began too late. He did play the violin in public in his teens, but he was so shy that once he performed with his back to the audience. He preferred playing chamber music at home with his brother and sister, with improvisations and occasionally playing his own compositions.

When it was time for him to go to college, as it was with Tchaikovsky, Schumann, and other artistic people, his family hoped he would become a lawyer. But he spent most of his time studying music and soon entered the new conservatory in Helsinki. There he met the pianist and composer Busoni, and they became close friends.

Another new friend was Armas Järnefelt, son of a distinguished general. Sibelius was a frequent visitor at the Järnefelt home, and there he met his future wife, the beautiful Aino. But as he had nothing to offer a prospective bride, Sibelius kept his passion to himself.

At the music academy he had an enthusiastic professor who understood that he was working with an extremely talented pupil, and he spent a great deal of time with Sibelius. "Martin Wegelius was the right man in the right place," Sibelius said later. Wegelius helped to draw Sibelius away from the violin and toward composition. He tried hard to interest his pupil in the music of Liszt and Wagner, but he never succeeded.

Sibelius would dutifully write compositions to suit the taste of his teacher while keeping secret pieces he wrote to please himself. After three years Wegelius gracefully gave in and encouraged Sibelius to write as he wished. Soon the young composer brought forth a string quartet that was performed; and because of it, he received a government award to study in Berlin and Vienna.

Sibelius had a hard time in Berlin. He was often penniless. He had inherited his father's inability to manage money, and he did not like what was going on musically in Germany. But one life-changing event occurred in Berlin—he met the conductor of the Helsinki Orchestra, Robert Kajanus, who later became one of Sibelius's ardent supporters and sympathetic interpreters.

One evening Sibelius heard Kajanus conduct his own composition, the *Aino* Symphony based on the *Kalevala,* the national epic of Finland, meaning "The Land of Happiness." This fired his imagination in an extraordinary way. For most of his creative life these Finnish folk tales, myths, and legends played a dominant part in his music.

In 1891 Sibelius returned to Finland and threw himself into the patriotic movement to free tiny Finland from the despotic rule of the giant Russia.

The Finns needed someone who had something vital to say, and what better way than through stirring music that spoke an international language.

Immersing himself in the verses of *Kalevala* and the works of other Finnish poetry, the patriotic and revolutionary Sibelius made his first musical setting as a choral symphonic poem, "Kullervo." It was an immediate and sweeping success in 1892, and soon Jean Sibelius became a symbol of Finnish patriotism.

The same year he married Aino Järnefelt. Also in 1892 he wrote his first great tone poem, *En Saga*, which evoked ancient Finland. As a critic said, "There are measures of introduction as fantastical as northern lights."

In 1893 Sibelius began composing the *Lemminkäinen Suite*, also known as *Four Legends of the Kalevala*, including the beautiful tone poem, "The Swan of Tuonela," one of his most haunting pieces of nature painting.

As a part of a series called *Tableaux of the Past*, Sibelius wrote "Finland Awakes," which later he rewrote as "Finlandia." It became the voice of the Finnish people in their struggle with Russia. The Russian government forbade the playing of "Finlandia" for a long time because it excited the public so much. Nevertheless, it was performed under various titles in different places, and as someone said, it did more than a thousand speeches and pamphlets could to promote Finnish independence. "Finlandia" is also beloved because it contains the hymn tune for "Be Still, My Soul."

Eventually the Russians were compelled to allow "Finlandia" to be played, but it took another hard twelve years before the Russians were driven out. Finally Finland had peace and freedom in 1919.

During the worst of the fighting Sibelius and his family nearly starved to death, but Sibelius never gave up his stubborn fight for freedom. For about five years after his marriage he had a heavy schedule of teaching to supplement their low income, but in the meantime Sibelius gained extraordinary popularity in Finland. In 1897 he received a government pension for life to free him for composition.

Sibelius's mother made a sincere effort to raise her children to be tactful and considerate of the feelings of other people. There are many stories to illustrate that Sibelius did take time to say a kind word to someone who needed it—often it was much longer than just a word—and he consistently avoided downgrading or discouraging young artists.

The one who bore the weight of everyday matters in the Sibelius home was his wife, Aino, and this covered a wide range of activities. Her husband was not a good businessman (true of many artists), and the family often lacked money. Also, at times Sibelius was as thoughtless and helpless as a child, particularly when composing a difficult piece. But what brought them through the troubled times was their genuine love and respect for each other and their sense of humor, which saved them over and over from senseless quarrels.

The couple had five daughters. One day a friend asked Sibelius, half in jest, if he would not have liked to have had a son. "Oh, no!" the composer answered spontaneously. "I have never in fact thought about it. My daughters are so dear to me, and I have had such pleasure from them that I could not have wanted for anything better." Aino was sitting close by mending her husband's socks. She added quietly and with her wonderful smile, "For my part I needed no other son than my husband!"

Aino Sibelius had an aristocratic and artistic background and recognized and appreciated her husband's uniqueness as a composer, a true artist whose music breathes of the land and waters of Finland, the pine forests, the deer, the sixty thousand lakes, and the long winter nights. "His work is my one and only concern," she told a friend. "I certainly won't say it has been easy, and to a certain extent I have had to restrain and keep a bridle on myself. But my destiny was as a gift from above."

After 1904 the Sibelius family moved to the country and lived in a large log house not too far from Helsinki. He called it Ainola after his wife, and they lived there for fifty years surrounded by trees and lakes, with birds and deer as their neighbors. This setting, so much to his liking, was the scene of his greatest creative achievements. Sibelius heard the sounds of nature and in an instinctive, uncontaminated way put down precisely what he heard. His astonishing orchestral effects were obtained by simple means. Concerning his composing, Sibelius explained, "Inspiration is like a butterfly's wings. Touch it and the magic is gone."

Between 1899 and 1924 Sibelius wrote seven symphonies. His First Symphony, which was strongly influenced by Tchaikovsky, was written in 1899. Then someone who approved of Sibelius's work gave a gift, and the family went to Italy. His Second Symphony was composed in Rapallo. This sunny, congenial composition was written in a room overlooking a beautiful garden of camellias, roses, almond trees, cypresses, and palms. Sibelius loved Italy and returned many times.

Around this time Sibelius wrote some incidental music for a play by his brother-in-law. Not realizing the value of the music, which has come to be known as "Valse Triste," Sibelius signed away the rights to it for an insignificant amount of money. As someone said, "Sibelius became one of the most popular composers in the world and among the most underpaid."

In 1908 Sibelius, suffering from an ear-throat infection, underwent thirteen painful operations. After the last operation, suddenly the doctor's young assistant reached down into Sibelius's throat and drew out the tumor. As he was going through this series of operations, Sibelius was convinced he was not going to live much longer, and his music changed in character.

In Finland they nicknamed his Fourth Symphony *Barkbröd*. It is bare and austere, as when after a winter there is little food, and bread is made from the bark of trees. The symphony is one of the most individual works in the early twentieth century, bringing to mind lonely landscapes of immense forests.

The music of Sibelius is powerful, rugged, and melancholy. One of his finest compositions is his Violin Concerto, an unconventional work with a Gypsy-like warmth.

In 1914 Sibelius was invited to be a part of a musical festival in Connecticut, and the same year he was presented with a doctorate by Yale University. In the presentation it was said: "What Wagner did for the ancient German legends, Doctor Sibelius has in his own magnificent way done for the Finnish myths. He has translated the *Kalevala* into the international language of music."

Sibelius wrote many songs, one of the best known being "Black Roses." Part of its fascination lies in the words, "for sorrow has black-petalled roses." The Swedish tenor Jussi Bjoerling has made a beautiful recording of it.

During World War I, Sibelius's fiftieth birthday was an occasion for a national celebration. The premiere of his Fifth Symphony was part of the festivity. For five years Sibelius worked on this symphony, writing and rewriting and polishing what was rewritten. It was worth the effort. Many consider the Fifth Symphony his greatest achievement, and his extraordinary originality as a symphonic thinker is everywhere evident.

As he grew older, his habitual self-criticism grew more and more severe. He made his last public appearance abroad in Stockholm in 1924, conducting his Seventh Symphony, which has only one movement. In 1926 his tone poem *Tapiola* had its debut in New York. *Tapiola* is to the northern woods what *La Mer* by Debussy is to the sea.

He promised the musical world that he was working on his Eighth Symphony, and he finished it several times, but it never pleased him. "I am my sternest critic," he said. "I won't discuss work I may discard." It never appeared.

In 1929 he stopped composing. There are many theories as to why he stopped. Sibelius had little sympathy with "Les Six," Schoenberg, or Stravinsky and did not feel in tune with the direction music was taking. He was certainly not going to follow them. Then his self-criticism intensified year by year, making it impossible to please himself. But we believe the major reason he stopped composing is that he had said enough and had the wisdom to know it. He clearly made up his mind that he had nothing more to express musically. As one examines the works of many artists, one cannot help noticing that some work on past the days of their creativity.

Then too one must understand that Sibelius gave generously of his time to other people. He was not only a great musician but a national hero. Strangers as well as friends, not only from Finland but from other countries, came to see him. He was unusually cordial to the stream of visitors, as well as helpful to various musical students. Sibelius was beloved by many people. When his wife, Aino, was seventy-five years old, a party was given in her honor. Sibelius delivered such a beautiful after-dinner speech that most of the guests had tears in their eyes.

On his ninetieth birthday he received more than one thousand telegrams, presents from all the Scandinavian monarchs, cigars from

Churchill, tapes of concerts from Toscanini, etc., and many performances were given in his honor.

When he was ninety-one, although forbidden by the doctor to do so, he climbed up the steep staircase early in the morning of his wife's birthday. He was carrying a huge bouquet of roses to give to Aino, just as on the day they began their lives together many years ago. He said, "I come now to court for a second time."

Their financial condition was poor most of their lives and worsened during World War II, but always someone helped them, as the time the New York Philharmonic Orchestra sent a gift to Sibelius thinly disguised as royalties.

One of the humorous stories of Sibelius and his generosity, even when he had little, was the day a beggar came to Ainola. Sibelius in his gracious manner visited with the man, and when the poor fellow left, he was wearing Sibelius's clothes. The composer said to his wife, "There goes Sibelius!"

He enjoyed telling his visitors, "I have always lived an unhealthy life." Then smiling and puffing on a cigar, he would add, "All the doctors who told me to give up smoking and drinking are dead, but I am quietly going on living."

Jean Sibelius wrote some imperishable music. He refused to be distracted by fads and fancies and worked unflaggingly to develop to the full the gifts within him. Like many other great artists, Sibelius felt that his work was divinely inspired.

When asked about his creativity, he spoke of having an inner urge and inner necessity to put down what he heard. This does not mean the notes flowed out of him without effort. Quite the contrary—there was hard work to do. But once the inner urge came, nothing could hold him back from composing. If for some reason he was hindered, he was miserable until he could get to work.

Jean Sibelius died at Ainola at the age of ninety-two, older than any other major composer.

<hr />

Recommended Reading

Levas, Santeri. *Sibelius: A Personal Portrait.* Lewisburg: Bucknell University Press, 1972.
Tawastsjerna, Erik. *Sibelius.* Berkeley: University of California Press, 1976.

<hr />

Recommended Listening

Concerto for Violin
"Finlandia"
Karelia Suite
Pohjola's Daughter
En Saga

"Swan of Tuonela"
Seven Symphonies
Tapiola
"Valse Triste"

Scott Joplin
1868-1917

*Composers generally have to make their start by
having somebody or something to write for.*

Gammond

While living in Sedalia, Missouri, Scott Joplin gathered together a double quartet that included two of his brothers. He was the leader, conductor, and soloist. The programs they prepared included popular songs of the day, plantation medleys, and, most important, new pieces written by himself. The group toured in several states, and in 1885 they went as far as Syracuse, New York, where Joplin sold his first two songs. The group disbanded in 1897, the same year he wrote the "Maple Leaf Rag."

Joplin went through a typical routine many artistic people experience, being turned down by a number of publishers who did not recognize that they were holding in their hands an important work. In Kansas City the publisher Carl Hoffman proved equally undiscerning about the merits of "Maple Leaf," but he did accept in 1899 a composition called "Original Rags." Its modest success proved a significant step in Joplin's career. He now gained the title "ragtime composer."

To earn a living, Joplin was forced to play in clubs, saloons, and gambling places, which he thoroughly disliked, as he was a modest, retiring person who did not appreciate the unwholesome atmosphere. But he did learn a great deal from the other black musicians and dancers he met, which helped him in his composing.

Because he was now known as a ragtime composer, the owner of a music store in Sedalia, John Stark, decided to hear Joplin's music himself; so he visited the Maple Leaf Club. Like Joplin, he had no taste for bawdy places. But when Stark heard Joplin play the "Maple Leaf Rag," he became very excited. In 1899 he bought it for fifty dollars and worked out a royalty plan for the composer. It did not happen immediately, but with Stark's perseverance the "Maple Leaf Rag" became a huge success of fairy-tale proportions. Scott Joplin became famous overnight. Stark later published many other rags by Joplin, including "Cascades," "Chrysanthemum," "Elite Syncopations," "Fig Leaf," "Nonpareil," and "Peacherine."

Success changed Joplin's life. Soon he married, bought a house, became a teacher, and with a thankful heart gave up his nightclub playing. In this period he composed a long succession of rags. As busy as he was, Joplin took time to help younger composers such as Joseph Lamb, Louis Chauvin, and Scott Hayden. Chauvin and Joplin wrote "Heliotrope Bouquet" before Chauvin died at twenty-four.

Scott Joplin was born in Texarkana, Texas, in 1868. His father was a former slave who worked for a railroad company and played the violin. His mother sang and strummed on the banjo. One of his brothers played the guitar, and Scott's instrument was the piano. His father deserted the family; so to support her six small children, Mrs. Joplin worked as a maid. She brought Scott along with her to her place of work, and one of the employers allowed the young boy to practice on the piano while she went about her chores.

Scott taught himself to play the piano at the age of seven, and then later was given some lessons by J. C. Johnson, partly of German descent. He introduced his talented pupil to the great European composers. Johnson, a churchgoing man, was the first to plant in the mind of Joplin the belief that the path of hope for the black people was education. We will see later that this is the theme of his unusual and original opera Treemonisha.

At sixteen or seventeen Joplin left home and wandered as an itinerant musician, spending eight or so years playing in honky-tonks, as there were no open doors for black musicians in those days. But these were years of continued learning for the quiet but determined Joplin. In a sense, ragtime composers served as musicologists, folk collectors who listened and absorbed the music all around them, and later organized it into anthologies, which they called rags. It seems fairly certain that the great march tradition of Sousa also had its influence on Joplin. Joplin's musical education was certainly strengthened by the church, where he learned something about faith and a lot about sound—how the sadness in a mournful song, for example, could be intensified by a persistent, staccato clapping, and that any song could be turned into a dance.

At a very early age Joplin had heard plantation songs and cakewalks and responded to the rhythm by tapping his foot and picking out the melodies on his mother's banjo.

When slaves were brought to the New World from Africa, a common practice among plantation owners was to group together the subordinates from different tribes. It added to their bewilderment until they learned to communicate with each other by means of drums, which they made out of whatever materials were available. Soon drums were outlawed when the white owners discovered that slaves were sending messages from plantation to plantation, but the ingenious slaves circumvented the law by "speaking" through heel-tapping and hand-clapping.

Music was the one effective means of communication for slaves, and rhythm could create as well as resolve tension. Singing became an essential part of their lives—when they picked cotton, unloaded cargo, or did other such chores. Their songs helped to make the long hours of work more bearable. We too can be uplifted on a hard day by putting on some cheerful Scott Joplin music.

Ragtime—that is, the "classic" ragtime—is written piano music. It covers a period from 1890 to about 1915. In this time, as well as later, it has been transcribed for other instruments, like the superb *Red Back Book* ragtime band arrangements; but it was originally written for the piano. Along with the many male rag composers, recent research has discovered over ninety women who also wrote ragtime music.

In ragtime, as in jazz, what makes its distinctive rhythm is the way the melody line is set against the bass line; that is, the melodic note is delayed or advanced for half a beat or for an eighth note while the left hand is kept steady. This is syncopation, or you could say, ragged time. Joplin never liked the term ragtime, and yet he is known as "the king of ragtime."

Ragtime is lively, rhythmic, and very bright—closely related to the blues and jazz. But what makes ragtime different is that it is not improvised music. It is written down and is to be played as written—and some pieces are very difficult. Joplin repeatedly told his students and fellow musicians, "Never play ragtime fast at any time." It takes a sensitive player to get the right tempo and feel the dignity of the music.

Ragtime is the first black music of the United States to achieve wide commercial popularity. It caused a musical revolution, as it was the first great impact of black folk culture on the dominant white middle class of America. Soon it became quite popular in Europe, influencing such important composers as Debussy, Satie, Stravinsky, Milhaud, Poulenc, and Hindemith. The American composer Charles Ives also was influenced by ragtime.

Ragtime is an American art form of the first order, and the classic ragtimes of Scott Joplin make one think of Chopin, because they are beautifully constructed and melodious. They have an unusually happy sound, an underlying nimble, foot-tapping rhythm that makes you want to move, exemplified in the "Stoptime Rag."

Those of us who are writers sit slumped over desks for long periods of time. We do not like to break our thoughts by taking a long walk or going for a swim, but it can be almost as invigorating to put on a Scott Joplin record and march, strut, and dance around the room and within ten minutes return to work, cheered and refreshed.

In the early 1890s Joplin went to Chicago and there became a friend of Otis Saunders. Saunders was an early believer in Joplin's genius and persuaded his modest friend to write down his music and have it published.

Joplin eventually wrote many pieces, including rags, songs, a folk ballet (*The Ragtime Dance*), two operas, and the enchanting "Bethena Ragtime Waltz."

After a series of marital difficulties, Joplin moved to New York City in 1907 and settled there with his second wife, Lottie Stokes, who took a great interest in his music and did her best to help him achieve his ambitions. Even with her enthusiasm and hope and his excitement about the opera germinating in his mind, there were difficult, sad years ahead for them.

Around the time he married Lottie, Joplin wrote a ragtime instruction manual to help musicians understand that ragtime music, when played correctly, is a respectable musical form. He issued the booklet himself in 1908, and he was the first black composer to have such a publication printed.

He continued to write rags and to travel, but soon he was hard at work on his second opera, the draft of which he had completed while still in St. Louis. In his lively interest for *Treemonisha*, Joplin was able to forget his disappointment over his inability to get his first opera, *A Guest of Honor*, produced.

By the end of 1910, a second draft of *Treemonisha* was completed, and Joplin was longing to find a publisher. His wife recalled years later, "What headaches that caused him!"

In 1911 he managed to get enough money to publish his opera himself. Regrettably, it was a failure. Joplin was crushed because he knew in his heart it was the best thing he had written. Moreover, he had invested years of struggle, as well as his diminishing income, on the composition. He had written both the words and music as well as designing the dances.

There is still one other reason its failure in his lifetime was such a crushing blow. The theme of *Treemonisha* is hope for black people through education. He knew he had an important message and was excited about communicating this truth through his opera. The opera is a fantasy with enough reality to appeal to the practical American mind.

The opening scene is a plantation somewhere in Arkansas after the slaves were freed and the white people have moved away. Treemonisha is the only educated person in the community, and her friends want her to lead them out of ignorance and superstition. When the chorus sings "We Want You as Our Leader," you know Joplin is remembering his childhood in Texarkana where there were no schools. The words and music are bright as well as poignant and the dancing exciting.

After Treemonisha agrees to be the leader of the freed slaves, the chorus sings and dances "Marching Onward." Once you have heard this lively music, you understand why it was such a bewilderment to Joplin that no one paid any attention to his opera.

After it was turned down by many publishing houses, he became increasingly depressed. Finally, in 1915 one performance was given at his own expense in a Harlem hall without an orchestra, scenery, costumes, or lighting. Joplin played the orchestra parts on a piano. The small audience was polite but not at all enthusiastic. To add to his sorrow, the black musicians in New York rejected him even more than the white people. They considered ragtime music lower class.

He was heartbroken and tried to forget it by getting back to the unfinished manuscripts cluttering his desk, but he was totally bewildered, unable to work, unable to play the piano, unable to teach. His last piece, "Magnetic Rag," he published himself in 1914, and it is one of his finest. Finally he had a nervous breakdown from which he never recovered, and in 1917 he was committed to a mental hospital. There he died April 1, 1917, at the age of forty-nine, the same day America entered the first World War. He was buried in an unmarked grave.

The sleeping beauty of American music, *Treemonisha* slumbered for over fifty years after his death until it was revived in 1972 by Robert Shaw in a performance in Atlanta. Joplin often said his music would only be appreciated fifty years after he died. The opera is now accepted as Joplin's finest work. Some consider *Treemonisha* the first great American opera. It was written many years before Gershwin's *Porgy and Bess* (1935). Some memorable moments in *Treemonisha* are "Aunt Dinah Blowed de Horn," "Frolic of the Bears," "We Will Rest Awhile," and "A Real Slow Drag."

Joshua Rifkin, an American pianist, stirred up interest in the ragtime music of Joplin in the early seventies by recording some of his pieces. "I felt the music should be treated seriously," said Rifkin, who is also a musicologist, "that it should be put out on a classical label with a dignified cover and literate notes." Schonberg in a review of the first Rifkin record stated, "Scholars, get busy on Scott Joplin."

At Chalet Chesalet we have a beautiful recording of *Treemonisha* by Gunther Schuller, who has been a key figure in the Joplin revival. Another Joplin enthusiast was Vera Brodsky Lawrence, a music collector and pianist. When she tried to find a publisher for a collected edition of Joplin's piano pieces, twenty-four publishing houses turned her down. Finally the New York Public Library agreed to print it, and it became part of the tremendous ragtime revival.

Scott Joplin devoted his life to creating a true art form and died believing himself a failure in this heroic mission. As his wife said, "You might say he died of disappointments. . . . He wanted to be a real leader, to free his people from poverty, ignorance, and superstition."

Another reason for the upsurge of interest in Joplin in the seventies was the film *The Sting*, released in 1973, which used Joplin's rag "The Entertainer" as the theme music. Several other rags are also featured— "Gladiolus," "Pine Apple," "Ragtime Dance," and "Solace." *The Sting* won the Academy Award for Best Picture of the Year in 1974, and the score and title song also won Oscars.

In 1975 *Treemonisha* received a full-scale production on Broadway, and in 1976, about sixty years after his tragic death, Scott Joplin was awarded the Pulitzer Prize for his contribution to American music. Undoubtedly there will be more awards to come. Perhaps someday Joplin's famous lost opera *A Guest of Honor* will be found. It is said he left it behind in a trunk full of belongings when he had to abruptly leave a Baltimore rooming house because he could not pay the rent. If you have an unopened trunk in your basement or attic, this would be the ideal moment to go treasure hunting!

Recommended Reading

Haskins, James. *Scott Joplin: the Man Who Made Ragtime.* New York: Doubleday and Co., 1978.

Recommended Listening

"Bethena Ragtime Waltz"
"The Cascades"
"The Entertainer"
"Eugenia"
"Heliotrope Bouquet"
"Magnetic Rag"
"Maple Leaf Rag"
"The Nonpareil"
Original Rags
"Solace"
Treemonisha (an opera)

CHAPTER 31

Ralph Vaughan Williams
1872-1958

*Two years of close association with some of the best
(as well as some of the worst) tunes in the world was
a better musical education than any amount of
sonatas and fugues.*

Ralph Vaughan Williams

*R*alph Vaughan Williams is considered one of the most important English composers of the first half of the twentieth century. His father was a minister who died when Vaughan Williams was a small boy. The family moved to the beautiful home in Leith Hill Place, Surrey, where his mother had lived. Both his parents came from families of distinction and independence. The Vaughan Williamses were eminent lawyers and judges. His maternal grandfather was related to Charles Darwin.

Even as a boy of six, Vaughan Williams was drawn to composing. To encourage his interest in music, his mother had a home organ built for him. He had an independent income that made it possible for him to have a very thorough education. His first teacher was an aunt. By the time he went to a preparatory school in Sussex, he could play the violin, piano, and organ.

In the next three years at Charterhouse, he switched from violin to the viola and also played with enthusiasm in the school orchestra. From Charterhouse he went directly to the Royal College of Music as a composition pupil of Parry. After two years he moved to Cambridge where he read history and music, and within three years he received a Bachelor of Music degree at Trinity College.

By this time Vaughan Williams knew he wanted to be a composer, but progress was slow. A cousin overheard a conversation at Cambridge: " . . . that foolish young man, Ralph Vaughan Williams . . . who continues to work at composing when he is so hopelessly bad at it."

Vaughan Williams himself admitted his "amateurish technique" in these years. Groves helped explain his slow beginning to us. "His early groping had much to do with a deep dissatisfaction with the English musical scene and an inability to see his own path," he said. But Vaughan Williams had years of studying and trying ahead before *he* understood what was wrong.

And so in 1895 he went back to the Royal College of Music for further enlightenment. In this period he met Gustav Holst, an English composer with a Swedish background, a man of sympathy, enthusiasm, and humor. They enjoyed each other and advised and corrected one another's music. The close friendship lasted until the death of Holst in 1934—almost forty years. Holst's best-known composition is *The Planets*. He wrote the music for a favorite Christmas hymn, "In the Bleak Midwinter."

Vaughan Williams studied composition with several teachers. One of them, Wood, had no confidence that his pupil would ever be a composer. Parry was the professor Vaughan Williams was especially indebted to. In later years Vaughan Williams remarked, "We pupils of Parry have, if we have been wise, inherited from Parry the great English choral tradition." That tradition began with Thomas Tallis, continued with Henry Purcell, and over the years finally reached the Wesleys. Parry picked up the tradition from them, and as Vaughan Williams said, "He has passed the torch to us, and it is our duty to keep it alight."

In 1897 he married Adeline Fisher. The same year he went to Berlin for further education. It is difficult to explain why he chose Germany, because temperamentally he was never able to identify with the German school. But there he went to have a few lessons with Max Bruch. As Schonberg commented, "Nothing much came of these."

In 1901 Vaughan Williams received a Doctor of Music degree at Cambridge, and shortly after joined the English Folk Music Society, which was the turning point of his life. We will return to that later.

Even though two of his compositions, the "Three Norfolk Rhapsodies" and "In the Fen Country," attracted a great deal of attention in 1906 and 1907, Vaughan Williams was still not satisfied with his technique. Off to Paris he went to see what Maurice Ravel could do for him. As he tried to explain, "In 1908 I came to the conclusion that I was bumpy and stodgy, had come to a dead end, and that a little French polish would be of use to me."

There could never have been two more different personalities—the Britisher Vaughan Williams, complete with pipe, big, stout, bearlike, "dressed with cheerful sloppiness," and the very French, tiny, dandified Ravel. One can imagine that Ravel scarcely knew what to make of the English invader! But Maurice Ravel did for Vaughan Williams exactly what he needed. He helped to release his pent-up creative energies.

After his visit to Paris and eight months of private lessons with Ravel, Ralph Vaughan Williams returned to England, considered his musical education complete, and at the age of thirty-six began to compose in all forms. He had the ability to profit by the examples of the many different musicians he learned from without his own artistic personality being colored by theirs.

As a composer, Vaughan Williams was motivated by three main sources—English folk song, English hymnody, and English seventeenth-century literature.

In 1902 Vaughan Williams was introduced by Lucy Broadwood to the systematic collecting of folk songs. He had begun to see that English music could not be revived by imitating foreign models. He needed to use native resources. The following year he heard an old shepherd in Essex sing "Bushes and Briars," and this intensified his interest in English folk songs.

A new stimulus came to him when in 1904 he joined the Folk Song Society. From then on Vaughan Williams regularly took folk song excursions and stayed in small towns to be among the people. He saturated himself in folk songs. For a period of nine years he collected tunes in Norfolk, Hereford, Surrey, and Sussex. "The knowledge of our folk songs did not so much discover for us something new," Vaughan Williams explained, "but uncovered something which has been hidden by foreign matter."

His discovery of a distinctively English expression is said to have opened a door for him as well as for other artists who might have otherwise remained ineffective, if not inarticulate. "As long as composers persist in serving up at secondhand the externals of the music of other nations," he said, "they must not be surprised if audiences prefer the real Brahms, the real Wagner, the real Debussy, or the real Stravinsky to their pale reflections."

Vaughan Williams learned after trial and error that mere transplanting of ready-made tunes could not satisfy him. In the two choral works *Toward the Unknown Region* and *A Sea Symphony*, with poetry by Walt Whitman, he began to show an individual way of writing music that was wholly his own, yet in another way distinctly native to England.

Béla Bartók, who traveled about his country, Hungary, also collecting folk songs, said, "The use of borrowed materials has nothing to do with the artistic results of a piece of music. . . . When you come down to it, Shakespeare borrowed, and so did Molière, Bach, and Handel. Everybody has his roots in the art of some former time."

In 1906 Vaughan Williams was invited to be music editor of *The English Hymnal*. He devoted months to this task, weeding out the bad and selecting the good. He also wrote some of the tunes himself, including the well-known "For All the Saints." Editorial work on *Songs of Praise* (1925) and the superb *Oxford Book of Carols* (1928) reveal his lifelong interest in the democratic sharing of music.

Besides the influence of the English folk songs, hymns, and Bach, he became acquainted with the great English choral music of the late 1500s. The spirit of Old England breathes through one of his best-known works, *Fantasia on a Theme by Tallis*, for string orchestra.

His *London* Symphony was first performed in London in March 1914.

Somewhat like Dickens, Vaughan Williams at times "quotes" the sounds of London—the Westminster chimes, the street cry of the lavender sellers, the hubbub of Bloomsbury, Big Ben, the serene flow of the Thames, etc. They are not clearly recognizable, but they are there.

Vaughan Williams had a lifetime habit of rising early to devote some time to music. He said that he felt a composer should not try to be original just for its own sake, because if you are, it will show in your music. He was primarily a melodist and shied away from chromatic harmony. He spoke for the common man through his music. He said a composer must reach his fellow countrymen before he can hope to have a universal audience.

From 1910 to 1914 he was at work on his ballad-opera *Hugh the Drover*, in which he truly captured the feeling of the English countryside. He completed it in August of 1914, calmly put it on a shelf, and at the age of forty-two joined the army. He spent much of the next four years in France working at menial but necessary jobs such as floor-scrubber, stretcher-bearer, and anything that a hardy, healthy man could do. Eventually he became a lieutenant so he could serve in the very midst of the fighting in France. No one knew he was one of England's most prominent composers.

When the war was over, Vaughan Williams returned to England and joined the staff of the Royal College of Music. He also became the conductor of the Bach Choir. Since 1905 he had been the conductor of the popular Leith Hill Festivals, and they continued until his death in 1958.

In 1921 Vaughan Williams composed the *Pastoral* Symphony, which became one of his most famous works. The agony that underlies much of this work is related to the composer's wartime experience. Around the same time (1924) *Hugh the Drover* was performed in London, ten years after it was shelved so he could go to war.

Kennedy said that Vaughan Williams "did not seek solace in religion after the war," which at the conscious level was probably true. But he did produce a succession of works, such as *Pilgrim's Progress* and the ballet *Job*, culminating in the mystical *Sancta Civitas* (a biblical oratorio mainly to words from Revelation), all of which suggest a deep concern with reaching toward a religious view of reality, though certainly not Christian. As someone who knew Vaughan Williams remarked, "His choice and interpretation of words plainly reflect the liberal humanitarianism of his family and of Parry, together with the ethic of his school mentors."

After the death of his wife in 1953, Vaughan Williams, at the age of eighty, married the poet and writer Ursula Wood. She described her husband as a "cheerful agnostic. He was never a professing Christian." Vaughan Williams viewed man as "a being darkly wise and rudely great, not by the grace and mercy of God, but by his own effort and courage. . . . " It is sad and most ironic to hear this about the writer of the music of "For All the Saints" and the editor of *The English Hymnal.*

In 1954 Vaughan Williams once more paid a visit to the United States on a lecture tour, visiting several universities. His last years were full of travel and activity, and always there was work in progress in spite of the deterioration of his hearing. Mention should be made of his often-heard *The Lark Ascending* for violin and orchestra and his beautiful songs "On Wenlock Edge," "The Five Mystical Songs," and "Silent Noon."

Ralph Vaughan Williams, composer, teacher, writer, lecturer, and conductor, had one of the longest creative life spans in history. He finished his Ninth Symphony only a short time before his death at the age of eighty-six. In this work he asserted himself as a composer of the modern age. For the first time he used a trio of saxophones. He made a notation that they should not behave like demented cats but rather remain their romantic selves. His was the music of a big man, a big spirit, and a very original thinker.

Recommended Reading

Day, James. *Vaughan Williams.* London: J. M. Dent, 1961.

Recommended Listening

Fantasia on "Greensleeves"
Fantasy on a Theme by Tallis
The Lark Ascending
Serenade for Songs (Blake) for Voice and Oboe
Symphony No. 3, *Pastoral*

Benjamin Britten
1913-1976

*It doesn't matter what style a composer chooses to
write in, as long as he has something definite to say
and says it clearly.*

Benjamin Britten

*A*nother of England's prolific composers in the mid-twentieth century
was Benjamin Britten. He was born on the feast day of St. Cecilia, the
patron saint of all musicians. His parents' home faced the North Sea, and
one can hear in his music his love for the sound of the sea. After his parents
died, he moved to a converted windmill in a little fishing village. He spent
long hours walking the windswept coast sorting out his musical ideas.

As a child the first music he heard was his mother singing to him selections from Schubert, Schumann, Bach, Handel, and Mozart. At two he
began to play the piano, and at five he started composing. When he was
seven, he read himself to sleep with musical scores of operas and symphonies. When he was sixteen, he received a scholarship to the Royal
College of Music. The only thing he wanted to do in life was to compose,
and at nineteen he was determined to earn his living through composition.
It was not easy, but he accomplished what he set out to do.

From these early beginnings flowed a distinguished career in both secular and sacred music. He rejected the tendencies of many composers to
ignore the church as a vehicle for great music and Christianity as a subject
for it. Some of his best-known sacred compositions are *A Boy Was Born, A
War Requiem*, the delightful *Ceremony of Carols, Rejoice in the Lamb*, and *The Holy
Sonnets of John Donne.*

He is best remembered for his operas *Peter Grimes, The Turn of the Screw*,
and *Billy Budd*. His opera *The Rape of Lucretia* includes two narrators who
make Christian comments on the pagan tragedy. Many in the audience
when this opera was performed were troubled and demanded, "Why drag
in Christianity?" But in the mind of Britten there was no question of "drag-
ging in Christianity." It had been there all the time. He felt it was morally
wrong to set a cruel subject to music without linking the cruelty to the hope
of redemption.

After the performance Britten said, "I used to think that the day when one could shock people was over—but now I've discovered that being simple and considering things spiritual of importance produces violent reactions!"

It was to the tune of one of Henry Purcell's hornpipes that Britten wrote one of his most popular works, *The Young Person's Guide to the Orchestra*—a lively and most exhilarating introduction to instrumentation. Purcell greatly influenced Britten's creativity.

"Britten-the-pianist closely resembles Britten-the-composer," said Rostropovitch. Britten had the ability to play songs by Schubert or Schumann or Haydn with such concern that he made the music sound as if it were his own.

In our Chesalet record collection there is a recording of the *War Requiem* conducted by Britten with the great Russian soprano Galina Vishnevskaya, the wife of Rostropovitch, singing. She and her husband were good friends of Benjamin Britten and his collaborator, Peter Pears. Her autobiography, *Galina* (1984), is immensely readable and exposes the cruelty of the Soviet Union to their great artists. Galina and her husband befriended Solzhenitsyn and literally saved his life before he was expelled from Russia.

Both Britten and Pears were pacifists, but they were granted exemption from going to war because they toured England giving recitals in small towns and villages, cheering the people who had never been to a concert before.

Benjamin Britten was undoubtedly one of this century's most gifted and disciplined composers. As in the parable of the talents, he multiplied his and proved to be a good steward of what God had given him. He was a metropolitan composer with a longing for a "micropolitan" existence. Whenever he could, he returned to the little fishing village. Being an intensely private person, there was a "Beware of the Dog" sign on his gate in seven languages. His pet was a tiny dachshund as gentle as its master.

In 1973 he became partially paralyzed after heart surgery and was able to work only for short periods. He died in 1976, and a friend said his end was "peaceful."

Recommended Reading

White, Eric W. *Benjamin Britten: His Life and Operas.* Berkeley: University of California Press, 1970.

Recommended Listening

A Ceremony of Carols
Peter Grimes: Four Sea Interludes
Rejoice in the Lamb
War Requiem
Young Person's Guide to the Orchestra

CHAPTER 32

Sergei Rachmaninoff
1873-1943

Nothing helps me so much as solitude [concerning how he composed].

Sergei Rachmaninoff

In 1941 Rachmaninoff made a transcription of Tchaikovsky's *Lullaby*, and it was performed in Syracuse, New York, on October 14. It was his last composition. Fifty-five years earlier in another country, another culture, another century, and another "world," the thirteen-year-old Rachmaninoff began his career as a composer with a transcription of Tchaikovsky's *Manfred* Symphony as a piano duet. Sergei and a friend played it for Tchaikovsky in the apartment of their music professor. From the beginning Tchaikovsky encouraged Rachmaninoff, and even today the name most often associated with the music of Rachmaninoff is Peter Ilich Tchaikovsky.

Sergei Rachmaninoff was born into a land-owning, well-to-do, aristocratic family in Oneg in the province of Novgorod not far from Petersburg in 1873. His grandfather was an exceptional pianist, and his mother, a lady of character and culture, was his first piano teacher. He began to play the piano at the age of four. The piano served another purpose in the Rachmaninoff home. Whenever the mother, Lubov, wanted to punish any of her six children, she made them sit under the piano.

Lubov had the entire care of the children as her husband was an irresponsible profligate whose gambling and reckless living had swallowed up the family fortune, including the Oneg estate. They were forced to move to Petersburg in 1882.

About the time the family settled into their small flat, a diphtheria epidemic struck the city. Several of the children became ill, and one of Sergei's sisters, Sophia, died. The father, already guilt-ridden, realized that this probably would not have happened had they been able to remain in the country. The accumulated humiliations of his careless living was too much for him. He abandoned the family, and his wife never saw him again.

Sergei was able to obtain a scholarship to the Petersburg Conservatory, but there he received no discipline; so he mostly played games with the other indolent students, had fun, and was a frequent truant from school. His cousin, Alexander Siloti, who had begun to make a name for himself as a pianist, realized the boy was throwing away his life and that without the example of a good father Sergei had tremendous need for discipline and study.

The only truly happy memories in Sergei's three years at the Petersburg Conservatory were the holidays at Borivoso. On these visits he would often accompany his grandmother to the services at the Russian Orthodox church where the sound of the church bells and the choral singing made a lasting impression on him.

Siloti knew one person who could rescue Rachmaninoff from following in the footsteps of his father—the eccentric but excellent music professor Nikolai Zverev. On the recommendation of Siloti, Zverev agreed to accept Rachmaninoff as his pupil in the autumn of 1885. Rachmaninoff was twelve. Abruptly this brought an end to Sergei's carefree Petersburg years, and it was the beginning of a totally new life in a strange city, Moscow.

He felt apprehensive about another move, but he was cheered by the realization that his talented sister Elena would soon be coming to Moscow. She had been accepted by the Bolshoi Opera House. Shortly before she was to leave for Moscow, she died suddenly from pernicious anemia. She was seventeen.

It was a dreadful shock to Sergei. As his grandmother kissed him good-bye—he had spent his last happy holiday with the grandparents—he was guarding carefully the one hundred rubles she had sewn into his jacket. On the train for Moscow, all he could think of was Elena. It was she who had first introduced him to the music of Tchaikovsky. Sergei particularly associated "None But the Lonely Heart" with his dear sister for the remainder of his life, and it helps one understand his tender regard for Tchaikovsky also.

The pupils of Zverev were chosen from the aristocracy, but not because of their wealth. If they were without means, like Sergei, but had talent, Zverev did not charge for the lessons nor anything else. He had a large extra bedroom in his apartment that accommodated two or three pupils.

Overnight Rachmaninoff's life changed from folly and fun to severely disciplined hard work, all revolving around music. There were two grand pianos in the apartment, and the practicing began at 6 A.M. There were also many classes to attend at the conservatory. Zverev felt that the social graces were an important part of education, and he saw to it that his pupils went to the latest concerts, operas, and plays too. The students were very glad for this part of their training.

Then Zverev had dinner parties in his own apartment, and the young musicians were required to play the piano for the distinguished guests. To illustrate how far Rachmaninoff had advanced in two years of intensive study with Zverev, this scene took place in front of Taneyev, the director of the conservatory. Zverev had four of his students (Rachmaninoff one of them) play on two pianos Beethoven's Fifth Symphony. When the four boys marched to the pianos without music, Taneyev, a legendary professor of composition, exclaimed, "Where is the music?"

Zverev replied calmly, "They play by heart."

Even after the performance, Taneyev was still muttering, "How is it possible?" An encore was requested, and the young stars played the scherzo from Beethoven's *Pastoral* Symphony—without music, of course.

To the end of his life Rachmaninoff astounded people with his amazing memory. A fellow pupil said of him, "His musical gifts surpassed any others I have met, bordering on the marvelous, like those of Mozart in his youth. The speed with which he memorized new compositions was remarkable."

The two most outstanding students of Zverev were Rachmaninoff and Alexander Scriabin. Scriabin also became an outstanding composer. He was a mystic, a complicated personality, and he became a philosopher-musician. Scriabin was deeply involved with the occult world and was influenced by Nietzsche, Wagner, and Eastern thought. His most widely performed compositions are *The Poem of Ecstasy* and *The Poem of Fire.*

After two years of study with Zverev, Rachmaninoff's growing proficiency as a pianist, his own compositions, and his increasing musical knowledge demonstrated the beginning of an excellent musician. He had made such rapid progress that Zverev and the other conservatory professors allowed him to study counterpoint with Taneyev. Taneyev had been a pupil of Tchaikovsky, and he became such an outstanding teacher that later Tchaikovsky took lessons from him!

Unfortunately in 1889 Zverev and the sixteen-year-old Rachmaninoff fell out. Zverev was training Sergei to be a pianist, and Taneyev and others were directing him toward composition. Rachmaninoff complained that he could not compose in the confusion of Zverev's apartment. He said he needed quiet and solitude. Of course, Zverev was indignant because of all he had done for him; and so, after four years, Rachmaninoff left. But it is true that Sergei Rachmaninoff would never, never have become one of Russia's greatest composers without the strong musical influence of Zverev in his life and Zverev's insistence on the necessity of an artist being a disciplined, hard-working person.

In the spring of 1892 Rachmaninoff graduated with honor from the Moscow Conservatory. The committee was unanimous in its decision to award him the highest mark, and Zverev was a member of the committee. After the ceremony Zverev followed his former pupil into the corridor and congratulated him, and the breach was healed. As a token of his genuine respect for Sergei and to show there was no trace of hard feelings, Zverev handed him his own gold watch. Rachmaninoff kept it the rest of his life.

In the same year, at the age of nineteen, Rachmaninoff wrote one of his most famous pieces, the Prelude in C Sharp Minor. As a result he became known all over the world, but personally he gained very little money from his masterpiece.

He wrote twenty-four preludes for the piano in about twenty years. Although Rachmaninoff was austere in appearance (people who knew Zverev commented on the resemblance of the manner and attitude of the two musicians—"All one big scowl," said Stravinsky), the preludes reveal a deep, warm, sensitive spirit.

The following year, 1893, Tchaikovsky and Zverev died. It was a double shock for Rachmaninoff, but the courage and resilience he had shown already in his life helped him to go on. He continued to compose, and to support himself he became a music teacher at a ladies' academy.

Rachmaninoff's First Symphony had its premiere performance in Petersburg. It was a complete failure. Later it was thought that the conductor was drunk, so it was played badly; but that was little comfort to Rachmaninoff. It was a horrible experience for him and cast him into deep depression. To the end of his life he suffered from melancholia and doubts about his talents.

While still trying to rise above the bouts with depression, he was invited to conduct and play in London in 1898, and he was invited back for the following season. But he returned to Russia in a worse mental state than before.

Finally some relatives persuaded him to see Dr. Nikolai Dahl, a psychiatrist. He visited the doctor every day for three months. As part of the treatment, he sat in a dark room while Dr. Dahl repeated these words: "You will begin to write your concerto. You will work with great facility. The concerto will be of excellent quality."

At the end of the treatment in the autumn of 1900, Rachmaninoff completed his Second Piano Concerto, which is one of his best-loved works. He also stopped excessive drinking. The concerto was dedicated to Dr. Dahl.

By 1901 Rachmaninoff had three new works ready. His Second Concerto genuinely moved the audience. A few weeks later Rachmaninoff and his cousin Siloti played the Second Suite, Op. 17. This was the first work completed after the return of his creativity. It is a dazzling composition, and a month or so before Rachmaninoff was married in 1902, Siloti was able to premiere *Spring*.

Natalia, Rachmaninoff's wife, had also graduated as a pianist from the Moscow Conservatory. On their extended honeymoon they visited Vienna, Venice, Lucerne, and Bayreuth. In Lucerne Sergei completed eleven songs, among them the beautiful "Lilacs." Other notable songs by Rachmaninoff are "In the Silence of the Night," "Floods of Spring," and "O, Do Not Grieve."

"Nothing helps me so much as solitude," he once said about his composing, but he did not find it in Moscow, where in 1904-1905 he became established as one of the ablest opera conductors in Russia. So in 1906 he abruptly moved his family to Dresden. There in virtual isolation he was able to write some of his best music, among which is the superb Second

Symphony. It was one of the most tranquil periods in his life, but he was there for only weeks or months at a time, because in these same years Rachmaninoff was conducting in Paris, Petersburg, Moscow, Warsaw, Berlin, England, Holland, etc. Also, the family (there were now two daughters) spent time at their country estate, Ivanovka, a place beloved by the Rachmaninoffs and important to his creativity.

Just before Christmas 1907, while back in Dresden, Sergei received word that he had been awarded the Glinka prize of one thousand rubles. Early in the new year he began work on an orchestral tone poem inspired by the painting *The Isle of the Dead* by the Swiss painter Böcklin.

The grim cypress trees, the dusky water, the small boat bearing a coffin are portrayed in music by a melancholy threnody of enormous intensity. The *Dies Irae* (Day of Judgment) theme, which haunted Rachmaninoff most of his life, appears in *The Isle of the Dead,* as well as in his three symphonies, *Rhapsody on a Theme of Paganini,* and other works. Leonard wrote, "Tchaikovsky had established a tradition that Russian music should wear the mask of tragedy."

Rachmaninoff's music belongs more to the nineteenth century than the twentieth; he was a traditionalist following in the footsteps of Tchaikovsky. In the world of music Rachmaninoff felt there was one supreme ruler—melody. His is singing music, and he teaches the doctrine of beauty. "In my own compositions, no conscious effort has been made to be original, or Romantic, or nationalistic, or anything else," said Rachmaninoff late in life. "I write down on paper the music I hear within me, as naturally as possible. I am a Russian composer, and the land of my birth has influenced my temperament and outlook."

He had an acute sense of his limitations and proceeded with his composing slowly, carefully, and steadily. Today people are beginning to realize that Sergei Rachmaninoff is a greater musician than previous generations had thought. As with any major composer, it takes but a few measures of his work to establish its identity.

In 1909 Rachmaninoff made his first American tour as a pianist. For this new challenge he composed his very beautiful but extremely difficult Third Piano Concerto. Besides the inner creative work Rachmaninoff did in order to prepare himself for a performance, he worked eight hours a day on his technique. He was an early riser and used his time well. The Russians are often intensely hard workers. Rachmaninoff was truly Russian.

Anyone who tries to play one of his piano pieces becomes aware of his dexterous fingers, the energy in the music, and the immense spread of his great hands. He could reach twelve keys. No matter where he was performing, even if playing to an almost empty hall, he always gave his best. And yet this highly gifted, shy, and sensitive artist was full of fears and lack of self-confidence most of his life. "I have not written a thing, but with God's help I hope I will."

Perhaps one of Rachmaninoff's best memories of his first American tour was his rehearsing and performing his Third Concerto with the great composer and conductor Gustav Mahler. Mahler exerted enormous effort to achieve what Rachmaninoff had written into the complex orchestral accompaniment. The members of the New York Philharmonic were quite disgruntled at the length of the rehearsal, but it was worth it. The performance was tremendously successful.

Rachmaninoff was urged to give more concerts in America, but with the extra money earned, he was now able to realize a dream and quickly returned to Russia—that is, as quickly as one could in the early part of the twentieth century. He bought an automobile, even had a chauffeur; but most generally Rachmaninoff was at the wheel looking as pleased as a twelve-year-old boy, with the chauffeur sitting beside him.

During the next few years Rachmaninoff served as conductor of the Moscow Philharmonic and was recognized as a powerful personality in the Moscow musical world. But by 1913 he had had enough of conducting and sought solitude in Switzerland and later in Rome in a small apartment where Tchaikovsky had once stayed. He wrote with enthusiasm about his haven: "All day long I spent at the piano or the writing table and not until the sinking sun gilded the pines of the Monte Pincio did I put away my pen." In this setting he composed *The Bells*, his favorite work. It is a choral symphony with words by Edgar Allen Poe.

By the summer of 1914 revolution and war in Russia had become a real menace. Many theaters closed for fear of revolutionists' bombs, but Rachmaninoff worked on composing his *Vesper Mass*, Op. 37. He had loved the Russian church chants from childhood. The work consists of fifteen hymns. The fifth, "Lord, now lettest Thou Thy servant depart in peace" (Luke 2:29), he wrote for his own funeral.

Right up until 1917 Rachmaninoff was so engrossed in his music he scarcely noticed what was going on around him. (Perhaps it would be fairer to say he knew the days were perilous, but he wanted to go on composing.) Suddenly, though, he began to sense the danger, as both he and his wife were aristocrats and landowners. He tried to concentrate on his Fourth Piano Concerto, but increasingly he became anxious for his wife and children.

At his most fearful moment, he received an invitation to give a concert tour in Sweden. Without trouble he was able to secure visas for the two daughters, his wife, and himself. In Petrograd they boarded the train for Finland, each carrying a small suitcase and about two thousand rubles. They were on their way to freedom, but as Walker said, "His mother and most other members of the family were still in Russia together with his music, his pianos, the orchestras, the Bolshoi, his friends, and the workers on his estate, his horses, his pictures, his motor car, and his personal belongings. The things that reassure people who they are and remind them where they belong were all abandoned."

In Finland they had to cross the countryside in a sleigh because of a furious snowstorm. Rachmaninoff probably wondered if he would ever see the lilacs at the Ivanovka gate again. He never did.

When Rachmaninoff moved to America in 1918, he had to make a choice. He had spent the first thirty or so years of his life as a composer, conductor, and pianist. Because he had little solitude for composing, and America had several renowned conductors, he chose to be a pianist.

Rachmaninoff became a fixture in the music life of the free world, and nearly every year for the next twenty-five years he gave scores of concerts, not only in the United States but also in Europe. Never again did he go back to Russia.

He worked diligently at his career but generally made time for holidays in the summer. Finally in 1931 he bought a home, patterned after the Ivanovka estate, on the shore of Lake Lucerne in Switzerland. Here Rachmaninoff wrote one last superb composition, *Rhapsody on a Theme of Paganini* for piano and orchestra.

Rachmaninoff said, "I know that while I am working I feel inwardly somehow stronger than when I do not work. Therefore I pray to God that I can work up to my last days." And he did. He died of cancer at the age of seventy, becoming an American citizen five weeks before his death.

Recommended Reading

Walker, Robert. *Rachmaninoff: His Life and Times*. England: Midas Books, 1980.

Recommended Listening

The Bells
Concertos No. 2 and 3 for Piano
Isle of the Dead
Preludes for Piano, Op. 23 and 32
Rhapsody on a Theme of Paganini
Songs: "Lilacs," "In the Silent Night," "Floods of Spring," etc.
Symphony No. 2
Vocalise

Arnold Schoenberg
1874-1951

If it is art, it is not for all, and if it is for all, it is not art.

Arnold Schoenberg

*T*he only instruction in composition Arnold Schoenberg had was study-ing counterpoint for a few months with a musician friend, Alexander von Zemlinsky (1872-1942). Yet today Schoenberg is known as the most contro-versial and cerebral composer in history. Rosenfeld called him "the great troubling presence in modern music."

In reply Schoenberg said, "I personally hate to be called a revolution-ist, which I am not. What I did was neither revolutionary nor anarchy." His followers are completely in accord with him. They feel Schoenberg carried to a logical conclusion the culmination of the thousand-year-old tradition of European polyphony. But there are other outstanding musicians who feel differently. The famous Swiss conductor Ansermet, in speaking of the break-down in communication between composer and audience, said that perhaps the new music was so alien to the normal processes of thought and aural experience that it was based on a faulty aesthetic.

Arnold Schoenberg was born in Vienna. Both his parents enjoyed music. By the age of eight he began to study the violin and soon after made his first attempt at composing. When his father died suddenly, the young Schoenberg had already left school in order to devote his life to music. Because of this unexpected tragedy, he grew up in straitened circumstances. Nearly all his life he struggled financially. He went to work in a bank to earn a living and composed in off-hours. Schoenberg studied and worked entirely alone, and basically was a self-taught composer. But as is the custom in Vienna, he used to meet daily with Zemlinsky and other musicians in a cafe to exchange ideas. Through Zemlinsky he was introduced to the advanced musical circles in Vienna, which at the turn of the century were under the 'spell of *Tristan* and *Parsifal.* All of this was part of Schoenberg's learning experience.

Basically a philosopher, Schoenberg had a strong taste for abstract speculation and the German reverence for "the idea." He had long periods of not composing while thinking through and developing his theories. There is no doubt that Arnold Schoenberg had one of the most original minds of all time and that his influence has been overwhelming.

Like many Austrian-Jewish intellectuals of his generation, he became a Roman Catholic. Then for a while he turned toward Protestantism. But in 1933 when Hitler came to power and Schoenberg was forced to leave Europe, he found it spiritually necessary to return to the Hebrew faith. Schoenberg was a seeker after truth until he died, but it is not clear what he meant by the word *truth.* He said once, "My religion needs no God, only faith."

In 1899 Schoenberg composed in three weeks the sextet *Verklarte Nacht* (Transfigured Night.) Everything that he wrote was composed in an incredibly short time because it was already worked out in his mind. The piece met with outrage, and when the audience hissed the performers, they sat down calmly and played it again. The composition uses the chromatic idiom of Wagner's *Tristan.* There are restless modulations, wandering sounds, and a building up of tension. It is written in the Expressionistic style reminiscent of the paintings of Munch, Kirchner, and Kokoschka. The music has exaggerated, wide leaps and extreme ranges to portray hyper emotion. Today it is one of Schoenberg's most popular works.

After his marriage to Zemlinsky's sister, Mathilde, the couple moved to Berlin in 1901. In order to earn their living, the serious, intellectual Schoenberg accepted a position conducting operettas and music-hall songs. It is hard to believe, but he even wrote a cabaret song; however, it was never performed because it was too difficult.

Soon they were back in Vienna, and they moved in with Zemlinsky. Because he was a gifted teacher, Schoenberg gathered about him a band of disciples. The two key pupils who helped to advance his ideas creatively were Alban Berg and Anton Webern. Most of his students worshiped him, and they helped to sustain Schoenberg in the fierce battle for recognition that was ahead of him. The group became known as the "Second Viennese School." In his textbook *Theory of Harmony* he said at the beginning, "This book I have learned from my pupils." In 1900 some of Schoenberg's songs were performed, "and ever since that day," he once remarked, "the scandal has never ceased." It is curious that Schoenberg in his theory classes rarely taught his own music, but basically concentrated on the compositions of Bach, Mozart, Haydn, Schubert, and Brahms.

In 1903 he became acquainted with Mahler, who was one of his strongest supporters and promoters. When the Chamber Symphony, Op. 9 by Schoenberg was presented a few years later, the audience whistled and banged their seats to protest "such sounds," but Mahler sprang up in his box and commanded silence. Afterwards Mahler confided to his wife, Alma, "I do not understand his work. But then he is young and may well be right."

Schoenberg's move away from tonality can be observed in the Second String Quartet (1907-1908). In the last movement is a vocal part for soprano that opens with the words, "I feel air from another planet." This often has been symbolically interpreted in the light of Schoenberg's breakthrough to a new world of sound.

In 1909 he finished his Piano Piece, Op. 11, No. 1, the first composition ever to dispense completely with tonal means of organization and move toward atonality. The whole course of post-Romantic music exhibited a tendency toward atonality. Schoenberg never liked the word *atonal*. He preferred the word *pantonal*, but *atonal* is what has taken root, because it sums up for most people what Schoenberg's music expresses—the rejection of tonality.

In Western music, tonality is based on the principle that seven of the twelve tones belong to a key, while five lie outside it. Schoenberg took his departure from the last quartets of Beethoven, but the more powerful influence in Schoenberg's desire to emancipate the dissonance and to have greater freedom was Wagner. In *Tristan* Wagner had pushed chromaticism as far as possible while still remaining within the boundaries of the key. Schoenberg said that the time had come to do away with the distinction between the seven diatonic tones and the five chromatic ones, and so he took the next step and declared that the twelve tones must be treated as equals. In this decision Schoenberg did more to change the sound of music in the twentieth century than any other composer.

Hindemith, who was rooted in the Reformation and influenced by Schütz, Bach, and Handel, insisted that doing away with the tonic is like trying to do away with gravity in the physical world, resulting in chaos. He regarded the principle of tonality as an immutable law. Hindemith believed that order in a composition is symbolical of a higher order within the moral and spiritual universe, a doctrine taught by Augustine. As Machlis says, "Dissonance resolving to consonance is symbolically an optimistic act, affirming the triumph of rest over tension, of order over chaos."[8]

Schoenberg was greatly influenced by the Expressionist painters Wassily Kandinsky, Paul Klee, and Franc Marc, as well as the poets Stefan George and Richard Dehmel. Expressionism sought to describe the inner state of man in the twentieth century.

For a time Schoenberg studied with Kandinsky, and between 1907 and 1910 Schoenberg painted a large number of paintings. The hallucinatory visions of the Expressionist painters brought forth distorted images on the canvases, and in like manner musical Expressionism rejected what had hitherto been accepted as beautiful. Expressionism was "the last gesture of a dying Romanticism." It was a suppressed, violent, agonized, distorted

---

8. J. Machlis, *Introduction to Contemporary Music* (New York: W. W. Norton, 1961), p. 338.

Romanticism of an anti-Romantic time in history, and the music of the age turned to atonality to try to express in notes what the artists were putting on canvas. Schoenberg once said, "There is only one greatest goal toward which the artist strives: to express himself."

Also in 1909 Schoenberg wrote his atonal monodrama *Erwartung* (Expectation). It is an eerie story of a woman who wanders through the woods by night seeking her unfaithful lover. When she finds him, he is dead. Schoenberg wanted to portray how, in moments of fearful tension, one relives the whole of one's life. The work has a single character and requires a huge orchestra. Schoenberg explored the world of fear and dreams. In his music, agony of soul often reigns unrelieved.

In 1912 he wrote *Pierrot Lunaire* (Moonstruck Pierrot). One feels as if the music is suspended, because in order to avoid tonal centers and a place of return and rest, Schoenberg used illogical root movements and no resolution. Pierrot Lunaire is like surrealist poetry. Some feel it is his most significant score. The tone poem is a parallel to T. S. Eliot's *The Waste Land*, a series of fragmentary dramatic monologues about the decadence of modern man.

The contralto part is not to be sung, but the rhythm must be kept while the voice only suggests pitches and immediately moves away from them. (This is called "speech-song.") It is extremely difficult to perform. Any means of exaggeration is used in order to communicate extreme human emotions. Schoenberg was searching for some other way than the text to give unity in the composition, as if he were writing music for words that had no meaning for him. One is reminded of Munch's painting *The Scream*. Schoenberg, like the Dutch painter Mondrian, rejected the laws of nature and then had to set up his own laws, which instead of giving more freedom are more demanding and restricting.

In 1913 Schoenberg completed *Die Glückliche Hand* (The Lucky Hand) with libretto by himself. In one scene the composer-painter uses both sound and color. A crescendo goes from red through brown, green, and blue-gray, to purple, red, orange, yellow, and finally white.

In the same year Schoenberg had his first triumph with the performance of *Gurrelieder* in Vienna. It is considered the "grand finale" of the whole Wagnerian, post-Romantic era. When called to the stage by applause again and again, Schoenberg, remembering the hostility the public had shown toward his earlier works, bowed to the conductor, bowed to the orchestra, but in no way would he acknowledge the audience. "For years those people who greeted me with cheers tonight refused to recognize me," he said. "Why should I thank them for appreciating me now." Schoenberg had a love-hate relationship with Vienna, as Mahler did before him.

Another key work is the great unfinished oratorio *Jacob's Ladder* (1917), based on the idea of reincarnation. In the text Schoenberg said, "One must go on without asking what lies before or behind."

For seven years Schoenberg did not write music while clarifying his thinking about how to reject tonality and still have unity rather than chaos. Thus the "twelve-tone" method was invented. The emphasis of the twelve-tone method, or serial writing, as it is also called, is intellectual and abstract. It is a rigidly organized system and moves within an extremely narrow expressive range. A *row* consists of the twelve tones of the octave in any order the composer decides. All twelve notes must be heard before any one recurs. This is to avoid a sense of return and resolution, or having one note sound more important than the others. All twelve notes are of the same importance. As Grout says, "Stated baldly, the theory *may sound* like a recipe for turning out music by machine." But he explains that it is not so. If the technique has been mastered, the twelve-tone row no more inhibits a composer's spontaneity than do the rules for writing a tonal fugue.

The twelve-tone row or serial technique represents Schoenberg's concept of "perpetual variation" (a fragmented contrapuntal music without a base). It is used to project moods of anxiety and fear. "It is significant that the perpetual variation of the basic row functions somewhat like the ragas of Hindu music," says Grout.

In 1918 Schoenberg founded the Society for Private Musical Performances with the intention of giving artists and art-lovers a real knowledge of modern music. Not only was the music of Schoenberg performed, but also that of Berg, Webern, Bartók, Mahler, Debussy, etc. In the final concert in 1921 *Pierrot Lunaire* was given.

In 1923 Schoenberg's long silence was broken, and in the Five Piano Pieces of Op. 23, in the last of the set, the new twelve-tone row technique was revealed. The same year Schoenberg's wife died. The following summer he married Gertrude Kolisch, and in 1925 he was appointed professor of composition at the Berlin Academy of Arts. Here there was a favorable attitude toward experimental art, but with Hitler coming to power in 1933, Schoenberg had to leave Germany. He went to the United States and eventually joined the faculty at the University of California in Los Angeles where he continued to teach and compose. He wrote in 1947 *A Survivor from Warsaw*, expressing grief over the victims of anti-Semitic persecution.

His American period in which he wrote a mixture of twelve-tone and diatonic compositions was not as productive as the years before because of ill health. He was unable to finish his opera *Moses and Aaron*, completing only two acts before he died. He wrote the libretto himself, and it is considered a masterpiece. It is based on the conflict that Moses is unable to communicate his vision, and Aaron can communicate but does not really understand. In Schoenberg's story Moses speaks of the "unknowable, impersonal God," which is the opposite of the truth. The Bible emphasizes the personal God whom anyone can know through Jesus Christ.

Schoenberg said, "I believe that art comes not of ability but of necessity." He became a composer in spite of all that was against him. He was very disciplined, not only in his life but in his music. Every trace of frivolity is missing. He was always burdened by serious, philosophic thoughts and labored over his compositions as if they were mathematical problems.

He grew increasingly rebellious and iconoclastic with each succeeding work and continued to penetrate deeper into the world of musical abstraction. Schoenberg aimed to strip music of human emotion, feeling, and relationships and wanted to produce music that was brief, thoroughly objective, and unemotional.

At times his egomania approached that of Wagner. Schoenberg said of himself, "I have discovered something which will guarantee the supremacy of German music for the next one hundred years." On another occasion he said, "Genius learns only from itself; talent chiefly from others." He seemed to take a grim pleasure in being the "troubling presence" of modern music. After he completed his Violin Concerto in 1936, he commented, "I am delighted to add another unplayable work to the repertoire."

Toward the end of his life, Schoenberg was a bitter man and resentful that he was neglected. Because of his inner torment, he became increasingly distrustful and irritable. Pablo Casals visited Arnold Schoenberg a few months before his death, and he found the composer sad and depressed because he thought he had done harm to music.

Schoenberg, in speaking about what he believed, said, "There are comparatively few points on which I strictly adhere to the Bible." Yet, interestingly enough, his last completed composition was Psalm 130, *Out of the Depths I Cry to Thee* (*De Profundis*, Op. 50b). It is a twelve-tone work for unaccompanied choir. According to Struckenschmidt, in it we hear "the daemonic compulsion that governed his music."

The teaching of Schoenberg, with his "uncompromising style and extraordinary originality," profoundly influenced two of his pupils, Alban Berg (1885-1935) and Anton Webern (1883-1945). Berg adopted most of Schoenberg's methods of construction, but he used them with more freedom that allowed for progressions in harmony and tonal-sounding chords. Berg, the Expressionist, was drawn to librettos of violence and unusual behavior. In his opera *Wozzeck*, a classic of the "Second Viennese School," he turned to the unconscious and irrational in his flight from reality, using themes of existential menace and death. *Lulu* is a more complex, abstract opera based on the twelve-tone row. Lulu is the eternal type of *femme fatale* "who destroys everyone because she is destroyed by everyone." It is a story of murder, blackmail, and sexual perversion—to the final degradation of the aging heroine on the streets of London. When Berg composed, he locked himself in a darkened room with the windows closed even in summer. His was essentially a tragic, morbid, pessimistic view of life that accorded with the intellectual climate in the twenties. He fought against chronic ill health and died at fifty of blood poisoning.

Anton Webern wrote lonely, strange music that was almost never performed in his lifetime. As a young man he admired Wagner, then studied with Schoenberg and followed the road of atonality. He grew increasingly partial to fragmentary themes and broad leaps. These fragments are pieced together into a mosaic consisting merely of brief, seemingly unrelated sounds. Webern built upon the Schoenbergian doctrine of perpetual variation. Sometimes a single tone became Webern's entire theme. It is sound for sound's sake with a sense of hovering suspension. This "pointillist" manner has had a vast influence, especially on his disciples Boulez and Stockhausen, as well as his concept of total serialization, which means complete control of the sonorous material. In Webern's *Five Orchestral Pieces,* the longest composition lasts a minute, and the shortest nineteen seconds. Webern wanted extreme brevity. It is music that hovers on the brink of silence.

John Cage studied for a while with Schoenberg in California, but he turned from the iron-clad twelve-tone system to the opposite extreme of "chance" music.

In conclusion, the twelve-tone row is limited as to the spectrum of human emotions it can express. True, it effectively reflects the atmosphere of fear, despair, and hopelessness prevalent in our moment in history. It is the right background music for the many threatening and horror-filled films being shown today. Twelve-tone compositions often end with a question, leaving the listener "up in the air," describing vividly modern man's sense of nonresolution. As Francis Schaeffer said in *How Should We Then Live?* "This stands in sharp contrast to Bach who, on his biblical base, had much diversity but always resolution. Bach's music had resolution because as a Christian he believed that there will be resolution both for each individual and for history."

Milton Babbitt (1916-), a mathematician and composer of twelve-tone music, says, "I believe in cerebral music." He explains that one should no more expect the layman to understand present-day music than one would expect him to understand advanced physics or mathematics. I began this chapter with a quotation from Schoenberg: "If it is art, it is not for all, and if it is for all, it is not art."

It is not surprising that Arnold Schoenberg felt at the end of his life that he had done harm to music. A musical system that appeals only to an elitist group of scientists and abstract philosophers must be based on a faulty aesthetic, as Ansermet suggested. The twelve-tone music and all the variations that have followed have no joy, no humor, no optimism, and no sense of delight in God's world.

Every great artist has a worldview, and certainly Schoenberg is a key composer in music history. "We have arrived," says Paul Henry Lang, "at the age of the philosophical composer in the sense that he is not content, as a creator, with musical expression but feels compelled to present his music as an illustration of philosophical ideas." As art historian Hans Rookmaaker said in a lecture: "What started in the philosopher's study is now in the hearts and minds of the whole Western world." The philosophical music of Schoenberg is a vivid illustration of this. His influence has spread widely.

Then it opened the door to electronic music that eliminated the performer, and today we have a "machine listening to a machine."

Schoenberg loved Bach's music, but tragically he did not understand the spiritual content of Bach's life and music. In place of the freedom, joy, and musical vitality of Bach, "Schoenberg took the body of music and stripped it of flesh, muscle, heart, and pulse, leaving it just a skeleton" (Stuckenschmidt).

I am not saying that the twelve-tone row should not be used. It does express some aspects of life extremely well, but it is a limited system with a negative outlook. The prophet Jeremiah was also confronted with disaster and human despair throughout his life, but because of his faith in the infinite, personal God, he was able to say, "Of this I remind myself, therefore I still have hope: Because of the Lord's mercies we are not consumed; His compassions never fail. They are new every morning; great is Thy faithfulness" (Lamentations 3:21-23, *Berkeley*).

Recommended Reading

Reich, Willi. *Schoenberg: A Critical Biography.* New York: Praeger Publishers, 1971.

Stuckenschmidt, H. H. *Arnold Schoenberg.* London: John Calder, 1959.

Recommended Listening

Schoenberg: Chamber Symphony in E, Op. 9
De Profundis, Op. 50b
Erwartung
Five Piano Pieces, Op. 23
Gurrelieder
Moses and Aaron
Pierrot Lunaire
Variations for Orchestra, Op. 31
Verklärte Nacht
Berg: *Wozzeck*
Webern: *Five Orchestral Pieces,* Op. 10

Charles Ives
1874-1954

*My work in music helped my business, and my work
in business helped my music.*

Charles Ives

Some critics have concluded that Charles Ives's business career was a
handicap to him as an artist, but he himself never felt this to be true. He said
that he learned much about life through the experiences he had in the field
of insurance. He told one of his friends, "You cannot set an art off in the
corner and hope for it to have vitality and substance. . . . Art comes directly
out of the heart of experience of life and thinking about life and living life."
In the mind of Charles Ives, this is the background for the artist, and he
learned it from childhood: there should be nothing exclusive about art.

For example, in his Second Symphony he quotes tunes such as
"Columbia, the Gem of the Ocean," "Camptown Races," "Old Black Joe,"
"Turkey in the Straw," etc., and at the end of the fourth movement, there is
a real bugle reveille. The composition ends like a Fourth of July celebration—with a big, loud *bang*. It is fresh, vital music, individualistic yet not
provincial. It is typical Ives, including the popular and the serious, and thoroughly American music when most composers in the United States were
merely echoing European voices.

Charles Ives considered it his duty as a Yankee and Puritan to scorn
pleasant, easy-to-listen-to, comfortable music. At one of his rare performances, the orchestra members struggling to read his illegible composition
ended up in chaos. Ives said admiringly, "Just like a town meeting—every
man for himself. Wonderful how it came out!"

He knew society would not pay him for the kind of music he wanted
to write, so he decided to look for work. His father, whom he greatly
respected, felt that a person could keep his music interest stronger, cleaner,
bigger, and freer if he didn't try to make a living from it.

As an organist Charles earned a small amount, and his first job in an insurance company paid him five dollars a week. Small beginning, but two decades later Charles Ives and his business partner and lifelong friend, Julian S. Myrick, had the largest insurance agency in America. For Ives, selling life insurance was challenging because it gave him an outlet for serving others while finding his own financial independence to get on with his music. He was convinced that the protection of the family and the home was a mission. He genuinely enjoyed helping people.

Endless stories could be told of his generosity. He was an extremely sensitive, shy man who had a love for the ordinary person. He was a paradox though—this quiet, gentle man had a *very* excitable nature. He was a pacifist, but he became a battler if something irritated him.

During the same twenty years or so that he was in the business world, Charles Ives was composing at night, on weekends, during holidays, working in isolation, concerned mainly with putting down the sounds he heard in his head. He did show some of his manuscripts to a few conductors and performers, but after a number of rebuffs he stopped looking for other musicians to understand his music. He did not want to be influenced or discouraged by criticism, and so he quickly gave up trying to interest anyone in his compositions.

How did this successful New York insurance man, whose business acquaintances had little knowledge that he was a musician, let alone a composer, become one of the most independent artists who ever lived? Mainly by sticking to his creative individuality and originality and not allowing the critics to tell him how to compose.

Today Charles Ives is recognized as one of the greatest, most original, experimental, and daring composers in the history of America. In the best sense of the word, he was a true eccentric, one of the strangest personalities music has known, and his career is without parallel. One hears over and over in his music remembrances of revival meetings. He loved the enthusiastic singing, loud and often off-key. To Ives this was life—so why shouldn't his music reflect the true sounds? He also delighted in putting down the varied outdoor sounds of nature on a summer day in New England.

Few of us have the energy and drive that Ives had or the genius, but even Charles Ives burned out and had to abandon both careers during the first World War. From 1930 until his death in 1954, he was a semi-invalid; however, in his twenty or so years of composing, he produced a sizable body of work.

Ives was far ahead of his time. Sometimes a well-meaning friend would suggest that he try to write music people would like—nice music (Ives despised the word *nice*). "I can't do it," he would answer. "I hear something else!" Perhaps the most amazing thing about Ives's music is that he was using advanced modern techniques and idioms such as polytonality, polyrhythms, polymeters, microtonal and tone clusters long before Schoenberg, Stravinsky, Milhaud, Debussy, and Cowell.

This is one of the most astonishing characteristics about Ives's music.

These modern composers knew nothing about him, and he knew nothing about them, and yet he was ahead of them. As David Ewen said, "In any book on our present-day avant-garde movement, Charles Ives must be the first composer to come under discussion." He is an authentic master.

Ives is the fountainhead of American modern music. Every American writing music today is more independently and confidently himself because of Ives's courage and perseverance. Ives now holds a unique place in American musical life. His most important music was composed between 1896 and 1921, but he remained almost unknown until the last years of his life. More about that later.

This Connecticut Yankee was born in Danbury on October 20, 1874, and began studying music with his father, George Ives, at age five. George Ives conducted one of the best bands in General Grant's army during the Civil War. Afterwards George was a music teacher, a bandmaster, and a great cornet player. He taught his son composition, theory, orchestration, and how to play the cornet, piano, and organ. He also grounded him in Bach, Beethoven, and Stephen Foster.

Charles's father was an original personality, not taken seriously by the people in Danbury. He had an endless curiosity about the sounds of music and encouraged his son to experiment musically with echoes and many other sound effects all around them, which stimulated Charles's imagination. However, the father insisted that his son learn the rules before breaking them. Charles's mother was a church organist, but in the Ives's home conventional listening habits were not encouraged.

Charles began to compose at an early age and was outstandingly musical. He was somewhat torn, though, about his total involvement in music, because he liked both baseball and football, not only as a spectator but also as a player. Later in life he recalled, "When other boys on Monday mornings on vacation were out driving the grocery cart, riding horses, or playing ball, I felt all wrong to stay in and play the piano." But in time whenever there was a choice between the ball park and the piano, he went straight to the piano.

To keep Charles's mind alert, his father would have him play "Swanee River" in one key, and he would play the accompaniment in another key, or he would have his son play two different melodies in two different keys on the piano at the same time. "You must stretch your ears and strengthen your musical mind," his father told him repeatedly. And Charles did.

It was natural that Ives loved band music. Whenever a band was marching in Danbury, and it was frequent in those days, Charles would follow them. Sometimes two bands would arrive simultaneously from opposite directions, each playing a different tune. This experience of hearing the mixture of two melodies and the joining together of alien tonalities and rhythms excited him, and it had a permanent impact on his creativity.

When Charles Ives entered Yale in 1894, he brought along some of his compositions, one being "A Song for Harvest Season," for voice, cornet, trombone, and organ pedal—each in a different key! His professor, Horatio Parker, severely rebuked him for his musical heresies, and after several unpleasant encounters, Parker testily asked, "Must you hog all the keys?"

Rather than spend his four years in open rebellion against the approved manner of writing music, Ives settled down and composed according to the rules. He wrote his First Symphony while at Yale and turned out an impressive number of "correct" compositions. The fact that his father, who was so close to him, died while he was a freshman undoubtedly influenced him. He remembered his father's admonition to learn the rules of music before breaking them. Ives was not a primitive artist but one highly educated and trained, as well as a deep thinker.

After he graduated from Yale, Ives shared an apartment with friends in New York City—they called it Poverty Flat. The demands on his time were enormous. He went to night school to learn something about law, enjoyed baseball, went to the insurance office every day, and still found time for his composing.

Soon after Ives and Myrick formed their company, he married Harmony Twichell, the sister of one of his Yale classmates. In his wife he found a wonderful partner. She was a beautiful, young lady who had trained to be a nurse and was able to care for her husband in a dedicated and responsible way. Harmony never doubted his genius and allowed his music to come before everything else.

She was the daughter of a clergyman, and going to church meant a lot to her. In later years Ives said, "Mrs. Ives never once said or suggested or looked or thought that there must be something wrong with me. She never said, 'Now why don't you be good and write something nice, the way they like it?' Never. She urged me on my way to be myself and gave me her confidence."

Ives did not have much extra time during those years of living a dual life, but nevertheless he made a point of playing with his nieces and nephews or teaching them something about music when they would visit. His nephew Brewster, who actually lived with the Iveses for a while, described a concert to which his uncle took him.

"We sat in the back row," he said. "His music wasn't played until toward the end of the concert. . . . It started with what sounded like discords, and there were protests from the audience that you couldn't miss . . . boos and catcalls. Uncle Charlie tapped me on the knee and said, 'Think we better go home.' It hurt him no end, but it didn't dim his enthusiasm for composing one iota." This helps to explain why Ives did not enjoy hearing his music played. He went to few concerts and rarely listened to the radio or records or read newspapers. He was single-minded and did not want to be influenced by others.

Brewster also remembered with joy his Aunt Harmony reading aloud to them, particularly *Heidi* and other wonderful stories. The Iveses' first home in New York was a modest apartment. They had no children of their own but adopted Edith, whom they adored. After Ives became more prosperous, he was able to buy a house in New York and a farm in West Redding, Connecticut, that became their beloved retreat.

In 1939 Edith married a young attorney, George Tyler. One of his vivid memories of life in a small New England town was Mrs. Ives reading to her husband every night after dinner and to whomever else happened to be there. "She would read all the novels of Dickens one after the other right through," Tyler said, "and then on to Thackeray and maybe Jane Austen. When she finished their favorite novels, why she'd start right over again."

Tyler added with a smile, "I often think of them sitting beside the fire in Redding in the evening. We would all sit back, and Mrs. Ives would read to us, sometimes for as long as two hours after dinner."

Absurdity and a sense of humor were part of Ives's personality. He was forever telling jokes, and he loved puns. In one score he wrote, "From here on the bassoon may play anything at all." He was sometimes as mischievous as a schoolboy. Concerning the "Fourth of July" from his *Holidays* Symphony, he wrote to the copyist: "Please don't try to make things nice! All the wrong notes are *right*. Just copy as I have, I want it that way." In his "Essays Before a Sonata," published at his own expense as a part of the *Concord Sonata*, he wrote, "This volume is now thrown, so to speak, at the music fraternity, who for this reason will feel free to dodge it on its way—perhaps to the wastebasket."

To prove that not everyone threw the essays into a wastebasket, one friend told Vivian Perlis, author of *Charles Ives Remembered*, "He says more in that book than Yale can give you in four years."

Central in Ives's works are his four symphonies and the *Holidays* Symphony. In his compositions he stressed American folk and popular music such as jazz, ragtime, military marches, patriotic songs, and hymns. Some works include sounds of circus parades and revival meetings that reflect his memories of life in New England. He quoted some 150 tunes in his music.

His intense activity in two careers impaired his health, and he was forced to abandon both professions. One day in 1926 he came downstairs with tears in his eyes and told his wife he was finished with composing.

As nobody seemed to want to hear his music, he had two works printed at his own expense. In 1919 he published the *Concord Sonata* and, accompanying the music, "Essays Before a Sonata." The *Concord Sonata* is recognized by some critics as the greatest music composed by an American. It is not really in sonata form but rather a collection of impressions attempting to express the spirit of transcendentalism associated with New England.

The four movements are "Emerson," "Hawthorne," "The Alcotts," and "Thoreau." Ives was strongly influenced by Emerson's mystical philosophy in which the spiritual is exalted above the material. As Chase said, "Ives was a blood-brother to the Concord bards, achieving in music more than half a century later what they achieved in literature and thought."

In 1922 Ives sent out a volume of *114 Songs*. These works were distributed with no cost (except to himself) to libraries, music critics, colleges, and whoever asked for them. They caused scarcely a ripple as far as the public was concerned, but they did catch the attention of Henry Cowell and Nicolas Slonimsky particularly. Coauthor Jane Stuart Smith had the privilege of singing the song "Evening" from one of these original volumes in her senior recital at Hollins College in 1947.

Ives's songs have spontaneity. One of the finest is "General Booth Enters into Heaven" with words by Vachel Lindsay. Many of these songs, such as "At the River," "Circus Band," "The Side Show," and "The Greatest Man," are a vital contribution to art song in America.

People began to recognize Charles Ives when the American pianist John Kirkpatrick played the *Concord Sonata* at a recital in Town Hall in 1939. It took him years to prepare for it as the notation of Ives was worse than Beethoven or Puccini—almost impossible to read. There were no bars, no designated tempo, because Ives said that tempo varies with what kind of day it is when the music is played!

Kirkpatrick repeated the piece several weeks later. At the age of sixty-five Ives was discovered by the American public. A few years later, in 1947, his Third Symphony was performed, and Ives received the Pulitzer Prize. His reaction was typically Ivesian. He exclaimed, "Prizes are badges of mediocrity. Prizes are for boys. I'm grown up."

He sent half of his Pulitzer award to Henry Cowell who was ill. Ives also was most generous to a journal called *New Music* that helped to print modern scores, but naturally he would not allow them to print his works. Also he helped to pay for Slonimsky's tours in Paris, Berlin, and Budapest.

The Third Symphony has a nostalgic quality of a church service of bygone days. In the first movement one hears "What a Friend We Have in Jesus" and "There Is a Fountain Filled with Blood"; "Just As I Am" is in all three movements. This brings to a climax the tradition of American hymnody from which our major musical impulse sprang for nearly three centuries.

It is true that the music of Ives is sometimes flawed, but it is always vital and interesting. In one of the essays he wrote, "Beauty in music is too often confused with something that lets the ears lie back in an easy chair." His music is not banal nor imitative like many of his contemporaries. There is an experimental, unfinished quality to his music. Mainly he heard his music in his imagination. Undoubtedly more performances would have helped to smooth out some of the roughness. As Schonberg observed, "He did not have a very good technique; in some respects he had a terrible technique. What he had was genius and a new way of hearing."

One of his most frequently performed orchestra works is *The Unanswered Question*. The strings represent silence, the trumpet the perennial question of existence; the flutes attempt to find a satisfactory response but never succeed. The stereophonic effect of this massed counterpoint is yet another example of Ives's creative originality.

Ives was a strong believer in life after death and was sure he would see his father again. Even though it is not easy to sift out where he stood biblically because of the influence of Emerson and Thoreau, he certainly heard the truth all through his life and quoted so many of the hymns with a clear Christian message. His wife regularly read the Bible to him and their daughter, Edith.

One of his first critics, Lawrence Gilman, who recognized Charles Ives's true importance, made this statement: "His music is as indubitably American in impulse and spiritual texture as the prose of Jonathan Edwards." When you hear the wheeze of a harmonium, the squeaky, out-of-tune violins, and off-key singing in his compositions, remember he is attempting to present life as it is, and as we learn so well as we live on, no one's perfect.

Recommended Reading

Perlis, Vivian. *Charles Ives Remembered.* New Haven: Yale
  University Press, 1974.
Chase, Gilbert. *America's Music.* New York: McGraw Hill
  Book Co., 1966.

Recommended Listening

"General William Booth Enters into Heaven"
Sonata No. 2, *Concord*
Songs
Holidays Symphony
Symphony No. 2
Symphony No. 3
"Three Places in New England"
The Unanswered Question
Variations on "America" for Organ

Maurice Ravel
1875-1937

Early in his life Ravel chose as his motto:
"Inspiration is but the recompense of daily labor."

*M*any people, critics included, have a false understanding of creativity. They give the impression that if one is a gifted person, an individual destined to be a composer, a painter, or a writer, whatever that gift is, it simply pours out of one. One critic wrote, "Ravel made music as easily as an apple tree grows apples"—a completely false statement. Ravel, who was secretive about how he composed, admitted this much: "I did my work slowly, drop by drop. I tore it out of me by pieces." His strong love of discipline proved to be his greatest aid as a composer.

To better understand Maurice Ravel, one has to know his background. He was born on the Basque coast in France near the Spanish border. His father was Swiss, and his mother was Spanish. Three months after Maurice was born, the family moved to Paris.

His father, Joseph Ravel, wanted to be a concert pianist. For several years he attended the Geneva Conservatory, but he had an equal interest in mechanics and inventing. Finally he decided to be an engineer. Joseph Ravel made wonderful toys for his boys, and Maurice had a lifelong interest in mechanical games. Later when he was learning the intricacies of composition, he found that working with chords and keys was as absorbing as taking apart and putting together a mechanical toy. Joseph Ravel never lost his love for music, particularly the piano, and took a profound interest in his son's musical development.

Madame Ravel was more of a comrade to her two sons than a mother. As a young woman she had been a model in one of the largest high-fashion companies. Both boys adored their parents and received all the care and attention that their circumstances allowed. It never occurred to Ravel to seek a wife, as he had such a secure and supportive situation at home.

After his father's death, which was a tremendous grief to Maurice, he depended more and more on his mother. A friend said, "No other woman could have lived with Maurice—his habits were too irregular." He would get up late and often worked all day in his pajamas.

About seven his mother would say, "It's seven, Maurice. Soon we shall have supper."

"Impossible. I must take a little walk first."

Hastily he would put on some clothes over his pajamas and go out.

About 10 P.M. his mother would have the servant bring her supper, and about eleven or twelve, oblivious of the hour or that he was inconveniencing anyone, Maurice would return. The entire time he had been working over his music in his mind.

Maurice Ravel was a born musician, destined for music from early childhood. "Even as a small child," he said, "I was receptive to every kind of music." This tiny, indefatigable man—he looked like a stylish jockey who seemed made of steel—was an artist to the fingertips.

Having very strict standards concerning his art and the freedom to work according to his wishes, achievement within limitation seemed to him the highest order of accomplishment. His self-critical attitude about his music, his unswerving purpose and discipline resulted in some of the finest music of the early twentieth century. It continues to be widely performed today.

Most of his life, until his health failed, Ravel worked carefully and slowly, polishing each composition like a jewel, so that his total output was comparatively small—only about sixty works. He was never content unless his compositions were perfect or as nearly perfect as anything can be in this world. Stravinsky called Ravel a "Swiss watchmaker."

Because he had such high standards, he sometimes spent a year or more on a single composition. As a result he became one of the most faultless composers of the twentieth century, though by some critics considered clever rather than profound. Even in his early youth he knew that all he wanted to do in life was to compose. "It's a good thing I took up music," he once said, "because I'd never be able to do anything else."

Rhythm was the fountainhead of Ravel's art. Many of his orchestrated works have been produced in ballet form at one time or another because of the profound sense of rhythm that makes his music especially fitted for interpretation through dance.

One of Ravel's first published works, in 1895, was *Habañera*. It is without parallel, as it revealed his great capability at the first printing. It was originally for two pianos and four hands and was later arranged for orchestra.

Ravel began to take piano lessons at seven and entered the Paris Conservatory when he was fourteen, where he studied for the next sixteen years! One of his teachers, in an excess of fury, called Ravel a "criminal" because he worked at the piano with such little enthusiasm; but Ravel's artistic aspirations were already toward creation, not interpretation. Also he was sensitive about his small stature, which included having small hands; and so, wisely, he chose to write music rather than play it imperfectly.

His composition teacher at the conservatory was Gabriel Fauré. Among Fauré's many pupils was Nadia Boulanger, who later became one of the most prominent contemporary composition teachers. Because of the marvelous influence of order in the teaching they received, twentieth-century music has been greatly enriched. God does use music to help bring order in His world. It is in a sense "the arithmetic of sound," and when music is distorted, as much of it is today, only more chaos can result. Fauré helped Ravel become master of his tools.

From the beginning of his musical career, Ravel followed a clear, direct path. He learned through his study of the classics, especially Mozart, that in order to know your own technique, you must learn the technique of others and that no one ever finishes learning a technique. Ravel was never afraid to imitate.

Through hard work Ravel learned his craft, which allowed him great freedom. Single-mindedness in the midst of diversity characterized his music. He was Classical in his desire for order. When he innovated as a harmonist, he drew unexpected but logical conclusions from old principles. One cannot help loving his Classical purity and yet contemporary feeling. Ravel was never old-fashioned, nor did he write poor music. He chose quality above quantity.

A year after he entered Fauré's class in 1898, his music had its first public performance. It was a dismal failure. One year later he was invited to conduct his *Shéhérazade* Overture. This performance was a fiasco as well. And a few years later, his failure to win the Prix de Rome after four attempts caused a public scandal. The same year, 1903, he composed the song cycle *Shéhérazade* and in 1904 the String Quartet in F, dedicated to Fauré—both fine works.

Ravel turned these disappointing experiences to good. Since the critics lacked the capacity to understand his music, he decided to ignore them. From then on he built up an armor against criticism, and throughout the rest of his life he seemed indifferent to either praise or censure and worked only to satisfy his inner urge. He would finish a composition and then turn his attention to a new one.

Another influence on Ravel was the eccentric genius Erik Satie, whose insistence on brevity, clarity, and simplicity also stimulated Debussy, Stravinsky, Poulenc, and others. Besides his musical genius, Satie had a wild sense of humor. He wore a fireman's red hat to a performance one time so the critics would recognize him. We can thank Satie for the humor we find in Ravel, Debussy, Stravinsky, and Poulenc.

Ravel's music has great wit and sparkle. To really appreciate Ravel, though, we must understand that beneath his seeming indifference was an ardent heart and a deep capacity for feeling. As a friend observed, "Ravel actually had an excess of temperament rather than a lack of it—a sensitivity hidden but profound—a strange combination of Spanish ardor and French restraint, together with the precise attention to detail which is characteristic of the Swiss."

The first piece of Ravel's to be favorably received and that helped to make his name a household word was, *Pavane pour une infante défunte.* It is a stylized dance for a dead Spanish princess. In this same year, 1899, his *Shéhérazade* Overture met with both approval and catcalls.

Maurice Ravel could not have survived without family and friends. Ricardo Viñes, who was at the conservatory with him, was his best friend. Viñes became a celebrated concert pianist and did much in the early days when Ravel was an unknown young composer to bring his music before the public. Their two mothers also became friends. It was a joy for them to speak Spanish together and talk about their country.

For a period of time Ravel and Viñes met with a group of young artists. The last member to be admitted was Stravinsky. They were a lively group, but as Fargue said, "We had more or less the same tastes, which was lucky for people as hot-headed as we were." Their interests ranged from Chinese art, many of the French poets, Cezanne and van Gogh, Chopin, the Russians, and Debussy.

One night when Ravel and Viñes were crossing a street in Montmartre on the way to a meeting, a rough-looking man bumped into them. He rudely pushed them aside and growled, *"Attention les Apaches!"* This was a word of insult in Paris and applied to social outcasts, so they got the idea to call their group *"Société des Apaches."* Everyone was delighted.

Ravel regularly gave his friends extra stimulus by bringing along heaps of Russian music. Borodin was his favorite. The group all became acquainted with the B Minor Symphony by Borodin, and they used the first eight notes of the symphony as a means of identification. One could whistle, hum it, or play it, and if you were an Apache, you knew a friend was near. This opportunity to exchange ideas in an encouraging atmosphere stimulated Ravel's artistic development.

Impressionist composers, as well as painters, loved the effect of light on water. We find this in the music of Ravel as he imposed his own form and order, like Cezanne, rather than letting his expression degenerate into formless fantasy. When he was twenty-six, Ravel wrote his first great water piece, *Jeux d'eau,* from which a whole new piano technique developed. Influenced by Liszt, this is a brilliant description of rippling waters inspired by the sound of fountains, cascades, and streams.

In the same year his father died, 1908, Ravel wrote another exciting water piece, "Ondine," from a group of three pieces called *Gaspard de la Nuit,* which is one of the high points of his art.

Also in 1908 Ravel wrote *The Mother Goose Suite* as a set of piano pieces for four hands for the pleasure of Mimi and Jean, the gifted children of his friends, the Godebskis. Ravel, in a sense, was always trying to escape from reality. He preferred to create his own world. He was like a spoiled child who never left fairyland. His shyness vanished when he was with children or animals. He not only understood cats—he could speak their language. When he moved into his small villa, Le Belvedere, a Siamese cat family shared his quarters.

He avoided tragedy in his art, and his favorite themes were Spanish rhythm, dance, comedy, and enchantment. He was a master of color and design, elegance, and polish. Melody is also everywhere in Ravel's music. In 1912 *The Mother Goose Suite* had a most successful appearance at the Theatre des Arts in Paris. Nijinsky told Ravel, "It's like dancing at a family party."

Ravel's most important work was his ballet *Daphnis et Chloé*, commissioned by Diaghilev, which has become a twentieth-century classic and one of the finest ballets France has produced. It is often performed also as an orchestral suite. He began it in 1909 and finished the score in 1912. It was first danced by Nijinsky.

To learn and be refreshed, the following year Ravel went to Clarens, Switzerland, for a couple of months. He had been there five years earlier when his father was ill. Clarens was also a favorite retreat for Stravinsky.

Ravel learned much about orchestration from the Russians, Berlioz, Chabrier, Saint-Saëns, and Johann and Richard Strauss; but his sound is different from those composers. There is a rich, colorful texture in the orchestration of Ravel. He enjoyed this part of his work more than any other because he thought orchestrally. To him, it was like a fascinating piece of machinery that he found challenging to fit together.

There are many stories about Ravel's habit of tardiness, but it was not simply due to negligence. He did not hear the clock strike eight or ten. In his mind he heard violins, oboes, and a harp playing. Regarding one of the infrequent concert tours Ravel made, Marguerite Long told of his "legendary abstractedness."

"At every stage of the journey," she said with a smile, "he forgot his baggage, or lost his ticket, or his watch, or kept his mail (or mine) unopened in his pocket. . . . " She added, "But his good nature never forsook him. He only laughed at his absentmindedness." It should be added that at the first presentation of *Daphnis et Chloé* Ravel arrived late.

During World War I he served as an ambulance driver. In 1916 his beloved mother died, and in 1917 he was discharged from the army for health reasons. From then on a great loneliness came over him that never really left him. Insomnia, which had begun during the war, increased to alarming proportions and was a torment to him.

He composed *La Valse* in 1920. He found some consolation in creating music in his deep depression. The piece is a tragic setting of postwar Vienna, a symbol of a dying world indulging in its last dance. A couple of years later he orchestrated Mussorgsky's *Pictures at an Exhibition*. To hear this after the original piano setting takes one's breath away at Ravel's ability to orchestrate so skillfully.

Because of his inability to sleep and his restlessness, he sought relaxation in the night clubs of Paris, where he heard much American jazz. To Ravel, jazz was the most important contribution of modern times to the art of music.

Even though he was lonely and restless, he still had his sense of humor. In 1925 he wrote his second opera, *L'Enfant et les Sortilèges* (text by Colette). It is one of his most tender works and presents a child's world of enchantment, full of imagination. The duet of the cats is memorable.

In 1928 Ravel was commissioned by the famous Ida Rubenstein to orchestrate a dance for her. What she requested had already been done by another composer, and so almost as a joke Ravel wrote *Bolero*. Immediately it became a sensation and is still one of his most performed works. It is an orchestral variation of a melody repeated nine times—the melody with its counter-subject remains the same with changes only in the growing crescendo of the orchestra. By the end of the piece, the whole audience is stamping their feet and clapping their hands to the mounting excitement of the rhythm. He was told that at the premiere a woman had shouted, "He is mad!" Ravel answered with a smile that she understood the piece.

Ravel completed two piano concertos in 1931, one for Paul Wittgenstein, who had lost his right arm in the war and asked Ravel to compose a work for the left hand only. His creative power seemed almost gone, but a visit to Spain, something he had longed to do for years, gave him a surge of energy, and he completed the two concertos.

In 1932, as a result of an automobile accident, and also from the years of little sleep, violent smoking, heavy wine, and highly seasoned food, Ravel had a breakdown. In the following years he began to lose control of his arms and legs. His mind remained normal, but he no longer could compose or play the piano. He had brain surgery and never recovered from the operation. Ravel died December 28, 1937, in a Paris hospital at the age of sixty-two.

As Gilbert Chase expressed it so well, "Ravel's music has been compared to those French gardens in which the trees and shrubs are trimmed to precise shapes and the flowers laid out in well-ordered patterns."

Recommended Reading

Goss, Madeleine. *Bolero, the Life of Maurice Ravel.* New York: Henry Holt and Co., 1940.
Roland, Manuel. *Maurice Ravel.* New York: Dover Publications, 1972.

Recommended Listening

Alborada del Gracioso
Bolero
Concerto in D for Left Hand
Concerto in G

Daphnis et Chloé
L'Enfant et les Sortilèges
Gaspard de la Nuit
Jeux d'eau
Ma Mère L'oye
Pavane pour une infante défunte
Quartet in F
Shéhérazade
Sonatine for Piano
La Valse

Manuel de Falla
1876-1946

*Spanish music is intensely alive—music inseparably
allied to its natural partner, the dance, has always
been the life beat of the Spanish people.*

Anonymous

*T*he household into which Manuel de Falla was born in 1876 was musical, and both families of his parents had been settled in the Andalusian city of Cádiz for several generations. Jane Stuart Smith has had a personal interest in Cádiz for years as her great-uncle, William Wirt Wysor, was appointed American vice-consul to Cádiz from 1893 to 1897. A most interesting book containing his letters from Cádiz has been written called *Old Sherry*. It was from near Cádiz that Columbus sailed to America in 1492.

Manuel de Falla's first piano teacher was his mother, and when Manuel was eleven, the two of them took part in a public performance of Haydn's *Seven Last Words of Our Saviour*, arranged for piano duet, a work originally composed for one of the churches in Cádiz.

He acquired the rudiments of theory from two local musicians, but the youthful Falla furthered his education by analyzing and studying with avid curiosity every piece of music that held an intense interest for him. Wagner's scores were a particular challenge to Manuel. Early in life he formed mental habits of self-discipline.

For a while Falla was undecided between a musical and a literary career, but around 1893, after hearing a series of symphonic concerts in the Museum of Art at Cádiz, he determined to devote himself entirely to music. Through these concerts Falla was introduced to the works of Grieg. The marked national character of Grieg's music, his harmony and absence of development, stimulated in Falla an intense desire to create something similar with Spanish music one day, which of course he did in a most imaginative and fiery way.

He was further encouraged to be a composer of Spanish music by attending some private concerts of chamber music held in the home of a

Cádiz amateur, Viniegra. Here Falla participated as pianist and played some of his own compositions (later destroyed). Attending operas and listening to sacred music increased his enthusiasm for composing music himself.

In the late 1890s Falla went to Madrid to study. After several failures in trying to compose *zarzuelas* (a native type of comic opera), he met Felipe Pedrell, a most fortunate meeting for both musicians. Pedrell was in a discouraged moment. He had much to teach, and few pupils understood what he was trying to communicate; but Manuel was ready for what he had to say.

Beginning in 1902 Manuel de Falla studied with Felipe Pedrell for three years and emerged aesthetically strengthened and with a vivid realization of the hidden creative values in Spanish music. Pedrell emphasized that each nation should base its art music on the native folk song, but allow the artist to use his imagination to make the music his own invention and not repeat it note for note. Falla went on record that he owed a great deal to Pedrell. The same year he began studying with him, Falla composed an Andalusian song, "*Tus Ojillos Negros*," which was very popular.

In 1905 Falla's lyrical drama *La Vida Breve* (Life Is Short) won the prize offered by the Academy of Fine Arts in Madrid for the best opera submitted by a Spanish composer, but it was not performed until 1913. Then he also won an award for piano-playing, which was a surprise to him as his real interest was composing; but it led to his establishing himself as a successful teacher.

For two years Falla taught piano in Madrid and at last was able to carry out a long-cherished ambition—to visit Paris. He went on a seven-day excursion that lasted seven years!

Even though he was obliged to live in cramped quarters because of meager resources, Manuel de Falla received immense inspirational and practical benefits in this cultural center of Europe. He said later that without France he could have achieved nothing. In the history of modern Spanish music an entire chapter could be written about the part Paris played in its development.

In Paris Falla made friends with Debussy, Dukas, and Ravel, who were all keenly appreciative of the values inherent in Spanish music. Many of the seemingly novel ideas associated with Impressionism were already found in Spanish folk music. In acquiring his orchestral technique, Falla was guided mainly by Albéniz, Debussy, and Dukas.

In 1908 Ricardo Viñes played Falla's "Four Spanish Pieces" for piano at a concert in Paris. They were dedicated to Albéniz, who died the following year. In 1911 Falla played his "Four Spanish Pieces" at a concert in London. Then in 1913 *La Vida Breve* was successfully produced in Nice, and the same year it appeared at the Paris Opéra-Comique.

At the beginning of World War I, Falla left France and went back to Madrid. In 1915 *El Amor Brujo* (Wedded by Witchcraft) was presented at the Teatro Lara. Later he rearranged it into a ballet with songs. Nearly everything in *El Amor Brujo*—rhythm, cadence, mode, and sonority—may be traced to the *cante jondo*. It is an example of imaginary folk art, and rightly famous is the stirring "Ritual Fire Dance."

There is in the music of Spain a passionate, deep melancholy underlying the outward brightness and seeming cheerfulness of the Spaniards, and Manuel de Falla's music is the true *cante jondo*. To describe briefly the *cante jondo*, it is the peculiar Andalusian-Gypsy type of folk song, "a deep song welling up from an immemorial past through the heart and mind of an artist who embodies the finest qualities of his race." Both *La Vida Breve* and *El Amor Brujo* are notable examples of *cante jondo*, the sinuous, florid, semi-oriental cantilena of Andalusia.

The years 1914 to 1920 were intense ones for Falla. He was frail in physique but full of nervous energy. His *Nights in the Gardens of Spain*—three symphonic impressions for piano and orchestra—had its first performance in the Teatro Real in the spring of 1916. This masterly work, so exquisitely sad, expresses that tragic sense of life innately a part of the Spanish soul.

Another large-scale work of this period was *El Sombrero de Tres Picos* (The Three-Cornered Hat), which was performed in London in 1919 by the Diaghilev Ballet Russe with designs by Picasso. The orchestration, influenced by Stravinsky, suggests a transfiguration of the guitar. It is the most humorous of Falla's works, and he gained world fame with the first performance. It is considered one of the great ballets of the century.

Falla did another comic opera, *Fuego Fatuo*, based on music by Chopin. His last exploration of the *cante jondo* is in *Fantasia Bética* for piano, composed in 1919 and dedicated to Rubenstein.

Falla's instrumental technique was often conditioned by effects peculiar to Spain's national instrument, the guitar. Albéniz and Granados were masters of the piano, but with Falla Spanish music found complete orchestral utterance. It should be mentioned that with few exceptions he chose the texts for his compositions.

Also in 1919 he wrote a chamber opera for puppets and singers based on an episode from Cervantes's *Don Quixote*. It was called *El Retablo* (Master Peter's Puppet Show). The work was commissioned by the Princess de Polignac and first presented in her home in 1923. In *El Retablo* Falla turns to the Classical tradition in Spanish music.

Falla settled in Granada around 1920 and remained there until 1939. A person of deep human sympathy and alertness, he was soon surrounded by a group of intellectual friends, including the great poet Garcia Lorca, who was killed in the Civil War. Here Falla remained in a small cottage even during the Spanish Civil War. He taught music and had a strong influence on twentieth-century Spanish composers. Also he was instrumental in organizing festivals to maintain interest in native folk songs.

One of his last outstanding works, *The Castilian Concerto* for harpsichord, flute, oboe, clarinet, violin, and cello, was dedicated to Wanda Landowska. His keyboard style shows a kinship with Scarlatti and his pupil Soler.

Until 1934 Falla traveled frequently as a performer and conductor of his music. In that same year when he came to Barcelona to conduct a concert of his music, Falla became very upset at the bombings that occurred in the night. His nervous tension heightened at the sight of growing lawlessness and convinced him that tragedy was about to fall on Spain.

His health worsened in the next few years. In 1939 he went to Buenos Aires to conduct four very successful concerts. He was urged to stay in Argentina, and he and a sister settled in the resort town of Alta Gratia de Córdoba. Because of his delicate health and the various disasters of the Spanish Civil War, he was unable to finish a vast cantata about Columbus, *L'Atlántida*, which he had worked on for twenty years.

In *La Revue Musicale* Falla said, "It is essential not to compose in an egoistic way, for oneself, but for others. . . . Yes, to work for the public without making concessions: that is the problem." He continued, "It is necessary to be worthy of the ideal within oneself and to express it, sometimes with immense labor, with suffering, and then to hide the effort, as if it were a well-balanced improvisation achieved with the simplest means."

Manuel de Falla is considered the most distinguished Spanish composer of the twentieth century. "As the man, so the music," wrote Chase. "Not a superfluous note, not an ounce of padding. It is difficult to imagine a figure more Spanish in type than this slight man, thin and alert . . . with eyes of flame." He was enthusiastic, passionate, and imaginative but very disciplined, contemplative, and a perfectionist.

It is true that Falla wrote comparatively little music because of his striving for perfection, but each composition is a major one of highest quality.

Manuel de Falla died in Argentina in 1946 at the age of seventy.

It is impossible to talk about Spanish music and not say a word or two about Albéniz and Granados.

Isaac Albéniz
1860-1909

*Never has music achieved such diversified, such
colorful impressions [speaking of Albéniz's piano
suite* Iberia*].*

Claude Debussy

*I*n Spain, said Cervantes, the newborn babe comes dancing forth from its
mother's womb. Isaac Albéniz was very Spanish. At four he appeared as a
pianist, having received his first lessons from an older sister. When he was
seven, his mother took the mischievous Isaac to Paris to study with
Marmontel, the teacher of Bizet and Debussy. Albéniz's musical gifts were
exceptional. He would have been admitted to the conservatory, but in a playful moment he threw a ball at a large mirror and smashed it.

He returned to Spain for further study, but having a spirit of adventure, at nine he stowed away on a ship for Puerto Rico and lived as a
vagabond life for several years. Part of the time he earned his living by playing the piano in places of entertainment, and during these years of wandering he arranged a recital tour that extended from Cuba to San Francisco.
He attracted attention to his skillfulness by turning his back to the piano and
playing it with the backs of his fingers!

Finally he earned enough money to pay his way back to Europe. Soon
he was penniless again, but it was spread about how gifted he was, and he
was given a royal grant that enabled him to study in Brussels and Leipzig.
Also he went to Weimar and Rome to receive lessons from Liszt.

After more traveling, studying, and giving concerts, he "settled" in
Barcelona in 1883. There he married his piano pupil, Rosina Jordana.
Giving up his career as a concert pianist when he was thirty, he began to
compose music. Albéniz was greatly influenced by Pedrell. In 1893 he went
to Paris where he met Dukas, Fauré, d'Indy, and Chausson.

Albéniz's masterpiece is *Iberia*, a suite of twelve brilliant and fascinating piano pieces that evoke the sights and sounds of Spain and reproduce
the rhythms and other characteristic features of Andalusian music.

His compositions are saturated with the color of Spain. They suggest
the hot blood of the Gypsy, the brilliance of the southern sun, and the

intense, controlled movements of the Spanish dance. Almost all the works of Albéniz are for the piano and inspired by Spanish folklore. Everyone should hear his *Tango in D.*

In 1903 Albéniz moved once again, this time to Nice. He had Bright's disease and went to Cambo-les-Bains in the Pyrenees for treatment. He died there shortly before his forty-ninth birthday, having lived a full life. He left unfinished two piano works, *Navarra* and *Azulejos,* the latter completed by Granados.

Enrique Granados
1867-1916

*Although his technique and his aesthetic approach
stem from Chopin and Liszt, Granados achieved a
truly original work with the* Goyescas.

Gilbert Chase

*E*nrique Granados first supported himself by playing the piano in restaurants and giving private concerts. Like Albéniz and Falla, he studied with Pedrell, and he too had a passionate interest in Spanish folk music. In the early part of the twentieth century, he wrote four operas, which were produced in Barcelona with little success.

In his youth Granados began to compose his *Spanish Dances* for piano, which are charming pieces. Because he was such an excellent pianist, he wrote magnificently for the piano. He was somewhat influenced by Albéniz, but the works of Granados have a peculiar simplicity that is his style, especially in his many songs and piano pieces. The dominant aesthetic trait of Granados is his feeling for the spirit of Madrid at its most colorful and romantic moment in history.

His masterpiece, *Goyescas*, is based on pictures and tapestries of the great Spanish painter Goya whom he greatly admired. They were written as two sets of piano works—six in each book. To hear "The Maiden and the Nightingale" played by Alicia de Larrocha is a sublime musical experience. Later he turned these pieces into an opera by the same name. Because of World War I, it could not be given at the Paris Opera House, which had accepted it in 1914.

It was performed two years later at the Metropolitan Opera House in New York with moderate success. Granados, who had a great fear of ships, decided to attend the premiere with his wife. On their return to Europe their ship, the *Sussex*, was torpedoed in the English Channel by a German submarine. Granados was already in a lifeboat when he saw his wife struggling in the water. He jumped in to save her, and they perished together, leaving six children. Both Albéniz and Granados died at forty-eight. What a loss for Spanish music.

Recommended Reading

Chase, Gilbert. *The Music of Spain*. New York: Dover Publications, 1959.

Recommended Listening

Falla: *El Amor Brujo*
    Nights in the Gardens of Spain
    Seven popular Spanish songs
    Three-Cornered Hat
    La Vida Breve
Albéniz: *Iberia*
    Suite Espanola
    Tango in D
Granados: *Allegro de Concierto*
    Goyescas
    Spanish Dances

Béla Bartók
1881-1945

*His best works are the reflection of one of the
strongest musical minds of the twentieth century.*
Harold Schonberg

*B*éla Bartók was a small, fragile man who suffered ill health much of his life; yet he had a will of iron. In spite of the seeming neglect of his music by the public in his lifetime, Bartók has become one of the most vital forces in twentieth-century music. This lone and enigmatic figure had a profound nationalistic spirit and became one of the greatest ethnomusicologists of all time.

Bartók was born in what is now a part of Romania (then Hungary). His father died young, and his mother began to teach him piano at the age of five. A serious, quiet child in poor health, he was unable to play with other children and therefore spent much time listening to his mother's songs and stories.

His mother recognized his musical talent and with indomitable ambition sacrificed in every way necessary that he might have the best possible training. Already composing at nine, playing in public at eleven, he entered the Royal Academy of Music in Budapest when seventeen, where he acquired a reputation as a brilliant pianist.

He studied with a pupil of Liszt and early disregarded the seeming "superficialities" of Liszt, considering him more important than Wagner or Strauss for the future of music. In 1905 he had an extended visit to Paris. He received no prizes, but his outlook in many ways was broadened. He graduated with honor from the Budapest Academy of Music and as a result was appointed to the faculty as professor of piano in 1907. He continued teaching there until 1934, although he was a reluctant teacher because of his reserve. He was at times almost a recluse in his love of solitude.

Throughout his life Bartók suffered financial difficulties, sometimes poverty, partly due to his uncompromising character. This did not curb his enormous zest as he continued his intense music study and composition.

His first important work for orchestra, *Kossuth*, was a symphonic poem on the life of a Hungarian patriot, which reflected the influence of Strauss. Soon after, he became very interested in Hungarian folk music. He met Zoltan Kodály in 1900, and they were swept up in the Hungarian nationalistic movement. In 1905 Bartók and Kodály began their fruitful trips to the remotest parts of Hungary, recording thousands of peasant tunes. Their first publication was *Twenty Hungarian Folk Songs* in 1906. By the end of his life Bartók had transcribed about eight thousand tunes ranging over Central Europe, Turkey, and North Africa. Among his more amiable works are the *Romanian Folk Dances* (1915).

As with Vaughan Williams, what Bartók called "peasant music" greatly influenced his composing. His originality developed as a result of this discovery. "The use of borrowed materials has nothing to do with the artistic results of a piece," he said. "After all Shakespeare, Molière, Bach, and Handel borrowed. Everybody has his roots in the art of some former time." He succeeded in transmitting folk music into something universal. The study and classification of folk songs occupied a good part of Bartók's energy for the rest of his life. As Machlis said, "His was a rare example of artistic creativity going hand in hand with a gift for scientific research."

Bartók was strongly attracted to the peasants, learning not only their music but their character and whole way of life. When collecting melodies, he lived most of the time in the open, eating simple food. In retrospect he said, "Those days I spent in the villages among the peasants were the happiest of my life. In order really to feel the vitality of this music one must, so to speak, have lived it."

There is great severity in much of his music and a sense of alienation, pessimism, and emptiness. One strains to hear a cheerful melody once in a while, but there was a deep spiritual void in Bartók's life that is reflected in his music.

He was a virtuoso pianist and is considered today one of the masters of modern piano-writing. The summary of his piano style are his 153 piano pieces, *Mikrokosmos*, which has become a basis for the study of the music of our time. His piano piece "Allegro Barbaro" (1911), with its pounding rhythm and harsh sonority, either repels or attracts. Bartók often treats the piano as a percussive instrument, which one senses in the barbaric vigor of his music and the dissonant, complicated Magyar rhythms.

In 1909 Bartók completed his first quartet. Through the years he eventually wrote six quartets, considered among his greatest music and the most important since Beethoven. Bartók had a profound veneration for Beethoven's last quartets. The Second Quartet contains some of the most beautiful music Bartók wrote. His profound pessimism is powerfully expressed in his Sixth Quartet.

He wrote three stage works: the opera *Bluebeard's Castle* (1911), the ballet *The Wooden Prince* (1916), and the pantomime *The Wonderful Mandarin*

(1919). This last work caused a scandal because of the questionable subject matter and the harsh sounds. Having received such severe criticism, he wrote nothing more for the stage.

His struggle for recognition as a composer was a bitter one. Each new work presented in Hungary was received with antagonism, crushing his spirit and nearly breaking his heart, but he pursued unswervingly his own individual path.

In 1923 Bartók divorced his wife and entrusted her and their child to the care of his sister in order that he might marry his young piano pupil, Ditta. He continued to support his mother, refusing to leave his country while she was still alive in spite of the growing threat of Nazism. He spoke out against the Nazis in an uncompromising manner, thereby endangering his life. By 1937 he forbade broadcasts of his music in Germany and Italy.

When his mother died in 1939, he left Hungary because of "the robbery and murder of Nazism." He went to America by way of Switzerland. He became acquainted with the young Swiss conductor Paul Sacher of the Basel Kammerorchester. As a result of their friendship, Bartók wrote three of his best works: *Music for Strings, Percussion, and Celesta, Sonata for Two Pianos and Percussion,* and *Divertimento.*

Bartók said that he desired to free music from the tyrannical rule of the major-minor keys in order to expand tonality. A way to that freedom came through his study of Hungarian folklore where he discovered numerous pentatonic tunes and modal scales. He deliberately refrained from the serialism of Schoenberg. Bartók's music is tonal, but much of it is powerful, savage dissonance with little melody.

His years in America were not happy. He and his second wife had little money, and they were anxious about friends and relatives in Hungary from whom they rarely had news. Concerning his health, he wrote to a friend, "It appears there is a disorder in my blood-picture, so they poisoned me with arsenic. . . . A few weeks ago, I said, 'Tell me, doctor, exactly what my ailment is! Choose a nice Latin or Greek word and tell me.'" It is not clear whether or not the doctor told him, but he had leukemia; and as he grew weaker, he was no longer able to appear in public. His last concert was with his wife, Ditta. They played his *Concerto for Two Pianos and Orchestra.*

For a time he was given a position at Columbia University where he worked on a collection of folk songs. He spent his last years in quiet neglect living in a tiny apartment on West 57th Street. In writing to a friend he said, "Our situation is daily getting worse and worse. I am rather pessimistic. I've lost all confidence in people, in countries, in everything."

Bartók longed for the "brotherhood of nations" and romantically believed that modern, alienated man might create deeply personal art by turning to some pure and precious source. The source he sought was vague and idealistic. It was not to God that he turned for inspiration, for early in his life he professed to be an atheist.

Bartók spoke of the Bible and religion in this manner: "It's odd that it says in the Bible, God created mankind, though it is really the other way around: Mankind created God.

"It's odd that it says in the Bible, the body is mortal, the soul immortal, though the opposite is also true: The body (matter) is eternal, the soul (that is, the form of the body) transitory."

No wonder Bartók felt himself set apart, predestined to a lonely existence. He loved and appreciated the music of Bach, but he never understood the source of Bach's inspiration, the living and holy God.

Toward the end of his life Bartók wrote some of his finest compositions. The *Concerto for Orchestra*, which was commissioned by Koussevitzky for a thousand dollars, was his last completed work and has proved to be one of his most popular today. Actually a symphony in five movements, its brilliant, imaginative sonorities overflow with feeling and emotion.

When he realized he was dying, he worked feverishly to complete his Third Piano Concerto in order to leave his wife an inheritance. On his deathbed he lamented, "The trouble is that I have to go with so much still to say."

When he put down the last bar of the Third Piano Concerto, Bartók wrote *vége*, the Hungarian word for "the end." It was the end of his life, but as a composer it was by no means the end. Within a few years of his death Béla Bartók became one of the most-played of all modern composers. He wrote very original, distinctive music with remarkable rhythmic invention. The aggressive percussion, the dissonance, and the crisp strength of some of his compositions is strangely at variance with the outward appearance of the little composer.

If you have been brought up on Bach, Handel, Vivaldi, Schubert, and Mozart, it is difficult to listen with joy to the music of Bartók, but as Charles Ives's father said, not only to his son, but to all of us, "You must stretch your ears and strengthen your musical mind."

Recommended Reading

Stevens, Halsey. *The Life and Music of Béla Bartók*. New York: Oxford University Press, 1964.

Recommended Listening

Bluebeard's Castle
Concerto for Orchestra
Concerto No. 3 for Piano
Dance Suite
Divertimento for Children
Mikrokosmos
Music for Strings, Percussion, and Celesta
Six Quartets
Romanian Folk Dances

CHAPTER 38

Igor Stravinsky
1882-1971

*For a beginner, in whatever field, there is only one
possibility, namely to submit himself to an external
discipline, with the double aim of learning the
language of his profession and, in the process, of
forming his own personality.*

Igor Stravinsky

A friend (and Stravinsky had many friends) said that Stravinsky looked like "a deeply preoccupied grasshopper." He was small of stature (five feet, four inches), and, to change the metaphor, he was a dapper, birdlike, lively, little man. Stravinsky was close to ninety when he died. He lived long enough to be recognized as the world's greatest living composer. Harold Schonberg of the *New York Times* felt that Stravinsky had the strongest influence on the early part of the twentieth century, Arnold Schoenberg and his pupils on the latter part. Stravinsky was the least hidebound and dogmatic and the most accessible of the great twentieth-century composers.

Igor Stravinsky was born near St. Petersburg in 1882. Since his father was a famous operatic bass, Stravinsky grew up in a musical atmosphere. The home was a center of culture, as the parents loved not only music but books and art also. He began piano lessons at nine. Stravinsky said that as a child, he was very lonely and reserved, partly because it was difficult for him to reveal his feelings. When he was still a boy, his mother took him to the opera. There he saw and heard Glinka's *A Life for the Tsar.* He had already played through some of the music on the piano, and that performance was an unforgettable experience for the future composer.

Even though music was an important part of his life, his parents wanted him to study law, which he did. At the university he became a friend of Rimsky-Korsakov's youngest son. After Stravinsky proved himself to be a diligent student of music, he began three years' study of composition with Rimsky-Korsakov. After a year and a half under such excellent teaching (Stravinsky became one of the great orchestrators), he began his first symphony.

About the same time that he graduated in law from the university, he married his cousin, Catherine Nossenko. It was the custom in the Stravinsky family to go to the country in the summertime, and Stravinsky promised Rimsky-Korsakov that while there he would send him a composition. By this time a strong bond of friendship had developed between the teacher and pupil. Stravinsky worked hard on his composition, *Fireworks*, and within six weeks it was mailed. In a few days the parcel returned with a message written on it: "Not delivered, owing to the death of the addressee."

Before his death, Rimsky-Korsakov had arranged for some of Stravinsky's music to be performed. In the audience was Sergei Diaghilev, director of the famous Russian Ballet Company, who had a genius for spotting talent. Diaghilev was a strong personality, and he inspired, stimulated, and dominated the music and art world between 1909 and 1929, calling on such talents as Debussy, Ravel, Matisse, Picasso, Cocteau, Satie, Poulenc, to mention a few.

Upon a single hearing of the *Fireworks*, Diaghilev commissioned Stravinsky to write an original ballet. Stravinsky chose a theme from an old Russian legend, and *The Firebird* was first performed in Paris in 1910. Overnight Stravinsky became famous. *The Firebird* was the first really modern ballet. It was followed in 1911 by *Petrouchka*, which revolted against the sweet sound of Romanticism. Then in 1913 came *The Rite of Spring*. The premiere, as Onnen describes it, "led to a very memorable scandal of the type of which Paris possesses an unquestionable monopoly."

When we listen to *The Rite of Spring* today, we cannot grasp how shocking the ballet was to the Parisians, because our ears have heard such an unbelievable array of sounds and noise since 1913. We have become unshockable listeners.

Stravinsky felt the scandal was the fault of Nijinsky, the choreographer. There were some rather indecent scenes. But the music was extremely new and in itself had a startling effect on the listeners, who had come for the usual Romantic sounds and sights. *The Rite of Spring* set off an earthquake in the musical world. It was to the first half of the twentieth century what Beethoven's Ninth Symphony and Wagner's *Tristan* were to the nineteenth century. It had a profound influence on other composers with its shattering rhythmical force. It is a masterpiece of controlled violence requiring a large orchestra. Stravinsky said that Debussy had the greatest influence on his writing of *The Rite of Spring*.

About one year after that explosive evening, *The Rite of Spring* was performed as a concert number with tremendous success. The new rhythm of the *Rite* was as important as the rhythm of jazz, because something like it appears in most of Stravinsky's later compositions and in the music of a majority of composers after 1914. In a sense, Stravinsky has restored to music a healthy, unwavering pulse. Many of his compositions are suitable for dancing. His music makes a clean sound. He is never sentimental. His is a coldly intellectual art. Stravinsky said that the purpose of music is "to create order between things, and above all, an order between man and time."

Stravinsky's music could be thought of as "thinking in sound." He said that the musicians of "my generation and I, myself, owe the most to Debussy."

Stravinsky continued to work in close collaboration with Diaghilev, but during World War I the Stravinskys lived mostly in Switzerland. He particularly enjoyed being in Clarens on Lake Geneva, as it had meant so much to Tchaikovsky.

In 1917 the Russian Revolution shook the world. In addition to Stravinsky's understandable concern for relatives and friends, he was now cut off from an important part of his financial resources. He took a strong stand against the Communist regime and did not return to his country for years. Soon after hearing of the revolution, Stravinsky was confined to bed with a nervous affliction. Years later he wrote about those days: "I found myself, with nothing in my pocket in a strange land, in the middle of a war, and so, whatever happened, I had to provide a means of existence for myself and my family. The only consolation I had," he added laconically, "was that my friends Ansermet and Ramuz were hardly in a stronger financial position than I."

The three friends, pooling their various abilities, went to work. The Swiss writer Ramuz wrote a libretto adapted from a Russian story, Stravinsky composed the music, and Ansermet was the director of *L'Histoire du Soldat* (The Soldier's Tale). It is a story of a soldier who barters his violin (the symbol of his soul) for the allurements of the Devil. It was a very economical production, using few instruments and showing the influence of jazz. All they lacked was financial backing. Happily Werner Reinhart, the famous theatrical director, was staying in Winterthur. They contacted him and interested him in their project. Soon they had the money. At the time *L'Histoire du Soldat* was not one of the most successful of Stravinsky's works, but today it is widely performed. To help himself get back on his feet again, Stravinsky wrote various piano works and began appearing as a concert pianist and conductor. He always loved the piano.

As soon as World War I was over, Stravinsky moved to France and lived in various places there for about twenty years. In Paris he was in contact with artistic circles, including Erik Satie and "Les Six." Stravinsky moved and traveled a great deal, and wherever he went, he was composing. In his French period he abandoned the Russian features of his earlier style and adopted a Neoclassical idiom. It was a tremendous effort to change. One can see in studying Stravinsky's music that nearly every major work is preceded by a minor composition for a smaller orchestra.

In his Neoclassical period Stravinsky was drawn to the clear forms of the Baroque and Classic styles. He treated them in his ultramodern fashion. He felt that music should not attempt to carry a message or mean anything in itself.

His work is that of one of the supreme logicians in composition. The music of Stravinsky is not meant to please an audience nor arouse its passions; and because of this, his music has a lean sound. Personally I prefer a rounder sound, but I admire him because of his concern for discipline, clarity, and tradition. He deplored the refusal of many artists to submit to the discipline of an established order. I believe that Stravinsky's music, as a whole, commands more respect than love.

He wrote another ballet for Diaghilev, *Pulcinella*, in 1920. In it Stravinsky plunged straight into the refreshing stream of the eighteenth-century Italian tradition. *Apollo* (1928) was the last of Stravinsky's ballets to be produced by the Russian Ballet Company. In 1929 Diaghilev died, and the ballet company melted away.

In 1930 Stravinsky wrote his *Symphony of Psalms* dedicated to the glory of God. Grout says that it is one of the great works of the twentieth century, a masterpiece of invention, musical architecture, and religious devotion. It is exceedingly terse and compact, lasting no more than twenty minutes. Here is Stravinsky at his best, inspired by a sincere religious conviction. Robert Craft, in his book *Conversations with Igor Stravinsky*, tells of the incident when Stravinsky was asked if one must be a believer to compose in the forms related to the church. Characteristically Stravinsky answered with directness: "Certainly, and not merely a believer in 'symbolic figures,' but in the Person of the Lord, the Person of the Devil, and the miracles of the Church." He added, "Religious music without religion is almost always vulgar."

Stravinsky had a genuine humility before God. It is not surprising to learn that he began his day with prayer. He recognized that the "principal virtue of music is a means of communication with God." "The Church knew what the Psalmist knew: Music praises God," Stravinsky commented in *Conversations*. "Music is as well or better able to praise Him than the building of the Church and all its decoration; it is the Church's greatest ornament. . . . The music of the nineteenth and twentieth centuries—it is all secular— is 'expressively' and 'emotionally' beyond anything in the music of the earlier centuries; the 'angst' in *Lulu* . . . or tension in Schoenberg's music. I say simply . . . that 'left to our own devices,' we are poor by many musical forms." Stravinsky started the "Back to Bach" movement and said that the heart of every musician's study should be the cantatas of Johann Sebastian Bach.

With still over thirty years of his life ahead of him, Stravinsky had to undergo many radical, difficult changes. In 1938 and 1939 his wife, daughter, and mother died, and because of the outbreak of World War II, he left Europe to go to the United States, even though he had become a French citizen in 1934.

After a year or so, he and his new wife, the painter Vera de Bosset, settled in Hollywood. In 1945 Stravinsky became an American citizen. Over the years some critics and listeners became disconcerted by his various changes of style, but we need to remember that he was a man who lived in three worlds. With his lively mind he was always interested in what was going on around him. At no time was Stravinsky content to rest on his laurels. He was always eager to venture in new directions and explore fresh musical territory. Ramuz in a letter to Stravinsky said, "What I perceived in you was an appetite and feeling for life, a love of all that is living; and that for you all that is living is potentially music."

By now, many of the idiosyncrasies that proved upsetting at a first hearing of Stravinsky have fallen into proper perspective. Nadia Boulanger spoke of the wonderful continuity that underlined the whole of Stravinsky's work.

In 1951 Stravinsky conducted the first performance of his opera *The Rake's Progress*, with words by W. H. Auden, at the Theater La Fenice in Venice, one of his favorite cities. It is his only full opera and is in the style of Mozart. While working on this score, he invited Robert Craft, a young American musician, to assist him. It was successful, and soon afterwards Craft became his musical assistant.

Craft's liking for the serial technique influenced Stravinsky to study the works of Schoenberg, Berg, and Webern. Gradually he introduced the twelve-tone row into his last works, such as the *Requiem Canticles*. These works are much briefer than his tonal compositions, but they still sound like Stravinsky. Even the serial technique went through the Stravinsky filter. These pieces make up only a small part of his total work. Stravinsky had an amazing ability to change and renew his musical thought. He never believed in using a formula. Each of his compositions has a different instrumental specification and a different sound. One can always expect the unusual in Stravinsky.

In Stravinsky's music there is no padding. He did all his composing at the piano, and he must have listened over and over to what he was writing to purge out unnecessary notes. Stravinsky was probably the first completely successful anti-Wagnerian in that he discarded the entire Wagnerian apparatus in favor, first of Russian nationalism, then Neoclassicism, and last his American period. His was a complete rupture with Romanticism. A certain tidiness characterized his intellect, his work habits, and his way of life.

He had his *small* idiosyncrasies though, as his wife, Vera, enjoyed writing about in a letter to a cousin in Moscow: "Igor's day is carefully routined. It begins with a headache which, however, is dispelled or forgotten in the shower. His bathroom, incidentally, looks like a prescription department in a pharmacy. . . . The vials of medicines, all neatly labeled in Russian by Igor himself, may be counted to the hundreds, and that, as the Americans say, is an underexaggeration. A branch-office drugstore has gone into business on his night table . . . they are so mixed up with the sacred medals that I fear he will swallow a Saint Christopher some night instead of a sleeping pill. Igor once told me that he acquired his taste for medicines at the precocious age of five. . . . It follows that he is also concerned with the health of people near him. Puff your cheeks in his presence and very likely he will give you a carminative; or cough . . . and instantly one of his silver pillboxes will appear and you will be obliged to swallow a grain of antiplague or other sugar-coated placebo—as I suppose them to be" (Stravinsky and Craft, *Conversations*).

Because Stravinsky had a long, productive life, obviously I have been able to mention only some of his compositions, but there is still one I want to call to your attention, and that is *Threni*. It was his first work to be conceived exclusively in the twelve-tone technique. It has enormous dignity and restraint. He wrote it in 1958, and the words are taken from the Lamentations of the prophet Jeremiah. In *Threni*, according to Machlis, we see that Stravinsky's "personal belief in man's need to submit to God works hand in hand with his equally strong belief in the artist's need to submit to order and discipline. Given this conception of art, it should have come as no surprise that Stravinsky ended by submitting to the most severe musical discipline our age has yet devised."

Although Picasso was an atheist and Stravinsky a person who respected God, nevertheless one finds certain parallels between these two artistic friends who knew each other from the ballet days in Paris. Each was a brilliant craftsman. Both of them used distortion for expressive purposes, and in their long lives they had various stylistic periods.

Ill health caused Stravinsky to slow down in his last years, though as late as 1970 he was working on instrumental transcriptions of some of Bach's preludes and fugues. Igor Stravinsky died in 1971 in New York City and was buried next to Diaghilev on the Island of San Michele near Venice at his request. His extraordinary personality lives on through his music and the many books written about him.

Recommended Reading

Austin, William W. *Music in the 20th Century / From Debussy Through Stravinsky*. New York: W. W. Norton, 1966.

Stravinsky, Igor and Craft, Robert. *Conversations with Igor Stravinsky*. London: Faber and Faber, 1958.

White, Eric Walter. *Stravinsky: A Critical Survey*. New York: Philosophical Library, 1948.

Recommended Listening

Apollo
Le Baiser de la Fée (The Fairy Kiss)
Firebird Suite
L'Histoire du Soldat (The Soldier's Tale)
Orpheus
Petrouchka
Pulcinella
Renard (Fox)
Le Sacre du Printemps (The Rite of Spring)
Song of the Nightingale
Symphony of Psalms
Threni

CHAPTER 39

Sergei Prokofiev
1891-1953

I hate imitation. . . . I do not want to wear anyone else's mask. I want always to be myself.

Sergei Prokofiev

*T*o test the accuracy of his hearing, Prokofiev, in 1917, decided to write a piece of music without the help of the piano; and so for a practical reason, he limited himself to the use of conventional chords. His symphony, which develops from themes, sums up the Classic elements almost to perfection—the formal balance and constraint, clarity, and urbane point of view. "It seemed to me," said Prokofiev, "that if Haydn had lived in this century, he would have retained his own style of writing while absorbing certain things from newer music."

Prokofiev called his work the *Classical* Symphony. "First, because it sounded simple," he explained, "and second, out of pure mischief—'to tease the geese,' and in secret hope that eventually the symphony will become a classic."

His "little joke" became a big success. The *Classical* Symphony, which antedated Stravinsky's new Classicism, was one of his first successful compositions, and it remains popular today. It is a gemlike, high-spirited work lasting only thirteen minutes.

Maria, Prokofiev's mother, devoted her life to the musical development of the gifted boy, and both parents wanted their son to have a good general education also. At one time Maria traveled all the way to Warsaw to find the right person to teach Sergei French. Louise, the new governess, was young and good-natured, and though she preferred to go to Moscow or St. Petersburg, she moved to the country when Maria promised to teach her how to play the piano.

Sergei did learn some French, but Louise became extra valuable when it turned out she was a wonderful copyist for his manuscripts. Prokofiev's manuscripts were not only sloppy but dirty. When Louise had to leave the

Prokofievs, his mother told him he must now learn to write music properly, because a poorly written manuscript was an offense to teachers, printers, and publishers. With time and much perseverance, he developed such a beautiful handwriting that when asked to show a rough draft, he would hand over a very legible, clean piece of music and nonchalantly say, "This is it."

Sergei Prokofiev was born in the Ukrainian village of Sontsovka. His father was the director of the enormous estate of a wealthy family who never lived there. Sergei in his childhood and adolescence knew no privations. He was brought up in luxury like a young prince in his own kingdom and attended not only by his mother but a staff of servants.

"While my mother was awaiting my birth, she played the piano for as long as six hours a day," Prokofiev later reported. "Thus, the future little human being was formed to the accompaniment of music."

Sergei began composing at five or six, and by nine he had written a partially developed opera. It was actually performed at the estate of a wealthy, music-loving uncle. When he was ten, his mother took him to Moscow to have his first professional instruction. Through friends of the family they were introduced to the celebrated and eccentric teacher Taneyev. Permanently attached to the door of the little house where the professor lived was the sign, "Sergei Taneyev is not at home."

Taneyev told Maria her son should learn the basics of harmony and counterpoint. Like Rachmaninoff, also a pupil of Taneyev, Prokofiev balked at the idea of strict rules. In the Moscow hotel where he and his mother were staying, Prokofiev preferred to sit by the window and write down the number of trolley cars passing by rather than study. Taneyev suggested they have the composer Glière come spend the summer months with them to help Sergei learn composition.

Glière did help Prokofiev to enjoy working on theoretical exercises and solving the problems of harmony. The teacher made it seem more like a game than tiresome work. Prokofiev loved chess. In fact, he once said that had he not become a musician, he would most probably have become a professional chess-player.

Glière's two summers with the Prokofievs helped Sergei to accept that he needed to examine the theoretical subjects, but most of all he enjoyed expressing his own musical ideas in his own way. Besides music and chess, Prokofiev was interested in astronomy and botany.

By the time Prokofiev entered the Petersburg Conservatory at thirteen, he brought along a number of his own compositions. In the ten years he was there he had many outstanding teachers, and although he did graduate with the highest honors in 1914, he caused untold anguish there with his radical music and his utter frankness on any subject. Like a spoiled child, he spared no one's feelings. He would have nothing to do with traditional music that stemmed from Chopin and Liszt. Loudly he insisted that the piano was a percussion instrument, and he played it with an unrelenting muscular exhibitionism that caused some of his teachers to cringe. One of the professors spoke of young Prokofiev as "very talented but rather unpolished." Stravinsky likened him to a porcupine "full of splinters."

As a graduation present his mother treated Sergei to a trip to England in 1914. There he met Diaghilev, the famous head of the Russian Ballet Company, who probably did more than anyone else to popularize Russian art abroad, always in a grand manner. Prokofiev and a group of other music-lovers were enthusiastic followers of Diaghilev's theory: "Pure art for art's sake."

When Prokofiev played his Second Piano Concerto for Diaghilev in his typical muscular way, a friend remarked in French, "This is some kind of wild beast!" (He quickly apologized when he learned that Prokofiev understood French.)

Prokofiev did eventually write several ballets. *The Prodigal Son* with designs by Rouault is considered one of the masterpieces of modern ballet. Also *Cinderella* and *Romeo and Juliet* are among Prokofiev's well-known ballets.

In the years when there was great unrest in Russia, Prokofiev was hard at work on a number of brilliant pieces. The *Scythian Suite* was the result of a commission by Diaghilev, but it was rejected; however, working together, they devised an idea for a ballet called *The Buffoon*. It took years before it was produced, but in that same period a number of splendid works came from the pen of Prokofiev. One of his outstanding compositions is the Third Piano Concerto.

Prokofiev was one of the greatest pianists of the age, and he did make a large and important contribution to Russian piano music, especially his sonatas. He was a very hard-working and disciplined artist. His opus numbers exceed 130. Throughout his life he would ask himself, "What have you accomplished today?"

By 1917 revolution had engulfed Russia, but Prokofiev worked on. However, when the spring of 1918 arrived, he was ready to leave his disturbed country and went to the United States by way of the trans-Siberian railway and Japan. He received one of the first passports issued by the Soviet government.

The permission was granted by Lunacharsky, the Soviet first minister of education and arts. Prokofiev announced in his blunt, comical way, "I have been working very hard and would now like to breathe a little fresh air."

"Don't you find we have enough fresh air here?" asked Lunacharsky.

"Yes, indeed I do," said the composer, "but I would like some ocean air."

On his passport was stamped: "For health and business reasons." It was a risky step Prokofiev was taking. He had to borrow money, and he didn't know if he would be accepted in America or ever be able to come back to Russia.

He stayed two months in Japan giving recitals. Then on the long journey across the Pacific, he worked on his opera *Love for Three Oranges*. The New York critics found his music "alarmingly ultramodern and an anarchy of noise and steel." The mechanistic style of Prokofiev became his badge of identification. In the newspapers and music journals he was called "the age-of-steel" composer or the "Cossack Chopin of the future generation."

The Russian composer, new to America and its ways, fared better in Chicago. There he met Cyrus McCormick, who introduced him to Frederick Stock, the conductor of the Chicago Symphony. The Opera Company of Chicago contracted to perform *Love for Three Oranges*, but certain circumstances arose, and they found it necessary to postpone it. In the meantime, Prokofiev became very ill with both scarlet fever and diphtheria. With his amazing energy, he recovered and tried giving piano lessons to earn a living, but with little success. So he began to work on another opera, *The Flaming Angel.*

In the next few years he gave a series of concerts in California and made several trips between America and Europe. Finally, in 1921 the Chicago Opera company gave a splendid production of *Love for Three Oranges.*

It was a great success with the audience and critics, but two months later it fell flat in New York City. It was not heard again in America for about thirty years, and then it was revived by the New York City Opera Company. In the hands of more imaginative people, overnight it became a box-office attraction, but too late for Prokofiev to enjoy his success, as he was back in Russia, very ill. To add to his distress, he was being severely attacked by the Soviets for his "bourgeois formalistic music."

In 1923 Prokofiev moved to Paris, and for the next ten years this was his home and the axis around which his musical life revolved. Paris was in a period of exciting fruitfulness. In almost every field of art there were exciting and daring changes.

Stravinsky was the leading anti-Romantic, and then there were "Les Six"—Milhaud, Honegger, Poulenc, Auric, Durey, and Tailleferre. These French composers, following the pattern of Satie, who used typewriters and sirens in *Parade*, attacked the excesses of German Romanticism with satire.

Among the artists also working with incredible energy and imaginative ideas in Paris were Picasso, Braque, le Corbusier, Ernst, Dali, etc., and it was Serge Diaghilev in one brilliant stage piece after another who brought together the new music and the new art of Europe. At this point Diaghilev was no longer producing only Russian ballet.

Prokofiev's mother came to Paris in 1920 in poor health. His wife, Lina, a singer whom he had met in New York, was very kind to her. They were both at her bedside when she died in 1924. Prokofiev, who had been very attached to his mother, felt the loss deeply, and it took him some time to get back to his composing.

Because of the pressure of his work and all the traveling he had to do to earn a living, Prokofiev began to have a growing desire to see his home country, if only to visit. He noted in his journal: "On January 18, 1927, at Bigosav, I put my foot on Soviet territory." He and his wife, Lina, were enthusiastically welcomed, but all Prokofiev could think about was that he was seeing through the car's frosty windows a Russian winter, a real winter, which he had truly missed all the years he had spent abroad.

After this first visit to Russia in many years, he knew that he would return again. As he explained to a friend in Paris, "Foreign air does not suit my inspiration because I'm a Russian. . . . My compatriots and I carry our country about with us. . . . Here I am getting enervated. I risk dying of academism."

Shortly before he returned to Russia in 1932, he had been weighing his own music and found it in need of overhauling. He began to strive for greater simplicity and more melody. In the last two decades of his life, he composed in greater abundance than ever.

Soon after his arrival in Russia, he wrote his Second Violin Concerto with his new emphasis on lyricism and Romantic melody. In this work he achieved a fresh, modern style with his own individual sound and a clarity similar to Mozart's. Also he wrote scores for various Russian films including *Lieutenant Kije*, *Alexander Nevsky*, and *Ivan the Terrible*.

In the war years he wrote a series of important works: the opera *War and Peace*, Piano Sonata No. 7, the String Quartet No. 2, the Flute Sonata in D, and the Fifth Symphony, which is neo-Romantic and like Brahms. These were clearly the works of a master.

Prokofiev's sense of humor was one of his greatest assets as a creative artist, and his comedy became less violent in these years. He composed many charming piano pieces and songs for children, and he is perhaps best known for *Peter and the Wolf*.

He said that he was always on the lookout for new melodic themes, which he wrote in a notebook as they came to him. When he was ready to write a piece of music, he had accumulated enough themes to make half a dozen symphonies. "Then the work of selection and arrangement begins," he explained with a smile.

The first years back in Russia Prokofiev was relatively happy because he was honored and respected, but there is little doubt that he was politically naive. When he finally saw what was happening to other artists, writers, musicians—Shostakovich, for example—it was too late.

Shostakovich (1906-1975) was the first to feel the harshness of the Communist Party with its insistence on socialist realism. Stalin wanted to make all artists propagandists for the state. In 1936 Shostakovich's opera *Lady Macbeth of Mtsensk* was performed in Moscow. It was reported that Stalin stormed out of the theater in a fury, wild with rage about the "degenerate music."

In time Shostakovich was ruined as a composer by the Soviet Union's emphasis on conformity and gearing one's creative work to the intellectual level of the broad masses. The government constantly intimidated him, and as he tried to write simplistic music to please the masses, it destroyed his immense and personal skill as a serious composer. This great composer died a slave to communism. Both his son and grandson, also musicians, defected to the West.

In 1940 Prokofiev left his wife and two children and married a militant Communist with personal connections at the top of the Kremlin hierarchy. His first wife, Lina, was imprisoned in various labor camps on false charges for nine years.

Because of his mounting discontent with himself and Russia, his health deteriorated, and in 1944 he almost died after a sudden heart attack. He suffered two other attacks, but each time he returned with amazing courage to his composing. Writing music or books and other artistic expressions are extremely helpful means for finding release from sorrow, pain, and anxiety.

It was not long before Prokofiev also came under attack by the Soviets and was forced to ask pardon for his music. His *War and Peace* was condemned as formalistic. The 1948 Central Committee Resolution squashed any lingering ideas of individuality or artistic freedom in Russia.

All adventurous music was banned, the country was closed to outside contamination, and all art in the Soviet Union became a vehicle for Soviet propaganda. A dreadful pall of dull uniformity fell over Russian art, literature, and music. No longer did Russian artists have anything to offer the world. Prokofiev, as Shostakovich before him, was reduced to turning out pallid and uncontroversial scores of artistic inconsequence.

Sergei Prokofiev was a great talent used and crushed by the Soviet state. Under the Communist system the people were the property of the state, and no Soviet citizen, no matter how great his achievements, could enjoy freedom. His work always had to serve the interest of the state, which of course had taken the place of God. As Solzhenitsyn said, "Communism is the most dreadful engine of oppression on our planet."

Ironically Prokofiev died the same day Stalin died, March 5, 1953. Prokofiev is one of the most often played of twentieth-century composers. "In his best music," Schonberg said, "he did hit an exposed nerve of the century."

Recommended Reading

Seroff, Victor. *Sergei Prokofiev: A Soviet Tragedy*. New York: Taplinger Publishing Co., 1979.

Recommended Listening

Alexander Nevsky
Cinderella
Concerto No. 3 for Piano
Concerto No. 2 for Violin
Lieutenant Kije
Love for Three Oranges

Peter and the Wolf
Romeo and Juliet
Sonata for Flute and Piano
Sonata No. 7 for Piano
Symphony No. 1, *Classical*
Symphony No. 5

CHAPTER 40

George Gershwin
1898-1937

Above all, Gershwin had melody.

David Ewen

*T*here were two vital sources of inspiration for twentieth-century music. Diaghilev's Ballet Russe brought to Paris an incredible concentration of talent—dancers, painters, set designers, composers, etc., and, secondly, from America, jazz. In fact, many countries consider jazz America's best-known export.

Jazz is an Afro-American term for syncopated music with free improvisation. (The most used rhythm pattern of jazz is ♪♩♪ , stressing the weak beat.) Jazz is a type of native American music first played extemporaneously by black bands in southern towns at the turn of the century. The heart of jazz is rhythm, originally based on improvisation, but later it was arranged by such superb musicians as Duke Ellington and Fletcher Henderson. The difficulty of arranging jazz is that it's hard to get everything on paper as the music is very complicated rhythmically.

The convergence of the folk-born forms of ragtime and blues into classic New Orleans jazz is one of the basic developments in the history of American music. Usually, ragtime is for the piano (Scott Joplin), blues for a solo (Bessie Smith), and jazz for a band.

New Orleans has been called the birthplace of instrumental jazz, with such great musicians as King Oliver on cornet and Louis Armstrong exciting listeners with his trumpet. Most early jazz-players were black, and much of the Afro-American music is "hot," be it a spiritual, a work song, a banjo tune, or a jazz piece. Although, of course, there is now "cool" jazz also.

Jazz has gone through many different styles, such as rags, blues, boogie-woogie, swing, bebop, progressive jazz, and so on. In fact, a recent *Time* magazine cover article was entitled "The New Jazz Age," telling about the

Marsalis brothers from New Orleans who are in the center of an exciting jazz renaissance.

Now we must turn to George Gershwin. He is one of the most gifted musicians the United States has produced. His music is American to the core, as well as very much his own style. One can always recognize Gershwin's music. He was born in Brooklyn, New York, the son of Russian-Jewish immigrants. His was a very close-knit family of four children. The attitude in the home toward religion was casual, and there was no musical background from his parents.

When his mother had an upright piano moved into their living room, Gershwin suddenly fell in love with music. He began to study seriously at the age of ten. Before this he had been involved only in sports and street games. But now his interest focused on music. He was infatuated with it and developed a lifelong absorption with his newly discovered art.

One of his early teachers, Charles Hambitzer (1881-1918), had a profound influence on Gershwin. He considered his pupil a genius and introduced him to great piano literature, such as Liszt, Ravel, Debussy, and Bach. Gershwin also admired Stravinsky, Schoenberg, and Berg. The boy had a vital, searching curiosity, and although he was never proficient at sight-reading music, he loved improvisation and inventing tunes.

In 1914 he left high school and went to work at fifteen as a Tin Pan Alley song-plugger for the Jerome Remick music publishing company, where he heard the good and the bad. Among the good were the songs of Irving Berlin and Jerome Kern, who became close friends with Gershwin. Gershwin soon was involved in the world of Broadway. (Kern's *Show Boat* is America's finest light opera.) Gershwin had begun to keep a little workbook, which he always had with him, to jot down melodies when they came to him.

At Remick's he made friends with the song-and-dance team, Fred and Adele Astaire. He made a prophetic comment to them, "Wouldn't it be great if I could write a musical show and you could be in it?" Years later, in 1924, this prophecy came true in *Lady Be Good,* marking the advent of the Gershwin musical.

His first great song hit, "Swanee," was made famous by Al Jolson. In 1924, when Gershwin was twenty-five, Paul Whiteman, who wanted to make jazz respectable, commissioned Gershwin to write *Rhapsody in Blue.* Gershwin wrote it in three weeks. Composer Ferde Grofé then orchestrated it. The work is a combination of Lisztian rhapsody and jazz. It was Gershwin's first attempt at a large musical form. He became popular overnight and soon was world famous and wealthy. Later a biographical film about Gershwin was produced entitled *Rhapsody in Blue.*

At the end of a long, rather dull concert in New York's Aeolian Hall, Gershwin at the piano brilliantly played *Rhapsody in Blue,* with its opening clarinet glissando (which necessitated a new technique for playing the clarinet). The audience was electrified. Though some critics were lukewarm, the public loved it and still does. Musical critics often misunderstood Gershwin, but he had the good sense not to listen to them and continued with his own unique style.

With the success of *Rhapsody in Blue* (recognition came early in his life), Gershwin acquired a five-story house near Riverside Drive in New York City and moved the entire Gershwin family there. When he needed privacy, he went to a nearby hotel because the house was too full of people and bustle.

His music is brilliantly alive today, still fresh and filled with ingenuous rhythmic patterns. Following the extraordinary success of *Rhapsody in Blue,* Walter Damrosch of the New York Symphony commissioned Gershwin to write the Concerto in F Major.

It is reported Gershwin went out and bought a book on how to write a concerto. Whether he needed its information or not, he succeeded brilliantly, as this is the first work in a concerto form by an American composer to enter the permanent repertoire of symphonic music. Gershwin certainly had the gift of melody, although he was not trained to handle the big forms.

Haunted by a lack of conservatory training, he continually sought to improve his composing by studying with various outstanding teachers until the end of his life. He always aimed for the best. For two years he studied counterpoint with the avant-garde composer Henry Cowell. Few composers have been so assiduous in seeking improvement as Gershwin.

He wanted to study with Ravel, but Ravel asked him, "Why do you want to become a second-rate Ravel when you are already a first-rate Gershwin?" Then he went to Stravinsky for advice. When Stravinsky heard that he made over $100,000 a year, Stravinsky exclaimed, "In that case perhaps it is I who ought to take lessons from you!"

Dynamic, physically attractive, and always well dressed, with a radiant personality, Gershwin was the center of an adoring circle of friends, including Kay Swift and Mabel Schirmer. Very sociable, he wanted people around him even when composing. He played the piano constantly and tended to compose late at night. Gershwin was rarely on time for appointments (like Ravel). Yet he was utterly charming, sweet, and absorbing, for music was his labor of love.

He played his own compositions with enthusiasm, improvising with a brilliant flair at many elegant social gatherings, delighting all in his usual round of parties. He loved to play *his* music and said, "You see, if I don't play, I don't have a good time!" His friend and interpreter Oscar Levant quipped, "An evening with Gershwin is a Gershwin evening."

Multitalented, he was also a good painter. He had a large income, so he began to collect modern paintings—early Picasso, Gauguin, Derain, Matisse, Chagall, Utrillo, Rouault, and others. Quite an athlete, he and Schoenberg enjoyed playing tennis and discussing composition. His last painting was of Schoenberg. Gershwin never married, as he was always busy and surrounded by family and friends. Music was his main interest and love. So, like many other composers who never married, such as Handel, Beethoven, Brahms, Ravel, and Poulenc, he was completely single-minded.

Gershwin was anxious to keep busy, unhappy when not working. Excitement nurtured his temperament. In 1928, while on vacation in Europe, he met everywhere enthusiastic crowds. How he did it in his hectic, glamorous life is difficult to understand, but he was always composing, even during holidays. With the usual big cigar in his mouth, he wrote the symphonic tone poem, *An American in Paris*. This was later made into an excellent film with Gene Kelly dancing. Like F. Scott Fitzgerald, Gershwin personified the sophisticated Jazz Age of the twentieth century. Both men were distinguished American artists, and, sadly, both died young.

An American in Paris is the story of a young man strolling about Paris, enchanted with the wonder of the city, yet stricken with the "blues," homesickness for America. The exciting score even includes taxi horns. In the music there is an effective blues section along with jazz and dance elements.

Gershwin proved that jazz can be used in larger compositions and was not confined to dance halls and bars. His music is called "symphonic jazz." His wish was to make "a lady out of jazz," built on the rhythm pattern of jazz ♪♪♪ . Many composers have been influenced by Gershwin—Milhaud, Poulenc, Copeland, Barber, and Bernstein—to mention a few.

Gershwin had a spontaneous lyric gift. As he said, he had more tunes in his head than he could write down in a hundred years. He wrote many successful Broadway musicals, including *Oh, Kay, Funny Face, Girl Crazy, Strike Up the Band,* and *Of Thee I Sing* (which won a Pulitzer prize). Stars such as Fred and Adele Astaire, Ginger Rogers, Gertrude Lawrence, and Ethel Merman performed in these Broadway hits, adding to his fame. His brother Ira was brilliant at finding the right words, writing many of Gershwin's lyrics. They worked together in a remarkably professional manner. George was known as "Mr. Music" and Ira was "Mr. Words."

A great admirer of Schubert, Gershwin also wrote exquisite songs: "Somebody Loves Me," "Love Walked In," "The Man I love," "Fascinating Rhythm," to mention a few. His music is full of optimism, vitality, and freshness. Gershwin rarely wrote sad music, though there is that lovely touch of nostalgia in many of his melodies.

In his *Preludes* for piano, he blended blues and jazz sounds with the Romantic piano tradition. Musicologist Abram Chasins said, "He was the only composer I ever heard who could make a piano laugh." Gershwin wanted to bridge the gap between popular music and the concert hall; in other words, from Tin Pan Alley on Broadway to Carnegie Hall. In his own unique way, he combines elements of blues, spirituals, ragtime, and jazz with harmonies of Ravel ("blue notes" flattening the third and seventh degrees of the diatonic scale). He was not a jazz composer, but used jazz and blues to create his own sound. In George Gershwin there was something of the Russian, the European Classicist, and the American Jew fused together. He regarded jazz as American folk music.

Lastly, we come to his master work and a giant stride in his music, the folk opera, *Porgy and Bess.* It is American in every note and our best opera—

filled with melodies and drama. Gershwin wrote it in 1935, just two years before his death. It had a lukewarm reception, but now it is performed the world over, including at the Metropolitan Opera and La Scala. *Porgy and Bess* is a remarkable work, filled with deep insight, poignancy, and compassion.

The superb lyrics were written by his brother Ira in conjunction with DuBose and Dorothy Heyward. The story is set in Catfish Row, a run-down, poor area on the waterfront of Charleston, South Carolina. Even a hurricane is included. Gershwin spent months on Folly Island, South Carolina, soaking up the idiom of the Gullah blacks of Charleston, their shouts and different ways of life. He felt at ease in this setting because he knew Harlem from childhood. This opera contains no actual Negro melodies. It is all Gershwin's original music, such as "Summertime," "I Got Plenty o' Nuttin'" and "It Ain't Necessarily So." He called himself a modern Romantic and chose to be himself in spite of the critics.

Gershwin bridged the gap between serious and popular music. His songs delighted the nation, and his improvisations were phenomenal. He wrote music for films in Hollywood, such as *Shall We Dance?* with Fred Astaire and Ginger Rogers, though he much preferred New York. Woody Allen's film *Manhattan* has an all-Gershwin sound track.

Toward the end of his life he suffered from bad headaches and dizziness and was suddenly taken ill with a brain tumor. Following an unsuccessful operation, he died in Hollywood, July 11, 1937. After Gershwin's death at thirty-eight, Schoenberg said, "I grieve over the deplorable loss to music, for there is no doubt that he was a great composer."

Recommended Reading

Ewen, David. *George Gershwin: His Journey to Greatness.* New
York: The Ungar Publishing Co., 1986.
Jablonski, Edward. *Gershwin.* Boston: Northeastern
University Press, 1990.

Recommended Listening

An American in Paris
Concerto in F Major for Piano and Orchestra
"I Got Rhythm" for Piano and Orchestra
Lullaby for String Quartet
Porgy and Bess
Preludes for Piano
Rhapsody in Blue for Piano and Orchestra
Songs

Francis Poulenc
1899-1963

*I have sought neither to ridicule nor to mimic
tradition, but to compose naturally as I felt
impelled to.*

Francis Poulenc

Francis Poulenc and Arnold Schoenberg were as different as Winnie the Pooh and Eyeore in their outlook on life and in their creativity. Shortly after World War I, Poulenc and his friend Milhaud were invited to visit Schoenberg at his home in Mödling on the outskirts of Vienna. Poulenc, who was not a philosopher, went along reluctantly. Austria was still suffering from poverty and inflation. There was an air of depression everywhere, although the Schoenberg house and garden were well kept. Inside, however, was worse than outside, as the walls of the various rooms were lined with Schoenberg's Expressionistic paintings, mostly facial studies in which only the eyes were visible (reminiscent of Kokoschka's influence).

As soon as the formal greetings were extended, the conversation became incomprehensible to Poulenc, who listened without comment as Schoenberg and Milhaud gravely discussed abstract philosophy and the twelve-tone row. Poulenc found it doubly hard to concentrate with all the eyes peering at him from the portraits on the walls, and he kept glancing out the open window at a small boy playing in the garden. Suddenly the child lost control of the ball he was bouncing and, as if it were "on target," the missile flew through the window and landed in the center of the soup tureen, spraying a thick brown liquid over the table and all those around it. As James Harding says, "The diversion was not unwelcome to Poulenc. His interest in Schoenberg, genuine though it was, can be explained by the attraction of opposites."

Francis Poulenc, the Parisian musician par excellence, was born in Paris not far from the Presidential Palace of the Elysée. His father, a successful businessman, was part owner of a drug company. His mother, a thoroughgoing Parisian, was interested in the arts, especially the theater. She played the piano well and gave Poulenc his first lessons when he was five. He loved hearing his mother play Mozart, Chopin, Schubert, Schumann, and Grieg, all of whom influenced his music. Schubert's *Winter Journey* songs made a lasting impression on him.

Poulenc was a rather sickly child, born after his parents had been married many years. He was the delight of the household, and even as a man, Poulenc was like a charming, overgrown schoolboy. Early in life he decided to be a composer. His father saw to the completion of his academic education first but allowed the piano lessons to continue. At an early age Poulenc was dictating compositions to his mother.

As soon as Poulenc's mother had taught him all she knew, she put him in the hands of various teachers. His most important teacher, Spanish pianist Ricardo Viñes, was an outstanding interpreter of Debussy, Ravel, de Falla, and Satie. Viñes not only introduced the fifteen-year-old Poulenc to as much music as possible, especially contemporary music, but also to Erik Satie and to another of his pupils, George Auric. After Poulenc became famous, he said of Viñes, "I owe him everything."

Poulenc became a brilliant pianist, although his own solo piano music is somewhat too facile. His splendid Concerto in D Minor for Two Pianos, showing the influence of Mozart, still has the unique and beautiful Poulenc sound. Poulenc and Auric became lifelong friends. Poulenc was awed by Auric's musical knowledge, brilliance, and sophistication and was inspired to work harder himself. The friends played through stacks of music that covered Auric's piano, went to concerts, and made friends with other musicians and artists they met in cafes.

A number of young composers were encouraged by Erik Satie and Jean Cocteau to give concerts in a Montparnasse studio. Six of these musicians—Francis Poulenc, George Auric, Darius Milhaud, Arthur Honegger, Germaine Tailleferre, and Louis Durey—became known as "Les Six." The name came into being through the critic Henri Collet when writing about a concert given by them. "Les Six," bound only by personal friendship and a desire to stand against Wagner and the German influence as well as Impressionism, had little in common other than their youthfulness, high spirits, and the desire to further their compositions. Musically they had no unifying aesthetic.

Poulenc was the youngest of "Les Six," and his piece *Rapsodie Negre* (Negro Rhapsody) launched "Les Six" as well as himself. The composition made an impression at its first playing because of the color, spice, and vigor of Poulenc's style. It had a melodic freshness all his own. He was only eighteen.

Before we go on with Poulenc, mention must be made of Erik Satie (1866-1925), who influenced many of the French composers. He had his eccentricities and weaknesses, but laziness was not one of them. He was a tremendous worker, "much more ant than butterfly," said Jean Cocteau. "Satie teaches what in our age is the greatest audacity—simplicity." His ballet *Parade* (about a circus), written for Diaghilev, with scenario by Cocteau and sets by Picasso, had a profound impact on modern theater. On one concert platform Satie appeared in a fireman's shining brass helmet so he would not go unnoticed. He has been called the "father of humor in modern music." One of his many quotes is, "I want to compose a piece for dogs, and I already have my decor. The curtain rises on a bone." He was a rebel, but not in an angry way.

His insistence on extreme brevity, clarity, and simplicity had a great influence on his friend Debussy, on Stravinsky, and later on the early compositions of Poulenc. Twentieth-century music owes much to Erik Satie. Simply expressed, his goal was to create an "everyday music" for everyday people—music that is down to earth, stripped of pretensions and ivory-tower seclusion. "All great artists are amateurs," said Satie. One of "Les Six," Milhaud, in speaking of Erik Satie, said, "The purity of his art, his horror of all concessions, his contempt for money, and his ruthless attitude toward the critics were a marvelous example for us all."

In 1918 Poulenc was called to military service in France. This interrupted his musical career, though while in the military he did write three exquisite piano pieces, *Trois Mouvements Perpetuels*. These are melodic, cheerful, Parisian two-part inventions of vivid charm without development or complication. Already one is aware of the importance of rhythm and jazz in Poulenc's music. After his release from military duties, he returned to composition with even greater zest.

In 1919 Poulenc composed his first songs to the poems of Guillaume Apollinaire. *Le Bestiaire* (Bestiary), with woodcuts by Raoul Dufy, is now a much-sought-after rare book edition. Poulenc is a musical counterpart to the painter Dufy. Raoul Dufy (1877-1953), best known for his lively decorative paintings, used bright, cheerful colors and a simple style to portray the world as he saw it. He was an artist who never really lost his enjoyment and appreciation of life, even after he became badly crippled with arthritis. Someone said that Dufy always looked like "an amazed cherub." He captured sensations in all their freshness and immediacy. He painted a happy world. He too loved music and painted individual instruments as well as entire orchestras.

Even though Poulenc already had a reputation as an able composer, he felt he did not really know how to write music correctly. So at the age of twenty-one he went to an excellent teacher, Charles Koechlin, to study harmony. His weekly exercises consisted of chorales in the form of four-part harmonizations on themes of Bach. He worked hard for three years, and this was the whole of his formal education in the theory of music. As Hughes says, "Poulenc probably composed more from instinct and aural experience than any major composer of this century." He had a deeply musical temperament.

Once Poulenc tried to write a string quartet. Unsatisfied, he threw it in a Paris sewer. Basically he wrote compositions in small forms. He never wrote a symphony, but some of his chamber works, such as the Sonata for

Oboe and the Sonata for Flute, are filled with beautiful melodies. His wood-wind music, for which the French are famous, is polished and witty. Poulenc learned orchestration mainly from listening to recordings and then examining the scores meticulously to learn how to get the sounds he liked.

Among the many artistic people Poulenc knew in Paris was Igor Stravinsky. It was Stravinsky who suggested to Diaghilev that "Poulenc might be able to compose a good ballet." *Les Biches* (The House Party) premiered in Paris in 1924. For this, his first big work, Poulenc wrote the scenario as well as the score, and it was a success. The sets and costumes were by Marie Laurencin and the choreographer was Nijinska, Nijinsky's sister.

Poulenc was well into his thirties before he began to write his finest songs. Today he is known as the greatest exponent of the art song in the twentieth century. His more than 130 songs include several song cycles. The dominant element in his music is melody, and his songs often begin immediately with the voice. He began to write more sensitively and powerfully after he started to accompany Pierre Bernac in song recitals. In my student days at Juilliard Music School, we often went to concerts at Town Hall in New York City. A memorable evening was a concert given by Francis Poulenc and Pierre Bernac. Afterwards my friends and I went up to thank these wonderful artists for their music. In my excitement, after I had expressed my appreciation, not knowing what else to say, I asked Poulenc how to pronounce his name. With an amused smile he answered, "It rhymes with bank."

Poulenc had a keen ear for poetry, and he ranks with Bizet and Debussy, both of whom are known for the excellence of their settings of French poetry to music. Poulenc had a vast literary and artistic knowledge. Some of his favorite poets were Apollinaire, Eluard, and Max Jacob.

His *Concert Champêtre* (Rustic Concerto, 1928) for harpsichord and orchestra, composed for the great harpsichordist Wanda Landowska, with an emphasis on rhythm, was written to show that the harpsichord is not an archaic instrument. This music is filled with the laughter and sunshine that we invariably associate with Poulenc.

Poulenc's nature had contrasting sides—the lighthearted and the sacred, the rebel and the conservative, the boisterous and the melancholic. In the 1930s two incidents occurred that had a profound effect on him and caused him to think more deeply about life and death. For the first time Poulenc had financial problems, and then in the middle 1930s his deeply religious nature was awakened by the tragic death of his close friend Ferroud in an automobile accident. Soon afterwards he began composing religious works, and with his wonderful compassion and humanity, they are, according to biographer David Ewen, "some of his noblest and most spiritual writing."

To understand Poulenc, we must realize that he placed great value on being regarded as lighthearted, charming, sophisticated, even frivolous. His friends were always happy when he walked into a cafe because they knew he would make them laugh, but behind his spontaneity and cheerfulness was hidden inner turmoil. As a friend observed, "Poulenc has two faces. One is smiling, the other serious." Poulenc, not one to speak about his private life, on a rare occasion described himself as "a melancholic character who likes to laugh like all melancholic characters." For years he was considered the clown of "Les Six," but his later years and music took on a more serious tone.

After turning back to his Roman Catholic faith in 1936, Poulenc began writing a series of religious works. He is considered one of the major composers of liturgical music in the twentieth century. In 1937 he wrote the Mass in G for unaccompanied mixed choir, dedicated to his father. There was little church music of consequence being written in France at the time, and Poulenc brought the needed astringent touch that helped revive liturgical music. His choral works show his greatest originality and richness of thought.

Poulenc brought a remarkable and telling simplicity to church music, which in France seemed imprisoned until released by Poulenc's lightness of touch, satire, and wit. The majority of his choral works are for a cappella choirs. Poulenc is one of the few modern French composers to reintroduce an authentic religious note into French music. In all of Poulenc's religious compositions there is a mingled sweetness and humility, a tenderness and simplicity of heart that causes the music to remain in the memory. A conservative, Poulenc never lost contact with the past. He had something to say, and he said it with style and personality from his heart. He pursued a lifelong study of Bach.

Poulenc spent the war years, 1940-1945, mostly in Paris. In 1943 he composed music to Louis Aragon's haunting reflection on the Nazi occupation of France. Entitled simply "C," it is one of the most magnificent of his songs.

Some of Poulenc's most delightful music is found in his setting of the children's story *Babar, the Elephant*. His *Les Animaux Modèles,* a ballet based on the fables of La Fontaine, is rich in harmony and orchestration.

Between 1953 and 1956 Poulenc worked on the music for *Dialogues of the Carmelites*. The text was taken from the superb play by George Bernanos. Poulenc followed the words with great care. His intention was to make the words heard. The voice is of prime importance, never the orchestra. It is an intensely emotional work.

One very snowy day in the Swiss Alps we built a fire in the fireplace, found both the music and the words, and listened to a recording of the *Dialogues* from beginning to end. It made a lasting impression and reminded us how often we only half listen to music. To heighten one's appreciation of music, it is helpful to follow the score and listen carefully to the words when there are words.

The story is about a group of Carmelite nuns who refused to disband during the French Revolution and consequently suffered martyrdom. The main theme is the psychology of fear. While composing the opera, Poulenc had a nervous breakdown. He spent several weeks in a clinic wrestling with the terrible twins self-doubt and fear of death. He was unable to work for months. Poulenc, like his heroine Blanche, lived in fear of everything and of nothing, of liberty and constraint. The final scene of martyrdom, as the nuns mount the guillotine, is unforgettable. At the last Blanche has victory over fear as she goes to her death trusting in the triune God of the universe. One feels it is Poulenc's victory too.

Poulenc, as many great artists, borrowed countless melodic ideas from such composers as Mozart, Chopin, Franck, Tchaikovsky, Mussorgsky, Chabrier, and Puccini. It was not that he had no ideas himself, but because of his love for the music of these composers, he made their music a part of his own works. The music of Poulenc is as personal as any composed in this century. He had a gift of improvisation and a free melodic abundance; yet he worked very hard at composition, always composing at the piano. Milhaud spoke of "the fresh charm of Poulenc's music." Music was melody to Poulenc. His clear, simple art renewed the wonderful tradition of Scarlatti and Mozart.

One of Poulenc's most scintillating works is *Gloria*—a joyful, radiant piece of music. Poulenc is, as much as anybody in this age, "a merry man of God in his music," and he received the same kind of reproaches as Haydn with his high-spirited religious music. Poulenc undoubtedly responded much the same—that the thought of God made him happy. *Gloria*, written in 1959, is in the style of Vivaldi. It has six sections, with each part very much a contrast to the next. It is a sincere composition, deeply felt and filled with sunshine.

Poulenc never married. Like Schubert, friendship was everything to him, and he had a large circle of friends. He loved Paris, but he also enjoyed his home, garden, and flowers outside the city. He was a connoisseur of painting, poetry, food, and wine. He owned several small works by Braque, Dufy, Marie Laurencin, Matisse, and Picasso.

Poulenc died suddenly of heart failure on January 30, 1963. His date book, which ordinarily was filled with many future appointments, had no entry beyond the day on which he died, and he left behind no unfinished compositions. As Erik Routley says, "Francis Poulenc's death in 1963 was one of those events which made one feel that a light had gone out." Poulenc was not the universal composer in the sense that Beethoven and Mozart were, but he sang his song, and it was beautiful.

Recommended Reading

Harding, James. *The Ox on the Roof.* New York: St. Martin's Press, 1972.

Hell, Henri. *Francis Poulenc.* London: John Calder, 1959.

Meyers, Rollo. *Erik Satie.* New York: Dover Publications, 1968.

Recommended Listening

Poulenc: *Animaux Modèles*
       Concert Champêtre
       Concerto in G Minor for Organ and Orchestra
       Concerto for Two Pianos and Orchestra
       Dialogues of the Carmelites
       Gloria
       Mass in G
       Trois Mouvements Perpetuels
       Sonata for Flute and Piano
       Sonata for Oboe and Piano
       Songs: *"Le Bestiaire," "Tel Jour," "Telle Nuit,"*
           "Sanglots"
       Story of Babar, the Elephant
Satie: *Parade*

CHAPTER 42

Dmitri Shostakovich
1906-1975

The tragic horror of a trapped genius.
Yehudi Menuhin

*I*n her splendid autobiography, Galina Pavlovna Vishevskaya, the famous Russian opera star, said, "Shostakovich's music is the soul of the twentieth-century Russian people." The great violinist Yehudi Menuhin made this observation about Shostakovich, "The tragic horror of a trapped genius." It is recorded in the fascinating book *Testimony—The Memoirs of Dmitri Shostakovich*, by Solomon Volkov.

Shostakovich was a child of the Soviet state where Communist ideology destroyed all spiritual values in its path. Everyone feared everyone else. Shostakovich called the Soviet Union, "An insane asylum of a country."

"No Soviet composer would even think of touching on the subject of religion. Soviet music has been forcibly cut off from one of the richest of all art soils—religion. Russian music from which all trace of spirituality has been erased seems like a monstrous concept," wrote Richard Anthony Leonard in *A History of Russian Music.*

We want to examine in this chapter whether the greatly talented composer Shostakovich was able to develop to the full his artistic capacity under the rule of a police state, in a society where culture was officially controlled by a Communist Party dictatorship over the arts.

One of his popular pieces is the energetic "Polka." It is lavishly orchestrated with a kind of circus humor that can be expected of Shostakovich. It is from his ballet *The Age of Gold* (1930). The story involves a team of Soviet athletes who win an international soccer match. Shostakovich had a passion for soccer and would drop everything to see a match. There is tremendous sarcasm in his music, a sense of mockery and wit.

Dmitri Shostakovich was born in Leningrad. Of Polish ancestry, his family belonged to the Russian intelligentsia. His mother, Sofiya, a gifted pianist, recognized her son's talent and gave "Mitya" his first piano lessons before he was ten years old. After the sudden early death of her husband of pneumonia, she sacrificed greatly, doing the most menial jobs in order to send her son to the Leningrad Conservatory, where he entered at the age of thirteen. Often the family (there were two sisters) had barely enough to eat.

Shostakovich was a brilliant pianist, highly trained in the Russian tradition. He chose to be a composer and began to write music at the age of fourteen. He was shy, unassuming, self-critical, high-strung, and fun-loving in his youth, with a strong sense of fairness, honesty, and integrity. He was helpful to younger colleagues. Just before his mother died, she said, "I have discharged my not-so-easy duties as a mother."

Glazunov, head of the Leningrad Conservatory and himself a remarkable musician, was very impressed with the talents of Shostakovich and helped him to receive several grants and special food rations.

Shostakovich soon became the center of attraction among musicians, but because of harsh conditions at the conservatory, he developed tuberculosis and was in and out of sanitariums. He also had heart trouble and severe arthritis. He suffered poor health the rest of his life; yet he was a tremendous overcomer and worker.

In severe times of poverty he helped his family by playing the piano to accompany films in movie theaters that were cold, drafty, and filled with smoke. Later under Stalin's regime, he wrote an enormous amount of film music, mostly with the theme of revolution. As Stalin loved films, Shostakovich wrote "safe music" that would please this despotic leader of the Soviet Union. It is mostly forgotten now.

For his graduation from the conservatory at the age of nineteen, he wrote his Symphony No. 1, which gained international recognition. This symphony revealed his great talent and helped to establish his reputation as a born symphonist, an artist with superb natural talents and first-rate academic training. He was on his way!

In the second movement scherzo of his first symphony, the piano is featured prominently. This is prophetic of many of Shostakovich's sardonic movements to come. It shows remarkable orchestration at such an early age. Eventually, he was able to conceive a whole symphony in his mind before writing it down. He needed no special environment to compose music. Even noise did not distract him. The symphony was the center of Shostakovich's creativity. He wrote fifteen of them.

Shostakovich was a remarkable pianist, able to achieve brilliant and rich keyboard effects. His Concerto No. 1 for Piano, Trumpet, and Orchestra is especially appealing. His trios, piano sonatas, preludes, and other piano music reveal his magnificent piano technique.

By nature a theater composer, he wrote two operas—*The Nose*, which is brilliant entertainment, and *Lady Macbeth of Mtsensk* (1932), of even greater significance. The latter was the pivotal work in his entire career and one of the most powerful operas of the twentieth century. This unrelenting, realistic opera met with international success for several years, until it was performed for Stalin in the Kremlin. (Stalin means "man of steel.") There was a vicious attack in *Pravda* against Shostakovich entitled "Muddle Instead of Music" in 1936, probably written by the notorious Zhdanov. The article turned many against Shostakovich.

From that point on, he was always under the threat of Stalin, seeing himself as a condemned man in a vast prison. Like many other people at that time, Shostakovich kept a small suitcase packed and ready to flee the country. The police usually came for their victims at night. Shostakovich could not sleep. He lay listening, waiting in the dark.

"The Great Terror" with its witch-hunting under the club of Stalin had begun in the 1930s, during which countless millions of people were murdered. Many of Shostakovich's friends simply disappeared. Stalin was one of the worst, most ruthless political criminals in history. He was morbidly superstitious and mad (or demon-possessed); he caused more harm than all the abnormal kings or czars of Russia's past put together. Shostakovich called Stalin a beast and a butcher, as human life meant nothing to him. No one dared to even whisper that Stalin was crazy. His system of lies and slander and his secret police were everywhere. His envy of anyone other than himself being praised caused him to be merciless and extremely dangerous.

Political ideology entered into the music of Shostakovich, and he was forced to work on two planes—one, producing propaganda pieces in order to save his life, and the other, serious works of artistic purpose. This made for unevenness of quality. His obvious borrowing made for too many notes, cheap ideas, and a rather crude sense of humor. He wrote rapidly only after the whole composition, including the orchestration, was in his head. He never rewrote his music. Under the fear of death at Stalin's order, he "put on a mask he wore for the rest of his life." He knew that millions were perishing in the gulags (slave labor camps).

His Fifth Symphony was much influenced by Beethoven, whom he considered the forerunner of the revolutionary movement, and by the huge symphonies of Mahler (who also suffered the fear of death, as shown by his theme in *The Song of the Earth*—"Dark is life, dark is death"). Shostakovich's majestic Fifth Symphony, with its brilliant orchestration, was a triumph at its first performance and even pleased Stalin. The composer was now writing "safe music," and art was turned into a Soviet vehicle of socialist realism. Modernism in Soviet Russia was dead.

Stalin inflicted severe trials and humiliation on Shostakovich and yet rewarded him with high honors (a cat-and-mouse game). Also the music of Prokofiev and Khachaturian was condemned by Stalin. Both were accused of "bourgeois formalism" by that most bourgeois Stalin.

In the book *Testimony*, Shostakovich is quoted: "I have thought that my life was replete with sorrow and that it would be hard to find a more miserable man, but when I started going over the life stories of my friends and acquaintances, I was horrified. Not one of them had an easy or happy life. Some came to a terrible end. Some died in terrible suffering, and the lives of many of them could easily be called more miserable than mine.

"And that made me even sadder. I was remembering my friends and all I saw was corpses, mountains of corpses; and the picture filled me with a horrible depression. . . . I've described tragic events . . . and several repulsive figures. . . . Perhaps people younger than I would be free of bitterness that has colored my life gray."

His Symphony No. 7 was composed in 1941 during the Leningrad siege while he was a fire warden. It was famous at the time, but with its heavy ideological emphasis, it is of less interest today. No other composer has been bound in so political a role. Yet Shostakovich is considered the greatest Russian symphonist of the mid-twentieth century.

His Symphony No. 10, written after Stalin's death in 1953, contains some of Shostakovich's greatest music. In it he sums up the Stalin era, giving us lugubrious slavic melancholy. The second movement is a "musical portrait of Stalin." It is inexorable, merciless music, like an evil whirlwind. But Shostakovich was entirely a product of Soviet training. He was committed to the ideals of the Soviet society in which he grew up and suffered so much, so in 1963 he finally joined the Communist Party.

His later symphonies, of which he wrote fifteen, have been severely criticized in the West for bombast, emptiness, and over-extension. But he continued to receive all kinds of honors. Leonard, in his excellent book, *A History of Russian Music,* says, "Shostakovich is, in short, an artist of superb natural talents. He is also a weather vane, shifting obligingly with the winds of either political or musical ideology."

Shostakovich loved the compositions of Mussorgsky, whose music had a great influence on him. Mussorgsky was a member of "The Mighty Five" or "The Mighty Handful." He was the greatest of them and is best known for his brilliant opera *Boris Godunov.* In his harmony, Mussorgsky is one of the most original of all composers. With Ravel's orchestration of Mussorgsky's *Pictures at an Exhibition,* the finale, "The Great Gate of Kiev," is impressive. Here we have the grandeur of czarist Russia. None of "The Mighty Five"— Balakirev, Cui, Rimsky-Korsakov, Borodin, and Mussorgsky—were professional musicians.

A nihilist and pessimist, Shostakovich said, "There is no afterlife." At another time he said, "I'll be frank. I don't have much faith in eternity." The image of death dominated his later works, and he was obsessed by the fear of death.

His was a life of fear and despair, yet he never gave up. He produced a vast output of music and was also a dedicated teacher. He was terribly shy and nervous, modest, awkward, embittered, with a malicious wit, and suffered frequently from bad health, yet he had a gentle and noble character. "My gray and miserable life," he said, and one hears in his music "the huge complex of human passions and sufferings." His music is filled with pessimism and gloom.

Some of the best music he wrote is found in his chamber works, the fifteen quartets, especially the Eighth Quartet, but he was pessimistic about much of his music. He said, "The majority of my symphonies are tombstones." Another time he said, "Awaiting execution is a theme that has tormented me all my life."

The theme of the Fourteenth Symphony is death as the grim reaper. "Death is all-powerful," he said. "Don't fool yourself. They wanted the finale of the symphony to be comforting. To say that death is only the beginning. But it's not a beginning; it's the real end. There will be nothing afterward, nothing." This symphony is a setting of eleven poems about death (dedicated to Benjamin Britten). There is no redemption in Shostakovich's music. No resolution. Only "a mood of desolation and loneliness."

How very sad that Shostakovich did not understand Christianity. Just these few words would have freed him had he been presented with the truth and *believed* it: " . . . that by His death Christ might destroy him who holds the power of death—that is, the devil, and free those who all their lives were held in slavery by their fear of death."

Many other great artists suffered terribly in Russia. Tolstoy was excommunicated; Pushkin was relentlessly followed by the secret police; Dostoevsky was sent to Siberia; Rachmaninoff, Stravinsky, and Glazunov, to mention a few, fled Russia; Shostakovich and Prokofiev endured agony; Russia's finest woman poet, Anna Akhmatova, greatly admired by Shostakovich, suffered terribly under Stalin; Solzhenitsyn was exiled for nearly twenty years. Russia has had a tragic but fascinating history.

Recommended Reading

Seroff, Victor. *Dmitri Shostakovich: The Life and Background of a Soviet Composer.* New York: Alfred A. Knopf, 1943.

Volkov, Solomon. *Testimony: the Memoirs of Dmitri Shostakovich.* New York: Harper and Row, Publishers, 1979.

Recommended Listening

The Age of Gold
Concerto No. 1 for Piano, Trumpet, and Orchestra
Lady Macbeth of Mtsensk
Preludes for Piano
Quartet No. 8
Symphony No. 1
Symphony No. 5
Symphony No. 10
Trio No. 2 for Piano, Violin, and Cello

CHAPTER 43

Shakespeare's Influence on Great Composers

This master singer of the world.

Halleck

If a person should master Shakespeare and the Bible, he would find all that is greatest in human thought. With the exception of the Scriptures, Shakespeare's dramas have surpassed all other works in molding modern English thought," wrote Halleck, a professor at Yale University.

The works of Shakespeare and the Bible are the perfection of English, and they have had the most lasting influence on Western art, literature, and music.

William Shakespeare was born in April 1564 at Stratford-on-Avon, located in one of England's fairest rural settings. The beauty of the region deeply influenced him, as he was a close observer of God's world, the world of nature and human beings.

His schooling was fairly brief but intense. Besides Latin, the required works in English were the catechism, Psalter, *The Book of Common Prayer,* and the New Testament. Many echoes from the Bible and the prayer book are found in the writings of Shakespeare. In fact, he refers to the Bible more often than any playwright of his day. The Scriptures not only gave him the conviction of a moral universe under God, but having a Christian background and framework helped to fire his imagination. The adjective most used in describing Shakespeare is "gentle," implying that he displayed the qualities of a man of good character.

After his marriage to Anne Hathaway (they had three children), he went to London in his early twenties in order to provide for his family. Throughout the next twenty strenuous years of his amazing career as an actor and playwright, Shakespeare wrote his glorious plays and poetry.

He was considered Queen Elizabeth's greatest subject, and, having earned fame and fortune, Shakespeare retired to a quiet life with his family in Stratford-on-Avon at the age of forty-eight. He died there at fifty-two.

One reason for the popularity of Shakespeare is the number and variety of his characters. They included people from all walks of life, and sometimes they seem more real than people living around us. One loves Shakespeare because of his profound understanding of human nature, his kindness, his humor, and his lack of harsh judgment on the imperfections of men and women.

No person with a searching mind can study Shakespeare without becoming a deeper and more varied thinker and without securing a wider comprehension of human existence, its struggles, failures, and successes. After association with the bard for a season, our minds are quickened, and the dull, ordinary, hard routine of life "does suffer a sea-change into something rich and strange."

It is true that the triumphs of the theater are ephemeral; however, many memorable quotes from Shakespeare are lodged in our minds today:

"Parting is such sweet sorrow . . . "
"What must be, shall be . . . "
"In the twinkling of an eye . . . "
"All the world's a stage . . . "
"Catching a cold . . . "
"What's in a name?"
"Brevity is the soul of wit."
"The time is out of joint . . . "
"The quality of mercy is not strained . . . "

Shakespeare loved music and introduced it into most of his plays. Good music expressed to him the order one finds in the universe, which he longed for in the pressures of his life. Most of the composers in this book were inspired by the Bible and the works of Shakespeare. Ben Jonson, a contemporary of Shakespeare, said of him, "He was not of an age, but for all time."

During the full flowering of the English Renaissance many composers, such as Thomas Morley, set Shakespeare's words to music. It was almost impossible to perform Shakespeare without music, for each act of a play was announced with formal trumpet fanfares. Both Henry VIII and his daughter, Queen Elizabeth, were excellent musicians. During their reigns England was referred to "as a nest of singing birds."

In the English Baroque period Henry Purcell, England's last great composer before the twentieth century, wrote the music for his finest opera, *The Fairy Queen*, an anonymous adaptation of Shakespeare's *A Midsummer Night's Dream*. Also writing in London in the Baroque period was Handel. Charles Jennens, a friend of Handel, chose the words for *Messiah*. He was an enthusiastic Shakespeare scholar. Handel in his operas and oratorios was influenced by the characterizations of Shakespeare, partly because of the wondrous musicality of his verse.

Mozart is compared to Shakespeare in that he too created believable women. Shakespeare's depiction of women of various types is one of the wonders of his genius.

Mozart's friend Haydn is compared to Shakespeare because of his "London Symphonies" and his success in London. Haydn's famous song "She Never Told Her Love" has a Shakespeare text from *Twelfth Night*.

It is startling to realize that every major composer of the Romantic period was inspired by Shakespeare. The whole force of the Romantic movement was enriched by literature. The Romantics merged the arts and tended to remove boundary lines between music and poetry.

Beethoven enjoyed reading Shakespeare and said, "If you want to understand my piano sonata *The Tempest,* read Shakespeare's *The Tempest.*" Schubert, a contemporary of Beethoven and probably the world's greatest songwriter, set two of Shakespeare's poems to beautiful music—"Hark, Hark, the Lark," and "Who Is Sylvia?"

Berlioz had a lifelong enthusiasm for Shakespeare, who had a tremendous impact on his creativity. Berlioz said, "Next to God it is Shakespeare who has created the most." Among Berlioz's finest works are *The Overture to King Lear; Romeo and Juliet,* a dramatic symphony with magnificent music; and his opera *Beatrix and Benedict,* (based on *Much Ado About Nothing*).

At the age of seventeen, Mendelssohn, inspired by his reading of Shakespeare, composed his incomparable overture to Shakespeare's *A Midsummer Night's Dream,* and years later he added about a dozen pieces to this enchanting orchestral suite full of charm and grace. Mendelssohn's friend, Schumann, a true Romantic, was deeply influenced by reading Shakespeare, Goethe, and Byron. For him poetry and music were closely united.

Liszt remarked, "I recognize in Shakespeare the secretary of the world who held up the mirror to nature." Liszt wrote a symphonic poem, *Hamlet.* Liszt's son-in-law, Wagner, saw in himself " . . . a fulfillment of the combination of Shakespeare and Beethoven." Wagner also said, "The tragedies of Shakespeare stand unquestionably above those of the Greeks." Wagner's second opera was taken from Shakespeare's *Measure for Measure.*

Verdi, the most Shakespearean of all opera composers, spent a great deal of time reading Shakespeare and considered him "the greatest authority on the heart of man. . . . I prefer Shakespeare to all other dramatists." Three of Verdi's finest operas are his early work *Macbeth* and his last two operas—*Otello* and *Falstaff.* The genius who made Verdi's final triumphs possible was Shakespeare.

Brahms loved to read Shakespeare, and one of his excellent songs is from *Twelfth Night*. His contemporary Tchaikovsky wrote his first enduring masterpiece, *The Overture to Romeo and Juliet,* while teaching at the conservatory in Moscow. Later he wrote overtures to *Hamlet* and *The Tempest*. Dvorak wrote an overture to *Otello*, and Fauré composed *Shylock*.

Debussy read Shakespeare with enthusiasm and longed to write an opera based on *As You Like It*, but he was too ill. He did compose incidental music to *King Lear*.

One of Sibelius's greatest songs is the music to Shakespeare's "Come Away Death."

Vaughan Williams wrote the Shakespearean opera *Sir John in Love* and his glorious "Serenade to Music" with words from the *Merchant of Venice:*

> *How sweet the moonlight sleeps upon this bank!*
> *Here we will sit and let the sounds of music*
> *Creep in our ears: Soft stillness and the night*
> *become the touches of sweet harmony.*

Benjamin Britten wrote an outstanding opera, *A Midsummer Night's Dream,* considered the most successful Shakespearean opera since Verdi. Bartók and Stravinsky wrote music for selections from Shakespeare's works. Prokofiev's *Romeo and Juliet* is among his finest works.

William Walton, one of the most important creative figures in modern English music, wrote marvelous compositions for three film productions of Shakespeare plays: *Henry V, Hamlet,* and *Richard III* (acted by the foremost Shakespearean actor of his day, Sir Laurence Olivier).

Russia's greatest poet Alexander Pushkin (called the Russian Shakespeare) read Shakespeare over and over to the end of his life. Pushkin's great drama *Boris Godunov* introduced the style of Shakespeare's historical tragedies to the Russian stage. Nearly all Russian composers have been influenced by Pushkin's writings and have set his works to music.

Shostakovich said, "Shakespeare's tragedies are filled with music. It was Shakespeare who said that the man who doesn't like music is not trustworthy. Such a man is capable of a base act of murder. . . . Shakespeare was a seer. Man stalks power walking knee-deep in blood [referring to Stalin]. Stalin hated *Hamlet* and *Macbeth,* as they reminded him of the millions of deaths he was responsible for. . . . When I read Shakespeare, I listen to his music." Shostakovich wrote compositions for *Hamlet* and *King Lear*.

Countless other composers were inspired by Shakespeare, to name a few: Salieri (*Falstaff*), Rossini (*Otello*), Bellini (*I Montecchi* and *Capuletti*), Gounod (*Romeo and Juliet*), Thomas (*Hamlet*), Weber (*Oberon*), Balakirev (*King Lear*), Smetana (*Richard III*), Saint-Saëns (*Henry VIII*), Micholai (*The Merry Wives of Windsor*), Elgar (*Falstaff*), Delius (*A Village Romeo and Juliet*), R. Strauss (*Macbeth*), Barber (*Anthony and Cleopatra*), and Tippet (*Midsummer*).

The father of the great French organist, Messiaen, made a noted French translation of Shakespeare, and when Messiaen was eight years old, he read out loud all of Shakespeare's thirty-seven plays.

Some of Shakespeare's romantic comedies, such as *Twelfth Night,* could be called musical comedies. There have been many Broadway musicals based on Shakespeare's works, such as *Kiss Me, Kate*, and countless films, like *Julius Caesar*. Over two hundred operas have been based on his plays. Surely Shakespeare is the greatest writer of the ages and the world's most popular author.

Recommended Reading

Chute, Marchette. *Shakespeare of London*. New York: E. P. Dutton, 1949.

Schmidgall, Gary. *Shakespeare and Opera*. New York: Oxford University Press, 1990.

Jane Stuart Smith and Betty Carlson. *Thoughts on Art, Literature and Humor*. Huemoz, Switzerland: Le Petit Muveran Publishers, 1987.

Recommended Listening

Elizabethan Songs

Beethoven: Piano Sonata *The Tempest*

Mendelssohn: *A Midsummer Night's Dream*

Berlioz: *Romeo and Juliet*

Verdi: *Otello, Falstaff*

Tchaikovsky *Romeo and Juliet*

Vaughan Williams: "Serenade to Music"

Britten: *A Midsummer Night's Dream*

Walton: *Henry V* film music

CHAPTER 44

Christmas Carols

... in psalms and hymns and spiritual songs,
singing with grace in your hearts to the Lord.

Colossians 3:16

*T*he most musical time of the year is the Christmas season when people crowd our churches to partake of joyful music. This is God's provision for dreary days, especially those who believe in the Incarnation of Christ. One of the glories of Christmas music is that it varies from the simplest carol of folk song origin to the great oratorios by the masters of music, such as the *Christmas Oratorio* of Schütz, Bach's *Christmas Oratorio,* and Handel's *Messiah.*

When one sings *noel* (French for birthday), it is a sign of Christmas joy at the birth of Christ.

The earliest noel reminds us that carol-singing is not a twentieth-century innovation or even a medieval custom, but goes all the way back to the Nativity itself. The first Christmas song was sung by the angels: "Glory to God in the highest, and on earth peace, good will toward men," with the result that the shepherds made haste to see Jesus and then spread the good news, glorifying and praising God.

For many around the world Christmas is the busiest and happiest time of the year with the cheerful sound of Christmas carols filling the air. Groups of carolers walk about singing Christmas songs, and music seems to be everywhere, celebrating God's gift to us of His Son.

The word *carol* comes from an old French word *carole,* meaning a round dance, suggesting that carols were originally dancing songs. Most of the old carols have a refrain; they are songs that are sung by a choir and danced in a circle at the same time—in other words, a choral dance.

Both songs and dances were part of worship in the early ages of mankind. Dancing is the "poetry of motion" heightened by singing. Of course, the song/dance has often been misused, such as in the orgy of the Israelites dancing about the golden calf, as described in the Bible. A positive use was when Miriam, the prophetess, took a tambourine in her hand, and all the women followed her with tambourines and dancing to praise God for the safe passage of the Israelites through the Red Sea.

When King Saul and David returned from a victorious war against the Philistines, the women met them, singing and dancing joyful songs with tambourines and lutes. In 2 Samuel 6:14-15 David, wearing a linen ephod, danced with all his might before the Lord in an act of thanksgiving.

It is thought that Hebrew poetry actually owed its origin and unique characteristics to the choral dance. In fact, it began by caroling. It is evident that the sacred hymns were sung by two choirs opposite each other (antiphonal), and the movements of the dance suggested the parallelism of the verse. The dancers and singers were members of a choir.

The Lord Jesus Christ did not look with disfavor on social festivities that included wholesome dancing. The carol, or dance, echoes Paul's understanding of the fruits of the Spirit (Galatians 5:22-23)—that we Christians are to be joyful and cheerful, obviously not all the time, but certainly more often than most of us are.

The carol and the mystery play (which reenacts a Bible story) are an emancipation from centuries of medieval church suppression of the dance and drama. In the mystery and miracle plays the songs used were carols. One of these was the "Coventry Carol." This music, a true masterpiece of simplicity, was sung by the women of Bethlehem just before Herod's soldiers came to slaughter the children.

St. Francis, with his jovial singing, in order to combat the kind of heresy and heathenism that denied the Incarnation, is thought to have instituted the custom of the adoration of the Nativity scene.

A famous near-secular carol from the Middle Ages is "The Boar's Head." It is still sung at the Christmas dinner at Queens College, Oxford, as the cooks bring in the traditional feast. According to the story behind the carol, a scholar was reading Aristotle while out walking. Suddenly a wild boar leaped out of the bushes. The student overcame the beast by stuffing Aristotle down his throat; a triumphant victory of the academic over the brutish! The head was severed by the scholar, and he took it back to college for dinner.

One of the greatly loved medieval advent plainsongs is "O Come, O Come, Emmanuel." In that era only the priests were allowed to sing. Like Gothic architecture, plainsong melodies were anonymous—in a sense the work of all the people combined.

The Renaissance in the fifteenth century brought a resurgence of the carol, as the modern spirit of humanism dawned on the Middle Ages. With a greater freedom of thought there was a renewal of man's interest in himself and the world he lived in. He now could look at life as having the possibility of joy in itself and not merely as preparation for an existence to come.

In the Renaissance the leisure time of all classes was taken up with music and dancing. The unifying element that held together cultural life was music. An important factor in the Renaissance was the rise of music printing.

One of the great Christmas carols of the high Renaissance is "In dulci jubilo," known in English as "Good Christian Men Rejoice." It belongs to the "Macaronic Carols." These are carols in two languages—lines of Latin interspersed with vigorous phrases in the vernacular. Fable tells us that "In dulci jubilo" was sung by the angels to the writer, who was drawn thereby to dance with his celestial visitors.

Carols were connected with the simple, natural things of this world, yet they insisted on the reality of the unseen world. The words were a light-hearted acceptance of theological profundities. Usually, the purpose of carols was to sing of the Trinity and to teach about Christ and the Christian faith.

Luther (1483-1546), father of the Reformation, said, "I feel strongly that all the arts, and particularly music, should be used in the service of Him who has created and given them."

Until Luther's time the congregation was silent, as only the priests were allowed to sing, but Luther wanted the people to share in the joy of praising the Lord through hymn-singing. Not only did Luther write the fine German Christmas carol "Von Himmel Hoch" ("From Heaven Above to Earth I Come"), but he also introduced the Christmas tree with lights (candles), which was to give the impression of stars over Bethlehem.

Another fine German Christmas carol is "Es Is Ein Ros' Entsprungen" ("Lo, How a Rose E'er Blooming"), written by the composer Michael Praetorius (1571-1621). His work helped establish the Lutheran church music style in Germany, preparing for the development that culminated over one hundred years later in J. S. Bach. Bach wrote a great deal of Christmas music, including his *Christmas Oratorio*.

A French proverb says, "The French sing or pipe, the English carol, the Spaniards wail, the Germans howl, the Italians caper." This reminds us that carols, like folk music, are sung in many countries and, with their simple freshness and spontaneity, are ever popular.

Although there are Easter and secular May Day carols, carols are most generally associated with Christmas, such as the "Lullaby Carol":

> *What child is this, who, laid to rest,*
> *on Mary's lap is sleeping?*
> GREENSLEEVES

Many of the carols we sing now are from the seventeenth and eighteenth centuries and are still beloved today: "Silent Night, Holy Night" (Austrian), "Angels We Have Heard on High" (French), and the English ballads "God Rest Ye Merry Gentleman" and "The First Noel." There are also cherished American carols: "It Came upon the Midnight Clear," "O Little Town of Bethlehem," and "We Three Kings of Orient Are," the negro carol

"Go Tell It on the Mountain," and the Appalachian carol "I Wonder as I Wander."

Actually, Christmas carols and Christmas hymns tend to overlap. Christmas hymns like "O Come All Ye Faithful," "Joy to the World," and "Hark, the Herald Angels Sing" are always included in Christmas celebrations. Women poets have written three choice Christmas songs—Mrs. Alexander's "Once in Royal David's City," Christina Rossetti's "In the Bleak Midwinter," and "Thou Didst Leave Thy Throne" by Emily Elliott.

We cannot overestimate the importance of carols, which, in part, led to our modern music based on the dance. One of Benjamin Britten's outstanding modern works is *The Ceremony of Carols.*

Carols are still being written today because we Christians take pleasure in celebrating the joy of Christmas. Two recent carols written by Jane Stuart Smith are "Sweetest Gift of My Possession" (words by Linette Martin) and "Lo, Newborn Jesus" (words by Christina Rossetti).

The *Oxford Book of Carols* is a treasure trove of wonderful music. Part of the editorial work was done by the distinguished English composer, Vaughan Williams, who found fresh inspiration in those memorable carols. Perhaps nothing is more necessary than to increase the element of joy in music—the joy that carols give to us.

Recommended Reading

Dearmer, Vaughan Williams, and Shaw. *The Oxford Book of Carols.* London: Oxford University Press, 1964.

Routley, Erick. *The English Carol.* London: Herbert Jenkins, 1958.

Recommended Listening

Britten: *A Ceremony of Carols*
Kings College Choir of Cambridge:
  A Festival of Lessons and Carols
  Procession and Carols on Advent Sunday
Vaughan Williams: *Fantasia on "Greensleeves"*
Christmas at L'Abri
Christmas with the Trapp Family Singers
Christmas Night: Carols of the Nativity, Conductor, John Rutter
A Festival of Carols, Conductor, Robert Shaw

Postlude

*T*he arts are not extraneous or a luxury in life, but they are a vital and essential part of our existence. Who can look at stars, the rising moon over Swiss Alps, the amazing variety of wild flowers in the springtime, hear great music, and read great literature and not know that our Creator God loves beauty? God expects us to have dominion over the earth through the different creative gifts He has given us.

Art comes from our being made in the image of God, and we know God is for the arts and has relegated to men and women wonderful gifts of creativity. Often these gifts have not been used for God's glory, however; nor do all artists acknowledge where their skills have come from, which does make us sad. Nevertheless, we can delight in great paintings, architecture, literature, music, and so on, remembering that the living God gives us richly all things to enjoy (1 Tim. 6:17). We do need to ask for discernment, though, so we will seek that which is wholesome and beautiful.

In order not "to walk into the future backwards," we must be careful not to shut ourselves off from the culture around us and, particularly, from the developments in twentieth-century music. Those of us at L'Abri Fellowship are deeply interested in saving the good in culture. We warmly affirm the following statement by J. G. Machen: "The Christian cannot be satisfied as long as any human activity is either opposed to Christianity or out of all connection with Christianity. . . . The Christian, therefore, cannot be indifferent to any branch of earnest human endeavor. It must all be brought into some relation to the gospel."[9]

We have seen clearly in these chapters that God has given incredible

---

9. J. G. Machen, *Christianity and Culture* (Huemoz, Switzerland: L'Abri Fellowship, 1969), p. 4.

gifts to His created men and women and the liberty to use them. We have also seen that there are different points of departure. Bach chose to draw on the Scriptures, "the well of life," for his inspiration and creativity, and he affirmed repeatedly that he wrote his music to the glory of God and with the help of Jesus. Most critics agree that Bach is the greatest composer of all time. A contemporary of Bach, Andreas Werckmeister, spoke of music as "a gift of God to be used only in His honor."

It is interesting to observe that many of the composers included in this book have acknowledged their indebtedness to Bach, such as Schumann, Chopin, Liszt, Fauré, Vaughan Williams, Rachmaninoff, Bartók, Poulenc, and others. With his profound Christian understanding, Bach has had an enduring influence in music history in terms of health, strength, and order.

Less than one hundred years after Bach, as the influence of the Enlightenment with its rejection of biblical Christianity began to be felt, Dr. Charles Burney in his *General History of Music* wrote that music is an innocent luxury, unnecessary indeed to our existence, but a great improvement and gratification of the sense of hearing.

Now that we are near the end of the twentieth century, humanism, leading to despair, has taken over much of music. "My religion needs no God, only faith," said the philosophically orientated Schoenberg, and he placed great emphasis on expressing oneself. As individuals turn further and further from the personal, infinite God, the Giver of gifts, the more dehumanized and twisted will be that which he or she creates. We have already arrived at the computer age with man thinking himself a machine listening to a machine.

We are not speaking of something unimportant, although some may feel that art, music, and literature are the extras in life. Alfred Einstein in his book *Greatness in Music* made this startling statement: "Artistic greatness is both more permanent and universal than historical greatness." Remembering that the Christian church from the first made use of the arts, we should be challenged to have them take their proper place again. As Martin Luther said, "I feel strongly that all the arts, and particularly music, should be placed in the service of Him who has created and given them." The arts in a Christian framework are an act of worship, and we should be willing to work on them, striving to make artistic statements worthy of the Lord in whom we believe.

There are no simple answers. We may have raised more questions than we have been able to answer. We are not against change and modern techniques, although some will weaken and some strengthen the content. The marvelous message of Christianity should not be presented in an old-fashioned way. There is the lostness of man, but ultimately the Christian should be hopeful and not write music that is harmful in this fallen world. We are called to make a personal contribution either as producers or appreciators of art.

One thing is certain—we cannot really pay for great art. It is a gift.

These composers wrote their music at great cost, both mentally and physically, with so little in return, and yet they persevered. When there was no alternative, some of these composers—such as Berlioz, Joplin, and Ives—published their own works.

Although many of these musicians were not truly appreciated in their lifetime, they have eventually been discovered. Part of the problem is that time alone can determine what is great art. We consider these composers our friends and want to have the joy of introducing them to you. It is not enough to listen to their music in a cursory fashion, because one's understanding and appreciation is vastly enriched through knowing more about the musicians' lives and struggles.

If we are not producers of art, we can be those who are enriched and encouraged by the marvel of the gifts our living God has so generously given to other men and women. Because it is true that art, literature, music, etc., are important in our lives, we should be willing to take time to learn more. We have found out through our study of great painters, such as Dürer, Rembrandt, and Giotto, as well as reading the best in literature—Job, Jeremiah, the letters of Paul, Shakespeare, Dickens, the Brontes—that these great artists enlarge the boundaries of our own lives.

To some it might seem restricting to live in a small mountain village, but not when you are surrounded with good records and books and a radio that features classical music all day long and very possibly all night long too. But we prefer to rest our bodies and minds then in order to wake up refreshed and eager to give thanks to God for His wonderful gifts to all of us.

We hope there will be those who are encouraged to struggle and find solutions so that increasingly the great gift of music will be used for the glory of God.

—Jane Stuart Smith

About the Authors

---

*J*ane Stuart Smith graduated with honors in liberal arts from Stuart Hall and Hollins College in Virginia. She studied further at the Juilliard School of Music in New York and the Tanglewood Festival School of Music in Massachusetts. Her chief voice teacher was Maestro Ettore Verna. As a dramatic soprano, Miss Smith has sung in major opera houses in Europe and America. At present she lives in Switzerland where she is a member and the International Secretary of L'Abri Fellowship. She lectures on art, literature, and music. In her many years in Huemoz, she has originated and participated in numerous art and musical festivals, as well as giving concerts in the United States, Canada, and Europe with the L'Abri Ensemble.

*B*etty Carlson has a B.A. degree from Grinnell College, an M.S. from Oregon State University, and has also studied at the Conservatory of Music in Lausanne, Switzerland. Among the various books she has written are *The Unhurried Chase, A New Song from L'Abri, No One's Perfect,* and *Reflections from a Small Chalet.* She is a volunteer helper at L'Abri.

The authors have written five books together: *A Surprise for Bellevue, The Gift of Music, Favorite Women Hymn Writers, Favorite Men Hymn Writers,* and *Thoughts on Art, Literature, and Humor.*

Music in the Flow of History and the Arts

	PERIOD	MUSIC	ARTS
ANCIENT HISTORY	4500 1100 B.C. Egypt Assyria Babylon Persia	Biblical Psalms	Pyramids Palace of Sargon II Ishtar Gate Persepolis
CLASSIC	1100 B.C. A.D. 500 Crucifixion of Christ A.D. 33 Greek Roman Etruscan	History of Western Music Begins c. A.D. 200 8 Modes	Acropolis Pompeii
MEDIEVAL	500 A.D. 1400 Byzantine Romanesque Gothic	Gregorian Chant Polyphony Ars Antique Ars Nova	Mosaics Cathedral Pisa Cathedral Chartres Dante

RENAISSANCE	1450 1600
	Quattrocento
	Cinquecento
	  Reformation 1517
	  Counter-Reformation
		Okeghem
		Josquin Des Prés
		Luther Chorales
		·Genevan Psalter
		Palestrina
			Giotto
			Da Vinci, Raphael,
			Michelangelo
			
			Dürer, Cranach
			Rubens

BAROQUE	1600 1750 Early Baroque High Baroque	Schütz Vivaldi, Bach, Handel	Rembrandt, Milton
NEO-CLASSIC	18th CENTURY (Age of Reason)	Haydn, Mozart Beethoven, Schubert	David Schwind, Goethe
ROMANTIC	19th CENTURY 1st Half: Romanticism 2nd Half: Nationalism Post-Romanticism Impressionism	Mendelssohn, Liszt, Chopin, Wagner, Verdi, Brahms Tchaikovsky, Dvorak Mahler Debussy, Ravel, Delius	 Delacroix Repin Van Gogh Monet, Cezanne, Sisley
AGE OF SCIENCE	20th CENTURY Expressionism Abstract Many Styles Nonobjective	Schöenberg (Atonality, Twelve-tone Row) Berg, Webern Bartók Satie, Stravinsky (Jazz) Poulenc Electronic Music (Machine) Stockhausen, Cage (Chance)	Kandinsky, Kokoschka, Munch, T. S. Eliot Gris, Braque Picasso Dufy, Matisse Duchamp Pollock

Select Bibliography

Apel, Willi. *Harvard Dictionary of Music*. Cambridge, Mass.: Harvard University Press, 1969.

Arnold, Denis. *The New Oxford Companion to Music*. Oxford: Oxford University Press, 1983.

Bukofzer, Manfred F. *Music in the Baroque Era*. New York: W. W. Norton, 1947.

Burney, Charles. *A General History of Music*. London: G. T. Foulis and Co., 1935.

Chase, Gilbert. *The Music of Spain*. New York: Dover Publications, 1959.

Durant, Will. *The Story of Philosophy*. New York: Simon and Schuster, 1953.

Einstein, Alfred. *Music in the Romantic Era*. New York: W. W. Norton, 1947.

Ewen, David. *Ewen's Musical Masterworks: The Encyclopedia of Musical Masterpieces*. New York: Bonanza Books, 1949.

Grout, Donald Jay. *A History of Western Music* (revised). New York: W. W. Norton, 1973.

Grove, George. *Dictionary of Music and Musicians*. New York: Macmillan, 1928.

Julian, John. *A Dictionary of Hymnology*. New York: Dover Publications, 1957.

Lang, Paul Henry. *Music in Western Civilization*. New York: W. W. Norton, 1941.

_____, and Bettmann, Otto. *A Pictorial History of Music*. New York: W. W. Norton, 1960.

_____, and Broder, Nathan, eds. *Contemporary Music in*

Europe. A Comprehensive Survey. New York: G. Schirmer, 1965.

Leonard, Richard Anthony. *A History of Russian Music.* New York: Minerva Press, 1956.

Lloyd, Norman. *The Golden Encyclopedia of Music.* New York: Golden Press, 1968.

Machlis, Joseph. *Introduction to Contemporary Music.* New York: Golden Press, 1968.

_____. *The Enjoyment of Music.* New York: W. W. Norton, 1963.

Reese, Gustav. *Music in the Renaissance.* New York: W. W. Norton, 1959.

Sadie, Stanley, ed. *The New Grove Dictionary of Music and Musicians.* London: Macmillan, 1980.

Schaeffer, Francis A. *How Should We Then Live?* Old Tappan, N.J.: Fleming H. Revell, 1976.

Scholes, Percy A. *The Oxford Companion to Music.* London: Oxford University Press, 1974.

Schonberg, Harold C. *The Lives of the Great Composers.* New York: W. W. Norton, 1970.

Slonimsky, Nicolas. *Baker's Biographical Dictionary of Musicians* (revised). New York: Schirmer Books, 1984.

Thompson, Oscar, ed. *The International Cyclopedia of Music and Musicians.* London: J. M. Dent and Sons, 1975.

Glossary

Anthem: A short choral work usually based on Scripture and performed in some Protestant churches by a chorus and soloist.

Antiphonal singing: Two soloists or groups alternating the singing of a religious text such as a psalm.

Atonality: A contemporary practice in which no principle of key is observed.

Ballet: A theatrical art form using dancing to convey a story theme or atmosphere.

Baroque: German and Austrian music of the seventeenth and eighteenth centuries marked by improvisation, contrasting effects, and powerful tension.

Cantata: A work for several solo voices and a chorus, much like a short oratorio or an opera but without acting.

Canticle: A liturgical song taken from the Bible.

Chant: A simple harmonized melody used in some churches for singing unmetrical texts, principally psalms or canticles.

Chorale: A hymn or psalm sung to a traditional or composed melody.

Classical music: Music of a more formal nature with emphasis on beauty and proportion rather than on emotional expression.

Concerto: A piece for one or more soloists and orchestra, usually in symphonic form with three contrasting movements.

Concerto grosso: A Baroque orchestral composition with a small group of solo instruments contrasting with the full orchestra.

Counterpoint: A part or voice added to another part. Combination of parts or voices each significant in itself, resulting in a coherent texture.

Dissonance: An unresolved musical note or chord.

Enlightenment, the: A philosophic movement of the eighteenth century marked by questioning of traditional doctrines and values, with a tendency toward individualism and an emphasis on the idea of universal human progress.

Folk song: A song originating among the peasantry of any race, transmitted orally from generation to generation and usually sung without accompaniment.

Libretto: The text of an opera or oratorio.

Lied: A type of solo vocal composition that came into being as an outcome of the Romantic movement. The poem chosen is of high importance and not a mere passenger for the tune.

Modulation: Change of key in the course of a passage.

Opera: Drama set to music.

Oratorio: A music composition using soloists, chorus, and orchestra. The subjects generally are taken from the Bible. There is no acting, and scenery is not used.

Orchestration: The act of scoring for an orchestra.

Overture: Instrumental music intended as the introduction to an opera or an oratorio.

Psalm: A hymn accompanied by stringed instruments. The book of Psalms is the oldest book of songs still in use.

Reformation, the: A sixteenth-century religious movement marked by rejection or modification of much of Roman Catholic doctrine and practice and the establishment of Protestant churches.

Romanticism: A literary, artistic, and philosophical movement originating in the eighteenth century characterized by reaction against Neoclassicism and emphasis on imagination and emotions with a predilection for melancholy.

Score: The copy of a musical composition in written or printed notation.

Serenade: A work for chamber orchestra, resembling a suite.

Sonata: An extended composition in several movements for one or two instruments.

Symphony: A usually long and complex sonata for orchestra.

Tonality: Loyalty to the key scheme of a composition.

Twelve-tone row (or serial technique): A composing procedure employing the dodecaphonic scale in which the twelve notes are considered to be all of equal status.

Index